Organization Practice

A Social Worker's Guide to Understanding Human Services

F. Ellen Netting

Virginia Commonwealth University

Mary Katherine O'Connor

Virginia Commonwealth University

Boston ▪ New York ▪ San Francisco
Mexico City ▪ Montreal ▪ Toronto ▪ London ▪ Madrid ▪ Munich ▪ Paris
Hong Kong ▪ Singapore ▪ Tokyo ▪ Cape Town ▪ Sydney

Series Editor: *Patricia Quinlin*
Editor in Chief, Social Sciences: *Karen Hanson*
Editorial Assistant: *Annemarie Kennedy*
Marketing Manager: *Taryn Wahlquist*
Editorial-Production Administrator: *Annette Joseph*
Editorial-Production Coordinator: *Holly Crawford*
Editorial-Production Service: *Lynda Griffiths, TKM Productions*
Composition Buyer: *Linda Cox*
Electronic Composition: *TKM Productions*
Manufacturing Buyer: *JoAnne Sweeney*
Cover Designer: *Kristina Mose-Libon*

For related titles and support materials, visit our online catalog at www.ablongman.com

Between the time Website information is gathered and then published, it is not unusual for some sites to have closed. Also, the transcription of URLs can result in unintended typographical errors. The publisher would appreciate notification where these occur so that they may be corrected in subsequent editions.

Library of Congress Cataloging-in-Publication Data

Netting, F. Ellen.
    Organization practice : a social worker's guide to understanding human services / F. Ellen Netting, Mary Katherine O'Connor.
        p. cm.
    Includes bibliographical references and index.
    ISBN 0-205-31759-6
        1. Human services. I. O'Connor, Mary Katherine. II. Title.

HV40 .N2479 2003
361--dc21

2002023214

Printed in the United States of America

10   9   8   7   6   5   4   3   2   1   RRD-IN   07   06   05   04   03   02

DEDICATION

Both of us have had the good fortune to have been encouraged and challenged by many intelligent and courageous women. We owe much of what we have made of ourselves and our lives to those women. And both of us have been the recipients of loving mentorship from two special women for whom this book is dedicated.

Ellen dedicates this book to Doris Quillin McCoy, her maternal aunt. From early childhood, she spent wonderful times in Aunt Doris's and Uncle John's apartment on Grove Avenue in Richmond, Virginia—just blocks from where the Virginia Commonwealth University School of Social Work houses her office today. Aunt Doris is a constant reminder of the importance of relationship, commitment, and human kindness.

Mary Katherine dedicates this text to Celia O'Connor Forrer, her aunt, godmother, and friend. It was Auntie who first encouraged a 5-year-old to use the library and a 16-year-old to consider opening doors to opportunity by going to college halfway across the country. Her strong spirit and quick, compassionate intelligence have been a great inspiration both personally and professionally.

We hope the work we have accomplished here continues a grand tradition established by these two women for us and for others. We dedicate our work to them as a way of saying thank you for their amazing influence.

CONTENTS

LIST OF TABLES

LIST OF FIGURES

PREFACE

When we decided to co-teach the planning and administration practice courses at Virginia Commonwealth University (VCU), we faced a surprising challenge. In order to find a contemporary theory text to support our curriculum, we were forced to search for a text outside the field of social work that would fully ground our students in contemporary theoretical debates and research about organizations. This was difficult because we knew students (somewhat like us) would feel overwhelmed with the massive amount of material being published on organization theory and wonder why so little of it had to do with social work. We selected a huge volume, *The Handbook of Organization Studies,* a collection of very complex readings written by scholars from multiple disciplines (Clegg, Hardy, & Nord, 1996). We think we convinced at least some of our students that the text was leading edge, but we were also told that students saw the book as "bad-tasting medicine"—very important to one's professional development but not always easy to swallow. It was not until they graduated and began to practice that a few came back and sheepishly told us that we probably ought to keep requiring that massive volume, or at least recommend it as a valuable resource to the next generation of students.

Although students admitted to having had their eyes open to completely new ways of understanding organizations and organizational behavior, they also were overwhelmed with the sheer volume of the handbook. The next fall, we began using a less formidable text by Shafritz and Ott, and we are now using their latest edition (Shafritz & Ott, 2001). Excerpting readings from various primary sources, *Classics of Organization Theory* provides an overview of the various schools of thought about organizations. On the downside, however, this is another book of readings, not an integrated text nor written for students of social work.

Our goal for the practice courses was to temper the required readings from these challenging books on organization theory by providing a timely and useful classroom commentary on social work leadership within organizations. We also assigned readings in texts on program planning, controversial issues in social work, and performance evaluation, all written by social work educators. Spanning the deep gulf between theoretical content and these latter readings has continued to be a challenge and the major reason we decided to write this book.

It is interesting that there are a number of contemporary texts on community *practice* (e.g., Hardcastle, Wenocur, & Powers, 1997); policy *practice* (e.g., Jansson, 1999); macro *practice* (e.g., Netting, Kettner, & McMurtry, 1998), which includes communities and organizations; generalist *practice* in larger settings (Meenaghan & Gibbons, 2000), and advocacy *practice* (Ezell, 2001; Schneider & Lester, 2001). In addition, a number of social work texts focus on administration and management (e.g., Brody, 2000; Patti, 2000). But there are no texts on organization *practice*—how one works and survives in organizations.

Given our experiences in locating appropriate books for our courses, we decided to write a theory-based, thought-provoking textbook on organization practice for the next generation of social work leaders. We wanted to conceptualize organization practice as a broader concept than agency practice. Because of this, we have defined *agencies* as provider organizations that deliver services and *social workers* as leaders in organizations that provide direct services. But social workers are also leaders in organizations that advocate for change, make policy, plan service delivery systems, and educate and train persons who deliver services. We think it is essential to have a text that integrates material on how social workers can understand human services within organizational arenas in ways that are different from what is available in the current social work literature.

We see organization practice as being broader than what administrators and managers do. All social workers practice within organizational contexts. Our concern is that if *all* social workers do not *understand* how organizations work and how people behave in these complex structures, they are essentially disempowered in the very arenas in which they are likely to spend the majority of their professional lives. They will have little chance to change organizations, much less use these settings as places from which to launch their community, policy, advocacy, and administrative practice efforts. We wanted to provide an integrated source of information for those beginning their practice in organizations. More than that, we wanted to develop materials to prepare students for future practice within organizations that are structured and staffed much differently from the way they were in the previous century.

To this end, we formed a collaboration grounded in both traditional and alternative approaches to organizational change. Our diverse backgrounds have proved to be essential to the development of this book. Schooled in a traditional planned change approach, Ellen brings to our partnership the ability to articulate fully the importance of outcome-based change and a substantive area in gerontology. Mary Katherine's perspective is based on the assumptions underlying alternative paradigms. She brings to our collaboration a rich background in multicultural community and organization practice with children and child welfare services.

In 1998, we coauthored "Integrating Gender into Human Service Administration, Organization, and Planning" in *The Role of Gender in Practice Knowledge: Reclaiming Half the Human Experience* as our first published collaboration (Netting & Rodwell, 1998). We discovered that we enjoyed the challenge of looking at things differently. We became intrigued with the exploration of nondominant approaches. In 1999, *Affilia* published our article titled "Teaching Our Students about Collaborative Approaches to Organizational Change" in which we began to question how we have taught organization change as if organizations conformed to a set of established principles (O'Connor & Netting, 1999). Our experience told us that organizations were surprising us at every turn, exuding cultures that were anything but conformist. We continued to co-teach the two-semester practice courses on planning and administration on both the VCU Richmond and Arlington, Virginia, campuses while we wrote this book, so that we could test our ideas in the classroom. The conceptualization of this textbook has emerged (and is continuing to emerge) from these collaborative writing and teaching efforts.

We have written *Organization Practice* to provide social work students adequate material in organization theory and in the use of different practice approaches designed to guide their leadership in organizational settings. We believe all social work students must fully understand the assumptions that drive the theories they embrace and that they must be able to act on those theories by understanding a variety of practice approaches within organizations. If they cannot do this, then they will not be leaders in organizations that address complex social problems. This book is theoretically driven with attention to historical and postmodern theories of organization and of organizational behavior. Our intent is to provide students with a critical lens for understanding organizations and multiple professional roles as leaders and change agents within them.

Attention must be given to the preparation of the next generation of social work organizational leaders who will be capable of maximizing the strengths within a diverse work force of colleagues. This book will help in that preparation by highlighting specific critical thinking skills targeted at understanding multiple perspectives, managing complexity, and developing collaborative approaches in organizational decision making within a well-developed social work frame of reference.

Having described what this book is intended to be, it is important to describe what this book is not. *Organization Practice* is not a text on administration and planning. A number of excellent resources in social work focus on social work administration (e.g., Lohmann & Lohmann, 2002; Kettner, 2002) as well as on program planning. In the pages that follow, we will refer to this literature, but our intent will be to set a broader frame—to elaborate four approaches to organization practice that will require students to engage in critical thinking. We explore the full landscape of diverse organizational types in which social workers practice. Social workers should not be limited to work in a particular domain or type of organization; today's students must fully expand their vision of potential practice settings and the leadership possibilities within them. This book does not provide specific models for practicing within different organizations. Instead, it provides a framework for understanding organizations and the practice within them. This has been accomplished in the following ways:

- Framing the entire text are explicitly stated assumptions about organizations and organizational behavior. Readers do not have to guess about what assumptions undergird each chapter and are encouraged to consider their own assumptions (and to critique ours) in light of provocative examples.
- The book is completely dedicated to organization practice within the field of social work.
- All social workers—regardless of focus, specialization, or concentration—are targeted, because all social workers will have to practice within organizations at some point in their careers.
- The book focuses on the importance of self-awareness and critical thinking in organization practice.

- The principles of the NASW Code of Ethics illustrate how values and assumptions can be used to assess organization practice approaches so that readers are aware of the implications of their choices in selecting different approaches.
- The text goes beyond the narrow definitions of *human service organizations* and includes all organizational settings in which social workers practice, many of which are not considered traditional human service agencies. Examples are drawn from planning and advocacy organizations across public, nonprofit, and for-profit sectors.
- Classical, contemporary, and emerging theories are categorized according to what they offer the practitioner in organizational settings so that they will be useful to social work students and practitioners.
- Drawing on an expansive and complex interdisciplinary literature, every attempt is made to integrate the latest in organizational thinking into the language of social work and to make it manageable for the reader.
- Terms are boldfaced as they are introduced and defined throughout the chapters. These terms cover all aspects of organization practice discussed in the book and can be found in the Glossary.

In the writing process, we have stretched ourselves and challenged one another to discover multiple ways of conceptualizing organization practice. We hope readers will find *Organization Practice* provocative, and we look forward to hearing from you so that we can learn from one another. This book is only the beginning of a journey on which we are embarking, and we invite our readers to join us in discovering new ways to understand, thrive in, and change organizations. Let the journey begin!

ACKNOWLEDGMENTS

A book such as this does not spring into existence without many important influences and supports. Certainly, what we have produced would not have been possible without the people who have been closest to this effort. We gratefully acknowledge their presence in the good and useful aspects of the book, while also being clear that any of the problems or weaknesses contained within are ours alone.

We thank our planning and administration students (even those who thought theory was "way boring") for their willingness to play with these ideas even when they were not so well developed and for their insightful and practical feedback to various versions of the text. If other students think the work speaks to them, it is because of the conversations we have had with our own students.

Also we are grateful to Dean Frank R. Baskind and the faculty of the Virginia Commonwealth University School of Social Work for supporting our research leave, which gave us the time to write and test the ideas. Particular appreciation is due to our friends and colleagues, David Fauri and Jaclyn Miller. David's collegiality across courses, his critical reviews of initial versions, his confidence in us, and his participation as a willing playmate have greatly strengthened our work. Jaci's thoughtful review of initial drafts of our materials and her invaluable assistance in helping us conceptualize organizational diagnosis have guided our thinking. To Jon Singletary, our student success story, we cannot thank you enough for reviewing initial versions and gently moving both of us to postmodernity.

To our friends in the publishing world, acknowledgments are also necessary. Thank you to David Estrin for well-targeted critical feedback, moral support, and friendship through the years; to Judy Fifer for believing in us; to Janice Wiggins for development work and for her initial, encouraging enthusiasm; and to Pat Quinlin for joining us in the middle of the process and offering enthusiastic support. We also gratefully acknowledge the following reviewers for their suggestions, which contributed in making this a better book: Kathy Byers, Indiana University; Felice Perlmutter, Temple University; and Jim Wolk, Georgia State University.

Finally, a special thank you goes to Peter M. Kettner for listening to us ramble on about the ideas in this book and for encouraging us to move beyond the traditional, and to Dennis Saleebey for telling Mary Katherine on the day of her dissertation defense that she really had not finished her analysis of Burrell and Morgan's multiple paradigms.

PART ONE

Setting the Stage

Part One, which consists of four chapters, begins with a broad overview of the organizational landscape in which professional social workers find themselves. Next is a brief historical review of organizational theory development in order to frame definitions of those organizations involved in human service activities. The use of critical thinking and self-awareness for leadership in organization practice follows. Last is an introduction to a framework to guide understanding of the complexity of organizing human services, which is expanded in Part Two.

The Organizational Landscape

In Chapter 1, we introduce knowledge about organizing structures in human services, and provide an overview of many types of organizations, such as social service, planning, advocacy, and host organizations. The goal is to emphasize how complex the landscape is and how impossible it is to place organizations into mutually exclusive categories.

We also elaborate on the multiplicity of organizational types that dot the landscape, the myth that human service organizations are the only domain in which social workers practice. Throughout the chapter, we provide examples of different types of organizations responding to human needs, illustrating their similarities and differences with a focus on values of the social work profession and their practice implications. We do this because we believe that effective social work practice within organizations (whether they are nonprofit, for profit, public, alternative, quasi-governmental, ethnic, faith based, feminist, or a host of other formal and informal structures) is dependent on organizational designs that reflect value congruence among the problem, the service, and the ethical demands of the social work profession. Social work practitioners are in unique positions in comparison to other helping professionals because of their simultaneous responsibility to attend to the client and the context of the problem. The complexity of the organizational leadership challenge requires that social work leaders understand the variety of structural options in order to expand the resources to ethically and effectively serve those in need.

Complex Organizations

Throughout the history of the development of formal and informal organizations and ways to study them, there has been an intense need to structure organizations and the behavior within them in order to achieve organizational goals. We begin Chapter 2 with an example of how this search for order has led to expectations and assumptions about organizations that may not necessarily manifest themselves in reality. In this chapter we introduce theoretical perspectives that have framed thinking about complex organizations over the last century.

Here, we underscore the necessity of understanding the organization practice context, and the limits of past efforts in this regard. We also introduce emerging perspectives on organizational power, politics, and culture. Chapter 2 concludes by emphasizing the importance of critical thinking and self-awareness in contemporary practice, leading to that focus in Chapter 3.

Critical Thinking, Self-Awareness, and Organization Practice

In Chapter 3, we emphasize social work attitudes, values, and skills needed for contemporary organization practice. We contend that social workers bring a particular perspective to the positions they assume and to the enactment of change, which is a regular, ongoing process within all organizations. From this perspective, then, there is an assumption that all social workers must be organizational leaders. We also assume that social workers are tied to some organizational structure—whether they are private practitioners within the confines of a small group or public officials within a complex web of bureaucratically entangled relationships. Social workers are not free agents, practicing without organizational sanction.

Regardless of where social workers perform their roles and engage with others, they work within complex contexts of multiple organizational relationships, requiring the use of multiple skills for effective practice to occur. Conscious use of self is an essential element of this perspective, as is critical thinking about all aspects of practice. Not only does the social work frame of reference demand program designs and services that are sensitive to the populations served, but those designing and implementing the services must be equally conscious of their own needs and biases. It is not only the clinician who is challenged to manage personal and professional boundaries but also the policy advocate, administrator, program coordinator, planner, and supervisor who must embrace the same professional challenges.

We introduce the NASW Code of Ethics as a template for critical analysis of professional organization practice in order to manage this challenge. We also focus on the inevitability of value conflicts in organizations that do not always reflect social work principles, along with some of the choices that will inevitably result. This chapter develops one of the important frameworks for the rest of the book: organizational leadership based on introspection and critical thinking about available knowledge. Here, the tools are provided to uncover the professional ethical conflicts due to complexity, diversity, and the social justice mission of the profession.

A Framework for Organization Practice

A framework is introduced in Chapter 4 that will shape the discussion throughout the rest of the book. Building on the reader's awareness of the personal assumptions one brings to organization practice, this chapter focuses on how one's assumptions can lead to different outcomes within the same organization. To illustrate how this happens, we draw from the work of Burrell and Morgan that distinguishes four paradigms that one might bring to organization practice: functionalist, radical structuralist, interpretive, and radical humanist. The assumptions that undergird these four very different worldviews are illustrated through discussions of philosophers of science, theories of organizations and organizational behavior, and a well-known instrument for determining personality types.

Multiparadigmatic thinking for organizational analysis and planning is essential for successful human service organization practice that appropriately operationalizes social work values in diverse environments. With the organizing framework in Chapter 4, the reader is ready to investigate the theories in each perspective that can guide understanding of organizations and the practice within them. This understanding is foundational to successful human service organizational change. Chapter 4 serves as an overview and introduction to the remaining chapters in the book.

CHAPTER

1

The Ever-Changing Landscape of Organizations and Human Services

This book focuses on the knowledge and skills social workers rely on to professionally work and survive in organizations. *All* social workers engage in organization practice, regardless of the focus of their practice. In this chapter, we want to impress upon the reader the importance of competent organization practice, because most social workers will work within, and with, many different organizations throughout their professional careers. We define **organization practice** as working and surviving in organizational arenas by making changes that address the needs of multiple stakeholders and constituencies and that reflect a strong grounding in professional values, critical thinking, and self-awareness.

To understand the current role of organizations in professional life, it may be helpful for the reader to think about how he or she views work. Many years ago, a worker in an agency might have aspired to remain in the same organization for years and to "move up" in that agency. Today's employment expectations are much different. It is more typical for people to change jobs frequently. It is also more typical for agencies and services to go into and out of existence. Examining organizations as practice arenas must be squarely placed within the broader societal context of changing expectations of what one looks for in a job and how employees define themselves within the world of work. In subsequent chapters, we will elaborate on the importance of this self-awareness.

The United States is an organizational society, composed of many different organizations that perform various functions. Today, few persons could describe themselves as untouched by multiple organizations, whether in the form of grocery stores, schools, specialty shops, hospitals, human service agencies, or a plethora of other structures. Organizations are an integral part of a contemporary lifestyle, and they are arenas in which the exchange of resources occurs on a regular basis. They may be situated in defined geographical communities or they may transcend geography, connected by technological innovation in virtual organizations. Their purposes and structures are as varied as their numbers.

This chapter describes the full and ever-changing landscape that is comprised of organizations that advocate for, plan, fund, and deliver human services. We begin by briefly examining human service organizational practice arenas and making some beginning comments about assumptions often held about organizations.

We then focus on how organizations are defined. Most of this chapter is devoted to an overview of the types of organizations that support and deliver human services in the United States. This means that we include those organizations that do not always define themselves as "human service agencies," since many organizations not solely in the business of providing human services may host components, units, or individuals that deliver human services. Successful modern-day practice requires that social workers identify human service programs delivered by agencies that were not previously viewed as traditional providers.

In addition, there are organizations that deliver no human services directly but perform support functions, such as providing funding, planning for and overseeing human service providers advocating for special population groups; and/or educating and training those persons who do provide services. These organizations often have staff who review grant applications and determine who will be funded, contract for services with local providers, set priorities among competing human service needs, formulate and interpret policy, advocate for change, and influence technologies used in service delivery. They are very much a part of the human service enterprise, even though they are not direct providers of human services.

We take an expansive view of human service work, encouraging professionals to recognize that there are no clear-cut, separate sectors in which human service work is conducted. Thus, we expose one of our many assumptions in writing this book—that contemporary human service work occurs through traditional, alternative, and emerging auspices and that many organizations are involved in the formulation and interpretation of policy, in influencing provider agencies, and in the daily delivery of human services. Given the ever-changing landscape of human service delivery, mapping this landscape is a challenge.

Organizational Practice Arenas

Rothman, Erlich, and Tropman (2001) help to define the large system practice we wish to emphasize by identifying three "specific social spheres in which the process of community intervention is played out . . . the *community* itself; *organizations*, both formal and informal, within the community; and *small groups* of various kinds, particularly task-oriented units such as committees, commissions, boards, and the like" (p. 3). They consider communities, organizations, and groups to be critical arenas for intervention, "the social settings and systems in which practice takes place" (p. 9) and they indicate that intervention "may prove frustrating and fruitless unless observation, diagnosis, and understanding have come first" (p. 10). Persons who seek to change communities find that they must work with various organizations and groups that claim community membership. These three arenas are anything but mutually exclusive in that communities, organizations, and groups overlap and interact.

Social workers, in both their personal and professional lives, by virtue of being a part of these complex arenas, are tied to numerous organizations that relate to and even formally affiliate with various communities and groups. Social workers are professionally affiliated with an organizational structure or structures—whether they are private practitioners within the confines of a small group practice or public officials within a complex web of bureaucratically entangled relationships. Few social work professionals are free agents who can afford to practice without the support of an organizational base. The few who operate as independent consultants or solo practitioners interact with and depend on a multitude of organizations for their survival. Organizations may even be the object of their interventions. So, social workers in their work encounter multitudes of organizations within their communities. Regardless of where social workers perform their roles and engage with others, they work in and with organizations, interfacing with multiple organizations. Social work is practice within context, and organizations are an essential part of that context. In addition, each of these organizations will have distinctive cultures, requiring the use of multicultural skills for effective practice to occur.

Some theorists view organizations as situated in uncertain, turbulent environments in which they are constantly responding to constraints (things they cannot change) and contingencies (things about which they have to compromise and negotiate). This popular view of organizations will be explored in detail in subsequent chapters. Yet, it is not just the environments in which organizations operate that are uncertain and turbulent, but organizations face internal uncertainties and turbulence as well. Organizations are dynamic, changing entities that are situated in dynamic and changing communities. Given the nature of these settings, to be successful, social workers must understand as much as possible about these dynamics.

Organizations that support and deliver human services vary in how they are structured, and it is important for practitioners to know how the organizations within which they practice are put together. One often hears the term *formal* used to describe an organization. This implies that there are also *informal* organizations. It is not always easy to define clear boundaries between what is a formal and what is an informal organization. For example, a group of committed citizens may organize to provide services to persons in need. In the process of organizing, they may develop a statement of purpose, rally the support of volunteers, and structure their services. They are technically an informal group. But what happens when they decide to form a nonprofit corporation so that they can receive funding from outside sources? If they are incorporated, they are formally recognized as a nonprofit organization. They may still have the same purpose, continue to use volunteers, and structure their services the same way, but they are no longer just a "group"; they are an "organization." Perhaps there are degrees of formality. We cannot state clearly when a group becomes a formal organization or when service delivery becomes formalized. We are just pointing out that even though groups, organizations, and communities can be conceptualized as three arenas in which social workers practice, they are interconnected and their boundaries are not always clear and distinctive.

Some Beginning Comments

Before examining the concept of organization and focusing on those that engage in human service delivery, we would like to release you from some of the constraints of order, finality, and logic that can accompany the student enterprise. Some of you may be hoping that you will find some universals that you can apply to all organizations, that the human service delivery system will make sense once you've studied organizations, and that practicing in organizations will be easier having read this material. If any of these thoughts sound familiar, we offer some alternatives to consider.

First, we (and others), will frequently refer to organizations as *systems* and to human service delivery *systems*. Do not be fooled by these references to *systems*. The word *system* may lead you to think of something that is logical, consistent, and definable as it works, but you will encounter many organizations (perhaps most) that seem very unsystematic. They are not transparent; neither will you see their order or the logic of the work. This may not be because you "just don't get it." It could be that these systems just don't make sense without understanding the full context in which they operate, or it could even be that they don't perform like systems at all. It could be that your assumptions about how things should work are so different from the assumptions held about the organization by others, that you are experiencing a clash in cultures. Do not despair, for this presents an opportunity to learn about a different culture. Some organizations may have similar characteristics, but every organization will have its own uniqueness. Some will be so unique that they will be different from those you have previously experienced. Do not jump to any conclusions about what you are experiencing until you can fully understand the major aspects of the cultural context of that organization.

Second, students often approach the study of human service organizations with the assumption (or hope) that the reason they don't quickly see how the whole service system works is because they haven't yet learned enough about how individual organizations work. As they learn more, they discover that the human service system may seem fragmented or hard to understand. Frustration occurs because there is a deep-seated assumption that someone somewhere conceptualized the system and understands the "master plan." Let us assure you—there is no one overriding master plan. Sometimes there are few, if any, overriding plans at all. Other times there are multiple plans of how the system should work, plans that have not been coordinated or even articulated, or plans that may even contradict one another. If you can't make sense of the delivery system, it is possible that the delivery system doesn't make sense. This is understandable when one thinks historically about how numerous organizations and groups emerged to address diverse needs in local communities. They did not arise simultaneously in a rational, concentrated effort to provide care. Some actually originated in protest to others that did not respond to the needs of invisible groups in the community. The landscape of human service delivery, therefore, is rich in diversity, offering the social worker an assortment of perspectives. It is the exceptional situation when there is a unified jointly held vision of human service delivery in a local community where organizations, though differing in structure and culture, mesh together to accomplish common goals.

Third, no matter what we say, there will be exceptions to every rule. Any attempts to define, categorize, or classify organizations are only that—attempts. If you know of an organization that does not conform to what we say throughout this text, then it is because you know of an organization that does not fit. It is probably not that you "don't get it" or that the organization in question should be made to conform in order to do it "right." Let us be clear in our message: We are attempting to provide some manageability in examining this landscape when in actuality we know that disorder and chaos are likely the way many systems creatively solve the problems associated with human service work. Organization practice, therefore, requires one to be constantly assessing and reassessing situations. This is why you are here—to learn about organizations so that you will become knowledgeable and skilled in a highly complex arena of practice and so that you can learn about and respect the many dimensions of difference in organizations and still professionally survive and thrive.

Defining Organization

One can find as many definitions of organizations as there are writers on organizations. For our purposes in a text that focuses on diversity in organizations, we are comfortable with the definition offered by Shafritz and Ott (2001), who define **organizations** as "social unit[s] with some particular purpose" (p. 1). They contend that "the basic elements of organizations have remained relatively constant throughout history: Organizations (or their important constituencies) have purposes (which may be explicit or implicit), attract participants, acquire and allocate resources to accomplish goals, use some form of structure to divide and coordinate activities, and rely on certain members to lead or manage others" (p. 2). These characteristics vary, depending on the environment in which an organization operates.

Other definitions use different words, but say essentially the same thing. For example, another group of writers say that an "organization is a cluster of roles held together by coordination and a mission. . . . Structurally, an organization needs roles, coordination, and mission" (Lakey, Lakey, Napier, & Robinson, 1995, p. 6). *The Social Work Dictionary* defines organizations as "formally structured arrangements of people, tools, and resources brought together to achieve pre-determined objectives through institutionalized strategies" (Barker, 1995, p. 266). This definition contains a number of assumptions in several terms: *formal structure, predetermined objectives,* and *institutionalized strategies.* We know organizations that have very informal structures, have no predetermined objectives (only broad, diffuse goals), and have not institutionalized their strategies nor intend to do so. A critical examination of definitions and word usage such as these may uncover assumptions, intended or unintended.

Shafritz and Ott's (2001) definition is to the point and we agree with their assumption that there is something "social" about this unit or arena by the very nature of multiple people being involved. They also assume there is "some particular purpose" for this social unit to come together. *Purpose* is a broad, inclusive word that could include goals and objectives, but does not have to do so. And there may be multiple purposes, depending on the organization.

Organizations as Collections of Programs and Services

Certainly Shafritz and Ott (and others) offer reasonable definitions of what an organization is, but we are more specifically concerned with understanding those organizations that support and deliver human services. These organizations have concerns about people and their needs that make them somewhat different from organizations in general, yet most of the organizational literature is not directed to these type organizations. We also recognize that not *all* organizations that deliver human services are full-time human service agencies, nor *everything* a human service organization does is focused on direct service delivery to clients. Organizations that fund, plan, advocate, and/or educate are in the human service business, even though they are not direct providers of services. If such organizations are social units that come together for a purpose, then these organizations often find ways to pursue that purpose in the form of programs.

Programs

Programs have been defined as "pre-arranged sets of activities designed to achieve a set of goals and objectives" (Netting, Kettner, & McMurtry, 1998, p. 300). Human service programs directly focus their activities on addressing specific client needs, whereas other programs support these human service efforts, focusing on such areas as fund-raising, public relations, or advocacy. Sometimes, entire organizations will be devoted to these support functions. For example, a state human service department may be an oversight and planning agency for those providers who deliver services locally. Similarly, a foundation that funds a program initiative to provide case management for troubled youth is supporting direct service grantees who implement its program.

Martin and Kettner (1996) say that a human service program

- addresses an identified social problem
- represents a significant proportion of the total activity of an organization
- has goals and objectives (either formally stated or implied)
- has designated resources, including personnel (because no activity or endeavor can take place without resources)

"These four criteria—and particularly the first criterion—rule out administrative activities such as personnel, finance, facilities management, clerical pool, and the like from being considered human service programs" (p. 22). Nevertheless, it should be noted that these other type programs are essential to organizational functioning.

In order to fully support direct client-serving programs, human service providers may have a variety of other type programs. For example, a human service agency could have

- direct service programs (to serve clients directly)
- staff development and training programs (to enhance staff abilities to serve clients)
- support programs (activities to support direct service programs such as fundraising, lobbying, or advocacy)

Direct service programs assist clients, usually attempting to make their situations better in some way. **Staff development and training programs** focus on staff, the intention being that because staff will have additional knowledge and skills, they will be able to do better direct service provision. **Support programs** may be program, organizational, or community based, with the intention being that their activities are processes that will lead to higher-quality programming.

Obviously, there are organizations that do not deliver direct human services but still have programs and still hire social workers. Roles that social workers play in these organizations are reflected in titles such as *advocate, trainer, planner, policy analyst, administrator, monitor, evaluator,* and *program officer.* Other organizations, called *provider agencies,* hire social workers in direct practice roles to implement programs through the provision of services.

Services

A **service** is a specific intervention. For example, a service could be counseling or receiving a mobile meal. Both are human services, for they directly impact individuals in need. Although one is less concrete (counseling) than the other (a meal), both services might be linked in a senior citizens' program designed to address both the psychological and nutritional needs of older persons. Programs tend to be comprised of multiple services. Although organizations do not always conceptualize their activities as programs composed of services, it is helpful to use this framework in looking at how human services are delivered.

This conceptualization is also useful in separating what is occurring in a human service organizational context as it attempts to meet clients' needs. At times within the service system, funding sources and other persons in power do not immediately recognize the need for new programs and services. Even well-designed programs and innovative service technologies may require piloting within an organization before they will be embraced. Sometimes there are unpopular causes or population groups who are not served at all. In these cases, hopefully, programs, services, or even new agencies emerge in response to these unmet needs.

Traditional and Alternative Social Agencies

Traditional social agencies deliver socially acceptable programs to socially acceptable clients in need. Funding and community sanction flow from long established patterns of acceptance of the need to serve clients in the ways that are chosen by the agencies. These agencies may practice in very conventional ways. Traditional agencies can be seen as the operationalization of local opinions, doctrines, and practices as demonstrated in what is planned, who is included in program planning, who is served, and how services are rendered.

On the other hand, **alternative social agencies** are formed when a person or group of people believe that the social needs of specific population groups are not being adequately addressed by other human service agencies. They can develop through public or private efforts. Perlmutter (1988) highlights what she calls "some of the necessary elements for the planning and implementation of a new alternative agency. These include: (1) a committed group of initiators, (2) a clarity of mission, (3) a clearly explicated value framework, and (4) charismatic leadership for a sustained period of time. Finally, a new program requires committed staff members who are willing, and able, to earn minimal salaries as full-time or part-time professionals" (p. 1).

Alternative social agencies are typically small in size and very dependent on charismatic leaders and clear service missions. Such an agency may begin with a service delivery strategy or service ideology unlike any other in the service system. As these agencies mature or when leadership transition occurs, the organization may be very vulnerable. Its reputation and its funding may be at risk. If the agency survives, it may gradually become more established and eventually more traditional in its approach. Societal attitudes may shift expectations of service delivery. The alternative agency of today can become the traditional agency of tomorrow. Depending on the situation, the transition into more traditional service provision may actually bring new clientele into the delivery system rather than keeping them on the periphery. On the other hand, as the agency matures and develops, it may be difficult to maintain momentum while remaining steadfast to the original client population.

Table 1.1 summarizes potential differences between traditional and alternative agencies. Keep in mind that some agencies may have characteristics of both and that some agencies may be evolving from an alternative to a traditional approach. Also, those organizations that fund and support human service programs, rather than directly providing services, come in both traditional and alternative forms. For example, a state commission on aging may be a traditional governmental organization that funds local home- and community-based providers, whereas a national advocacy association for gay and lesbian elders may be considered a radical alternative organization.

TABLE 1.1 Differences between Traditional and Alternative Agencies

Characteristics	Traditional Agencies	Alternative Agencies
Clients	Fund, plan, or deliver socially acceptable programs to socially acceptable clients in need	Are formed to advocate for or deliver services to groups whose needs are not being met by other agencies
Funding	Have funding that flows from long-established and multiple sources	Do not have well-established funding sources, which poses a risk to agency survival
Leadership	Have designated administrators and supervisors within a defined structure	Typically inspired by a charismatic individual who mobilizes volunteers and paid staff to action
Service Delivery	Are part of service delivery structures that are established by agency staff and protocols that have been used over the years	Must establish service delivery approaches, using client participation and evolving protocols
Size	Are typically medium to large in size, given available resources	Are typically small, given available resources
Staff	Offer staff salaries commensurate with local pay scales	Are heavily dependent on volunteers and staff who work for less than other agencies pay
Values	Operationalize dominant opinions, doctrines, and practices	Have guiding values and ideologies that run counter to dominant opinions, doctrines, and practices

Types of Organizations That Plan and Deliver Human Services

Public Agencies

By definition, public or governmental agencies are mandated by law at some level of government. A **public agency** in the U.S. context is established through a local, state, or federal system with the purpose of that agency contained in legal statutes. Examples of public agencies are local, state, or federal departments of human or social services, health, education, and aging. Public agencies are created through legislation and are charged with implementing public social policies. Since social policies are formulated, developed, debated, and eventually approved and enacted by public policymakers, public agencies inherit the controversies sometimes surrounding the social policies that mandate their programs and services. Their destinies as service entities are deeply imbedded in current and past political ideology.

Public agencies that deliver human services vary in how they are structured. For example, Ezell and Patti (1990) examined state-level human service agencies in Delaware, Florida, Minnesota, Oregon, South Carolina, and Utah. These six states were selected because they represented diversity in comprehensiveness (how many different services they provide), integration (how connected or interrelated their services are with one another), and centralization of services and decision making. Even though these researchers hoped to find "what is best" in terms of how public human services are structured, they reported that every state had something to offer and that each state's agency had strengths and limitations. In each state, various constituencies had different expectations, some of which conflicted. The design of state and local agencies represented compromises among diverse constituencies and the outcomes they would accept.

Public agencies are often large in size for reasons of efficiency because they are mandated to serve numerous population groups with multiple problems. However, this does not mean that they will look the same across states. In fact, given differences in regional and local resources and needs, it is questionable that they should look the same. We disagree when people say, "If you've seen one state bureaucracy, you've seen them all." They may appear hierarchical in structure, but there are many different ways to design an effective public agency, just as there are different ways to determine effectiveness. Because of the political context of the public agency, it is the political process of consensus building that determines public agency design and the scope of its services. Therefore, there will be much diversity in terms of what and how many programs an agency will have from state to state. This is also the case for what services each program will contain, how its programs will relate to one another, how centralized or decentralized its decision-making and authority structures will be, and how many branch offices it will have.

Private Agencies

Private agencies are a broad category of organizations, including those that are called nonprofit and for profit. Both are part of the human service enterprise.

Nonprofit Organizations

Nonprofit organizations are referred to as *nongovernmental, third-sector, voluntary, charitable,* or *tax-exempt agencies.* They have uncompensated, voluntary boards of directors who cannot benefit financially from the organization's profits. Any profit made must be reinvested in the organization.

Kramer (1981) began conducting cross-national research on nonprofit or voluntary organizations before it was popular to do so. He views nonprofit voluntary agencies as more bureaucratically structured than voluntary associations, "governed by an elected board of directors, employing professional or volunteer staff to provide continuing social service to a continuing clientele in the community" (p. 9). Kramer's definition has a definite social service slant, given his social work background.

Other definitions by professionals from other fields are slightly different. For example, Hall (1987) defines a nonprofit organization as a group of individuals who come together for one of three purposes: (1) to carry out public tasks that have been contracted to them by the government, (2) to perform tasks for which there is a demand that neither the state nor the market is addressing, or (3) to influence policy in any of the sectors. This is a more broad, highly political definition than Kramer's definition.

Just as nonprofit organizations are called *voluntary agencies,* they are also called *nongovernmental organizations (NGOs),* indicating that they are not publicly mandated. Lohmann (1989) points out that using the prefix *non* to describe an entire group of organizations is not particularly helpful. He compares naming a sector nonprofit or nongovernmental to defining lettuce as a mammal. "Lettuce is a non-fur-bearing, non-milk-producing, non-child-bearing, and non-warm-blooded nonanimal. Further, as a mammal, lettuce is highly ineffective, being sedentary and not warm-blooded. All other mammals are much faster. Lettuce is also remarkably non-agile and fails to protect its young. On the whole, lettuce is a miserable excuse for a mammal!" (p. 369). Lohmann's wit reveals the challenges posed by defining one sector (nonprofit) in light of another (for profit).[1]

Nonprofit agencies have been described over the years in numerous ways—as representative organizations of a defined body of the citizenry, as nonstatutory organizations, as nongovernmental organizations with an elected board of directors, as organizations supported by voluntary (nontax) dollars, and even as organizations that "feel" voluntary. We add to this laundry list the possibility that some voluntary agencies today do not feel voluntary at all. They are struggling to become more businesslike and in the process are having identity crises over who they really are. For us, what probably makes a nonprofit agency "voluntary" is that their board of directors must serve without compensation and are therefore volunteers.

The reason nonprofits are called voluntary agencies is largely attributed to the U.S. Internal Revenue Code (I.R.C.) that establishes special conditions regarding taxation. But numerous analysts have also attempted to classify nonprofit organizations in various other ways. For example, the Bureau of the Census has its own classifications separate from the Internal Revenue Service; the United Way developed a taxonomy many years ago (Sumariwalla, 1976); the Independent Sector spearheaded a project in the 1980s to create the National Taxonomy of Exempt Entities (NTEE) (Hodgkinson & Toppe, 1991); and the International Classification of Non-Profit Organizations (ICNPO) has its own classifications (Salamon & Anheier, 1992). Taxonomies and classifications tend to list types of agencies according to the services provided (e.g., health, housing, or youth development agencies). Obviously, many agencies deliver multiple services and would fall into more than one category.

Just to add to the complexity of the nonprofit landscape, and contrary to popular belief, nonprofit organizations can make profits. In fact, if they do not make profits, they may have little chance at stability and growth. The defining characteristic of a nonprofit organization is that it is barred from distributing profits, or net earnings, to individuals who exercise control over it. These individuals might be directors, officers, or members. Net incomes, if any, must be retained and devoted to the purposes for which the organization was formed (Hansmann, 1981). This means that any funds left over at the end of a fiscal year must be reinvested in the organization, not distributed to any constituency.

Another element that muddies the distinction between types of agencies in human services is the highly interdependent nature of the service delivery system. This interdependence is particularly notable between the governmental and the nonprofit environments. It is the rare nonprofit human service organization that does not count on a portion (sometimes a large portion) of its funding from governmental sources. Whether an agency depends on food subsidies to keep its day care costs low or on social service contracts to provide foster care, the independent, community-based, voluntary nature of nonprofits seems to be eroding. Services in the private sector seem to be almost as political as those in the government sector.

For-Profit Organizations

For-profit organizations are part of the commercial or market economy. They are businesses and must pay taxes. They have boards of directors who generally are compensated and they may have investors or stockholders, all of whom can benefit financially from the organization's profits.

For-profit organizations, which have always been part of the human service landscape, have become more involved in service delivery since the 1960s. For example, "between 1965 and 1985, for-profit centers and chains emerged as the fastest growing source of child care in the United States," increasing from 7 to 24 percent of the market niche serving the child care needs of employed parents (Tuominen, 1991, pp. 450–451). Another example is the nursing home industry that is predominately run by for-profit businesses.

With privatization, the once assumed distinctions between profit and nonprofit, governmental and nongovernmental entities are blurring. Many for-profit agencies are competing against nonprofits for governmental service contracts. In addition, nonprofit organizations may even create for-profit agencies to generate income that can be contributed to their causes. For example, for-profit thrift stores are often a stable source of income for nonprofit groups that are highly involved in human service delivery.

Therefore, a full picture of the human service landscape must include the linkages among and between organizations. To remain vibrant and relevant, for-profits, like nonprofit and public agencies, make connections with various groups and communities. We now turn to some of the ways in which organizations interrelate.

Relationships among Groups, Organizations, and Communities

Whether they are public, nonprofit, or for profit, organizations are often committed to or have allegiances with other organizations and with other arenas, such as groups and communities. These organizations may represent or be affiliated with economically and politically disadvantaged populations who are not served or are underserved by other human service providers. Community affiliations may be formed around certain ideologies, belief systems, values, or population groups. They may be formed when a particular group agrees to provide funding to a cause. Some of these relationships are more explicit or more formalized than others. For example, a public agency's mandate may be very specific in defining the population group to be served, and the special-interest groups who advocated for the social policy that created the agency will likely have strong feelings about how the organization carries out its mandate. A nonprofit agency may have evolved out of an advocacy group that wants to address the needs of homeless people and has become a more formalized organization committed to continuing their cause. A for-profit organization with a high commitment to social responsibility may contribute to service delivery by donating a portion of its profits to a charitable agency with which an affiliation is formed.

Whatever the type agency, some organizations are explicit in espousing their relationships for ideological, religious, legal, economic, and/or political reasons. It is impossible here to fully explore the many forms these connections can take or even all the terms used to describe them. Terms such as *association, affiliation, linkage, coalition, alliance, allegiance, federation,* and a host of others are heard in organizational corridors as members dialogue about interorganizational, group, and community relationships.

To illustrate the diverse external connections organizations can have, we briefly examine some typical ways of connecting through (1) association, (2) ideological community, (3) franchising, and (4) host relationship. It is important to note that these are not mutually exclusive categories, and are only examples of many ways in which organizations relate to one another, to groups, and to communities. An organization could have multiple connections of different sorts with various groups and communities. We do not intend for these examples to be all-inclusive, but we want to spark the reader's interest in how incredibly diverse an organization's relationships can be.

Associations

Kramer (1981) defines **voluntary associations** as "membership organizations which usually have a social purpose—a 'cause'—and usually seek to benefit their constituency" (p. 9). Billis (1993) calls voluntary associations "groups of people who draw a boundary between themselves and others in order together to meet some problem, to 'do something'" (p. 160). This definition sounds very similar to the definition we gave earlier for an organization—there is a structure, participants, and a purpose. The difference is that the boundary in a formal organization may be recognized by a charter and bylaws approved by the state's corporation commission. A voluntary association can technically exist without being legally formalized. On the other hand, voluntary associations can be highly formalized, such as the National Association of Social Workers (NASW), the Child Welfare League of America (CWLA), the American Association of Retired Persons (AARP), or the American Association of Homes and Services for the Aged (AAHSA). It can be argued that voluntary associations are so widespread that they are the "authentic roots or core of the nonprofit sector" (Harris, 1998, p. 144).

Voluntary associations may have individual or organizational members—sometimes they have both—and these members may even pay dues. For example, NASW members are individual social workers who identify with the profession. Members of AARP members are older persons who wish to affiliate with one of the largest lobbying groups in the country. **Umbrella associations** are "nonprofit associations whose members are themselves nonprofit organizations" and it is estimated that one out of every five nonprofit organizations belongs to an umbrella association (Young, 2001, p. 290). For example, CWLA and AAHSA have organizational members: CWLA attracts organizations that provide services to children, whereas AAHSA's affiliates are an assortment of nonprofit long-term care facilities and service providers that provide services to older persons. These associations often have national meetings at which their members come together for professional enhancement, political action, or socialization.[2]

It would be impossible to fully explore the nature of organizational associations in one chapter. However, it is important to note that multiple writers have developed typologies of interorganizational relationships—those situations in which more than one organization works in some way with others, thus cutting across formal organizational boundaries. For example, Bailey and Koney (2000) provide a continuum of associational types beginning with the concept of (1) affiliation; followed by (2) federations, associations, and coalitions; (3) consortium, networks, joint ventures; and ending in (4) mergers, acquisitions, and consolidations. Bailey and Koney view affiliations as the loosest form of connection in which two organizations typically relate, with both maintaining total autonomy. Federations, associations, and coalitions are moderately autonomous relationships in which both individual organizational goals and the goals of the member organizations are important. Consortia, networks, and joint ventures assume minimal organizational autonomy, whereas mergers, acquisitions, and consolidations require the organization to entirely relinquish its autonomy.

Research on associational structure is found in the globalization literature as attempts are made to understand the emergence of nongovernmental organizations (NGOs) in developing countries and international nongovernmental organizations (INGOs) (Brown & Moore, 2001). For example, Lindenberg (1999) reports the results of an international practitioner conference in which five associational structures are identified: (1) separate independent organizations, plus coalitions; (2) weak umbrella coordinating mechanisms; (3) confederations; (4) federations;

and (5) unitary corporate models. In this typology, independent organizations function on their own but may choose to collaborate loosely with others when it is convenient. These types of associations are transitory and typically focus on fleeting advocacy issues. Independent organizations with weak umbrella coordinating mechanisms are typically aligned with a central organization that has minimal power over the associated organization, whereas the confederation is one in which organizational members have ceded some degree of power to the central organization. Federations hold more centralized power, whereas the central unit actually makes resource and other important decisions for subsidiaries in the case of the unitary corporate model. Further exploring the federation concept, Foreman (1999) compares two U.S.-based organizations: World Vision International and Habitat for Humanity International. Both provide global relief services and both could be labeled as federations, yet Foreman illustrates how federations differ in their associational form. World Vision is a donor-member–dominated federation, whereas Habitat is what she calls a global bumblebee federation because of differences in their governance structures.

Many agencies are local representatives of national organizations. Prevent Child Abuse America and the Alzheimer's Association, for example, operate in various relationships with national offices. It is important to explore just how strong these associations are and how much autonomy local chapters or groups have from central or national offices. Other organizations are associated with local groups, and may not be associated with a state, regional, or national body.

One often hears the term *grassroots* to refer to a movement or effort occurring in a local geographic area. Grassroots associations are one type of voluntary association—a type that is highly dependent on volunteers.[3] Smith (1999) defines **grassroots associations (GAs)** as "locally based, significantly autonomous, volunteer-run, formal nonprofit groups that manifest significant voluntary altruism as a group; they use the associational form of organization and thus have an official membership of volunteers who perform all or nearly all of the work done in and by the nonprofits" (p. 443). Whereas the focus of much nonprofit activity has been on larger, more formal organizations having a wide scope of service, the grassroots association is comprised of local members who come together for a specific cause and are tied to a geographical community.

Never make assumptions about associations and what they mean, because no two organizations are exactly alike in their relationships with others. We now turn to relationships that illustrate various ways and reasons organizations choose to connect or identify with a particular group for ideological, cultural, or religious reasons.

Ideological Communities

Relationships with ideological communities may be more or less loosely constituted, but they add to the cultural identity of the organization and its reason for being. We now briefly explore three types of communities with which organizations might relate. Note that these type communities are not always geographical or place related, but may be related to "nonplace" communities (Fellin, 1995, p. 4).

Religious or Faith Communities.   **Religious affiliates** are social service organizations that publicly acknowledge a relationship with a religious group or faith community. Typically, they are separately incorporated as nonprofit organizations and have names such as Lutheran Social Ministries or Catholic Charities. Nonprofits with religious affiliations proliferated during the late 1800s and early 1900s and are still very much a part of the traditional human service network. Over the years, these organizations have been called *sectarian agencies, church agencies, church-related agencies, church affiliates,* and, more recently, *faith-based agencies.* Few assumptions can be made about the meaning of religious affiliation, for it will vary by agency. Few religious affiliates today serve persons only from the groups with which they affiliate; in fact, many denominations have always served persons from any faith tradition. These affiliates often receive public dollars to carry out their mission and it is often hard to distinguish what makes them "religious" (Ellor, Netting, & Thibault, 1999). Yet, they maintain an affiliation with a religious group, an ideological symbol that may hold different meanings for administrators, staff, and consumers.

Although faith-based groups have provided human services for hundreds of years, the debate over what constitutes a faith-based organization escalated in 2001 with the Bush administration's establishment of the White House Office of Faith-Based and Community Initiatives. This initiative underscored the "Charitable Choice" provision in the Personal Responsibility and Work Opportunity Reconciliation Act of 1996 (often called "Welfare Reform"), which sought to reduce barriers to faith-based groups interested in accessing public funds to provide human services. It is important to recognize that with these policy changes, the concept of a faith-based organization expanded beyond traditional nonprofit religious affiliates to include community-based congregations and groups, many of which are not formally incorporated as nonprofit organizations (Cnaan, 1999; Sherwood, 2000; Wineburg, 2001).[4]

Ethnic Communities.   Some agencies are related to ethnic communities. More than 20 years ago, Jenkins (1980) began studying the ethnic agency as a special form of social organization. She defined the **ethnic agency** as having the following characteristics: (1) serving primarily ethnic clients, (2) predominately staffed by persons who have the same ethnicity as the clients served, (3) having a majority of its board from the ethnic group served, (4) having an ethnic community and/or ethnic power structure to support it, (5) integrating ethnic content into its programs, (6) desiring to strengthen the family as a primary goal, and (7) maintaining an ideology that promotes ethnic identity and participation in the decision-making process.

Research on ethnic agencies continues, as illustrated by Cortes's (1998) study of Latino nonprofit agencies. He defines *Latino nonprofits* in the United States as those "whose missions focus on Latino community members." (p. 439). He adds that they are typically tax-exempt corporations with Latino boards of directors and led by Latino chief executives or they are voluntary associations dominated by Latino constituencies.[5]

Feminist Communities. Ideological relationships may be based on a feminist perspective of service delivery. A **feminist organization**, according to Martin (1990), "meets any of the following criteria: (a) has a feminist ideology; (b) has feminist guiding values; (c) has feminist goals; (d) produces feminist outcomes; (e) was founded during the women's movement as part of the women's movement (including one or more of its submovements, e.g., the feminist self-help health movement [or] the violence against women movement)" (p. 815). Feminist organizations emerge in various sectors. They can be nonprofit or profit making; their structures can vary; and they can be local or national in their domain (Martin, 1990). Feminist organizations use paid and volunteer staff in different ways (Metzendorf & Cnaan, 1992).

Organizations that affiliate with a feminist group or ideology are often alternative agencies that have emerged because traditional service providers have not been sensitive to gender differences. Hyde (2000) elaborates on the nature of feminist social movement organizations (FSMOs), asserting that "FSMOs are the embodiments of feminist theory and practice, and reflect varied missions, structures, issues, strategies and products. Examples include peace encampments, lesbian rights networks, economic development and micro lending institutions, cultural centers, displaced homemaker leagues, reproductive rights groups and credit unions" (p. 49). She identifies three major ideological streams with which feminist organizations may identify: liberation (socialist or radical), liberal (women's rights), and cultural (woman controlled) (Hyde, 2000, p. 50), underscoring the recognition that there are multiple feminist ideologies.

Having introduced multiple communities with their own ideologies with which organizations may relate, we now turn to another type of relationship: the franchise. Though this concept is long established in for-profit circles, it has relevance for both nonprofit and for-profit human service organizations.

Franchises

Many agencies are local representatives of regional, national, or even international organizations. Oster (1992) defines such a connection as a **franchise** relationship in which local agencies or chapters conform to the following traits:

1. "The franchiser transfers to the franchisee the exclusive right to use a trademark or sell a particular product. Often, though not always, this right is given over a particular territory.
2. In exchange, the franchisee pays the franchiser and may have to agree to purchase supplies or new materials from the franchisee. Typically, the fee involves some initial lump sum and then ongoing fees keyed to the level of business.
3. The franchiser provides some assistance to the franchisee, typically on technical, operating matters, and maintains some control of the way in which the business is operated.

4. Any residual profits and losses from the business go to the franchisee [which means it can go into providing more service]. (p. 224)

Nursing homes (e.g., Manor Care), assisted living facilities (e.g., Sunrise), and day care facilities (e.g., KinderCare) are recognized trademarked names of franchised for-profit agencies. They are also deliverers of human services. Consumers expect standard quality from franchised operations, just as they anticipate that hamburgers or milk shakes from a franchised company in any city in the world will be the same. Although nonprofit agencies may not think of themselves as franchises, there are numerous long-established exemplars where the franchised concept applies. Oster (1992) contends that "more than half of the top 100 charitable nonprofits are franchise organizations" (p. 226). Goodwill Industries and Planned Parenthood, for example, operate in franchise relationships with national offices. Goodwill Industries has 179 affiliates in the United States, whereas Planned Parenthood has 171 (p. 225). Local affiliates pay their national organizations a percentage of their operating budgets in exchange for the use of the logo and name, technical support, and various activities such as lobbying at the national level for policies relevant to agency needs. Restrictions placed on franchisees vary greatly.[6]

Host Relationships

Human services may be delivered by departments, programs, or individuals housed within host organizations. **Host organizations** are typically large agencies that deliver human services or employ social workers as part of what they do, but whose primary purpose is not the delivery of human services. Therefore, host organizations can be health care systems, school settings, the military, commercial enterprises, or various other organizations in which a unit or component delivers social services. Host organizations are often administrated and dominated by professionals who do not specialize in social work (Jansson & Simmons, 1986), and social workers are viewed as "institutional guests" (Auslander, 1996, p. 15). Clients do not typically come to a host organization for the purpose of obtaining human services, since that is not the primary function of the host organization. However, in the process of providing what clients need, host organizations may engage social workers or social service units to assist clients.

In the past, host organizations such as acute care hospitals had social work departments from which a group of social work professionals could operate in what was a highly specialized medical setting. However, as hospital structures have changed, departments have often been replaced by decentralizing individual social workers to various units or cost centers (e.g., oncology, pediatrics, trauma, etc.). Social workers often complain that there is a loss of identify when the subcultural unit no longer exists. They report feelings of isolation from their peers, for when the host "unit" disappears, it is replaced by individual social workers who work on multidisciplinary teams in various locations within the larger health care system. Professionals from other fields supervise these social workers. Yet, the organization still remains a *host* for the provision of social services even though the concept of social work *unit* or social work *department* no longer applies.

TABLE 1.2   Selected Types of Organizational Relationships

Types	Descriptions	Examples
Associations	People or organizations that voluntarily associate for a defined purpose—includes membership organizations and grassroots associations	National Association of Social Workers (NASW) Child Welfare League of America (CWLA) American Association of Homes & Services for the Aged (AAHSA)
Ideological Communities	Organizations that align with the ideologies and values of religious, ethnic, feminist, or other communities	Catholic Charities (religious affiliation) Latino nonprofit (ethnic affiliation) Women's shelter (feminist affiliation)
Franchises	Organizations that have a relationship with regional or national organizations and seek to carry out the same goals locally	Prevent Child Abuse America The Alzheimer's Association The United Way American Red Cross YMCA
Host	Organizations that house programs and services, but do not view social services as their only or primary mission	Social services in hospitals School social work services Parish social work programs EAP programs Family assistance programs (military personnel)

Examples of host organizations cut across sectors. Public utility companies may hire social workers to assist low-income clients with billing issues, and for-profit businesses may establish employment assistance programs (EAPs) to provide support for employees who are dealing with child and elder care issues. Religious congregations may hire parish social workers to provide services to persons within their local community. Military bases may have family service programs designed to address psycho-social needs. Legislators may hire social workers to assist with constituency services. With the diversity that has been showcased so far, it should be clear that a good portion of social workers are likely to find themselves practicing in organizations that do not always define themselves as human service agencies, but that definitely provide human services. Table 1.2 summaries the types of relationships we have just highlighted.

Policy and Politics as Context for Organizations

We have used the notion of organizational landscape because it makes sense to us, but also because geographical metaphors are often used to approach the complex array of organizations across the United States. Reed (1996) refers to the "contested terrain" of organizational theorizing, whereas Van Til's (1988) ground-breaking work is titled *Mapping the Third Sector*. Lohmann's *The Commons* (1992) reminds us that what used to be the grounds in each village where activity took place did not disappear, but were restructured into the vast assortment of groups, associations, clubs, and nonprofit organizations that bring people together in community. Ryan (1999) continues the metaphor in examining the "landscape for nonprofits" as does Patti (2000) in writing about "the landscape of social welfare management" (p. 3).

Contemporary researchers stress the importance of understanding this landscape by "tracing the development and differentiation of organizational forms through empirical analysis of the built environment" (Guerra-Pearson, 1998, p. 459). Organizational forming can be measured "(a) by incorporation dates; . . . (b) by address or stability in location after numerous temporary moves; or (c) by the movement from adaptive space or rebuilding and expansion on adaptive sites to purpose-built spaces" (p. 460). Agencies formed in the last two centuries have rich histories as they have developed, often in the interest of serving underserved population groups or carrying out the values of an affiliated group. In other words, in any community in the United States there are groups of human service agencies that have a history that can be examined in historical context in order to see how social services have been, and are being, delivered. This historical dimension of the landscape is important in a community context, but the sociopolitical underpinning of organizational life is also important.

We have previously reviewed many types of organizations and their relationships that comprise the landscape of human services. These relationships are shaped in the context of U.S. politics and policy. Therefore, we provide a very brief overview of trends that have influenced and are influencing the nature of human service delivery.[7]

Sectoral Politics

Two highly visible sectors have always existed in the United States: the public and the market. Many names have been used to describe each. The **public sector** is also called *governmental* and *state*. The **market sector** is broadly viewed as *the economy, the commercial, the business,* or *the for-profit sector*. Whatever they are called, the focus of most organizational theory and management literature has been on trying to understand and influence the organizations that comprise these two sectors. Entire professional fields are devoted to their study and to the preparation of the next generations of public administrators for government and business people for the market. But sectoral issues are political and the tensions between the public and market or private sectors are important to understanding organizational contexts.

Public Subsidies of Private Agencies

Public agencies have been contracting with private agencies for the provision of social services since the early 1800s. For example, debates over governmental subsidies to provide private charities were heard as early as 1808 in New York City when the New York Orphan Aslyum requested and was granted monies by the mayor (Guerra-Pearson, 1998, p. 460). Today, **purchase of service contracting (POSC)**, sometimes called *federalism by contract* or *private federalism*, occurs when public agencies engage organizations from other sectors to actually deliver government funded services. Salamon (1987) refers to this arrangement as **third-party government,** or making the private organization an agent of the public.

As the welfare state developed, many people believed that public agencies were the dominant provider of human services. Conservatives argued that government was destroying the voluntary sector and should be taken to task, whereas liberals complained about the inability of a weakened voluntary sector to provide services as a justification for expanding government's role. By 1980, however, over 40 percent of the money spent at all levels of government in the United States to support human services went to nonprofits. Another 20 percent subsidized for-profit providers, leaving less than 40 percent to be delivered by government agencies. "In other words, nonprofit organizations had become the deliverers of a larger share of government-funded human services than government agencies themselves" (Salamon, 1993, p. 19). The voluntary sector, in the form of nonprofit agencies, actually expanded during this time.

Renewed Interest in Nonprofits

During the 1980s, policymakers became more interested in what is called the **third sector**, also referred to as the *charitable, independent, tax-exempt, voluntary,* or *nonprofit* sector. Organizations in this sector have deep roots in the United States and elsewhere, but were of less interest to policymakers, organizational theorists, and scholars until the 1980s. Growing disillusionment with the welfare state and government fostered a search for alternative approaches to providing human services as persons with political power began to consider the third sector's potential as a legitimate provider of human services. Ironically, the third sector had always been a part of the human service landscape, but people in power did not always take it seriously. The third sector included activities such as voluntary action, advocacy, grassroots initiatives, and even social movements that were often designed to enhance the status or quality of life of population groups who were invisible or even unpopular. The third sector, combined with the for-profit sector, became very interesting to politicians bent on privatizing government services and taxpayers who were tired of "big government." The rediscovery of the third sector emerged when public-sector provision of services lost favor.

With this rediscovery, new forms of service delivery proliferated and recognition of the roles played by third-sector organizations increased. An entire new interdisciplinary field of nonprofit management was established. Now, nonprofit administrators are being educated in schools of public administration, business, management, and social work. A debate persists about where to place these professional programs that educate people to lead and manage third-sector organizations.

Recognition of the importance of the third sector was accompanied by a growing legitimacy in nonprofit scholarship. Kramer (1981, p. 9) identifies four organizational roles that nonprofit organizations typically play. The *vanguard* role is one in which the agency is designed to innovate, pioneer, experiment, and generally create new programs that government may eventually take over. The *improver* or *advocate* role casts the agency in a critic, watchdog, or even gadfly position in which it persuades and even pressures government officials to extend, improve, or create needed services. The role of *value guardian* occurs when a voluntary agency provides leadership in upholding certain ideologies, beliefs, or values to protect the interests of certain groups (e.g., racial, ethnic, cultural, religious). The role of *service provider* occurs when the agency delivers social services that government is not willing, is unable, or prefers not to deliver. This later role is performed when government contracts with nonprofits to deliver human services (1981, p. 9).

Van Til (1988) conceptualizes human service delivery within the context of a mixed economy, manifested through intersectoral relationships. No longer did it make sense to view three distinctive sectors, even academically, for, as Van Til points out, public, profit, and nonprofit organizations were in constant interaction with one another. There were even organizational hybrids emerging that were not owned by any one sector. Terms such as quasi-*this* and quasi-*that* were used to describe these new organizational forms on the human service landscape. For example, **quasi-nongovernmental organizations** (**QUANGOS**) were defined as private, nonprofit incorporations largely financed by government, created by government initiative, and serving an important public purpose (Pifer, 1983). In hindsight, the Community Action Agency that emerged out of the 1960s War on Poverty was a QUANGO.

For-Profit Marketization and Nonprofit Commercialization

During the 1980s, there was much talk about "the marketization of welfare," in which the delivery of services by for-profit firms increased. In addition, a "commercialization" of nonprofit activity was occurring in which nonprofit organizations were beginning to engage in for-profit activities. For-profit organizations had long been the primary providers of nursing home and day care services, but during the 1970s, they had expanded their scope of services as other segments of the population were targeted, such as working mothers, older persons, middle- and upper-income people in need of family counseling, drug treatment, adoption assistance, and so on (Salamon, 1993).

As government entered a retrenchment mode in the 1980s and nonprofits searched for new sources of revenue, they often turned to the market—targeting clients who could pay or had third-party payments attached. For-profit agencies that had been enticed into the social service arena during a time when government dollars had been more available had positioned themselves for a market niche in the human service arena. They continued to be involved (Salamon, 1993), and in some cases began to compete with nonprofit agencies in the community. All this may be about to be made even more confusing if the early efforts in the George W. Bush administration related to federal funding of faith-based services comes to fruition.

Continued Focus on the Bottom Line

Most theorists have focused on trying to understand for-profit organizations devoted to delivering products to consumers who can pay. There is a great deal of interest and money involved in figuring out how one can find, support, facilitate, and even cajole employees into doing quality work that will result in high company productivity. The shelves of popular bookstores are lined with eye-catching titles about quick fixes and management trends designed to sell books and to make businesses more competitive. Certainly, there is a service component to selling any concrete product (e.g., cars, appliances, books, CDs, etc.), and people may shop around until they get "good service," but the products themselves are quite discrete. If they work well or do what consumers want them to do, then sales will be up and consumers will be happy.

Today, one hears a great deal of talk about how human service agencies are becoming more like "businesses." Depending on the source, this statement may have multiple meanings. Being more like "businesses" may mean being more accountable, focusing on effectiveness and outcome measurement, being more efficient, turning more profits, and so forth. However, human services are very different from cable service and automotive servicing in that the target of human services is alive and in need. This distinction cannot be underestimated.

Conclusion

Since social work as a profession does not underestimate the importance and the possibilities of the human condition, we believe that social workers are poised to manage the complexities of designing and implementing needed programs and services. These programs and services will be administered by an incredible variety of human service organizations in highly politicized environments. These organizations will associate with diverse groups, organizations, and communities as they seek to define and redefine themselves in relationship to others. Social work practitioners will do the same, as they, too, seek to define who they are, what they represent, and where they prefer to work. Organization practice is the ability to work and survive in these challenging arenas by making changes that address the needs of multiple stakeholders and constituencies and to reflect a strong grounding in professional values, critical thinking, and self-awareness.

In reading Chapter 1, we hope that you have begun to recognize the challenges and opportunities within organizations that fund, plan, advocate for, and deliver human services. We also hope that you will have glimpsed just how intriguing this human service landscape is, and that your curiosity is sparked. In Chapter 2, we turn to different ways of defining, knowing about, and understanding these complex organizations.

ENDNOTES

1. For a thorough review of the nonprofit concept, see Lohmann (1992).
2. See Harris (1998) for challenges faced by voluntary associations.
3. See Smith (2000) for a detailed analysis of grassroots associations.
4. For a full historical understanding of faith-based human services, see Cnaan, (1999) and Wineburg (2001).
5. For a full discussion of the ethnic agency, see Chapter 6 in Iglehart and Becerra (1995).
6. For a full discussion of franchises, see Oster (1992).
7. We provide only a brief, introductory overview of what is a very complex political environment. For an in-depth historical account, see Axinn and Stern (2001).

CHAPTER 2

The Ongoing Search to Understand Complex Organizations

Chapter 1 provided a beginning sense of the structural and sectoral variation that is possible in organizations involved in human service advocacy, planning, oversight, and delivery. This organizational diversity makes generalizations and expectations about human service programs challenging. The **diversity**, differences that represent fundamental and instrumental variations, has long been a challenge for those interested in understanding the best ways to structure organizations and to manage human behavior within them.

In this chapter, we attempt to take the reader beyond the worn dichotomy between traditional and alternative agencies previously introduced, and redefine both types as complex and diverse organizations. Regardless of whether a contemporary organization is considered traditional or alternative in its approach to human services, it is already or is becoming more diverse in at least four ways. First, given the demographics of U.S. society, the agency will increasingly serve clients, consumers, or customers (depending on the language used) who have multiple backgrounds and characteristics. Second, the agency will increasingly hire staff and recruit volunteers who represent diverse cultures. Third, the agency will be developing and changing its own culture and, if it is large enough, will develop subcultures within its own boundaries. Last, when compared with any other organization, even those agencies that do similar things, it will stand as a unique culture amid other agencies with similarities and differences. Thus, the organization in question will be part of a diverse grouping of those organizations involved in the human service enterprise. Key to the very nature of contemporary organizations is that they are built around differences. The importance of differences cannot be ignored, for the very nature of being multicultural implies that differences are present (see Table 2.1).

Differences are not always viewed as strengths in organizations. In traditional bureaucratic agencies, attempts are often made to repress differences and to work toward standardization, routinization, and sameness. In some agencies, differences are viewed as problems to be reckoned with by those in leadership positions. Alternative agencies are less standardized, less routinized, less "the same." Yet, alternative agencies develop because attention to differences—often in the form of client groups who are not being served, much less valued—are not being addressed by traditional organizations. Alternative agencies are alternative to traditional agencies because they assume "other," nontraditional organizational forms and

TABLE 2.1   **Ways in Which Organizations Manifest Differences**

Organizational Aspect	Manifestation of Differences
Clients, consumers, customers	Increasingly diverse, having different backgrounds and characteristics
Staff, volunteers	Increasingly diverse, representing different cultures
Organizational culture	Developing and changing corporate culture, with subcultures developing within the organization
In comparison to other organizations	Having a unique culture among other agencies with similarities and differences

may project different values. Theories about alternative agencies are not always very well developed because they are newer in their emergence than traditional theories. This means that alternative agencies often have to use more established dominant approaches to service delivery or make their own way, often without much support or guidance. Being "other" means they are often defined by what they are not. Only in the last two decades has diversity become a significant topic for organizational theorists and researchers (Daly, 1998), and this focus on diversity is relevant to both traditional and alternative organizational forms. It is important to know how this transformation is occurring and what it means for social workers who practice in contemporary organizations.

In this chapter, we begin by examining the search for universals in which many organizational theorists engaged for many decades. We follow with an historical overview of how differences have been treated in organizational theory and why the recognition of organizations as being multicultural is a more recent phenomenon. Following this historical perspective, readers are asked to consider how they are going to function as employees, leaders, and service providers in twenty-first–century organizations that have or are quickly becoming diverse, multicultural, and, for many individuals, potentially exciting places to spend professional time. Last, we focus on the concept of organizational culture and its potential helpfulness in defining the contemporary organization.

The Search for Order

In Chapter 1, we gave the reader permission to recognize that just because she or he "doesn't get it" does not mean that there is a logical order just waiting to be discovered. One of the authors is reminded of when she graduated from her master's program in social work with a concentration in planning and administration. She kept waiting to be "found out" because the service delivery system just didn't "make sense" and somehow she knew it just must fit together in some logical manner. She discovered that she held deep-seated assumptions, based on organizational theories she had learned, theories that had espoused sets of universal rules to guide organization practice. For example, there *should* always be one supervisor for a person. Didn't everyone know that? There *should* always be an organizational chart with clear lines of authority. How could an organization exist without a visible structure? She was perplexed and discomforted when she encountered organizations with matrix supervisory structures and agencies in which no organizational charts had been developed. She couldn't figure out why people didn't just "fix" these obvious flaws in their agencies when she pointed them out. Logic, based on her own set of assumptions, just didn't always click with others who didn't seem to need this same kind of order. But from where did this need for order come? The assumptions that she brought to organization practice were literally tied to her view of the world and to the organizational theories she had embraced. She felt comfort in these theories because they supported her assumptions or perhaps she got her assumptions from being taught the theories. Either way, the problem came when she saw real-world practice that flew in the face of what she had learned to expect, practice in which differences were rampant.

Almost since the inception of organization studies, the goal has been to minimize difference in order to create predictable performance. Daly (1998) asserts that the "philosophical underpinnings of Western thought have resulted in [seeking] order to end chaos and uncertainty, suppress contradictions, and find the one perfect truth" (p. xiv). Organizational research has, for example, shied away from questions that might reveal privileges enjoyed by dominant members of the organization or the oppression of other members (Nkomo, 1993; Scott, 1992).

This drive for sameness and predictability viewed difference as a problem and standardization as necessary for an effective and efficient operation. Note that this is not intended to condemn early theorists who started without any previous understandings of what an organization is all about. The conceptualization and study of organizations had to begin somewhere and many of the things that were discovered about organizations are still useful today. However, what it does mean is that there was an incredible push to find the "one best way" to design organizations and to prescribe how people should act within them. Ironically, early organizations may have been structured similarly, but people were highly diverse. The result of ignoring those human differences meant that some staff people were able to "fit" and others were not, that some people were viewed as deserving clients and others were not.

Assumptions about Organizations

For many years, theorists have searched for ways to understand and to order organizations. Organizational scholars have even attempted to order and categorize the theories that have emerged. In 1961, Koontz classified organizational theories, referring to a "management theory jungle." Hutchinson (1967) categorized theories according to scientific management, environmental and human relations school, man (sic) as decision maker, and current theories of management. A bit later, Scott and Mitchell (1972) added neoclassical theory, systems concept, organization processes, and organization change. Bolman and Deal (1991) made sense of organization theories by categorizing them into the structural frame, the human resource frame, the political frame, and the symbolic frame. Farazmand (1994), on the other hand, cited three categories: instrumental rationality, which includes classical and neoclassical theories; systems theories; and critical and interpretive theories. All of these typologies attempted to order very complex ways of approaching organizations.

Shafritz and Ott (2001) identify nine major perspectives on organization theory:

1. Classical organization theory
2. Neoclassical organization theory
3. Human resource theory or the organizational behavior perspective
4. "Modern" structural organization theory
5. Systems theory and organizational economics
6. Power and politics organization theory
7. Organizational culture and sense-making
8. Organizational culture reform movements
9. Postmodernism and the information age

Shafritz and Ott's classification scheme is now in its fifth edition. Their second edition (1987) included the first five perspectives. Their third edition added "power and politics" and "organizational culture" as "two newer schools or perspectives of organization theory that literally did not exist when the first edition was published" (p. v). In fact, the organization culture perspective was so new that Shafritz and Ott (1987) referred to it as controversial and countercultural to existing organizational theory (p. 373). Their fourth edition added "sense-making" to the organization culture perspective and added two additional categories. We point this out to emphasize how the search for understanding organizations is ongoing and how new theoretical perspectives are continually emerging. Each perspective contains clusters of assumptions that often are not compatible with one another.

In 1997, Morgan published the second edition of *Images of Organization,* the first version of which had sold extremely well because it touched a chord with readers attempting to define and understand organizations. Morgan demystified what was often seen as "a kind of magical power to understand and transform the situations [successful managers and problem solvers] encounter" (p. 3). His premise was "that all theories of organization and management are based on implicit images or metaphors that lead us to see, understand, and manage organizations in distinctive yet practical ways" (p. 4). Defining **metaphors** as "attempt[s] to understand one element of experience in terms of another" (p. 4), he proceeded to elaborate on the metaphorical images most frequently used when people try to define and understand organizations. Morgan's list of metaphors follows:

■ Organizations as machines
■ Organizations as organisms

- Organizations as brains
- Organizations as cultures
- Organizations as political systems
- Organizations as psychic prisons
- Organizations as flux and transformation
- Organizations as domination

Morgan details each metaphor, identifies theories that reflect each metaphor, and examines the strengths and limitations of each. We encourage the reader to access this highly insightful book for a deeper understanding of how people construct their definitions and expectations of organizations through metaphorical understandings of what organizations are like. It is also helpful to consider what metaphors one currently uses when approaching an organization and how that establishes one's expectations of what will happen in that organization. For example, we have students who excitedly tell us that their field agencies are "just like a family!" As soon as we hear this, we know that their assumptions and expectations (and perhaps those of the organization itself) are tied to a family metaphor. We gently suggest that this metaphor is not only inappropriate but that it will set them and other organization members up for great frustration because organizations are not intended to be families.

Sources such as Shafritz and Ott (2001) and Morgan (1997) are readily available if the reader is interested in pursuing his or her various theoretical perspectives. Our intent in this chapter is to introduce traditional assumptions and concepts that have dominated thinking about organizations in the previous century and compare them to more contemporary conceptualizations of organizational life. We begin by briefly tracing efforts to understand organizational structure, organizational goals, and organizations and their social environment, including the major schools of organizational analysis and some of the metaphors they represent.

Traditional Approaches to Understanding Organizations

Almost from the beginning of research on organizations and organizational behavior there has been a quest to determine "how best to coordinate human efforts in the service of organizational goals" (Etzioni, 1964, p. 2). Early categorization schemes were similar in that there was assumed to be a "right" way to approach the organizational world and there were relatively narrow and precise definitions of organizations.

Classical Theories

The search for effectiveness and efficiency in organizations gave rise to various approaches to understanding and planning for change in organizations. The earliest such approach grew out of American industrialization at the turn of the twenti-eth century and was based on Frederick W. Taylor's *scientific management* (1911). Scientific management recognized no inherent conflict between the organization and those working within it. The assumption was that whatever was good for man-agement would also be good for labor: Higher productivity leads to higher profits, which means higher pay and therefore greater satisfaction. Using this model of analysis, it was assumed that material rewards were closely related to the work effort. It was important to understand the organization in order to make the worker respond with the greatest possible performance. Therefore, understanding the organization involved finding the best working procedures and equipment or tools, determining the best way to teach them, and then tying pay to output so that workers were induced to produce.

Shafritz and Ott (1996, pp. 29–37) categorize Taylor's scientific management in the classical organization theory perspective, along with theorists such as Max Weber, who is considered the father of the theory of bureaucracy, and Henri Fayol, who developed the first comprehensive theory of management. Classical theories were based on four fundamental assumptions:

1. Organizations exist to accomplish production-related and economic goals.
2. There is one best way to organize for production, and that way can be found through systematic, scientific inquiry.
3. Production is maximized through specialization and division of labor.
4. People and organizations act in accordance with rational economic principles. (Shafritz & Ott, 2001, p. 28)

Mechanistic approaches, generated from classical theories, continue to shape how organizations are defined and structured. It is little surprise, then, that Morgan (1997) framed these theories as machine metaphors in which routines, efficiency, reliability, and predictability were expected organizational characteristics. Yet, another metaphor is relevant here as well. One might ask why Taylor was so ada-mant about there being "one best way." Morgan explains that Taylor's metaphor of organization was the psychic prison in which there was no order. Taylor "was a man totally preoccupied with control...an obsessive, compulsive character, driven by a relentless need to tie down and master almost every aspect of his life" (1997, p. 221). Taylor's metaphor for organizations, and the accompanying assump-tions, led him to create ways to structure organizations as machines so that they would be controlled by managers. We hope that this illustration reveals to the reader how important it is to recognize the assumptions held by theorists and how those assumptions are translated into their work.

Recognizing Human Differences and Complexity

Since the late 1920s, much of organization theory developed in reaction to the clas-sical theories of scientific management and bureaucracy. The Human Relations School in the United States recognized workers' needs beyond the economic, and the often cited work of Elton Mayo and his research team beginning in 1927 at the Hawthorne plant in the Western Electric Company is seen as a breakthrough event. Mayo's team was attempting to fit workers into classical views of organizational productivity by manipulating various factors (e.g., lights, pay incentives, flow of materials). When workers were more productive, even when important factors were withheld, the research team reframed their study in social psychological terms, recognizing for the first time the importance of human differences (as opposed to mechanical similarities) within organizational life.

Understanding organizations, in what later became known as human relations or organizational behavior theory, meant paying attention to social and cultural needs, not just economic needs of workers. Shifting focus to social rather than physical determinants of output, the goal of human relations theory was to understand the real nature of workers' needs, their informal group life and its relationships to the organization, so that enlightened management could develop the steps necessary to meet workers' needs. Needs could be met when work and organizational structure were related to the social needs of employees. Given previous perspectives on organizations, human relations theory no longer viewed organizations as the "independent variable to be manipulated in order to change behavior.... Instead the organization [is] seen as the context in which behavior occurs.... The organization influences human behavior just as behavior shapes organizations" (Shafritz & Ott, 2001, p. 146). The list of human relations theory assumptions looks remarkably different from the earlier list of assumptions held by classical theorists:

1. Organizations exist to meet human needs.
2. There is a reciprocal relationship between organizations and people, both need one another.
3. Fit between individuals and organizations is important, otherwise both will suffer.
4. Good fit between organizations and individuals is mutually beneficial, in that human beings will find meaningful work and organizations will draw from people's strengths and talents. (Shafritz & Ott, 2001, p. 146)

The field of social psychology and organizational behavior was embraced by many as a reaction to the oppressive nature of classical theory, and there were other writers who strongly reacted to the classicists. Neoclassical theorists emerged as revisionists and critics of scientific management and bureaucratic theory shortly after World War II. The attacks of these theorists, vigorous as they were, did not result in a total abandonment of many classical concepts. Neoclassical theorists—such as Chester Barnard, Robert Merton, Herbert A. Simon, Philip Selznick, R. M. Cyert, and James G. March—expanded, modified, and revised classical organization theory (Barnard, 1938, 1968; Selznick, 1948; Simon, 1957), taking classical theory another step forward, beyond purely mechanistic or machine metaphors. Shafritz and Ott (2001) contend that neoclassical theorists "paved the way—opened the door—for the soon-to-follow explosions of thinking from the human relations,

'modern' structural, systems, power and politics, and organization culture perspectives of organizations" (p. 91).

Criticism of Traditional Approaches

Earlier traditions to understanding organizations fell short in helping decision
makers in complex organizations fashion structures and establish worker motivation to consistently achieve organizational goals. Even in the early days of organizational research, Etzioni (1964) saw that using organizational goals and their
measurement as a way to understand organizations was problematic for studying
and evaluating organizations. For him, asking how well an agency achieved what
it had been assigned to accomplish was more like "social criticism rather that scientific analysis" (p. 16) because agencies rarely totally achieve their goals. He com-
mented, "Ideals are more attractive than the reality which the organization attains"
(p. 16). Etzioni contended that with complete achievement of goals as the only measure of success, all agencies are judged to be ineffective and inefficient—a useless
product for any model of organizational analysis.

In 1964, Etzioni proposed an alternative, comparative "systems model."
Instead of comparing organizations to ideals about what they might be or might
achieve, he proposed that organizations be assessed in relation to other similar
organizations. A comparative model allowed a broader assessment of the organizational process other than merely the achievement of goals, thus allowing nongoal
activities to be considered. Benefits of this approach were not seen without concomitant costs. Though this allowed understanding beyond nongoal activities, it was
expensive and required more analytic complexity and skills on the part of those
wishing to reach organizational understanding. Lack of skills and lack of theory to
guide the question formation regarding complex organizations still resulted in this
approach's lack of feasibility.

As organizations developed more complexity in structure, expectations, and
participants, as well as in location and culture, organizational theories constructed
at high levels of abstraction were unable to aid in the framing of the specifics of a
particular study of organizations (Etzioni, 1961). In addition, the theories in use had
been built from very traditional views of social science, leaving no room for rigorous study of the more interpretive dimensions of organizational culture and politics. None of the theories and models in use aided the organizational researcher or
leader in looking at human meaning within organizational life, nor were they able
to aid in understanding or managing the diversity challenges of organization practice.

Beginning in the 1960s, a juncture in the development of organizational theory occurred. Alternative theoretical perspectives, each with its own assumptions
and foci, emerged from the 1960s to the turn of the twenty-first century. Shafritz
and Ott (2001) identify six different perspectives on organizational theory. We will
briefly mention several of the contemporary perspectives in the next section of this
chapter. These theories appear in more detail in later chapters, where we examine
different ways of knowing about and practicing in organizations.

The Emergence of Multiple Alternative Perspectives

Classical organizational theorists were structuralists. They wanted to know how to design the best form that would make an organization function most productively. The search for the "one best way" became a mantra of persons who ascribed to a Taylorist approach. Although bureaucratic theory was often viewed with disdain, large organizations often sought to structure themselves somewhat bureaucratically just to manage their complexity. Even though the human relations/organizational behavior perspective focused on the human element within organizations, the purpose was to get the human being in sync with the organization, thus enforcing a desired conformity. This, too, had implications for how organizations were structured and how people felt about them.

"Modern" Structuralist Organization Theory

"Modern" structuralist organization theory is distinguished from classical approaches by time. The classicists developed their perspectives prior to World War II, and the modern structuralists wrote after the war. Influenced by neoclassical and human relations and systems theorists, modern structuralists saw understanding organizations as requiring a more encompassing, balanced approach. In this perspective, it was assumed that conflict and strain within the organization were inevitable and not always undesirable. The goal was to understand the organizational/personal needs and issues, discipline and autonomy, formal and informal relations, management and worker perspectives, ranks' and divisions' perspectives, and the organizational environment both inside and outside the organization in order to understand the relationship between material and social rewards related to productivity. Though this perspective did incorporate elements of the approaches that came before it, at the base was an acceptance of conflict and alienation from a Marxian tradition. It was assumed that large, complex organizations had elements of shared interests and other interests that were incompatible. The organization served as a platform for power struggle rather than as a surrogate family. From this perspective, understanding organization required the understanding of the social functions of conflict in order to allow differences to emerge so that testing and adjustments in the organization could be made to ensure greater productivity (Shafritz & Ott, 2001).

As modern structuralist theory evolved, studies of organizations and behavior of those within them focused on understanding authority and its use, organizational structure, communication, control, leadership, and organizational interaction in its social environment. At this stage in development, researchers on organizations were concerned with both formal and informal elements of structure (Blau & Scott, 1962) and whether to structure an organization according to its products or its functions (Walker & Lorsch, 1968). Modern structuralists assumed that "most problems in an organization result from structural flaws and can be solved by changing the structure" (Shafritz & Ott, 2001, p. 198).

Building on the structuralist approach, the 1970s and 1980s saw the development of organizational research that attempted to understand and predict organizational behavior or create best decisions. The research focus was on describing important variables and the linkages between these variables that influence their effectiveness in organizations. Most of the attempts at understanding were based on quantitative studies at a high level of abstraction (Etzioni, 1975) rather than on detailed observations about single organizations. From this research, a conceptual framework evolved (Heydebrand, 1973) that identified the important dimensions of organizational life. One dimension involved studies of the nature and complexity of the organizational environment and organizational autonomy. Issues such as the complexity of the organization, the organizational age, and the organization's autonomy were studied.

A second dimension included organizational goals and task structure. Growing out of an interest in the interaction between the environment and autonomy, and their influence on organizational structure, this dimension looked at the number and diversity of major organizational objectives, geographic dispersion, variability of tasks, organizational size, organizational change, and dimensions of effectiveness. All of this was seen to be related to another dimension—internal structure. Here, the interest was in the division of labor: specialization, standardization, formalization, centralization, configuration, and flexibility (Heydebrand, 1973, p. 458). The technical complexity and skill structure of the organization was also at issue, as was the social environment. The social environment was operationalized to include such elements as involvement, rewards, and rationality.

The social environment and its relationship to managerial autonomy were also at issue. This led to yet another dimension of the conceptual framework: organizational coordination and control. In this dimension was included the concept of professionalization, including nonbureaucratic and bureaucratic approaches, forms of administration, decision making, and interorganizational networks. Together, these dimensions represented the determinants of internal structure. Organizations could be understood and the characteristics of organizations could be identified through this network of internal and external control clusters. In sum, the mathematical approach to understanding organization was the most technologically sophisticated. The hope was that understanding organizational size in relation to complexity and administration could statistically affect efficiency, satisfaction, flexibility, and productivity (Etzioni, 1975).

Systems Theories

In the late 1960s, systems theory came fully to the forefront of organizational thinking with the publication of two pivotal works written by Katz and Kahn (1966) and Thompson (1967). While structuralists had continued to focus on machine metaphors (albeit more flexible machines), early systems thinkers were firmly rooted in organism metaphors. Organizations were seen as species in which dynamic interactions transpired, in which there were inputs, throughputs, outputs, outcomes, feedback loops, and a whole range of terms describing interaction between organizations and their environments. Systems theorists recognized the importance of the changing environment. Thompson (1967) distinguished between the organization's task and general environments. *Task environments* included all those individuals, groups, and organizations with which an organization had interaction. *General environments* were defined as broader institutions of society reflected in things such as political structures or societal attitudes.

Different schools of thought within systems theory hold differing assumptions about organizations, raising interesting issues for critical thinking about organizations. Systems theories "differ on the kind of system social systems are" (Martin & O'Connor, 1989, p. 54). Social scientists have used five analogies to depict social systems: mechanical, organismic, morphogenic, factional, and catastrophic (Burrell & Morgan, 1979, Chapter 4). Depending on the analogy used, systems theory can be used to describe both traditional and alternative agencies. Table 2.2 summarizes these analogies.

Martin and O'Connor (1989) explain each of the analogies in Table 2.2. They see the *mechanical* analogy as viewing social systems as physical machines, derived from physics. This is a closed-systems approach, focusing on internal integration, and is how the early structuralists would have viewed an organization. One can almost hear the early theorists searching for the one best way to make people in organizations work as interchangeable parts and to locate the right structure that will maintain equilibrium within the system. This approach to systems has been highly criticized for ignoring both complexity and the interdependence of organizations and their environments.

The *organismic* analysis comes from biology and was a reaction to the machine analogy, much like the human relations and "modern" structuralists reacted to the classical and neoclassical theorists. In this analogy, society is viewed as a biological organism with interrelated parts that are functionally unified. Emerging in the 1940s and 50s as a reaction to the more mechanistic views of systems, the organismic analogy developed with advances in biology. Talcott Parsons is credited with having advanced this development in his structural-functionalist approach to systems that dominated theoretical circles between the 1950s and 1960s. "Structural functionalism and its progency, systems theory, provided an 'internalist' focus on organizational design with an 'externalist' concern with environmental uncertainty" (Reed, 1996, p. 37). According to Parsons, social systems had to perform four functions in order to survive: adaptation, goal attainment, integration, and pattern maintenance. In performing these functions, the goal was to seek homeostasis, a state of balance in which every part is working together and is integrating with the whole. Focusing attention on the status quo and attempting only incremental change, the organismic type of systems theory leads to a search for order and consensus. Martin and O'Connor (1989, p. 54) think that it is unfortunate that open-systems theory "has been used often with an organismic analogy and, as a result, is believed to have limitations that it does not have." This is why one will run into people who talk about how conservative or change adverse systems theory is. They are referring to the organismic type of systems theory that focuses on maintaining the status quo at all costs. Traditional organizations have often been

TABLE 2.2   Analogies Used by Social Scientists to Depict Social Systems

Analogy	Description and Principal Tendency
Mechanical	Assumes perfect coordination and integration of parts; Assumes that departures from equilibrium result in correct action to return to equilibrium; Assumes social systems are like machines; Emphasizes order and stability over conflict and change.
Organismic	Assumes high coordination and integration of parts; Assumes that departures from homeostasis result in corrective actions to return to homeostasis; Assumes society is like a living organism with different organs that cooperate closely to contribute to the survival of the whole; Assumes social systems are cohesive because of consensus of citizens, families, communities, etc.; Emphasizes order and stability over conflict and change.
Morphogenic	Assumes that social systems change constantly through interaction and exchange with their environment(s); Assumes that social systems are highly open; Assumes social systems may be orderly and predictable but may also be disorderly and unpredictable; Assumes that order may rest on coercion and domination as well as cooperation and consensus; Places about equal emphasis on conflict and change as on order and stability.
Factional	Assumes that social systems are divided into contentious factions that conflict over goals, priorities, resources and strategies; Assumes that the turbulent division of the system into factions is the principal tendency of the system; Emphasizes conflict and change over order and stability.
Catastrophic	Assumes that social systems are severely segmented and warring; Assumes that little order or predictability exists; Assumes that conflict may destroy some component parts; Assumes complete reorganization of the system is required if the system is to become less chaotic or conflictual; Emphasizes conflict and change over order and stability.

Source: From Patricia Yancey Martin and Gerald G. O'Connor, *The Social Work Environment: Open Systems Applications.* Copyright © 1989 Allyn & Bacon. Reprinted by permission. Adapted from G. Burrell and G. Morgan, *Sociological Paradigms and Organisational Analysis* (Aldershot, England: Ashgate, 1979), Figure 4.1, p. 67. Used by permission.

accused of behaving in this way, of not taking risks, and of focusing on organizational maintenance over client service.

Unlike mechanical and organismic analogies, morphogenic, factional, and catastrophic analogies focus on the dynamic and changing nature of social systems rather than attempting to deny those dynamics. Conflict is seen as a normal part of being an organization within a complex environment.

Morphogenesis means structure change, as opposed to **morphostasis,** which means structure maintaining. A *morphogenic* approach, then, views systems as capable of change. In actuality, the possibility that an organization will return to a previous state of stability is only one of many possible options. The expectation is that as organizations gain more knowledge and experience, they will indeed change their structures, forms, goals, policies, and a host of other factors. Thus, maintaining a steady state of equilibrium would mean that the system has not grown and developed. Systems theory based on a morphogenic analogy expects interaction with the environment to influence what occurs within the organization so that the organization adjusts accordingly. There is a sense of fluidity that comes from recognizing differences and learning from those differences. New organizational forms will emerge over time, hopefully leading to more highly ordered, complex systems (Martin & O'Connor, 1989).

Whereas a morphogenic analogy works well in an organization that has members who are in general agreement about direction and purpose, or at least get along reasonably well, a *factional* analogy views organizations as being somewhat fragmented among various, somewhat contentious, groups. This lack of cooperation is characterized by internal conflict, complete with contention, domination, competition, and lack of cooperation rather than harmony among members. Given that members change and staff turn over in organizations, a factional analogy may apply at times within systems and not be relevant at others, depending on the presence of contentiousness. This analogy is compatible with the morphogenic analogy because both assume that organizations are within ever-changing environments in which conflict and disorder are to be expected. The difference is that in the factional system, conflict among groups is occurring within the organization as well (Martin & O'Connor, 1989).

The last analogy is *catastrophic,* and like the previous two analogies just discussed, it assumes that social systems are in constant change. In this view of organizations, however, internal competition is harsh, severe conflict is occurring on an ongoing basis, and all aspects of the system are in flux. To survive, reorganization is ongoing and parts of the system may literally be on the verge of collapse. Again, like the morphogenic and factional analogies, organizations may move in and out of catastrophe (Martin & O'Connor, 1989).

These latter three analogies of systems theory bring organizations beyond a simple view that they are shifting in an environmental sea, attempting to regain stability and equilibrium. Instead, they recognize that organizations and environments are in a constant state of interaction and that organizations have various degrees of stability within. There is no expectation that organizations will remain the same; in fact, the potential for change is constant, and being able to change may make the difference in whether the organization grows, develops, and even survives as a viable entity. Change is a way of life in these open systems.

We will return to these systems analogies in subsequent chapters. At this point, it is important for the reader to realize that just because someone says that they use systems theory does not tell the full story. One has to know which type of systems theory is being used, the analogy in which it is grounded, and thus the assumptions that are held. Since there are many different types of systems theory, one can easily become confused.

Power and Politics Theories

Just as systems theory caught the attention of organizational theorists and scholars, the power and politics perspective on organizations also emerged in the early 1970s. Earlier recognition of conflict had been viewed as tension between formal structure (organization) and informal groups (workers); now, power and politics theorists viewed organizations "as collections of persons who used power and political activities in all their interactions" (Netting & O'Connor, 1998, p. 297).

Power and politics theorists reject the assumptions held by "modern" structuralists and systems theorists, both of whom assume that an organization's primary purpose is to achieve established goals. Power theorists view these assumptions as highly naive, rather viewing what happens in organizations as a constant struggle between power, politics, and influence. Goals are established as a result of ongoing maneuvering and bargaining, thus goals shift as power shifts. Formal authority, defined as legitimized power, is recognized as only one of many influences in organizations. In fact, other forms of power may prevail over authority-based power (Shafritz & Ott, 2001, pp. 298–303) when informal power and influence are exercised.

Thus far, we have touched on six of the perspectives identified by Shafritz and Ott (classical, neoclassical, human resource, "modern" structuralist, systems, and power and politics). Power and politics theorists begin to part company with the other five by questioning the fact that the quest for rationality within organizations is formalized. They point out how important the informal system is in actually making things happen (or not happen) in organizations. The power and politics theorists and the organizational culture and sensemaking theorists depart from accepted assumptions and begin to define organizations very differently. These later theories have been particularly helpful for alternative agencies that have sought guidance in understanding and organizing their organizations. Those particularly interested in feminist and alternative approaches have found these perspectives helpful, given that they challenge theoretical assumptions long embraced by more traditional agencies.

Organizational Culture and Sensemaking

Shafritz and Ott (1996) identify a number of emerging theories that comprise what they call the *organizational culture and sensemaking perspective*. Theories within this perspective not only challenge more traditional classical and neoclassical views of organizations but they also challenge assumptions held by "modern" structuralists and systems theorists about how decisions are made in organizations and why people behave as they do. "Modern" structuralists and systems theorists see organizations as rational, meaning that their purpose is to achieve agreed-upon goals (Shafritz & Ott, 1996, p. 420). A sensemaking perpective, however, contends that for organizations to be totally rational, they would have to be self-correcting collections of interdependent people who could come to consensus on objectives and methods, coordinate their activities through information sharing, and predict organizational problems and resolutions (Weick, 1992). Weick concludes that these conditions seldom exist in modern organizations. Yet, the basic assumptions of "modern" structuralists and systems theorists are that these factors must be in place, and once everything is ordered, the organization will function optimally. The organizational culture perspective literally assumes the opposite—that cultural norms, values, and beliefs guide what happens in organizations, not formal rules, authority, or rational behavior.

A leading theorist in organizational culture, Schein (1992) defines **organizational culture** as "a pattern of shared basic assumptions that the group learned as it solved its problems of external adaptation and internal integration, that has worked well enough to be considered valid and, therefore, to be taught to new members as the correct way to perceive, think, and feel in relation to those problems" (p. 12). Note that Schein begins with "shared basic assumptions." Yet, one often enters organizations in which those basic assumptions are so ingrained that they are often not even recognized on a conscious level. They may even be shared unconsciously by organizational members. Problems arise when a disjuncture occurs between what exists and what is needed internally or externally to maintain an organization's cultural norms.

Solving problems of external adaptation and internal integration refer to the ways in which organizational members go about working on their relationship with the larger external environment and dealing with issues internal to the organization. Schein (1992) contends that adapting externally includes (1) gaining a consensus on the mission, (2) establishing goals, (3) finding the means to achieve those goals, (4) finding ways to measure how the work is going, and (5) identifying strategies to repair things when goals are not being met (p. 52). According to Schein, if these five areas are minimally necessary for an organization to structure itself to survive in its environment, then there is great potential for misunderstanding when persons from different backgrounds enter the organization.

To further complicate the importance of being culturally competent, in large organizations there may be multiple groups (units, departments, branch offices, etc.) developing their own shared assumptions and approaches to the work of the organization. Therefore, within organizations, subcultures often develop. Subcultures may be complementary, but they may also experience times in which norms and values have to be clarified or even in which there is intergroup conflict that cannot be fully resolved.

By now it should come as no surprise that no matter what perspective is presented about organizations, there will be criticisms. If ever the reader believed that there really is a "one best way" and that emerging perspectives are moving toward finding that one magical organizational structure that would be perfect in planning or delivering human services, we hope we have dispelled the myth. Instead, according to Morgan, "One of the major strengths of the culture metaphor is that it directs attention to the symbolic significance of almost every aspect of organizational life" (Morgan, 1997, p. 146). Organizational culture and sensemaking theories do not simplify; they complicate the business of choosing organizational structure for delivering human services. At least from these perspectives, one can recognize just how challenging the task is.

As with all perspectives, the organizational culture and sensemaking perspective has limitations. Since this perspective has "crept" into the popular management literature, it has become almost commonplace in most organizations to recognize the importance of corporate cultures and subcultures. Although this recognition is a positive change in how people are seen in organizational contexts, critics worry that managers will label some cultures as "good" and others as "bad," moving toward a type of ideological control and attempting to engineer values. Certainly, managers have always attempted to influence attitudes, values, and norms in order to motivate employees, but the pressing movement to manipulate and shape culture could result in party lines and beliefs in "one best culture." If culture is a set of shared assumptions, as Schein points out, then one has to ask the question: Shared by whom? Culture and sensemaking perspectives, used by persons with mechanistic assumptions, could actually become tools of control, manipulation, and totalitarism. Morgan (1997) contends that the creation or enacting of culture can be a wonderfully empowering process and is often seen in the literature as a voluntary process in which workers participate. He adds, "We all construct or enact our realities but not necessarily under circumstances of our own choosing. There is an important power dimension underlying the enactment process that the culture metaphor does not always highlight to the degree possible. When this is taken into account, the culture metaphor becomes infused with a political flavor" (p. 152). This political flavor is what the power and politics perspective introduces into the mix and why these two metaphors (organizations as political systems and organizations as cultures) are beneficial in thinking about organizations in context.

Organizational Theories and Human Service Organizations

Table 2.3 summarizes some of the important contributions made by each of the perspectives just discussed. Keep in mind that each perspective (and the writings within each perspective) reflects certain assumptions that may contradict others. The point is that with the development of both classical and modern organization theories that reflect the complexity of postindustrial and technological societies, understanding organizations also becomes increasingly complex. Added to the global nature of many organizations and the multicultural profile of most U.S. work environments, the old ways of categorizing organizations may feel oppressive to persons in organizations intent on creating a more just work environment in

TABLE 2.3   Primary Contributions by Organizational Theoretical Perspectives

Theoretical Perspective	Primary Contribution
Classical theory	Recognized the importance of formal organizational structure and productivity
Human resource/Organizational behavior theory	Recognized the importance of individuals and groups, the informal "system," and their relationship to the organization
Neoclassical theory	Acknowledged organizational complexity
"Modern" structuralist theory	Transcended traditional, naive approaches to formal structure and provided a more comprehensive, balanced perspective of multiple sets of factors that relate within organizations
Systems theories	Viewed organizations as open systems within changing environments
Power and politics theory	Acknowledged the importance of influence, politics and informal power within organizations, beyond traditional views of authority as legitimized power
Organization culture theory	Recognized that organizations develop their own beliefs grounded in deeply held assumptions and values.
Sensemaking theory	Pointed out the ways in which organizational players reconstruct or "make sense" out of what happens

a more just society. Honoring diversity requires honoring diverse ways of understanding, communicating, thinking, and doing. It is our assumption that simply categorizing perspectives into ways of thinking about organizations is only a beginning step. To fully engage in organization practice, one must get beyond recognizing different perspectives or worldviews and actually be able to use different ways of understanding in one's work.

Each perspective presented in this historical recounting of attempts at understanding organizations brings with it certain insights and emphasizes particular aspects of organizational life while overlooking other essential elements. Even though these insights are only possible as a result of applying a particular perspective, much has been left unexamined. To date, no one approach has been able to capture fully the current complexity of organizational life. Organizational diversity includes elements such as purpose, structure, type, affiliation, and location as well as values, beliefs, and assumptions undergirding agency culture. Staff and client diversity includes gender, race, nationality, sexual orientation, attitudes, religion, values, and cultural diversity. Staff are often diverse in terms of the professions they represent. Individuals also reflect diversity within groups, including differences represented and covered by the Americans with Disabilities Act or the Age Discrimination Act. These multiple, and often overlapping, aspects of diversity are related to organizational behaviors and outcomes. It is no surprise that Cox (1993) asserts, "Managing diversity is among the most important management challenges of this decade" (p. x).

Social work leaders in human service organizations must think critically about their own and others' assumptions about organizations and organizational behavior. This includes recognizing major theories that have influenced and continue to influence their thinking about organizations. Critical thinking about organizations will inevitably lead to disagreement because no two people will hold the exact same assumptions. Being aware of the potential for clashes of assumptions and the need to clarify one's own perspectives are key to future organization practice.

Connecting Theories to Human Service Organizations

Organizational theories were not developed by persons in the business of planning and providing human services. In fact, when we assign theory texts to our social work students, they typically do not include any writers from the field of social work. Students are introduced to economists, business administrators, engineers, sociologists, and a host of experts in other disciplines. Early organizational theories were not focused on human service work, but on the work of business corporations. Therefore, connecting theories to human service organizations is not easy, given that human service organizations are somewhat unique in their work with consumers (not inanimate products) who bring their own perspectives to the interaction.

In the early 1980s, Hasenfeld (1983, pp. 9–10) distinguished six unique characteristics of human service agencies that made them different from other organizations, given their focus on working with and on people. First, the fact that their *raw material* consists of people vested with moral values affects most of their activities. For Hasenfeld, service technologies must be morally justified because every activity related to clients has significant moral consequences. A second important distinction is *goals*. The goals of human service organizations are vague, ambiguous, and problematic. This is not due to incompetence, but because it is far more difficult to agree about achieving desired "welfare" and "well-being" needs of people than it is to transform inanimate objects. Third, the *moral ambiguity* surrounding human services also implies that they operate in a turbulent environment. There are many interest groups with many perspectives and agendas, each attempting to achieve their values and aims through the organization. Fourth, human service organizations must operate with *indeterminate technologies* that do not provide complete knowledge about how to attain desired outcomes. Human nature is never as predictable as many of the elements in the natural sciences. Fifth, the core activities in human service organizations consist of *relations between staff and clients*. It is within relationship that change occurs. Change is the product of the human service enterprise, a much different product than in most businesses. Finally, human service organizations lack reliable and valid measures of effectiveness, and, therefore, may be more *resistant to change and innovation*. We would take a more critical stance on this sixth element and suggest that the expectations of achieving valid and reliable measures of effectiveness itself fails to recognize how human service agencies differ from other organizations. Perhaps alternative measures are needed to capture this very uniqueness. Figure 2.1 summarizes Hasenfeld's characteristics.

Hasenfeld's distinctions have been extremely helpful to persons trying to understand human service agencies in the last two decades. Today, there may be less distinctiveness between human service and other type agencies, but the points made by Hasenfeld are still relevant. He contends that "other types of organizations may exhibit one or more of these attributes, but it is the combination and interaction of all of them that makes human service organizations distinctive" (2000, p. 90). Human service work *does* involve moral values and consequences. Social workers *will* face dilemmas in deciding what approaches (technology) to use that will not do harm to clients. Agency staff will work closely with clients, and clients will need to be included in the decision making that leads to those results that will indicate program effectiveness. Like all organizations today, human service organizations operate in turbulent environments because people feel strongly (both positively and negatively) about programs that are designed to change the way people behave, feel, or perform.

Hasenfeld (2000) continues to write about human service management and administration, stressing the importance of locating theories that take into account the nature of human service agencies. He warns that appropriate theories and tools for business organizations will not always work for human service agencies and that social work administration practices "must be anchored in organizational theories that take into account . . . attributes [of human service agencies] . . . and they must be empirically verifiable" (p. 90). Thus, the nature of human service organizations requires persons who are skilled in thinking critically and acting competently in the face of competing values and expectations from various constituencies. The-

FIGURE 2.1   Hasenfeld's Six Unique Characteristics of Human Service Organizations

1. Consumers are raw material, consisting of people vested with moral values that affect most of their activities.
2. Goals are vague, ambigious, and problematic.
3. Moral ambiguity surrounds human services.
4. Indeterminate technologies do not provide complete knowledge about how to attain desired outcomes.
5. Core activities consist of relations between staff and clients.
6. Reliable and valid measures of effectiveness are lacking, making these organizations resistant to change and innovation.

ories that focus on power and politics as well as culture and sensemaking may be helpful in recognizing conflict as a normal part of life in human service organizations. These theories may also be helpful in understanding alternative agencies.

Conclusion

We began this chapter by distinguishing four ways in which organizations are diverse in terms of clients, staff, corporate culture, and within larger systems of agencies. Human resources, organizational psychology, and power and politics theories are particularly helpful in identifying and understanding diversity because these types of theories focus on individuals and groups within an organizational context. As the work force and consumers of human services become more and more diverse, there will be a greater and greater need for social work practitioners to use these theoretical constructs.

The search for order in organizational theory has become a search for understanding in a world in which organizations do not always make sense in traditional ways. The emergence of theories that go beyond purely rational ways of controlling people within organizations offer unlimited possibilities in critically thinking about organization practice.

We agree with Hasenfeld (2000) that human service work is moral work. Reviewing social work core values and ethical principles reveals that organizational values and premises may or may not always fit well with codes of ethics, professional standards, and even personal moral values. Organizational theories are also grounded in values that may or may not fit with the intent of social work leaders. The effective social worker must examine fit between organizational and professional values and look for ways to link the two. Programs and services within human service agencies—whether they are formal or informal; traditional or alternative; public, nonprofit, or for profit—are driven by cultural values that derive from a variety of historical, social, and political forces.

With the values of the profession in mind, we now to turn to Chapter 3, in which we focus on the use-of-self in organization practice and highlight the importance of critical thinking and self-awareness in leading and practicing in complex and diverse organizations.

3

Leadership, Critical Thinking, and Self-Awareness in Organization Practice

Chapter 1 defined organizations, examined different types of agencies that deliver human services, and ended with a brief overview of policies and politics across sectors and agencies. We continued that broad perspective in Chapter 2, as we reviewed ways organizations have been defined. In this chapter, we take a more "micro" focus by looking at individuals as leaders within the complex array of organizations that advocate for, plan, fund, and deliver human services. The primary message in this chapter is the importance of critical thinking and self-awareness for being an effective organization-based practitioner. We are assuming that when social workers enter an organization with knowledge of their own assumptions and the ability to think critically, they are better able to be a valuable member of organizations where persons from many different cultures and backgrounds come together. Being a *valuable member* does not mean that everyone will be grateful for your contributions. Others may not be aware of their own assumptions and may not always appreciate critical thinking skills that bring into question long-held beliefs, values, and practices. On the other hand, we do not think social workers have a choice of remaining passive, noncritical participants in organizational life if they are operating from the value base of the profession.

Since we are intent on creating not *just* organizational leaders, but *social work* organizational leaders, this chapter will also focus on social work core values and ethical principles that can be used to guide organization practice. If one is fully self-aware within an organizational context, one will discover that applying social work principles is a thought-provoking, and sometimes even paradoxical, challenge—possible only with the aid of well-developed critical thinking skills. Our concern is that social workers thoroughly recognize the implications of embracing certain values, and that they be able to identify those situations in which organizational theory and behavior comply with or contradict these values.

Leadership in Complex Organizations

For those readers who just relaxed because they do not plan to be an organizational *leader* and who think the contents of this book do not apply to them, we have a clear message to convey. We assume that every social worker has leadership responsibilities within any organization in which they work because leadership is not just a title or position like manager, administrator, or something only full-time macro-practitioners do. **Leadership** is an attitude about responsibilities in an organization based on professional skills and a set of values that compel an individual to act. Leadership may come from any organizational member, regardless of the formal authority and power structure in that organization. The clinician who knows what happens to clients on a daily basis has a responsibility to provide that information to others for targeting further service development. These actions demonstrate leadership skills. The line worker who visits clients in their home environments will know more about what really happens to the agency's clientele than will managers who may have ultimate programmatic decision-making responsibility. Sharing the information will shape the program. The line worker demonstrates leadership skills by carefully documenting what she or he is learning and is responsible for clearly conveying this information to others who have ultimate program or legal responsibility. The program director who is aware of low staff morale and who needs to find ways to promote teamwork will be a leader for his or her staff team even if it is primarily the agency director's responsibility to establish the staff tenor for the whole agency.

Leadership means having vision about what information is important to share and when to share it so that change can happen in organizations. Leaders do not just identify and assess a problem, but plan for and facilitate successful problem resolution. Problem identification and solution are skills and responsibilities of all social workers. This means that organizational leadership is a professional responsibility of every social worker, no matter what position one holds.

This approach to leadership and the change that can result is not new to social work. In 1978, Brager and Holloway wrote *Changing Human Service Organizations: Politics and Practice* in which they recognize that organizational problem solving and change had been relegated to two groups: top-level administrators and managers, and third-party consultants. They contend that their approach to change "inverts the usual lens by focusing on the ways in which organizational actors with less formal power can influence those with more formal power" (p. ix). Their book was designed to provide direction for human service professionals at *all* ranks to contribute to change that would benefit consumers. Concerned that too much of the previous literature had focused on theory without tying theory to practice, Brager and Holloway specifically discuss ways in which staff can influence change within human service organizations. They begin by focusing on conflicting ideologies in which organizations are products of larger societal values and beliefs and the tendencies of different groups within organizations to hold contradictory values. They use three sets of tactics introduced by previous writers (Brager & Specht, 1973; Warren, 1971)—collaborative, campaign, and contest—that may be used to approach change from within. **Collaborative tactics** are characterized by open communication in which people are willing to engage in problem solving for change. **Campaign tactics**, seen as a midpoint along a continuum between collaborative and contest, include "hard persuasion, political maneuvering, bargaining and negotiation, and mild coercion designed to educate and persuade others that change needs to occur" (p. 133). **Contest tactics** engage participants in conflict and pressure, in which the violation of social and legal norms may occur. Brager and Holloway's focus is on collaborative and campaign tactics, acknowledging that "contest tactics are rarely used in practice related to internal organizational change" (p. 133). See Table 3.1 for an overview of tactical approaches to change.

Two years later, Resnick and Patti (1980) published *Change from Within: Humanizing Social Welfare Organizations,* an edited volume designed to provide guidance about how to approach change within organizations "initiated by low-power persons in formal organizations" (p. vii). Similar to Brager and Holloway's earlier assertions, Resnick and Patti also recognize that little scholarly literature had at that time been directed toward how to go about making change happen. They comment, "Practitioners have been forced to rely on assumptions, analytic tools, and intervention techniques drawn largely from their clinical training, or more commonly, from personal judgment and experience. Reliance on these usually implicit sources of expertise has often resulted in practitioners viewing agency problems as the collective expression of individual personalities, rather than as organization phenomena per se" (pp. vii–viii).

Resnick and Patti go on to explain their rationale for organizational change. First, they explain that as organizations grow and develop, they become concerned about maintenance and survival, with the potential for displacing their original goals. **Goal displacement** occurs when an organization moves in different directions from its original purpose. For example, the leaders of an alternative agency could become so concerned over being able to survive financially that they might apply for any available funds, even if receiving the grant will mean taking the agency in a different direction from its original cause or purpose. Organizational change activities, then, would involve staff in attempting to refocus the organization's efforts, to align activities with original goals. Second, Resnick and Patti are concerned about increasing organizational size—as agencies become larger, they often become more hierarchical. Good communication in larger agencies may be more difficult to achieve, and staff at all levels and the clients they serve may not be heard by administrators. Third, they argue that staff who view themselves as change agents, whose voices can be heard, will be more engaged staff. Their com-

TABLE 3.1   **Approaches to Change**

Type of Tactics	Characteristics of Situation
Collaborative tactics	High communication among participants and a willingness to work together
Campaign tactics	Need to educate or inform participants so that they will be willing to cooperate
Contest tactics	Communication has broken down and there are persons/groups who are openly opposed to the change and unwilling to compromise

mitment to the important work of human service planning or provision will be stronger if they feel valued in their participation. "Involvement in change from below is the crucible on which organizational citizenship is forged" (p. 5).

Since these words were written, there has been an explosion of literature on organizational change, leadership, and culture. Some of this literature can be found in social work books and journals. For example, Kettner, Daley, and Nichols (1985) built on previous work and defined *planned change* as distinctive from *unplanned change* by four characteristics: "it is limited in scope, is directed toward enhancing the quality of life of clients, includes a role for consumers, and is guided by a professional practitioner who acts as a change agent" (p. 7). In their view, "the responsibility for initiating change in organizations and communities rests with every human service professional at any level who comes in contact with or has knowledge of a situation where the need for change is indicated" (p. 8).

Other social work texts continue to reinforce this theme that leadership within organizations is the responsibility of all social workers, regardless of organizational role. Netting, Kettner, and McMurtry (1998, p. 10) state that the person who calls herself or himself a social worker, but who is not willing to participate in organizational or community change, is not really doing social work. Social work, by definition, means working with people in context.

We are committed to this long-established tradition that every social worker can be a leader in initiating change, regardless of their organizational role. Our hope is that the reader will see the importance of both direct practice skills, accompanying understandings of human behavior, and the specifics of organizational skills from which to develop successful leadership for change. Our message in this book goes beyond what has been provided students of human service organizations in the past. Instead of just straightforward concrete planning and administration skills, social work leaders must develop the skills necessary to flourish in the chaos that accrues with multiple perspectives that produce different ways of doing the work of delivering human services in a multicultural environment. As agencies become more diverse in populations served, in approaches to service delivery, and in addressing political, economic, and cultural challenges, there may be no resolutions or "real" answers. Consider, instead, that there may just be informed ways of acting without the expectation of closure, definitive analysis, and guarantees. Social work leaders must therefore be open to considering multiple perspectives in which possibilities and opportunities can emerge.

From this standpoint, working in multicultural environments in ways that are socially "just" may mean that chaos and uncertainty will be the norm. We are giving you permission, as a future organizational leader, to stop fighting the chaos and, instead, to relish the challenges it offers to use your best critical thinking skills to work toward needed change. We hope that the approach offered in this chapter will begin to equip you to practice in complexity and ambiguity, recognizing possibilities, accepting challenges, and overcoming obstacles.

For direct practice or clinical students among our readers, serious effort will be given throughout the text to identifying the practice skills that a well-trained clinician can bring to leadership in organization practice. Much of what you have learned in direct practice—such as conducting multidimensional assessment, identifying problems, planning change, and managing barriers to change—will come in handy when translated into an organizational context, but we offer a word of caution. As Resnick and Patti (1980) made clear, organizations are not just collections of personalities; they are much more complex phenomena. We will now explore just how complex they are.

Critical Thinking and Self-Awareness Skills in Organization Practice

The importance of critical thinking in social work and other professional fields has been emphasized over the last decades. The difficulties have been in defining exactly what critical thinking means and then applying the concept in practice. Critical thinking entails sophisticated data collection and data analysis skills. It requires complicated judgments in the face of uncertainty because all the important data are never available for certain judgment. This lack of complete information has become an accepted norm when speaking of critical thinking within a clinical setting; it is discussed as *clinical judgment* (Miller, 2001). However, within organization practice, often the goal is to find an unambiguous *right* answer. This strikes us as unfortunate and actually counterintuitive, since organizations by design are much more complicated than individuals, families, or group systems, making a universal *right* answer even more impossible to achieve.

How one deals with the environment created as a result of critical inquiry depends on one's consciousness about self and personal expectations about work. Organization practice, like clinical practice, is actually a process of boundary management (Falck, 1988). In fact, according to Falck, most administrative challenges can be attributed to an inability to separate personal issues from professional ones. One's ability to choose an appropriate solution strategy in the face of an identified problem is largely based on being able to separate one's personal needs from the higher-order needs of the clients and the organization. This requires a well-developed sense of self and awareness of one's own strengths and vulnerabilities. Without this, the critical analysis will fall short of its potential. In sum, critical thinking based on self-awareness in organization practice is not for the faint of heart, but then social work isn't either.

The Role of Critical Thinking in Organizations

Critical thinking involves the ability to think in complex ways. Kroeger and Thuesen (1988) give some specific hints about this type of thinking. They have developed several hierarchies that take one from simple to complex thinking. The hierarchy of particular interest in organizational practice is related to information management and is summarized in Figure 3.1. With information, one starts at copying, the simplest form of data management, and moves to comparing, computing, compiling, analyzing, coordinating, and, finally, to the most complex process, syn-

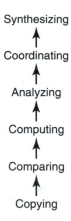

Synthesizing

Coordinating

Analyzing

Computing

Comparing

Copying

**FIGURE 3.1   Simple to Complex Thinking Hierarchy:
Information Management (Kroeger & Thuesen, 1988)**

thesizing. Examples of this hierarchy in organizations would include, as the simplest form, copying a report. The second level might include comparing that report to a similar report from last year. If the comparison shows that the reports cover similar items, then results could be tabulated and then compiled or organized. The next step would be drawing conclusions from the comparison of last year to this year. Coordinating would include providing this information to decision makers so that a focus could be determined for future action. The last, and most complicated, process includes synthesizing.

The determination of future action would not just be based on the data and the perspectives of those decision makers involved, but would also include an assessment of such aspects as the strengths and challenges in the particular context, including resources and other demands. When all that information is brought together, appropriately considered, and reduced for manageability, then synthesis for decision making has occurred. The ability to move from concrete descriptions to synthesis is at the core of critical thinking in organizations.

Gibbs and Gambrill say, "**Critical thinking** involves a careful appraisal of claims, a fair-minded consideration of alternative views, and a willingness to change your mind in light of evidence that refutes a cherished position" (1996, p. 23). The words *cherished position* should not be taken lightly. In thinking critically, assumptions held by oneself or others are examined carefully and could be changed, based on new or alternative information. The process is not an easy one if these assumptions are cherished, or tightly held, almost as immutable truths. Groups within organizations, even entire organizations, can cherish assumptions. You may recall from Chapter 2 that Schein (1992) calls this pattern of shared basic assumptions the basis of organizational culture. When consensus is so great as to create a perspective resembling a culture, the assumptions of that consensus are tenaciously held. Basic assumptions in organizations can come to be so taken for granted that one finds little variation in thinking or performance within a cultural unit. In fact, if a basic assumption is strongly held in a group, members will find behavior based on any other premise inconceivable. If, for example, the culture in a foster care unit is one of blaming biological parents, it is unlikely that anyone within the unit would actively consider the parents' strengths. Regardless of data, it would not be part of the assessment considerations because it would not occur to anyone to even think about strengths.

Such basic assumptions become like theories-in-use, which tend to be neither confronted nor debated and thus are extremely difficult to change. To learn something new that might allow change in this realm requires practitioners to resurrect, reexamine, and possibly change some of the more stable portions of their cognitive structures. Such learning is intrinsically difficult because the reexamination of basic assumptions temporarily destabilizes one's cognitive and interpersonal world, which can release large quantities of basic anxiety (Schein, 1992, p. 22).

People in organizations, as well as individuals and groups, may discover that their cherished assumptions are not congruent with what they are observing. Recognizing this discrepancy poses a dilemma—suffer the anxiety of moving to another assumption or hang on tenaciously to avoid the pain that accompanies change. Either choice is uncomfortable in its own way.

The Role of Self-Awareness in Organizations

Attending to this basic anxiety and understanding the destabilizing effect of critical thinking is central to self-awareness. Just as in direct practice, self-awareness within an organizational context requires an honest appraisal of oneself. There are many worthwhile discussions of self-awareness in relation to direct work with clients,[1] but few speak specifically to the need for this same level of self-consciousness within the organizational setting. We agree with Falck (1988) and believe that interpersonal patterns and perceptions within an organization are key to understanding organizational behavior.

The same level of scrutiny to reactions within the organization is as necessary as it is with an individual client. The organizational leader must be aware of personal biases, habitual distortions, and personal behavior that might contribute to the organization problem being addressed. These personal or internal elements may be contributing to the problem assessment or its solution.

Another area requiring honest scrutiny is personal style. It is necessary to know that the style in use is the appropriate style for the selected problem-solving strategy. If the organizational leader is naturally domineering, it must be clear that this dominance will produce the desired results. If one's style is naturally more shy or passive, will that type of communication pattern create the level of attention in others needed for problem resolution? Is natural assertiveness, confrontation, defensiveness, or a withdrawn pattern of communication warranted? The point of this assessment is the realization that what is natural in one's style may not be effective in each situation. With consciousness of the preferred style, and critical analysis regarding what is necessary with the people involved, the social worker desiring change can strategically choose a style that is more likely to succeed. If more assertive discussion is necessary in order to be heard, even if a more quiet approach is preferred, the more effective strategy can be implemented because of introspection, critical thinking, and appropriate skill development.

In addition, the organizational leader cannot assume that anyone's life experiences have been left at the door of the agency. A frank assessment of how one's life experiences may influence perceptions and judgments is essential for drawing valid conclusions regarding personal reactions to organizational experiences. The goal is to achieve personal reaction and reality congruence, but this is not possible until and unless the people involved are clear about how personal history shapes the lens with which they attempt to understand a situation. For example, experience of personal pain from abuse or neglect as a child may cause overidentification with a client or colleague in pain, to the degree that accurate appraisal of a situation is impossible. If a worker has had a history with controlling and critical parents, then critical feedback from those whose role it is to evaluate may not be received in the spirit it is intended. Similarly, if a worker has had a bad care-giving experience with an older relative, the employee might have difficulty working with older persons who remind him or her of that relative. An active effort to disentangle personal reactions from the current reality is essential not only for sensemaking in the organization but also for effectiveness.

According to Kondrat (1999), there are at least five types of self-awareness involving successively higher orders of consciousness skills and complex thinking skills. Though her work is linked to direct practice, it is also very relevant for organization practice. Our students suggest that there may actually be seven types of awareness, including preconscious and contextual types. Therefore, we combine these two types with the five identified by Kondrat.

Preconscious self-awareness is a transitional phase in which a person may recognize that he or she is not self-aware. This preconscious type is important because it is the beginning of the insight that something needs to happen differently. It is a triggering stage in which one accepts the possibility that something needs to change in the way one looks at himself or herself. One recognizes that self-awareness is not present.

To be self-aware in an organization, a social worker must first clearly experience awareness, and this is what Kondrat (1999, p. 459) calls *simple conscious awareness*. This type of self-awareness is when a lightbulb goes on in the worker's head. *Reflective awareness*, a third type, requires distancing from the contents of an experience for observation and critique. It involves getting beyond the lightbulb experience and beginning to analyze why one has felt a certain way or acted in certain ways. A fourth type, *reflexive awareness*, requires attention to and understanding of how personal history and the actual personhood of the practitioner impacts the situation under consideration. The fifth type, a more social constructivist version of reflexivity, is called *social constructive awareness*, and requires awareness of the mutual shaping that goes into meaning making within the organizational setting.

The sixth level, essential for organizational leadership, is *critical reflectivity*. This requires asking reflective questions about bias and intolerance. For example, one might examine the biases that "center on the relationship between seemingly unproblematic, everyday behavior and racially structured outcomes" (Kondrat,

1999, p. 468). The idea in this type of self-awareness is to accept the responsibility and the power to act to change the structures that support and sustain unequal outcomes in vulnerable groups inside and outside the organization. This type of awareness accepts the notion that organizational participants are not just passive recipients upon whom the organization acts but they are also active agents with responsibilities to challenge the status quo. This sounds remarkably similar to earlier visions of social work leadership within organizations (Brager & Holloway, 1978; Kettner, Daley, & Nichols, 1985; Resnick & Patti, 1980).

This critical reflectivity is essential in assessing not only personal beliefs and attitudes but also how the social/structural environment of the organization may be continuing or extending majority power and privilege to the detriment of the more vulnerable. Therefore, there is likely a seventh type of self-awareness in which the full implications of one's reflective questions and actions are assessed. We call this *contextual awareness*, where self-awareness meets the reactions, resistance, and consequences of change, understanding and accepting the external results of articulation of individual consciousness. Table 3.2 summarizes the types of self-awareness.

TABLE 3.2   Types of Self-Awareness

Level of Self-Awareness	Characteristics
1. Preconscious awareness	The person begins to recognize that she or he is not self-aware.
2. Simple conscious awareness	The person clearly experiences awareness.
3. Reflective awareness	The person is reflective, taking some distance from the experience so that he or she can observe and critique.
4. Reflexive awareness	The person must pay attention to and understand how personal history and the actual personhood of the practitioner impacts the situation.
5. Social constructive awareness	The person must be aware of the mutual shaping that goes into meaning making within the organization.
6. Critical reflectivity	The person must ask reflective questions about bias and intolerance, accepting responsibility and the power to act to change oppressive organizational structures.
7. Contextual awareness	The person recognizes the consequences of critical reflexivity—how her or his raising questions impacts others—sees himself or herself in the context of others.

The Practice of Critical Thinking

Some of the challenges to self-awareness can be overcome through clear, critical assessment. In writing this book, we hold numerous *cherished* assumptions. We assume that social workers have no choice but to think critically; otherwise, clients will not receive the best services one can provide. We assume that social work practice will be fraught with conflicts, some intentional and others totally unexpected. We know disagreements occur when different cherished assumptions collide. Depending on one's personality and style, conflicts may be tempered or ignited, but they will not be avoided. We also assume that organizations are arenas in which the potential for assumptions to clash will be accentuated by the sheer number of people who interact. But we also assume that this sets the stage for the social worker to engage in a challenging and stimulating work environment that will stretch one's ability to use professional judgment based on well-reasoned thought. In addition, we assume that all this stretching and reasoning is based on one's desire to do the best possible work one can offer clients. This may mean struggling with (and possibly even changing) some cherished assumptions along the way. We know this is not easy, but see if you can begin to address the questions in Figure 3.2.

According to Falck (1988), "The emotional, intellectual, and technical aspects of social work are subject to the conscious, rational, and planful use of oneself as a social worker" (p. 120). No critical thinking process will produce effective results without the self-discipline necessary to achieve a consciousness about how one uses oneself in the organizational context. Once conscious use of self is part of a practice vocabulary, then real critical thinking can begin. Gibbs and Gambrill (1996) contend that "critical thinking and self-awareness go hand in hand" (p. 9). They have identified a list of elements to consider in order to think critically (see Figure 3.3). We will briefly look at each in relationship to organization practice in order to aid in the development of a commitment to "reflect on the soundness of reasoning and a respect for the views of others" (Gibbs & Gambrill, 1999, p. 9).

Evaluate the Accuracy of the Claims. In this book and in the classroom, students will be overwhelmed at times with claims from professors and experienced practitioners about what one should and should not do. It will be important to evaluate the accuracy of these claims by assessing whether they are accompanied by

---

FIGURE 3.2   **Beginning Questions about Assumptions**

1. What are your assumptions about organizations and organizational behavior?

2. When, where, and how did you develop these assumptions?

3. If you think about an organization with which you are familiar, do all your assumptions hold up? If not, which ones don't and why?

4. Think about an organization with which you are familiar. What basic assumptions do you think drive this organization's culture?

FIGURE 3.3 Gibbs and Gambrill's (1996) List of Critical Thinking Elements

- Evaluate the accuracy of the claims.

- Evaluate arguments.

- Recognize informal fallacies.

- Recognize propaganda stratagems.

- Recognize pseudoscience, fraud, and quackery.

- Use language thoughtfully.

- Recognize affective influences.

- Avoid cognitive biases.

- Increase self-awareness.

clear arguments. It will be necessary to determine what criteria one will use to assess claims and when to ask whether the criteria have been tested for accuracy. For example, a social work manager might say, "It is best to diversify one's funding base and have multiple revenue streams, rather than depend too much on one source." A social worker hearing this statement would want to ask what evidence indicates that this claim should be embraced and whether that evidence is relevant to the type of agency to which the claim is being applied. It certainly may be the manager's experience, but would this principle apply to *every* situation? What about small, specialized, or alternative organizations that have only one program and only one source of funding? Is diversification of funding important within programs so that different services have different revenue sources?

Evaluate Arguments.   Evaluating arguments requires identifying the conclusion reached and then carefully considering the reasons stated for reaching that conclusion. Arguments may be unfounded if they are not logical, contain false premises, or do not move in an identifiable direction (Gibbs & Gambrill, 1996, p. 7). This direction does not have to be linear, but the direction must be identifiable and have its own logic.

Recognize Informal Fallacies.   **Fallacies** are actually mistakes in thinking that take skill to spot. Fallacies may occur when

- the premises do not support the conclusion
- broad generalizations are applied too liberally
- facts and positions are misrepresented
- emotional appeals are not grounded in facts

"Begging the question," "sweeping generalizations," and "straw person arguments" are all examples of fallacies. They work because they create confusion in communication. For example, in a unit meeting, a situation regarding clients is explained in such a way as to suggest that there is no service available to serve the clients' needs. When probed, the worker fails to understand the clarifying questions when the supervisor is trying to be very clear. A series of informal fallacies could be at work. The worker may be generalizing too broadly. The supervisor may be using excessive wordiness that obscures her or his message that lack of service is no excuse. The worker, who is adamantly sticking with the idea that a specific service unavailable in the agency is the only option, feigns lack of understanding in order to avoid scrutiny of his or her position. The result is lack of clarity and an inability to really assess what is happening.

Recognize Propaganda Stratagems.   Fallacies may actually be promoted in **propaganda strategies** in which someone tries to persuade or convince another person to come over to his or her way of thinking. Propaganda is used like a sales pitch. For example, consider this statement: "Programs under the auspices of nonprofit organizations, as opposed to those under for profits, will be more sensitive to clients because they are mission driven rather than revenue driven." This is an example of a broad generalization applied to an entire sector—nonprofit organizations—and one with tremendous emotional appeal. It is a misrepresentation of a situation by deceptively using part truths. The communication, though couched in informational language, is really meant to persuade, because no self-respecting social worker wants to be accused of defending a revenue-driven organization. A profit motive sounds so crass and unfeeling! Here, fallacies such as oversimplification and assumptions that mission and revenue are mutually exclusive opposites, and that all nonprofits (or for profits) conform to certain stereotypes are tactics. These tactics are used to persuade those receiving the communication that nonprofits aren't interested in making profits and that agencies that are interested in profits cannot be good for clients.

Recognize Pseudoscience, Fraud, and Quackery.   Spotting pseudoscience, fraud, and quackery also involves critical thinking. **Pseudoscience** occurs when claims are couched in scientific language, but these claims are not substantiated by word or number data. **Quackery** pertains to the promotion of unproven, even harmful, claims, whereas **fraud** is intentional deception and misrepresentation. Organizational life is fraught with opportunities to spot these type claims. For example, public relations materials are often couched in language that sounds scientific, such as, "The staff in this agency have over 100 years of combined professional experience in working with adolescents, and this organization has been a pillar in the community network of services for over 60 years." This may sound impressive until one realizes that "combined years of professional experience" doesn't say anything about quality and whether these professionals have continued to keep up to date. What if there are 100 professionals in the agency, and each one had only one year of experience! And the agency may have lasted in the community for 60 years, but what data support, much less define, its "pillar" status?

Use Language Thoughtfully. Gibbs and Gambrill (1996) emphasize the importance of thoughtful language. Not only do we agree with their emphasis but we also experienced firsthand, while writing this book, the awesome responsibility of using thoughtful language, because we know that no matter what words we use, there is the potential to be misunderstood. We have provided a glossary of terms at the end of this book because we found ourselves needing to define meanings for our own collaboration, and we see the advantage of sharing those definitions with our readers.

The writer of a popular book titled *Why Didn't You Say That in the First Place? How to be Understood at Work* (Heyman, 1994) contends that one should approach organizational life with the assumption that being misunderstood is normal. This is particularly true in multicultural and multidisciplinary environments. Armed with the misunderstanding assumption, one does not have to struggle with the surprise of finding out that colleagues didn't understand what you said or that you misunderstood as well. One just expects to be misunderstood, and then sets about trying to clarify what is meant. This removes the pressure to be understood, and when by some stroke of fortune one is understood the first time around, it becomes a bonus or cherished surprise that occasionally happens in one's working life. Even without the expectation of full understanding, approaching communication as a learning/teaching cycle meant to move toward further and deeper clarity helps to establish the carefulness that effective communication requires.

Recognize Affective Influences. Even when thoughtful communication is exchanged within an organizational context, Gibbs and Gambrill (1996) reinforce the importance of recognizing affective influences. Sometimes workers like one another so much that they are reluctant to disagree or just want to support another person's perspective. The context in which communication occurs and in which decisions that affect clients' lives are made is rife with affective influences that may be as subtle as a knowing glance between colleagues or as obvious as the authority and power differentials in a large bureaucracy. Add to the communication how age, race, gender, and ethnicity influences shape how people speak, hear, and understand, and the complexity of this affective dimension of communication becomes clear.

Avoid Cognitive Biases. Avoiding cognitive biases means recognizing tendencies "to accept initial assumptions without question, to think that causes are similar to their effects, and to underestimate the frequency of coincidences (chance occurrences)" (Gibbs & Gambrill, 1996, p. 9).[2] Biases do exist regardless of one's perspective on science and reality. Recognizing what biases one brings to one's work is a beginning to critical thinking, which leads to increased self-awareness. Being self-aware means asking why you believe what you do and considering if you can support the claims that you make. "Critical thinking encourages you to ask questions about your beliefs, values, claims and arguments. . . . It encourages you to be aware of what you know and don't know and to reflect on why you act in certain ways and what the consequences may be" (Gibbs & Gambrill, 1996, p. 10).

Increase Self-Awareness.   Although many of our readers are convinced that self-awareness and its accompanying critical thinking skills are a necessary component of one's professional repertory, we recognize that others may be less convinced, if convinced at all. Why might this be? First, it may be easier not to look honestly and thoroughly at oneself in order to be clear about strengths and challenges, needs and areas of personal risk within organizational life. Sometimes it is easier to go along with the status quo. In addition, in "ideal situations," critical thinking skills may work quite nicely, but we have encountered few *ideal* organizations. Raising more questions in already uncertain situations is not always an easy or a welcomed thing to do. Perhaps this is why you are in a social work program—you recognize that it takes a great deal of skill, and the support of other organizational members, to fully realize one's leadership potential in organization practice. See Figure 3.4 for questions to ponder about critical thinking and organization practice.

Critical thinking is useful in many aspects of professional life. The next section addresses another arena where critical thinking will be helpful. Critical thinking is particularly important when addressing what are essentially the moral underpinnings of the social work profession. When considering the core values of the profession, one immediately thinks of achieving what is *right*. But what is *right* may depend on navigating and critically thinking about many contexts, a very important context being the organizations in which social workers practice.

The Relationship of Leadership, Critical Thinking, and Self-Awareness

So what is the relationship between leadership, critical thinking, and self-awareness? Leadership is an attitude of responsibility that requires some type of action. It may be verbal action, such as speaking up. It may be mobilizing others to do something that needs to be done. It may be modeling action that exemplifies certain values and brings them to life. Whatever the type action performed, leadership requires other persons to observe or participate in that action. Leadership occurs in a context. It is not something that one keeps in one's head. It is not solitary.

However, effective leadership requires a grounding in self-awareness and critical thinking. Informed leadership is not action just because one wants to act;

FIGURE 3.4   **Beginning Questions about Critical Thinking**

1. What are the characteristics of critical thinking?

2. How might you practice thinking more critically?

3. Can you think of instances in which you recognized informal fallacies, propaganda strategies, pseudoscience, fraud, or quackery?

4. Think of an organization with which you are familiar. What are the *affective influences* that make a difference in how you relate to others in this organization and why?

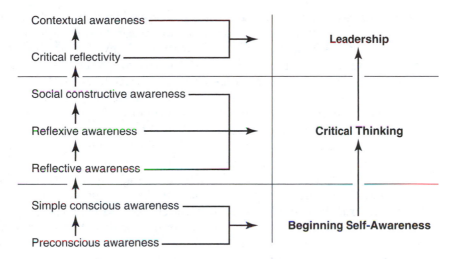

FIGURE 3.5　Self-Awareness, Critical Thinking, and Leadership

rather, it is action that has been carefully considered and that is responsibly based on information gathered. This does not mean that leadership cannot be spontaneous, but self-awareness will assist a leader in knowing when to act quickly and when to wait. Leaders must assess when it is appropriate and necessary to act, which cannot be consistently accomplished without critical analysis.

Figure 3.5 illustrates the relationship between leadership, critical thinking, and self-awareness. Note that self-awareness leads to critical thinking. Without getting beyond a beginning level of self-awareness, a person cannot think critically. As one moves to the more complex levels of self-awareness, critical thinking becomes a natural by-product. Critical thinking is the basis of productive leadership. The self-aware leader is armed with critical consciousness that results from critical thinking. This goes beyond personal needs to a larger awareness and is the resource needed to facilitate change. Notice that this relationship of self-aware, critical thinking and action is very similar to clinical role in individual family and group work.

Social Work Core Values in Organizational Context

Much has been made of the moral values inherent in human service work, especially professional social work. We pointed out in Chapter 2 that Hasenfeld (2000) views people work as moral work. It is moral work from two perspectives. First, it is moral work because it is the right thing to do—helping people in need. Social work has also been seen to be moral work because societal expectations of what is good and right tend to be operationalized in the types of social work activities that are supported at a given time in history. For example, society expected social workers to be intrusive when the larger society envisioned its right to act for clients' own good. Morality, as with all values, shifts as cultures and societies shift. Since social work typically is acting at the border between the individual and society, what is seen as professionally appropriate is a reflection of the interaction between the individual (including those in the profession) and society in general. Human service organizations, such as the social work profession, are expected to be a reflection of societal expectations about work with persons in need.

Some readers will argue that basic principles do not change and that there are overriding universal values that will withstand the test of time and are in fact "God given." These persons are **absolutists**. Others will argue that there is no one "Truth" with a capital T; instead, there are multiple truths because "ethical standards depend on cultural practices, political climate, contemporary norms and moral standards, and other contextual considerations" (Reamer, 1995, p. 48). These persons are **relativists.** You will have to determine which of these terms applies to you. These different ways of looking at values are based on different assumptions. When absolutists and relativists meet, they will likely encounter points over which they disagree (see Table 3.3). Understanding where you "naturally" fall on what might be called the relativist to absolutist continuum is another important aspect of self-awareness. What you do with this knowledge, then, becomes a part of the complex thinking challenge central to critical thinking. No matter what is written about ethics and ethical professional behavior, determining what is ethical depends as much on your perspective as an absolutist or as a relativist as it does on the content of any professional code.

Generally speaking, societal expectations of the social work profession are expressed in the ethical principles of the profession. The principles are the basis of societal sanction but they also have value implications for social workers working in organizations that provide human service programs and services. We use the National Association of Social Workers (NASW) Code of Ethics as a starting point for our discussion, even though we recognize that not all social workers are NASW members. We also know that many social workers follow the principles of specific constituency groups either concurrently with or before that of NASW. See, for example, the National Association of Black Social Workers (NABSW), the Clinical Social Work Federation (CSWF), and the Canadian Association of Social Workers.

TABLE 3.3   Beliefs of Absolutists and Relativists

Absolutists	Relativists
Basic principles do not change.	Principles change.
There are overriding "universal" values that stand the test of time.	Values change with time and context.
There is a Truth.	There are multiple truths.
There is one best way.	There are multiple ways.

In addition, regulations established for state licensing boards and human service agency standards also set ethical standards for practice (Reamer, 1998, p. 2).

Any look at the history of the social work profession will show that codes of ethics, regulations, and standards governing practice have been revised and amended as times change. Standards develop within an ever-shifting sociopolitical context. Expectations change as the context changes. The current code reflects where the social work profession is in this historical moment. The NASW Code goes a long way in explicating the current **social work perspective**. It is this perspective that recognizes the worth of the individual and the individual strengths and potentialities within the context of community rights and responsibilities. It has been said that social work has a "simultaneous dual focus" on the individual and the social context within which the individual finds himself or herself. It is this perspective that serves as a lens through which organization practice can be viewed and analyzed.

Regardless of how one views a code of ethics—as reflecting universal principles or as emerging and ever-changing—it is helpful to know *what* principles are currently espoused. The NASW Code of Ethics lists six core **values**, or dimensions of the profession held in high esteem, that are linked to six ethical **principles**, or standards for action related to the value. Table 3.4 lists these values and principles.

Now, assume you are a social worker in an organization that provides human services. First, you must be clear about your own personal, moral, and professional position vis-à-vis the values of the profession. You must hold yourself to professional practice congruent with the NASW Code. Remembering that practice is almost always organizationally based, congruence with the code must include the organization where you practice. We suggest if you use these core values and ethi-

TABLE 3.4   NASW Code of Ethics: Values and Principles (1996)

Value	Principle
1. Service	Social workers' primary goal is to help people in need and to address social problems.
2. Social justice	Social workers challenge social injustice.
3. Dignity and worth of the person	Social workers respect the inherent dignity and worth of the person.
4. Importance of human relationships	Social workers recognize the central importance of human relationships.
5. Integrity	Social workers behave in a trustworthy manner.
6. Competence	Social workers practice within their areas of competence and develop and enhance their professional expertise.

cal principles as a template to assess your organization's performance, you might find there are some values and principles that hold up well in the organization and others that do not. If you looked at the theories that guide management in your agency, you might find that the values and principles derived from the theoretical perspective do not mesh well with those articulated in the NASW Code of Ethics. We would be foolish to suggest that incompatibility between these core values and organizational behavior means that you can no longer work for this organization, or few social workers might be formally employed! However, we do believe that it is the professional social worker's responsibility to recognize when professional principles (whatever they are) are being violated and to assess just how egregious the violation is. In other words, the social worker who has critical thinking skills will be able to assess the fit of social work values and ethical principles with organizational behavior and then to determine what action is needed for a better fit. This is organizational leadership.

Social workers bring to their work a particular perspective of respect for the individual in the context of their own experience. This respect of the individual also shapes how a social worker engages in the enactment of change as a regular, ongoing process within all organizations. Conscious use of self is an essential element of this perspective. The social work frame of reference demands that designing programs and services that are placed within organizational contexts demonstrate sensitivity to the populations served. In human service organizations, social work attitudes, values, and skills are needed for contemporary organizational practice that assures appropriate sensitivity to people in need. To assure the presence of the social work perspective, self-awareness and critical thinking are essential. Figure 3.6 provides some beginning questions to consider.

Self-Awareness and Multiculturalism in Organizations

Imagine, then, that one enters an organization in which persons from diverse groups with different values and assumptions come together to achieve a purpose

FIGURE 3.6   Questions about Values and Ethics

1. Consider the six core values and ethical principles in the NASW Code of Ethics. How might you prioritize these values and principles? What is your rationale?

2. Think of an organization or a human service program with which you are familiar. How do the assumptions and values that guide this program fit with the NASW core values and principles? Do you think that it is important for programs to always fit? How do you think someone of a different age, gender, or ethnicity would respond?

3. Do you think that there are universal principles that pertain to all situations? Why or why not? Give examples.

or purposes. Think about how the group and subgroup cultures will interact within an organizational culture to create their own set of values and assumptions. Consider that we have not even mentioned the clients one serves and how they fit into this multicultural interaction, though it is for the purpose of serving clients that the organizational culture is established in the first place. Even if the teams and groups within this organization work well together and share certain values and assumptions, clients will bring their own values and assumptions to the interaction. Cox (1993) refers to the concept of **cultural fit** as "the degree of alignment between two or more cultural configurations" (p. 170). Social workers have to develop skills in assessing cultural fit in order to work toward organizational change when client diversity is not compatible with established organizational culture.

Self-awareness is essential in working with the complexities of a multicultural environment. Without awareness of prejudices and stereotypes regarding those different from oneself, an organizational member may be deceived into thinking that those biases and stereotypes are absent. The worker in a multicultural environment should have the honesty and humility to admit the limits in his or her openness to difference. With this admission comes the recognition of the level of care necessary in communication and judgments so that personal prejudices do not cloud the picture or alienate those with whom solutions must be forged. Self-awareness is a key to moving away from prejudices and stereotypical perceptions, but until full liberation from discrimination and oppression is possible, it is also the major tool for managing diversity.

The multicultural competency for which self-aware practitioners should strive has been labeled in the direct practice literature as *ethnic-sensitive* (Devore & Schlesinger, 1991; Lum, 2000) or *cross-cultural* (Harper & Lantz, 1996) *competence.* Helpful guidance for practice with the multiple cultures within and outside an organization can be found in this literature. However, even more precise guidance is provided regarding direct practice. Lum defines this practice as **minority practice**, "the art and science of developing a helping relationship with an individual, family, group, and/or community whose distinctive physical or cultural characteristics and discriminatory experiences require approaches that are sensitive to ethnic and cultural environments" (p. 6). For direct practice, most theorists suggest that practice must be shaped with a sensitivity to experiences of racism, prejudice, and discrimination as well as attention to the specific cultural belief systems and behaviors that might influence individuals' views of themselves, their world, and their possibilities. This same sensitivity is important to organization practice.

Many more details about competent multicultural practice will emerge throughout the rest of this book. For now, it is important to develop some elements of the type of respect that comprises effective multicultural practice. The first element of respect is self-respect. In order to risk the hard work of cross-cultural communication central to respect, it is necessary to feel good about oneself. It is impossible to respect others until people respect themselves. The second element of respect comes through dialogue. Real understanding is impossible without true communication. One can move through misunderstanding and anger through dialogue. Dialogue is only possible if all parties are fully present in the conversation.

Attention to the conversation is essential. This attention sometimes will require vigorous conversation, sometimes called *dialectical conversation.* At other times, respect occurs through silently bearing witness to the personal narrative of a colleague or client. A third important element of respect is curiosity and being humble about one's knowledge. Multicultural practice requires genuine interest in the stories, experiences, and perceptions of others. Genuine respect is only possible when one knows people's real thoughts, feelings, and fears. The real communication of these basic aspects of human experience comes through a fourth element—sense of safety. Safety is created when one communicates a sense of the other's worthiness, which is the fifth element. Figure 3.7 lists the elements of competent multicultural practice.

Lawrence-Lightfoot (1999) says that from these expressions of respect comes empowerment. Crossing the borders of difference through genuine understanding and respect allows everyone involved to gain more knowledge. This knowledge can be used to make decisions that will nurture self-confidence and self-reliance in organizations and social environments.

Conclusion

Social work leaders with the power and skills to effect needed changes in human service organizations must critically think about their own and others' assumptions about organizations and organizational behavior. Critical thinking in an organizational context will inevitably lead to conflict because no two people will hold the exact same assumptions. Being aware of the potential for assumptions to clash and clarifying one's own perspectives are key to organization practice, particularly as one works in increasingly multicultural organizations.

Social work core values and ethical principles reveal that organizational or program values and premises may or may not fit well with codes of ethics, professional standards, or even personal moral values. The effective social worker must examine fit between organizational and professional values and look for ways to link the two. This responsibility is equally important for the line worker and the manager. Micro- and macropractice are either impeded or enhanced by the capacity for reflexive, complex, critically analytical thinking in the organizational con-

FIGURE 3.7 Elements of Competent Multicultural Practice

1. Self-respect

2. Dialogue

3. Curiosity

4. Sense of safety

5. Recognition of worthiness

text. In addition, as programs are designed and redesigned to meet needs, social workers will need skills in multicultural practice to engage the chaos, sustain creativity, and maintain and construct effective and just organizations.

We now turn to Chapter 4, which will demonstrate that there are multiple valid ways of understanding organizations and the behavior within them. Understanding multiple approaches to organizations and the people within them is needed for effective organization practice to occur.

ENDNOTES

1. See, for example, Hepworth, Rooney, and Larsen (1997).
2. As you will see later, this is a rather narrow version of what constitutes a bias in that it underscores a certain set of assumptions about cause and effects that are not held in all perspectives about what constitutes acceptable knowledge. It also assumes that what is constructed cognitively is not necessarily real.

4

A Multiparadigmatic Framework for Understanding Organization Practice

Chapter 3 linked self-awareness, critical thinking, and leadership. In the previous three chapters, we encouraged readers to be mindful of their assumptions about types of organizations, approaches to working in increasingly complex organizations, and the compatibility of their work with social work values. We emphasized diversity as a major theme in contemporary organizations, reinforced in different sets of assumptions that different people bring to organization practice.

In this chapter, we introduce a framework for identifying and beginning to understand the genesis of these diverse assumptions and why they may be embraced with such fervor. First, we examine the concept of paradigm and how it relates to the continuing search for order and understanding among writers of both management and leadership literature. We then present four paradigms developed by Burrell and Morgan (1979) that will serve as a guiding framework for organization practice for the remainder of the book.

The Importance of Paradigm

People have different views of the world, embedded in assumptions that are important to them, whether they recognize them or not. Having read Chapter 3, we hope you are in touch with at least some of the assumptions you bring to organization practice. We have tried to be explicit about many of our assumptions in previous chapters because we recognize how they guide the material that we present in this book. Assumptions are embedded in diverse views of the world and in how people act within it. The term *paradigm* has been popularized in recent years and is loosely used in daily conversation to describe diverse worldviews. The concept of paradigm provides clues to why people believe there are certain ways in which an organization should do its work, including such things as what one person expects from another on a daily basis. A **paradigm** is defined as the general organizing principles governing perceptions, including beliefs, values, and techniques that describe what exists, where to look, and what the person can expect to discover (Ritzer, 1980). In keeping with this definition, we use *paradigm* to mean a worldview that contains a set of deep-seated assumptions that are so much a part of the person that it is often hard to step back and even know what those assumptions are. Paradigms, then, reflect the basic assumptions that order a person's world. These assumptions emerge in the context of the individual's experiences with others, organizations, communities, and the larger society. These assumptions also influence how one approaches self-awareness, critical thinking, and leadership.

In a way, paradigms are related to our earlier discussions of organizational cultures. When organizational members come together to design programs and services to carry out their agency's mission, they will act on their beliefs of what is valuable and important to do. These actions will be based on agreed-upon worldviews and assumptions. When conflict arises in the process, it can be due to different working styles or even to people having a bad day or many other related factors. However, when conflict escalates and people strongly feel that their views cannot be compromised, they may be working out of different paradigms in which different assumptions prevail. Just as changing an organization's culture is very difficult, it is not easy to communicate between individuals when they are coming from such different perspectives. Literally, their views of the world and how it works (or should work) are in conflict.

Conflicts in organizations are inevitable, and it is healthy to acknowledge them. To squelch conflicts of assumptions would be to ignore the strengths that come from persons embracing different paradigms. It would also mean sidestepping issues and not fully communicating with one's colleagues. In fact, recognizing differences among organizational stakeholders is so important that we hope to convince you to engage in what is called *multiparadigmatic practice* within organizations. **Multiparadigmatic practice** means being able to identify assumptions in use within an organization and then using one's critical thinking and practice skills to move in and out of different ways of thinking (paradigms). Leaders have respect for organizations and individuals who embrace different worldviews than their own and even make the conscious choice to work from a different set of assumptions when that is the best fit for the problem at hand. This is not easy. Individuals typically feel more comfortable in certain paradigms than in others. We believe, however, that it is necessary for the human service leaders of the future to be able to think and act multiparadigmatically in order to fully actualize their organization practice.

Just as we focused in Chapter 2 on different assumptions held by organizational theorists coming from different perspectives, there are diverse assumptions held by persons who have studied employees, managers, and leaders within organizations. To illustrate how these assumptions have shaped understandings of organization practice, we turn to a number of writers on management and leadership.

Assumptions about Managers and Leaders

It has long been recognized that managers can hold, and act on, different assumptions about employees. For example, according to McGregor (1960), Theory X managers assume that workers inherently dislike work and have to be closely supervised. Conversely, Theory Y managers see followers as eager to work and capable of participating in decision making. Similarly, Tannenbaum and Schmidt

(1958) identify a continuum between what they call the autocratic (boss-centered) and the democratic (subordinate-centered) leader, who hold different assumptions about managing employees. "The notion underlying these categories is that a leader tends to utilize a consistent way of interacting with followers and that this method is based on his or her philosophy and assumptions concerning human behavior" (Lewis, Lewis, & Souflee, 1991, pp. 194–195).

Four leading schools of research on leadership emerged during the twentieth century: "trait, style, contingency, and the new leadership paradigm" (Bargal, 2000, p. 305). Each approach was intended to explain the concept of leadership, and each had its accompanying assumptions. The trait approach, which predominated in the 1930s, 40s, and 50s assumes that leaders are born rather than made. Leaders are assumed to have certain personal characteristics, such as a need for power or achievement, and these traits are viewed as making them successful. The style approach emerged as early as the Ohio State University studies on leadership in the 1940s (Stogdill & Coons, 1957). Various scholars focused on leadership style, and their work continues to influence contemporary views of leadership (Bales, 1954; Likert, 1961). The style approach assumes that leaders can be categorized according to patterns of behavior, such as how they show consideration for their employees, define tasks to be done, and monitor employees in carrying out responsibilities (Bowers & Seashore, 1966).

Later, Blake and Mouton (1978) categorized management styles according to the attitudes displayed by leaders, attempting to categorize leadership behaviors on a grid rather than along only one continuum. Their widely cited managerial grid categorizes five types of leaders along two axes: concern for people and concern for production. Blake and Mouton believe that a leader who has both high concern for people and production is the ideal type for which managers should strive. Other writers use the terms *task* versus *relationship* for *production* and *people* (Reddin, 1970), and suggest that perhaps leadership is more situational than there being one ideal type for all occasions.

The contingency approach to leadership emerged during the 1960s. Theorists such as Fiedler (1967) emphasized the importance of context in determining what would work in any given situation. The assumption that context has to be taken into consideration is an important contribution. As theorists attempted to understand assumptions about leadership and its practical application to managing people within an organization, the concept of situational leadership emerged (Hersey & Blanchard, 1977) in which the fit between leader and follower has to be carefully assessed and then style has to be adapted.

We remember participating in the 1970s in very popular training exercises in which everyone tried to categorize one's assumptions about leadership. It was very typical for a trainer to come in, administer a tool, and then have everyone categorize themselves. In this particular event, the trainees were either vanilla, chocolate, or strawberry. As it was explained, vanillas had certain assumptions, chocolates had still others, and strawberries had others, yet all were equally important and valued (some people might like different flavors more than others, but there was no one right way). The point is to recognize that the assumptions held are different and that individuals tend to lead with their preferred assumptions.

We use this example to illustrate that there is nothing new about recognizing that people bring different assumptions to organizational leadership and management. This has been in the management literature for years. The difference now is that some managers/leaders are beginning to seek ways to maximize these differences rather than seeing them as barriers to productivity. This changing perspective is reflected in the new leadership approach, which contrasts with the trait, style, and contingency perspectives, all of which are grounded in a social psychological tradition (Bargal, 2000).

Tied to Burns's (1978) view of leadership, the new leadership approach views leaders as creators of vision, culture, and strategy. Terms such as *transformational* and *transactional leader* are used to portray an approach to leadership in which old assumptions are challenged and organizational cultures are created and changed. The overriding assumption in the new leadership approach is that change is inevitable and that a visionary leader can transform the workplace into a meaningful arena (Bargal, 2000).

Assumptions about Employees

Behavior in organizations has also been categorized, particularly since the development of the human relations theories of organizational behavior. Using Koontz, Hutchinson outlines six schools of management thought (Hutchinson, 1967, p.10): operational school, empirical school, human behavior school, social systems school, decision theory school, and the mathematical school. Pfeffer (1981), having a great interest in power within the organization, suggests four models of management theory: rational, bureaucratic, decision process/organized anarchy, and political power. Bolman and Deal (1991) suggest that theorists of leadership and management can be sorted into rational system theorists, human resource theorists, political theorists, and symbolic theorists. Historically, then, managers have been told to understand their subordinates by categorizing either their behavior or their attitudes. The idea is that through understanding, the manager can better plan, specialize, and use authority and leadership for organizing, controlling, and managing (Hutchinson, 1967).

An alternative to this controlling approach is the very popular Myers-Briggs test (Myers, 1998) built on Jungian theory and developed by Katharine Cook Briggs and Isabel Briggs Myers to allow "the constructive use of difference" (as cited in Martin, 1997). The Myers-Briggs model of personality is said to provide insight into how and why people understand and approach the world in different ways. It is based on the assumption that there are four dimensions of personality preferences. The first is how one directs energy (*extraversion* vs. *introversion*). The second is how one prefers to take in information (*sensing* vs. *intuition*). The third is how one prefers to make decisions (*thinking* vs. *feeling*). And the fourth is how one is oriented to the outer world (*judging* vs. *perceiving*). These preferences are combined into 16 different types, combining *I* for *introvert* or *E* for *extrovert* with *S* for *sensing* or *N* for *intuitive* and either *T* for *thinking* or *F* for *feeling* with *J* for *judging* or *P* for *perceiving*. The combination (see Figure 4.1) purportedly describes how one sees the world.[1] A paper-and-pencil questionnaire is used to assess type, where there is no right or wrong

FIGURE 4.1   Characteristics Frequently Associated with Each Personality Type

Sensing Types

Intuitive Types

Introverts

ISTJ Quiet, serious, earn success by thoroughness and dependability. Practical, matter-of-fact, realistic, and responsible. Decide logically what should be done and work toward it steadily, regardless of distractions. Take pleasure in making everything orderly and organized—their work, their home, their life. Values traditions and loyalty.	**ISFJ** Quiet, friendly, responsible, and conscientious. Committed and steady in meeting their obligations. Thorough, painstaking, and accurate. Loyal, considerate, notice and remember specifics about people who are important to them, concerned with how others feel. Strive to create an orderly and harmonious environment at work and at home.	**INFJ** Seek meaning and connection in ideas, relationships, and material possessions. Want to understand what motivates people and are insightful about others. Conscientious and committed to their firm values. Develop a clear vision about how best to serve the common good. Organized and decisive in implementing their vision.	**INTJ** Have original minds and great drive for implementing their ideas and achieving their goals. Quickly see patterns in external events and develop long-range explanatory perspectives. When committed, organize a job and carry it through. Skeptical and independent, have high standards of competence and performance—for themselves and others.
ISTP Tolerant and flexible, quiet observers until a problem appears, then act quickly to find workable solutions. Analyze what makes thing work and readily get through large amounts of data to isolate the core of practical problems. Interested in cause and effect, organize factors using logical principles, value efficiency.	**ISFP** Quiet, friendly, sensitive, and kind. Enjoy the present moment, what's going on around them. Like to have their own space and to work within their own time frame. Loyal and committed to their values and to people who are important to them. Dislike disagreements and conflicts, do not force their opinions or values on others.	**INFP** Idealistic, loyal to their values and to people who are important to them. Want an external life that is congruent with their values. Curious, quick to see possibilities, can be catalysts for implementing ideas. Seek to understand people and to help them fulfill their potential. Adaptable, flexible, and accepting unless a value is threatened.	**INTP** Seek to develop logical explanations for everything that interests them. Theoretical and abstract, interested more in ideas than in social interaction. Quiet, contained, flexible and adaptable. Have unusual ability to focus in depth to solve problems in their area of interest. Skeptical, sometimes critical, always analytical.

Sensing Types   *Intuitive Types*

Extroverts

ESTP Flexible and tolerant, they take a pragmatic approach focused on immediate results. Theories and conceptual explanations bore them – they want to act energetically to solve the problem. Focus on the here-and-now, spontaneous, enjoy each moment that they can be active with others. Enjoy material comforts and style. Learn best through doing.	**ESFP** Outgoing, friendly, and accepting. Exuberant lovers of life, people, and material comforts. Enjoy working with others to make things happen. Bring common sense and a realistic approach to their work, and make work fun. Flexible and spontaneous, adapt readily to new people and environments. Learn best by trying a new skill with other people.	**ENFP** Warmly enthusiastic and imaginative. See life as full of possibilities. Make connections between events and information very quickly, and confidently proceed based on the patterns they see. Want a lot of affirmation from others, and readily give appreciation and support. Spontaneous and flexible, often rely on their ability to improvise and their verbal fluency.	**ENTP** Quick, ingenious, stimulating, alert, and outspoken. Resourceful in solving new and challenging problems. Adept at generating conceptual possibilities and then analyzing them strategically. Good at reading other people. Bored by routine, will seldom do the same thing the same way, apt to turn to one new interest after another.
ESTJ Practical, realistic, matter-of-fact. Decisive, quickly move to implement decisions. Organize projects and people to get things done, focus on getting results in the most efficient way possible. Take care of routine details. Have a clear set of logical standards, systematically follow them and want others to also. Forceful in implementing their plans.	**ESFJ** Warmhearted, conscientious, and cooperative. Want harmony in their environment, work with determination to establish it. Like to work with others to complete tasks accurately and on time. Loyal, follow through even in small matters. Notice what others need in their day-to-day lives and try to provide it. Want to be appreciated for who they are and for what they contribute.	**ENFJ** Warm, empathetic, responsive, and responsible. Highly attuned to the emotions, needs, and motivations of others. Find potential in everyone, want to help others fulfill their potential. May act as catalysts for individual and group growth. Loyal, responsive to practice and criticism. Sociable, facilitate others in a group, and provide inspiring leadership.	**ENTJ** Frank, decisive, assume leadership readily. Quickly see illogical and inefficient procedures and policies, develop and implement comprehensive systems to solve organizational problems. Enjoy long-term planning and goal setting. Usually well informed, well read, enjoy expanding their knowledge and passing it on to others. Forceful in presenting their ideas.

answer, nor right or wrong types. The idea is that all types are good, just different (much like the example of vanillas, chocolates, and strawberries used earlier).

More and more, the Myers-Briggs test is being used to help people make better career choices and manage intimate relationships. It is used in counseling, parenting, business, teamwork, leadership and spirituality development, and education. The valid and reliable instrument seems to identify how the mind is used and how the individual feels most comfortable, natural, and, confident. It shows how people have different interests, ways of behaving, and ways of viewing strengths and needs for growth.

Isabel Myers believed understanding of differences is "useful whenever one person must communicate with another or live with another or make decisions that affect another's life" (Myers as cited in Myers & Kirby, 1994, p. 16). Since the 1980s, there has been a general public acceptance of the Myers-Briggs's characterization of ways people perceive and relate to the outside world, leading to a level of acceptance that there is no one "best style." It seems there is a growing acceptance that uniqueness brings strength, that different styles are useful, and that differing perceptions are assets. These attitudes are entering the organizational field with the recognition that personality type is related to career satisfaction and organizational competence (Tieger & Barron-Tieger, 1992), team members' types affect team building (Hirsh, 1992), and ways of describing and analyzing organizational situations set the stage for organizational change (Lawrence, 1993).

Although the Myers-Briggs is designed to respect differences, the tool has not always been used for that purpose. Management trainers have used the Myers-Briggs over the years to point out why different employees had different needs, but the message was often interpreted by managers as a way to understand why things were not working and to try to coral or manipulate employees to "get with the program." Thus, the Myers-Briggs instrument can be used to control the behavior of subordinates, even though that was not necessarily its intent. Until recent developments by postmodern theorists,[2] there was an assumption (or at least a hope) that there was a "one best way" of doing the business of organizing. Differences were recognized, but they were viewed as liabilities rather than strengths. Some managers searched for order and conformity rather than focusing on the strengths that exist amid diversity.

A Multiparadigmatic Approach

The continuing search to identify differences reveals that no matter how much a manager or leader would like to have people conform to a shared set of assumptions and create an organizational culture that reflects shared values, there will always be people who don't share assumptions or values. The reasons for and the depth of differences and the ability of anyone to change those differences vary. Categorizing differences in order to understand them offers some possibilities in organization practice. Managing the complexity of all this becomes the challenge, and a multiparadigmatic perspective has great potential in meeting that challenge. An important question, then, is: How does a person learn to think multiparadigmatically so that he or she can maximize strengths amid this diversity of strongly held worldviews?

Efforts to critically analyze organizations and the practice within them, with an eye to cultural competence and social justice, have been greatly enhanced by the work of Burrell and Morgan (1979). Their thinking helps to incorporate scholarship on organizations with more recent and seemingly contradictory efforts of modern and postmodern thinkers. In their classic work, *Sociological Paradigms and Organisational Analysis*, Burrell and Morgan provide a framework for making sense of the many competing and often contradictory theories of organization and organizational behavior. Their way of framing the multiple approaches to researching and understanding organizations is central to our thinking about social work practice within an organizational context. We see their framework as a useful way to organize and manage one's simultaneous attention to social work values, complex situations, and multiple perspectives. It is also compatible with the Myers-Briggs's efforts to promote understanding, respect, and acceptance of differences between people of different nations, races, cultures, and persuasions. These multiple paradigms have the potential to help people in organizations "to recognize and enjoy their gifts" (Briggs Myers & Myers, 1995, p. xv).

Basic Assumptions of Different Perspectives

In the remainder of this chapter, we provide an overview of Burrell and Morgan's work. Their multiparadigmatic thinking can become a conscious part of one's organization practice, thus enhancing one's ability to embrace the complexity and diversity of the work environment and to tolerate the frustrations of conflicts that come with differences. It is our hope that a multiparadigmatic understanding of organizations will help you, as it has helped us, to move from differences that block development to differences that empower.

Burrell and Morgan (1979) begin by identifying four different dimensions that become the axes of a four-cell matrix in which each paradigm is located. The first axis is formed by what they label *subjectivist-objectivist dimensions,* and the second

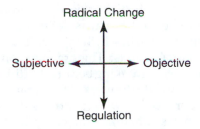

FIGURE 4.2 Burrell and Morgan's Four Dimensions
Source: Adapted from Burrell and Morgan (1979, Chapter 1).

is formed by *regulation-radical change dimensions.* Figure 4.2 illustrates how the dimensions could be visualized in a matrix. Keeping this matrix in mind, both sets of dimensions are defined next.

Subjectivist-Objectivist Continuum

Burrell and Morgan start with basic assumptions about the nature of social science in order to identify different paradigms. They begin by asking four basic questions:

1. What is human/social reality like?
2. How can, or do, we know this and how is knowledge about it transmitted?
3. What is human nature basically like?
4. What methodology do we employ to study or observe human/social reality? (1979, p. 3)

In responding to these questions, most organizational theories can be seen as either subjectivist or objectivist and these dimensions can be placed on a continuum:

Subjectivist  Objectivist

Theories based on a **subjectivist perspective** assume that social reality exists primarily in the human consciousness (a product of one's mind). The subjectivist would say the answer to question 1 is **nominalism**—human reality exists within the mind. In responding to question 2, a subjectivist would say that knowledge about reality is soft, subjective, and natural **(antipositivism).** From a subjectivist perspective, question 3 would be answered that human nature is based in **voluntarism**—people can be proactive in creating their own realities. Free human beings participate actively in the creation and construction of social reality, and reality must be experienced to be transmitted and understood. And last, a subjectivist perspective on question 4 would be **ideographic,** meaning that concern should not be focused on universal principles or an absolutist view. Instead, subjectivists emphasize what is unique and relative to the individual and the ways in which individuals create, change, and interpret the world. Asked what methods would be used to study organizations, subjectivists would prefer qualitative approaches.

Think about a person who might be described as subjectivist. From a values and ethics standpoint, that person would be a relativist, as defined in Chapter 3. Recall that a relativist does not abide universalism in which there is "one best way." Also imagine an organization that might be subjectivist. This organization would by definition be an alternative to traditional ways of thinking because traditional thinking seeks order through locating the best way to do the work of the organization.

Theories based on an **objectivist perspective** would address the four questions quite differently. In response to "What is human/social reality like?" an objectivist embraces **realism,** placing reality above and beyond individual knowledge. Question 2 would be answered by the objectivist as **positivism,** in which knowledge

TABLE 4.1 Subjective-Objective Approaches to the Social Sciences

Subjectivist Perspective	Objective Perspective
Nominalism (in the mind)	Realism (external)
Antipositivism (soft, subjective, must be experienced)	Positivism (hard, real, tangible)
Voluntarism (people create their environments)	Determinism (people are products of their environments)
Ideographic (analyze subjective accounts generated by "getting inside" situations of everyday life)	Nomothetic (use methods of natural science to test hypotheses in accord with scientific rigor)

Source: Adapted from G. Burrell and G. Morgan, *Sociological Paradigms and Organisational Analysis* (Aldershot, England: Ashgate, 1979), Figure 1.1, p. 3. Used by permission.

about social reality is hard and concrete. From this dimension, social reality exists outside the individual. The objectivist response to question 3 would be that reality shapes action and perception, which is **determinism**. People are not shapers of their own realities, but are products of their environments. Asked what methods would be used to understand this dimension, natural science methods can be applied to the study and understanding of social reality. This stance is called **nomothetic**.

Again, think about persons or organizations that hold objectivist assumptions. Not only is there "one best way" if one can only find it, but truth has a big "T." These persons and organizations are absolutists, as defined in Chapter 3. The organization would be traditionally organized in a bureaucratic and hierarchical structure. Objectivist individuals believe in universal Truth over which they have no control. They are the searchers who seek the *right* answers. They would never be accused of saying that everything is relative, and when they work with subjectivists, they will often be frustrated by their colleagues' alternative perspectives.

Table 4.1 provides an overview of subjective-objective dimensions and how they differ in their aproaches to the social sciences.

Regulation/Radical Change Continuum

In additional to their four questions about the nature of social science, Burrell and Morgan are also concerned about the nature of human society—the patterned associations between people over time. What assumptions influence, for example, how people come together (associate) in an organization? To answer this question, they identify two dimensions that create perspectives about society that were dominant in the literature, *regulation* and *radical change*, and place them on a continuum:

Regulation ◄————————————————————► **Radical Change**

Theories built on a **regulation perspective** assume that society is characterized by social order and equilibrium. Reality is ordered, if not rule governed, and knowledge for knowledge's sake is an acceptable result of rigorous, scientific inquiry. A regulation perspective is held by persons who embrace the status quo, and seek consensus rather than focusing on conflict. In a way, the search for order that we described earlier is based on this dimension.

On the other hand, theories grounded in a **radical change perspective** focus on deep-seated structural conflict, modes of domination, and even contradiction (change, conflict, and coercion in social structures). This perspective views reality as conflict ridden, if not chaotic. According to this perspective, knowledge for change or action should be the goal of scientific inquiry.

Table 4.2 provides a list of concerns based on the regulation versus radical change dimensions.

Four Paradigms

Taking the two continua just described, Burrell and Morgan form a matrix. The subjectivist-objectivist continuum forms the horizontal axis and the regulation-radical change continuum forms the vertical axis. Figure 4.3 reveals a four-cell typology in which assumptions based on different dimensions come together into four paradigms: functionalist, radical structuralist, interpretive, and radical humanist. Each paradigm represents a fundamentally distinct set of perspectives for analyzing organizations.

Notice the similarity between this organizing scheme and that of the Myers-Briggs typology. In fact, later we will illustrate how the personality types can be placed on these same subjective/objective and regulation/radical change continua. For now, it is important to see that just as the Myers-Briggs instrument identifies separate and unique types, the four paradigms define fundamentally different perspectives for the analysis of social phenomena. For example, leaders holding these different perspectives would develop different expectations for employee perfor-

TABLE 4.2   **Concerns of Regulation versus Radical Change Dimensions**

Regulation Concerns	Radical Change Concerns
1. The status quo	1. Radical change
2. Social order	2. Structural conflict
3. Consensus	3. Modes of domination
4. Social integration and cohesion	4. Contradiction
5. Solidarity	5. Emancipation
6. Needs satisfaction	6. Deprivation
7. Actuality	7. Potentiality

Source: Adapted from G. Burrell and G. Morgan, *Sociological Paradigms and Organisational Analysis* (Aldershot, England: Ashgate, 1979), Table 2.2, p. 18. Used by permission.

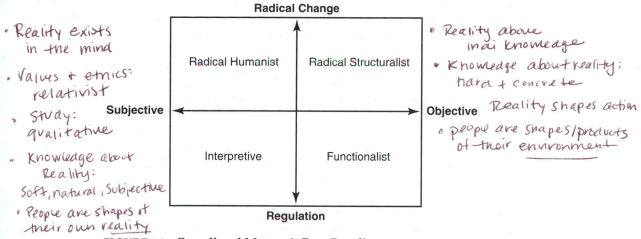

Handwritten margin notes (left):
- Reality exists in the mind
- Values + ethics: relativist
- Study: qualitative
- Knowledge about Reality: Soft, natural, Subjective
- People are shapes of their own reality

Handwritten margin notes (right):
- Reality above in ai knowledge
- Knowledge about reality: hard + concrete
- Reality shapes action
- people are shapes/products of their environment

Figure diagram labels:
- Radical Change (top)
- Radical Humanist / Radical Structuralist
- Subjective / Objective
- Interpretive / Functionalist
- Regulation (bottom)

FIGURE 4.3   Burrell and Morgan's Four Paradigms

Source: Adapted from G. Burrell and G. Morgan, *Sociological Paradigms and Organisational Analysis* (Aldershot, England: Ashgate, 1979), Figure 3.1, p. 22. Used by permission.

mance. These mutually exclusive paradigms define four alternative views of the social world based on different metatheoretical assumptions regarding the nature of science and of society. To understand the nature of all four is to understand four different, and oftentimes competing, views of society and of organizations in society.

Burrell and Morgan assume that all organizations can be located within the context of the four paradigms according to the assumptions that are reflected in the organization's work. To practice appropriately and to effect lasting change, one must understand the constraints and opportunities of each paradigm. This understanding will provide the flexibility to respond to very different expectations about what constitutes good organization practice based on different sets of assumptions about the role of organizations and the persons who associate within them.

One further note is important. These perspectives are mutually exclusive, alternative views. As such, they represent four different ways of seeing, knowing, and practicing. Certainly, one can operate in different paradigms at different times, but no organization or person can operate in more than one at any given time without confronting major contradictions in understanding and practice. In fact, when one encounters paradox in organization practice, it is likely that different, incompatible perspectives are trying to coexist. For example, consider the cognitive dissonance you would feel as a new worker entering what has been called a "collaborative organization." The agency director and your supervisor have both told you that everything is done collaboratively, yet you notice that "team meetings" include only upper administration. Decisions and directives flow to you hierarchically. You are never asked for input. In this example, the decision process is very hierarchical, coming from a functionalist perspective, while the upper administrators seem to articulate a collaborative mandate from an interpretive perspective. Lower-level workers in this organization are destined to live in the frustration and paradox created in this organization, which is attempting to work from two very different sets of assumptions—assumptions that actually contradict one another.

Another example of the difficulty in managing differences based on paradigmatic perspective might be more closely linked to personality type. You are a very pragmatic individual who feels comfortable only working with "facts." You could be a Myers-Briggs ISTJ (introverted, sensing, thinking, judging). You enter an agency where its members seem very much at ease with one another, very friendly, and very close. They like one another and share very intimate information all the time. They might all be ENFPs (extroverted, intuiting, feeling, perceiving). The decision process seems to be based on what "feels right," with little attention to evidence. You are astounded that they are so successful and well respected. You need empirical evidence to decide organizational direction and you don't wish to have organizational members become intimates like family members. Clearly, your approach to the work environment is coming from a more functionalist perspective. Your inclination will be to criticize the others' way of doing business. On the other hand, the rest of the organization appears to be functioning from a more subjectivist, interpretive perspective. Others will tend to criticize you for being too rigid and unfeeling. From either direction, dissonance is inevitable.

Burrell and Morgan's paradigm represents competing points of view with clearly defined boundaries and with different consequences for practice. We offer them as a way to move beyond the paralysis of cognitive dissonance into a comfort zone of paradox made possible by critical analysis and acceptance of ambiguity.

In the next section of this book, a full chapter will be devoted to each of these paradigms and to the organizational theories that emerge from each set of assumptions and result in different approaches to organization practice. Now, however, we will provide an introductory view of each of the four paradigms.

The Functionalist Paradigm

Radical Humanist	Radical Structuralist
Interpretive	Functionalist

We begin with the *functionalist* paradigm because it is from the assumptions within this paradigm that the majority of classical organizational theories emerged and evolved into "modern" structuralist thinking. Perspectives in this paradigm have influenced theorists who sought to describe (or even prescribe) a rational, orderly approach to work. The functionalist paradigm contains the dominant assumptions from which most organizations tried to function in the twentieth century.

In the functionalist paradigm, objectivism meets regulation. Therefore, realist, positivist, determinist, and nomothetic perspectives about social science are combined with a concern for the status quo, social order, consensus, social integration, solidarity, needs satisfaction, and actuality. In its overall approach, the functionalist paradigm seeks to provide essentially rational explanations of social affairs. It is pragmatic and problem oriented, seeking to apply the models and methods of the natural sciences to the study of human affairs. It tends to assume that the social world is composed of relatively concrete empirical artifacts and relationships that can be identified, studied, and measured through approaches derived from the natural sciences.

Most traditional positivists and postpositivists subscribe to this perspective, which has been well defined by persons such as Compte, Spencer, Durkheim, Pareto, Mill, Mead, and James. According to Burrell and Morgan (1979), the functionalist paradigm owes much to Marxist theory, German idealism, and sociological positivism.

For social work direct practice, Martin and O'Connor (1989, p. 78) analyzed the predominant social work practice theories according to the paradigms from which they were derived. They suggest that psychosocial casework, transactional analysis, family systems therapy, structural family therapy, conjoint family therapy, cognitive-behavioral approaches, problem-solving therapy, behavior modification, and reciprocal groupwork models all fit comfortably within the functionalist paradigm. In community practice, they place the social planning model there as well. In a later section of the text, we will more fully describe the basic assumptions of the major theories of organization and organizational behavior. At this point, it is sufficient to say that Burrell and Morgan (1979) would place a majority of organizational theories within the functionalist paradigm.

Myers-Briggs types might also be located in this paradigm based on similar assumptions about reality and what is valued. For example, persons described as ISTJs (introverted, sensing, thinking, judging)—with their realism, organizing abilities, and command of the facts based on logical pragmatism—can be seen to be functionalists. The ESTJs (extroverted, sensing, thinking, judging) and their need to analyze and bring into logical order the world of events, people, and things using current facts and realities are functionalists in their worldview. So, too, are the ESTPs (extroverted, sensing, thinking, perceiving), with their interest in how objects, events, and people work. Their tendency for logic and analysis of outer world and real-life experiences also places them squarely within the functionalist paradigm.

FIGURE 4.4   **Assumptions of the Functionalist Paradigm**

From the Objectivist Perspective
1. Reality is above and beyond individual knowledge.
2. Knowledge about social reality is hard and concrete.
3. People are products of their environments; they are shaped.
4. Natural science methods can be applied to the study and understanding of social reality.

From the Regulation Perspective
5. Society is characterized by social order and equilibrium.
6. Knowledge for knowledge's sake is acceptable.
7. Consensus, rather than conflict, is important.

Source: Adapted from Burrell and Morgan (1979, Chapter 1).

Finally, for the purposes of critical analysis, we can place approaches to the ethical principles of the social work profession within paradigms as well. A person or organization operating from the functionalist paradigm would approach the core values of service, social justice, dignity and worth of the person, importance of human relationships, integrity, and competence in ethical absolutist terms. Functionalists would be certain that there is "one best way" of defining and assuring what constitutes the core values of the profession and they would see core values as universal and unchanging. Functionalists would search for certainty and the reduction of conflict among competing values. Figure 4.4 summarizes the assumptions of this paradigm.

The Radical Structuralist Paradigm

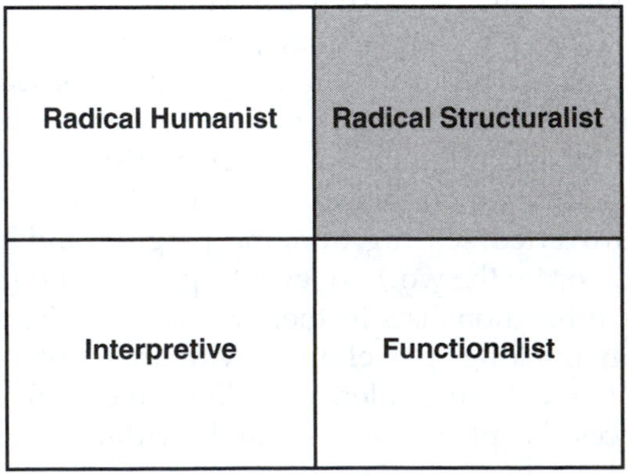

Radical Humanist	**Radical Structuralist**
Interpretive	**Functionalist**

The *radical structuralist paradigm* shares an objectivist approach to science similar to that of the functionalist paradigm, but it is directed at fundamentally different ends. Both paradigms are objectivist, but in the radical structuralist paradigm a commitment to radical change intersects with objectivism. Radical change focuses on modes of domination, contradiction, and deprivation. Objectivists assume that there is universal, rules-based knowledge, and in this paradigm that knowledge is gained for the purposes of radical change, emancipation, and potentiality. This perspective is realist, but concentrates on structural relationships to understand and generate fundamental conflicts on which will be based radical change at the class level. Radical structuralists focus on these structural relationships within a social world assumed to be realist, seeking to provide explanations of the basic interrelationships within the context of total social formations. People in this paradigm view contemporary society as characterized by fundamental conflicts that generate radical change through political and economic crises.

Martin and O'Connor (1989) could not identify direct practice theories that guide practice with individuals, families, or groups that fit into the radical structuralist paradigm. However, they place the social action model of community change in this paradigm. We include perspectives embraced by activists such as Saul Alinsky, the Black Panthers, and Latin American liberation theologians.

Generally, philosophers who take the position that science should serve to critique the status quo of social affairs fit within this worldview. Their interest is in class conflict leading to a revolutionary overthrow of hierarchy, power, and authority. Such thinkers as Weber, the mature Marx, Engles, Lenin, Bukharin, Coletti, Dehrendorf, Rex, and Miliband are radical structuralists, according to Burrell and Morgan (1979). Kantian and Hegelian influences are also present. Burrell and Morgan (1979) suggest that there is very little American or British organizational theory development in this paradigm. Rather, organizational theorists taking a radical structuralist perspective have more often developed the critique of the functionalist approach (p. 366). European organizational theorists, however, have developed several theories—including contemporary Mediterranean Marxism, Russian social theory, conflict theory (which can be seen as a subset of critical theory), and radical organization theory—that fit within the assumptions of the radical structuralist approach.

From the categories of personality types, the ISTPs (introverted, sensing, thinking, perceiving), with their need to understand how things in the real world work so they can make the best and most effective use of them, are likely radical structuralists. The ENTPs (extroverted, intuitive, thinking, perceiving), with their natural inclination to question and critique ideas and events in order to understand them, also share this worldview, although they may lack the need to bring order to the world like most radical structuralists. Finally, the ENTJs (extroverted, intuitive, thinking, judging), with their need to analyze and bring to logical order all aspects of their world, are radical structuralists, given their need to create plans for strategic action.

Radical structuralist social work practitioners share ethical absolutism with those taking the functionalist perspective. However, ethical decisions for them also require action to achieve such things as social consciousness, social justice, integrity, and dignity and worth of the person. Critique of the status quo without activ-

FIGURE 4.5   **Assumptions of the Radical Structuralist Paradigm**

From the Objectivist Perspective
1. Reality is above and beyond individual knowledge.
2. Knowledge about social reality is hard and concrete.
3. People are products of their environments; they are shaped.
4. Natural science methods can be applied to the study and understanding of social reality.

From the Radical Change Perspective
5. Society is characterized by deep-seated structural conflict, modes of domination, and even contradiction.
6. Knowledge for change and action should be the goal.
7. Conflict, rather than consensus, is important.

Source: Adapted from Burrell and Morgan (1979, Chapter 1).

ities to promote change would be seen to be unethical from this perspective. Figure 4.5 provides an overview of the assumptions held by radical structuralists. The radical structuralist paradigm holds objectivism in common with the functionalist paradigm, but contrasts with functionalists by embracing a radical change perspective.

The Interpretive Paradigm

Radical Humanist	Radical Structuralist
Interpretive	**Functionalist**

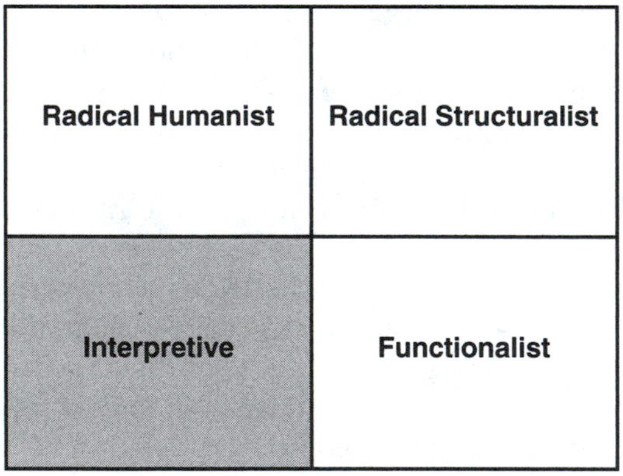

In the *interpretive paradigm*, subjectivism meets regulation. This paradigm is informed by a concern to understand the world as it is. It assumes that to understand the fundamental nature of the social world, it must be at the level of subjective experience. The interpretive approach seeks explanation of the reality of individual consciousness and subjectivity, within the frame of reference that people are participants as opposed to observers of action. It tends to be nominalist, antipositivist, voluntarist, and idiographic. The social world is seen as an emergent process that is created by the individuals concerned. Social reality is little more than a network of assumptions and intersubjectively shared meanings based on multiple perspectives. The problems of conflict, domination, contradiction, potentiality, and change play little part in this frame of reference because regulation predominates. Instead, there is much more orientation toward obtaining an understanding of the subjectively created social world as it is in terms of an ongoing process. The interpretive paradigm is involved with issues relating to the nature of the status quo, social order, consensus, social integration and cohesion, solidarity, and actuality. It assumes a relativist position in that the world, though ordered, is an emergent social enterprise that is continually being created. It assumes that meaning is created and that intersubjectively shared meaning influences decision making and behavior (Weber, 1947a).

Though there seems to be a natural philosophical affinity between the assumptions of the interpretive paradigm and the social work perspective, particularly in regard to the context dependence of individual experience, only a few social work practice theories are identified by Martin and O'Connor (1989) as belonging within this paradigm: client-centered therapy, problem-solving casework, and Gestalt therapy. More recently developed interventions guided by social constructionism, social constructivism, and symbolic interactionism also are a part of an interpretive perspective, as are all therapies under the rubric of narrative therapy.

Given their interest in socially constructed and socially sustained meaning and their assumption that meaning can only be understood in the immediate social context, Burrell and Morgan (1979) place Dilthey, Husserl, Schutz, Gadamer, Garfinkle, Berkeley, Heidegger, and Merleau-Ponty in the interpretive paradigm. It is clear that, like the functionalists, these thinkers were influenced by the German idealists, but they were more interested in understanding through **Verstehen** (complete understanding) than through positivism. Because of this focus on holistic understanding, some works of Kant, Weber, and Mead exhibit this paradigmatic perspective, while others (the majority of their work) fit within the functionalist perspective.

Until recently, few theories of organization could be placed within the interpretive perspective. However, the surge of organizational culture and sensemaking perspectives in the last two decades have emerged from assumptions held in the interpretive paradigm. Studies of the subjective experience of individuals within organizational contexts are guided by phenomenology, hermeneutics, phenomenological sociology, constructivism, ethnomethodology, and phenomenological symbolic interactionism.

For personality types, the ISFPs (introverted, sensing, feeling, perceiving), with their deep-felt connection with others, though the warmth and concern are not generally expressed openly, fit within the interpretive paradigm. The ESFPs (extroverted, sensing, feeling, perceiving) are excited about continuous involvement in activities and relationships. They show their caring in warm and pragmatic gestures of helping, which also places them within the assumptions of the interpretive perspective. With their driving force to understand whatever phenomenon is the focus of their attention, the INTPs (introverted, intuitive, thinking, perceiving) are also interpretivists. They want to make sense of the world. The ENFPs (extroverted, intuitive, feeling, perceiving), with their excitement and continuous involvement in anything new and their attention to the outer world of possibilities and a deep concern for others, also fit within this paradigm. However, their interest in possibilities for people might move them toward radical humanism.

Social workers coming from interpretivist perspectives are ethical relativists. Individualism, situational ethics, relativity, service, and importance of human relationships would be important measures of ethical behavior. However, understanding and analysis would take precedence over corrective action, since, from this perspective, change will naturally emerge from understanding. Figure 4.6 provides a summary of assumptions undergirding the interpretive paradigm.

Note that the interpretive and the functionalist paradigms both hold assumptions about there being order (regulation) in the world. Persons coming from these different perspectives would, however, disagree about how order comes to be. Whereas the functionalist would see order as superimposed by the environment, the interpretivist would see order as socially constructed. Both would seek consensus and would see the importance of understanding organizations as valuable, even if some action or change did not occur as a result of that new understanding.

The Radical Humanist Paradigm

Radical Humanist	Radical Structuralist
Interpretive	Functionalist

In the *radical humanist paradigm,* subjectivism connects with radical change. In this paradigm, the central emphasis is on human consciousness, believing that consciousness is dominated by the ideological superstructures with which humans interact and which drive a cognitive wedge between humans and true consciousness. Without true consciousness, fulfillment is inhibited or prevented. Emphasizing radical change, modes of domination, emancipation, deprivation, and potentiality from a subjectivist standpoint, this perspective rejects the concepts of structural conflict and contradiction in favor of a view of the social world that is nominalist, antipositivist, voluntarist, and idiographic. The major concern from this perspective is the release from the constraints that the status quo places on human development. Society is assumed to be antihuman; therefore, human beings must develop ways

FIGURE 4.6   Assumptions of the Interpretive Paradigm

From the Subjectivist Perspective
1. Social reality exists primarily in the human mind.
2. Knowledge about social reality is soft, subjective, and natural.
3. People can be proactive in creating their own realities.
4. Given that individuals create, change, and interpret the world, qualitative approaches to understanding are useful.

From the Regulation Perspective
5. Society is characterized by social order and equilibrium.
6. Knowledge for knowledge's sake is acceptable.
7. Consensus, rather than conflict, is important.

Source: Adapted from Burrell and Morgan (1979, Chapter 1).

to transcend the spiritual bonds and fetters that tie them to existing social patterns in order to realize full potential. The goal is radical change to release constraints that hamper human development.

There are no well-developed social work practice theories in the radical humanist paradigm. However, with the emerging interest in spirituality and holistic treatment modalities, fully developed approaches may be on the horizon. Some of the emergent practices—such as transpersonal work, transcendental meditation, and spiritual counseling—would fit here. Given the general assumptions of the perspective, it is doubtful if any fully formed theory (using the expectations of the functionalist perspective to define what constitutes theory) will ever develop due to the unabashed connection to an individualized subjectivist view of social reality.

The philosophers who can be placed in this paradigm have also been influenced by German idealism. They share a common concern for individual freedom of the human spirit. Burrell and Morgan (1979) place Kant, Hegel, Husserl, Lukács, Gramsci, the Frankfurt School, young Marx (before the influence of Engles), Habermas, Horkheimer, Marcuse, Adorno, Sartre, Illich, Castaneda, and Laing in the radical humanist paradigm, based on their emancipatory aims.

From an organizational theory perspective, the major theory that fits within the paradigm is what could be called *antiorganization theory* (Farmer, 1998) in that it suggests that any organization theory is naive since no organizations exist outside of individual consciousness. Therefore, any theory developed about organizations is misconceived and politically distasteful. There are, however, a few other theories that hold some of the major assumptions of the paradigm: anarchistic individualism, French existentialism, and one branch of critical theory. **Solipsism,** or the assertion that there exists no independent reality outside of the mind, would also fit within this perspective.

Personality types that could be said to fit in this paradigm include the ISFJs (introverted, sensing, feeling, judging), who value respect and a sense of personal responsibility. The ESFJs (extroverted, sensing, feeling, judging) use their senses to orient their feelings about current facts and realities that are overlayed with an active and intense caring about people. Preference for the inner world of possibilities, ideas, and symbols also place the INFJs (introverted, intuitive, feeling, judging), within this paradigm. This is also true for the ENFJs (extroverted, intuitive, feeling, judging) with their intuition that orients their feeling to the new and to the possible where working to potential engages their intense caring. The INFPs (introverted, intuitive, feeling, perceiving) are also within this paradigm by virtue of their intense caring about ideas, projects, or any involvement they see as important. They embody a concern for human potential. Finally, the INTJs (introverted, intuitive, thinking, judging) can also be said to share in this paradigm by virtue of their attention to the inner world of possibilities and their orientation to work intensely to make their visions into realities.

Social work practitioners from this perspective are ethical relativists who see ethical behavior as context embedded. Social justice as well as dignity and worth of the person would need a strictly individualistic analysis in order to determine what can be seen to be ethical and what should be done if it is not. Lack of action to right that which is wrong is unethical to radical humanists, given their desire for change. Figure 4.7 summarizes the assumptions of the radical humanist paradigm.

Note that the radical humanist and the interpretive paradigms have a subjectivist perspective in common. Persons in both these paradigms would agree that reality is a social construction, subject to change. However, the radical humanist would view the interpretivist as too focused on consensus to take on the important changes that need to be made. It is also important to note that the radical humanist and the functionalist paradigms have nothing in common. In fact, their assumptions are contradictions of one another.

FIGURE 4.7   **Assumptions of the Radical Humanist Paradigm**

From the Subjectivist Perspective
1. Social reality exists primarily in the human mind.
2. Knowledge about social reality is soft, subjective, and natural.
3. People can be proactive in creating their own realities.
4. Given that individuals create, change, and interpret the world, qualitative approaches to understanding are useful.

From the Radical Change Perspective
5. Society is characterized by deep-seated structural conflict, modes of domination, and even contradiction.
6. Knowledge for change and action should be the goal.
7. Conflict, rather than consensus, is important.

Source: Adapted from Burrell and Morgan (1979, Chapter 1).

Why Are Paradigms Important?

Why have we provided such a broad discussion of four different paradigms for analysis of organizations and organizational behavior? Wouldn't just providing our preferred approach be less confusing and possibly more convincing? If we had chosen only to present our preferred perspectives, the reader would have been left with holes in the analytical scheme that was developed. Instead, we think it is important to provide a broad intellectual source for understanding the complexity of organization practice.

We acknowledge that one could read about these paradigms and feel very frustrated, thinking that everyone is being put into boxes. Believe us, being put into boxes is probably one of the things we have resisted all our lives, and continue to resist. In fact, what we hope will be accomplished by the time you read this entire book is that you will understand the box of assumptions you bring to the world. Further, we hope you will be able to consciously move in and out of that box (paradigm), fully aware that there are alternative ways of knowing the world. As with personality characteristics, most people who are under stress or exploring new situations will tend to retreat to those assumptions (those boxes) in which they feel most comfortable, those modes of thinking that have made them who they are. The self-aware social worker will know when she or he chooses to operate from a paradigm in which there is the most comfort or familiarity, even if that paradigm is not congruent with the organizational context in which one finds oneself. However, the skilled practitioner will also be able to identify when one's own assumptions are in conflict with those of others, are incompatible to the degree that something has to change, and begin to find ways to maximize those differences as strengths. This is what multiparadigmatic practice is all about, recognizing where we and others are "coming from."

We also hope this discussion of paradigms, especially related to Martin and O'Connor's work, has begun to show some of the parallels that exist between direct social work practice and administrative social work practice, identifying some of the theoretical perspectives that both hold in common. We also hope that the analytical scheme provided by Burrell and Morgan allows one to pay attention to key assumptions in any theory of interest that will help identify the precise issues that differentiate theoretical approaches. For us, the four-paradigm configuration has been very helpful in organizing and making sense out of conflicting scholarship/ research and other data. It also allows one to see where information is missing, since most organizational theory work has been in the functionalist paradigm.

As we explore in depth each paradigm, one will see that most authors who approach organizations from alternative paradigmatic perspectives have often critiqued functionalists without really developing their own perspectives. It is our hope that this framework will become so interesting and exciting that you will build on some of the new postmodernist work to fully develop organization theory within each perspective.

Multiple paradigms allow respect for fundamentally different perspectives. "Fit" can happen in a variety of ways, because multiple paradigms expand the horizon of modes of theorizing, modes of behaving, and modes of approaching the business of organizing. Different concepts and different analytic tools are logically derived in each paradigm. This allows the ability to test to see if the methods of research being undertaken are true to the nature of the phenomena under study (including the assumptions of the context of the investigation).

More important, multiple paradigms validate the existence of respectable, different perspectives. Understanding the extent of the differences between these four worldviews will provide vehicles for bridging the real alternative realities for true communication and understanding. Multiparadigmatic thinking allows recognition of the degree to which you and your colleagues in organizations may be participating in mutually exclusive, although viably different, ways of seeing the world. We think facility in multiple paradigms is one clear way to move toward multicultural practice.

Multicultural practice leaves functionalist orthodoxy behind and expands one's possibilities to see organizations not just as mechanical or organistic but also as chaotic, socially constructed entities full of creativity and possibilities. This analytic scheme can become a tool for negotiating those possibilities. It is also a tool for negotiating life in organizations. The four paradigms give the multiparadigmatic thinker the ability to attend to key assumptions, thereby sorting out precise issues that might differentiate approaches to practice and problem solving within organizations. The four paradigms are a tool for analysis to determine where an organization is, has been, and where it might be possible to go.

The four paradigms together help in understanding the basic similarities and differences between organizations. They also help to locate one's own frame of reference in order to understand how certain theories, approaches, and practices are more appealing than others. Finally, they help to show how change in personal or organizational basic assumptions is so difficult. Change in metatheoretical assumptions is possible, but not often achieved in practice because the unconscious application of a paradigmatic perspective is so basic to the essence of the organization. Through conscious attention to paradigmatic perspectives, needs for change can be discussed across paradigms in order to achieve a more just environment in which to plan and deliver human service programs.

Conclusion

The search for order—whether it is designed to categorize managers and leaders, employees' attitudes and behaviors, or even organizations themselves—is ongoing. New perspectives are continually emerging as paradigms clash. Initially, categorization was aimed at helping managers control subordinates so that work could be accomplished more efficiently and effectively. The early models of categorization were built on assumptions about organizational life that are no longer universally useful. In order to respond to the multiple challenges of a diverse workforce in a diverse society, new ways of understanding organizations are necessary.

Though it was initially questioned because persons without academic credentials developed the categorizing typology and the test, the Myers-Briggs typology and test has become a well-respected instrument with broad-scale usefulness. Not only has it been useful in personal and family life situations but it has also contributed to better targeting of educational experiences and better superior/subordinate management techniques. The categories describe more than personality types; they are indications of worldviews of a paradigmatic nature as well. Myers-Briggs helps to elaborate how diversity can be understood and how the challenges of differences can be managed. There are differences. These differences have both positive and negative consequences, but the differences are not good or bad, just different.

Another tool for understanding and managing diversity is Burrell and Morgan's four mutually distinct paradigms that create four fundamentally different perspectives for analysis of organization. As a beginning assessment of their usefulness as a tool for analysis of organizations and organizational behavior, social work values and practice theories can be placed within the paradigmatic framework. This is true, too, for the major organization and organizational behavior theories. Finally, the personality types derived from the Myers-Briggs test can also be located within the paradigmatic structure.

We hope you noticed in our discussion of the classification process that organization theories are more likely to be found in the functionalist perspective, whereas personality types are more likely to be found in the radical humanist paradigm. No wonder there is a difficulty in integrating theory into practice! There exists little natural connection between these perspectives. The radical humanist perspective would suggest that the functionalist asks the wrong questions and uses the wrong methods, thus producing useless information. On the other hand, the functionalist perspective would question whether the radical humanist perspective could constitute a legitimate, rigorous way of knowing. In later sections of the book, it will be clear that each perspective has something to contribute to one's understanding of the world and to practice within organizations.

ENDNOTES

1. Those wishing to understand more about Myers-Briggs should see Briggs Myers and McCaulley (1985), Briggs Myers and Myers (1995), Denarest (1997), Hirsh (1992), Kroeger and Thuesen (1988), Lawrence (1993), Martin (1997), Myers and Kirby (1994), and Tieger and Barron-Tieger (1992).
2. See, for example, Fox and Miller (1995) and Hassard and Parker (1993).

Understanding Organizations

Theory and Practice

In Part Two, we continue to examine the Burrell and Morgan (1979) framework as a way of organizing theories and introducing approaches to organization practice. The four frameworks introduced in Chapter 4 will be elaborated on in separate chapters. Each elaboration is followed by an accompanying chapter illustrating how the assumptions of that particular paradigm influence the approach to practice in organizations based on those assumptions. The following questions are pursued in each practice chapter: (1) What are the characteristics of organizations most likely to operate from the assumptions of this paradigm? (2) How does one begin to assess this type of organization? (3) What language is used in these organizations? (4) What approaches to practice are most likely to fit within this type organization? and (5) What are the implications of paradigmatic assumptions for social work leaders in this type organization?

Functionalist Theories and Practice

Chapter 5 elaborates functionalist assumptions and focuses on those theories most tied to the functionalist paradigm. Classical and neoclassical organization theories fall within this paradigm, providing an historical perspective on positivistic assumptions that have been embraced by traditional human service organizations. Two types of systems theory (mechanistic and organismic) are included with their focus on inputs, throughputs, outputs, and outcomes. They are highly positivistic and assume that one lives in a rational world in which organizations should attempt to maintain stability in turbulent environments. This chapter will likely seem very familiar to the reader, as the majority of human service agencies have survived by at least attempting to conform to functionalist assumptions in which maintaining the status quo is a high priority.

Chapter 6 focuses on understanding practice within functionalist organizations. Practice in a functionalist organization may work well with the current push toward outcome measurement, which assumes that if one does certain things on the front end (inputs) and then knows what technologies to use with clients (throughputs), there will be ways to measure the quality of what happens (outcomes). Further, there is congruence with the belief that the only worthwhile outcomes are those that are measurable. This chapter demonstrates why planned change approaches in which incrementalism is appropriate also work well with the assumptions of this paradigm.

Radical Structuralist Theories and Practice

Chapter 7 focuses on the radical structuralist paradigm and its underlying assumptions. Theories that draw on these assumptions are in the power and politics and the postmodern traditions. Special attention is given within the broad power and politics theoretical umbrella to the important place of certain types of feminist and critical theory that question the status quo and demonstrate concern for the general nature of oppression and oppressed populations. The three branches of systems theory (morphogenic, factional, and catastrophic) that acknowledge conflict and change are also explored. The reader will see how organizational theories in this paradigm seek radical social change at the class level and immediately are faced with a challenge when encountering functionalist organizations bent on preserving the status quo.

In Chapter 8, practice within radical structuralist organizations is explored, with a focus on the importance of the dialectical nature of this enterprise. Ways in which power and politics are operationalized within these organizations are examined. Understanding the practice within radical structuralist organizations suggests change is anything but incremental; rather, it is intended to promote radical transformation of those who have been subject to oppressive (often functionalist) systems.

Interpretive Theories and Practice

In Chapter 9, the interpretive paradigm is examined and two emerging schools of organizational theory are highlighted: organizational culture and sensemaking theory. Rather than focusing on organizational structure or products, interpretive theories bring into view how individuals within the organization conform to norms that are often unstated and difficult for outsiders to understand and how organizations are socially constructed. Like their functionalist counterparts, interpretivist theorists are comfortable with the status quo, but they part company in how they view difference. Interpretivists are subjectivists who seek to understand organizations and the meaning that people find within them. They revel in diversity and although they seek consensus, they do so with the assumption that a new consensus will continually emerge.

Chapter 10 points out why practice in interpretive organizations is so different from work in radical structuralist and functionalist organizations. In interpretive organizations, to fully understand what is happening in one's organizational life is viewed as individually empowering in and of itself. Understanding this approach will also help the practitioner understand the standpoint of persons who do not find the search for meaning to be productive and why they may view change in interpretive organizations as soft, subjective, and difficult to achieve.

Radical Humanist Theories and Practice

Chapter 11 reveals the assumptions and theories derived from the radical humanist paradigm. Similar to their radical structuralist colleagues, radical humanists are tied to power and politics theories, critical theory, and certain branches of feminist theory and postmodern theory. An antiadministration approach to theory is introduced in this chapter, illustrating just how far apart functionalists and radical humanists are in their thinking and theorizing. The emerging nature of theory in this area forms a provocative backdrop against which to explore the nature of the radical humanist organization.

Chapter 12 introduces the last of the four chapters geared to understanding practice. This one focuses on understanding organization practice from a radical humanist view. This chapter reveals the paradoxical nature of practicing in an organization that is so individualistic that its goal is to empower individuals and respect difference at all costs. Clarity about the function of conflict should be possible. Conflict for practitioners in radical humanist organizations offers the potential for unlimited change possibilities and the free release of the human spirit.

Although we consider the radical humanist organization and the practice within it the hardest to fully comprehend, we think it will provide the reader with many possibilities for the future. We see it as a developing, alternative perspective from what is typically seen in human service agencies and one that may become very much part of viable organizations with global perspectives in the years to come.

The Final Chapter

The last chapter is where the reader can begin to measure his or her own level of understanding about organization practice for the twenty first century. We provide a model of critical analysis that allows even-handed consideration of the costs and benefits of structuring organizations from the different paradigmatic perspectives.

We also look at the strengths and challenges of organization practice from each paradigm, ending our considerations with a straightforward look at the types of leadership that are most congruent with each perspective. It is our hope that Chapter 13 will serve as a launching platform for future social work leaders to engage in thoughtful and competent organization practice that develops in response to changing contexts and changing needs.

5 Functionalist Theories about Organizations

In Chapter 4, we introduced the functionalist paradigm, and in this chapter we explore the theories and assumptions that fit within this paradigm. We will also investigate what we are calling functionalist organizations. Of the four paradigms, we begin with the functionalist paradigm because most traditional views of organizations are based on assumptions inherent to this worldview.

This chapter expands the description of the functionalist paradigm provided earlier, beginning with basic assumptions and followed by an elaboration of the order and control themes of this perspective on organizations. After this thorough paradigmatic grounding, the major organization and organizational behavioral theories that fit within this perspective are identified. The chapter closes with a critical analysis, so that the reader is left with an ability to judge what is gained and what is given up when approaching organizations from a functionalist worldview. We then transition to Chapter 6, which focuses on understanding practice within functionalist organizations.

We caution the reader that we are referring to the functionalist organization as a prototype, because today there may no longer be "pure" functionalist organizations. Even agencies that are definitely functionalist in nature may have units, programs, and/or staff members that operate under different assumptions. When this happens, organizational members and units will encounter paradoxes as differing assumptions clash. Once you read further into the book, it is our hope that you will understand why functionalist assumptions may collide with assumptions from other paradigms. But, first, let's focus on the themes and assumptions of the functionalist paradigm.

Functionalist Themes

Most traditional approaches to understanding organizations are based on assumptions held by the functionalist paradigm, and most of the theories that were developed during the early stages of organizational research are positivist and, therefore, functionalist in nature. These theories are based on the presumption that research and analysis of organizational data are exclusively rational and that research methods should be traditionally scientific. Therefore, organizational

Radical Humanist	Radical Structuralist
Interpretive	Functionalist

study should be oriented to carefully defined designs, including variables, sample, data collection, and data analysis. Further, there is an assumption that good organizational study is impersonal with the goal of prediction and control of persons and things within the organizational setting. Research is capable of producing generalized principles to guide the replicability of events and procedures in the organizational context. Once there is sufficient evidence, then it is possible to know enough about the organization to control both the process and the product of the organization. With sufficient information, order can be structured and activities within the organization can be regulated in a predictable manner.

The functionalist paradigm holds a traditional view of knowledge building about organizations that has its genesis in the natural sciences, where controlled experiments are the preferred method of knowing and understanding. This expectation and the assumptions upon which it is built present challenges for research and practice in ever changing, complex organizations where all the variables may not be known and order is not part of the organizing experience. To more fully understand these challenges it is helpful to look a bit more closely at the basic terms and assumptions that define the paradigm.

Assumptions of the Functionalist Paradigm

The functionalist paradigm is objectivist in its perspective. Recall that Chapter 4 presented four terms that define *objectivism*. Figure 5.1 provides a brief review of those terms.

The functionalist view assumes there is reality apart from the individual and his or her perceptions and that there are universal truths. The functionalist ontology is realist, assuming that what is known is independent of the human mind and that understanding anything is abstracted from an independent reality that exists "out there." Given this view, the accepted functionalist **epistemology,** or what can be known and how scientists can be expected to know it, is positivist. This means

FIGURE 5.1 Objectivism: Defining Terms

Realism (external)

Positivism (hard, real, tangible)

Determinism (people are products of their environments)

Nomothetic (use methods of natural science to test hypotheses in accord with scientific rigor)

Source: Adapted from G. Burrell and G. Morgan, *Sociological Paradigms and Organisational Analysis* (Aldershot, England: Ashgate, 1979), Figure 1.1, p. 3. Used by permission.

that theoretical propositions must be tested or built according to the rules of formal logic and based on methods derived from the natural sciences to create scientific (trusted) knowledge. Positivism seeks hard, real, and tangible knowledge. Knowledge can be acquired in this way because it is assumed that reality is deterministic, comprised of antecedents and consequences, making everything totally determined by a sequence of causes that can be identified or uncovered. This identification or discovery is the role of scientific research, including research about organizations.

Since the functionalist paradigm takes an objectivist position regarding human nature, humankind is viewed as rational, able to use reason to support a position. It is also thought that human experience is just as deterministic as reality, based on identifiable causes and consequences, which require only identification or discovery to be understood and managed. Human nature, like reality in general, is based on lawlike generalizations that describe everything about the human experience exactly the same way for all time. There is "truth," which means that the functionalist paradigm takes a nomothetic position that describes reality and human nature based on what is generally the case. This is a rule-governed reality.

Recall that the functionalist paradigm sits within the intersection of objectivism and regulation. Regulation, combined with a belief in universal truths, assumes that generalization is possible and desirable. This is why, according to Burrell and Morgan (1979), the functionalist perspective holds interest in maintaining the status quo and achieving social order. In this perspective, it is believed that consensus, social integration, solidarity, needs satisfaction, and actuality are possible. Figure 5.2 summarizes the concerns of this regulation perspective.

Now we turn to how the functionalist perspective guides organizational theory. But before we do, look at Figure 5.3, which was originally introduced in Chapter 4. This figure provides a quick summary of the basic assumptions of the functionalist paradigm. Keep these assumptions in mind, and return to this figure as often as you need, to see how many of the theories used by social workers and others in organizations fit within this paradigm. You may find that you recognize some, possibly all, of these assumptions because the organizations you have experienced may have been shaped by this perspective.

Figure 5.2   Concerns of the Regulation Perspective

Status quo

Social order

Consensus

Social integration and cohesion

Solidarity

Need satisfaction

Actuality

Source: Adapted from G. Burrell and G. Morgan, *Sociological Paradigms and Organisational Analysis* (Aldershot, England: Ashgate, 1979), Table 2.2, p. 18. Used by permission.

FIGURE 5.3   Assumptions of the Functionalist Paradigm

From the Objectivist Perspective
1. Reality is above and beyond individual knowledge.
2. Knowledge about social reality is hard and concrete.
3. People are products of their environments; they are shaped.
4. Natural science methods can be applied to the study and understanding of social reality.

From the Regulation Perspective
5. Society is characterized by social order and equilibrium.
6. Knowledge for knowledge's sake is acceptable.
7. Consensus, rather than conflict, is important.

Source: Adapted from Burrell and Morgan (1979, Chapter 1).

Functionalist Organizational Theories

Since the majority of theories that have been developed to guide our understanding of organizations and to further their study have emerged from the functionalist framework, it is sometimes seen as the *only* scientific approach to understanding organizations and the behavior within them. As you move further into the discussion of alternative perspectives about organizations, you will recognize that there are many other rigorous ways of understanding organizations. But we start with the theories that can be located within the functionalist paradigm because they will probably be the most familiar. They have the longest history of guiding organizational research and have received the most critical analysis. As the chapter develops, you will also discover that these theories present some of the most interesting challenges to organizational leaders in operationalizing a social work frame of reference. We think that the theories here may represent the most barriers to the challenges of future organizational practice within a multicultural society.

In Chapter 2, we focused on the search for order in understanding organizations. Shafritz and Ott identified nine major perspectives on organization theory. Most of the earlier perspectives developed based on functionalist assumptions. In this chapter, we focus on five of the major perspectives identified by Shafritz and Ott (2001):

1. Classical organization theory
2. Neoclassical organization theory
3. Human resource theory or the organizational behavior perspective
4. "Modern" structural organization theory
5. Systems theory and organizational economics

Each perspective is briefly discussed, along with some of the major contributors so as to fully develop the functionalist view of organizations and what constitutes acceptable behavior of organizational participants.

Classical Organizational Theory

Organizational theory really began during the industrial revolution in Great Britain and the United States. Theories were developed to manage complex economic organizations. These early theories have been grouped into what has been termed *classical* theories because they were the first, with their influence beginning in the late 1700s and continuing until the 1930s and even beyond. In Chapter 2, we introduced the four fundamental assumptions of this collection of theories. Table 5.1 reiterates these assumptions and ties them to the functionalist perspective.

It is within the context of classical theory that workers were understood not as individuals but as parts of a factory system, much like machine parts. The goal of classical theory was to guide understanding so that employers could take advantage of people, money, and machines for productivity. The goal was to locate the "best way" to organize for production.

Adam Smith (1776) is credited with creating the first method to structure organizations and the people within them so that people would be more machine-like in their work. He proposed that the best way of operating a factory was to centralize equipment and labor, have a division of labor, manage through specialization, and give attention to the economics of the competitive marketplace.

After this strong attention to structure, theorists focused on managing that structure and the people within it through the development of the science of administration. Henri Fayol (1916) was the first theorist to create a comprehensive theory of management, but because he was French and outside of the British/American mainstream, his real influence was not felt until his work was translated into English in the late 1940s. Fayol identified the important elements necessary to orga-

TABLE 5.1   **Classical Organizational Theories and the Functionalist Perspective**

Assumptions of Classical Organization Theories	Assumptions of the Functionalist Perspective
Organizations exist to accomplish production-related and economic goals.	Society is characterized by social order and equilibrium. (Regulation)
	Knowledge for knowledge's sake is acceptable. (Regulation)
There is one best way to organize for production, and that way can be found through systematic, scientific inquiry.	Knowledge about social reality is hard and concrete. (Objectivist)
	Natural science methods can be applied to the study and understanding of social reality. (Objectivist)
Production is maximized through specialization and division of labor.	Consensus, rather than conflict, is important. (Objectivist)
People and organizations act in accordance with rational economic principles.	People are products of their environments; they are shaped. (Objectivist)
	Reality is above and beyond individual knowledge. (Objectivist)

Sources: Adapted from Shafritz and Ott (2001, p. 28) and Burrell and Morgan (1979).

nize and manage an organization. His six principles—technical, commercial, financial, security, accounting, and managerial—still have currency today. His areas of
interest continue to present modern challenges: division of work, authority and
responsibility, discipline, unity of command, unity of direction, subordination of
individual interest to the general interest, payment of personnel, centralization,
chain of command, order, equity, stability of personnel, tenure, initiative, and
esprit de corps.

Probably the most famous and influential classical theorist was Frederick
Taylor (1916), who, with his principles of scientific management, proposed that
organizations could be more productive if designed scientifically. He believed this
design could be achieved through time and motion studies that would uncover the
fastest, most efficient, least fatiguing way of doing the business of the organization.
He assumed this would allow management to impose this best way on workers,
thus creating the best way of social organizing. From his early work came many
derivations by his followers who looked for ways of planning and systematically
controlling the work environment through scientific principles. One of the most
notable followers was H. L. Gantt (1861–1919), who developed the Gantt chart for
planning output so that ammunition could be tracked during World War I. **Gantt
charts** are bar graphs illustrating who is expected to do what task at what time. The

charts were used for other purposes than ammunition tracking following the war. Prior to computerization, Gantt charts were important guides to monitor progress in early social service agencies.

Other noteworthy contributors to classical theory were Max Weber and Luther Gulick. Weber (1922) characterized the core features of bureaucratic organization and the pattern of behavior that followed. Basically, his description of the ideal type of bureaucracy had the following dimensions:

1. Positions in the organization are grouped into a clearly defined hierarchy.
2. Job candidates are selected on the basis of their technical qualifications.
3. Each position has a defined sphere of competence.
4. Positions reflect a high degree of specialization based on expert training.
5. Positions demand the full working capacity of their holders.
6. Positions are career-oriented. There is a system of promotion according to seniority or achievement. Promotion is dependent on the judgment of superiors.
7. Rules of procedure are outlined for rational coordination of activities.
8. A central system of records is maintained to summarize the activities of the organization
9. Impersonality governs relationships between organizational members.
10. Distinctions are drawn between private and public lives and positions of organizational members. (Weber, 1947b; Rogers, 1975, as cited in Netting, Kettner, & McMurtry 1998, pp. 196–197)

Gulick (1937), influenced by Fayol, identified the major functions of management within a hierarchical, bureaucratic organization. Gulick's contribution includes his mnemonic, POSDCORB, for the seven functions of management—planning, organizing, staffing, directing, coordinating, reporting, and budgeting. Weber and Gulick's contributions, like Taylor's, are still present in the thinking of today's functionalist theorists.

From a current standpoint, all this work may look narrow and simplistic. An historical lens helps to identify the degree to which it was really ground-breaking thinking that was steeped in the assumptions of what is now called the functionalist paradigm. Classical theorists were seeking the best way to structure and manage organizations so that they would be consensus-based, rational collectivities that performed in the most efficient manner possible. But the challenge was so great that these early classical contributions led to the second major perspective identified by Shafritz and Ott (2001): neoclassical organization theory.

Neoclassical Organizational Theory

Most theoreticians who fit within the neoclassical tradition are placed there because they were critics and revisionists of classical theory. Their work occurred post–World War II. Although most thinkers of the time continued the interest in organizing for productivity, their criticism of earlier theoretical work was based on some or all of the following: rejection of the minimization of the humanness of organizational members, necessity of coordination of needs among bureaucratic units, the existence of internal-external organizational relations, and the need to under-stand organizational decision making (Shafritz & Ott, 2001). As statistical technol-ogy evolved, criticism also included the lack of empirical grounding for most of the classical thought. The neoclassicists created less a new approach than a modifica-tion of what had come before. Their developments were based on methods drawn from the behavioral sciences. Neoclassical theory presents a transition in the theo-retical movement from the overly simplistic, mechanistic perspectives of the classi-cal theorists to more contemporary thinking about complex organizations.

Two of the earliest critics of the classical approach were Chester Barnard and Herbert Simon. Barnard (1938) spoke of the necessity of cooperation among people within organizational settings for goal achievement. Further, he thought it was the executive's responsibility to establish the context for this cooperation by establish-ing a purpose and moral code of the organization and by instituting a system of formal and informal communication. These efforts were to ensure participants' willingness to cooperate because within these structures should be found induce-ments and other means of persuasion to achieve cooperation.

Herbert Simon (1946) rejected the theories of Fayol, Gulick, and others, calling their perspective "proverbs of administration" rather than principles of adminis-tration. He strongly reacted to those approaches dominated by excessive formalism and rationalism that he believed limited both organizations and individuals from making choices. He proposed that definition and accurate measurement of the objectives of administrative organization would move administrative practices from art to science. This could happen with sufficient scientific rigor to control for alternative explanations or effects of the studies. Simon (1947) focused on the importance of organizational decision making, introducing the concepts of "bounded rationality" and "satisficing decisions" to characterize the complexity of decision making within the context of formal organizations. **Bounded rationality** means that individuals, no matter how much information they collect, always make decisions within limits. Simon recognized that decision makers would never know everything there was to know about any situation, and so when a decision had to be made, they had to recognize the boundaries of their knowledge base. Decisions made without all possible information necessary for a fully considered decision is called **satisficing decision making.** Decisions are made within these boundaries because human beings do not have the intellectual capability to totally maximize possibilities; therefore, a perfect decision is not possible—only a satisfac-tory one. Though this moved organizational studies closer to the experience of organizational members, what was missing in Simon's theorizing was "politics, culture, morality, and history ... [which were] treated as random, extraneous vari-ables beyond the influence, much less control, of rational cognitive processes and organizational procedures. [They became] analytically marginalized, left outside the conceptual parameters of Simon's preferred model" (Reed, 1996, p. 36).

Neoclassicists can be credited with beginning the theoretical movement from interest in purely engineering elements in the organization to contextual elements of the organization's environment. With this change of interest came the involve-ment of another discipline in the study of organizations and organizational behaviors. Sociologists helped to establish that organizations are not isolated from the environments in which they are located. Talcott Parsons (1956) introduced the general theory of social systems as a way to analyze formal organizations. At the same time, other sociologists were interested in understanding the perspectives and behavior of those within organizations. Phillip Selznick (1948) found that persons within the organization were not purely rational, and without a recognition of this, managers were unable to cope with the nonrational. His well-cited case study on the Tennessee Valley Authority revealed that many people within that organization did not necessarily share the organization's goals. Without shared goals among workers, managers had to resort to what Selznick called *cooptation* as a means of controlling alternative perspectives and assuring conformity to the organization and its mission. Other sociologists, such as Melville Dalton (1950) and W. F. Whyte, also contributed to the neoclassical perspective. Dalton recognized the structural friction between line staff and organizational units, while Whyte looked at the consequences of stress and status on human relations within the organization.

In sum, all these students of organizations and organizational behavior collectively served as a transitional or evolutionary step between formal classical theory and its mechanistic dominance, to a recognition of the challenges of a more complex understanding of what is necessary to achieve more satisfactory management of behavior in modern organizations. Even the critics of rational approaches were often searching for the one best way, looking for new sources of power and authority, rather than stepping into a different set of assumptions representing an alternative worldview. Some critics began clamoring to understand how the sense of community among members could be recognized as an important element in organizational theory (Reed, 1996, p. 36). To examine the human side of organizations, we now turn to the third perspective identified by Shafritz and Ott (2001): human relations/organizational behaviorial theory.

Human Relations/Organizational Behavioral Theory

All the early theories of organizations were really attempts at dealing with organizational behavior by structuring organizations in ways that would control and standardize human behavior. After all, from a functionalist perspective, if one really believes that there is one best way to do business, then controlling human beings so that they do their work in that best way becomes the goal. Most early theories were used to guide the actions of the people in the organization. It was not until the development of the various aspects of human relations or organizational behavioral theory that this focus was finely tuned. It was at this stage that classical organizational theory was actually displaced, making room for the more creative approaches to understanding organizations. At this juncture, theorists realized that organizations were much more than variables to manipulate in order to change behavior of organizational members. Instead, organizations were understood as contexts within which behavior occurs. The people and the organization represent mutual, interactive influences through which people are shaped by the organization and the organization is shaped by the people within its boundaries.

The early studies of people in organizations gave rise to a new discipline, industrial or applied psychology, in which psychological findings from laboratory experiments were applied to organizational matters. The technology came from the emerging behaviorists and behavioral sciences that developed during and after World War II in response to the military need to find appropriate recruits and train them to meet military needs. Behaviorism provided the means to influence employees, their attitudes, and psychological conditions in order to impact productivity. Hugo Münsterberg (1922) helped to move organizational studies beyond behaviorism to the recognition that employees were humans, not machines, who needed to be treated as individuals in order to enhance employee productivity.

Recall that earlier we mentioned Elton Mayo (1933) and his famous study of the Hawthorne electric plant where results were achieved simply because the research was undertaken. Mayo's study represented a major breakthrough in understanding organizationally based social psychology, group relations, group norms, and issues of control and personal recognition. Researchers began to focus on humans as individuals, respecting their need for accurate information in order to make informed decisions based on free will within the organizational setting (Argyris, 1970).

More than 50 years of organizational behavioral research have focused on people's perspectives on jobs, organizational communication, work groups, one's own work, roles within the organization, and leadership. Few women can be identified as organizational researchers, but Mary Parker Follett's (1926) early work on communication and leadership style was the forerunner for much of the work on motivation. She focused on the manner in which orders were given, seeing orders as mutually agreed upon between leaders and followers in light of unique situations that could not always be anticipated.

Perhaps the most influential thinker regarding motivation is Abraham Maslow who, along with Mayo, set the stage for the clarifying ideas found in Theory X and Theory Y developed by Douglas McGregor. Maslow (1943), as a behaviorist, posited that all humans have needs and these are at the base of their motivational structure. Needs were viewed as hierarchical and once a need was met it no longer served as a motivator, so that when lower-order needs were met, higher-order needs became motivating forces. Herzberg (1966) looked at motivation from a different perspective, investigating intrinsic and extrinsic motivators. He found that extrinsic elements, such as working conditions and pay, kept down dissatisfaction but did not serve as motivators, while workers were intrinsically motivated by the use of their creativity and intelligence. Building on need recognition, McGregor (1957) outlined two different assumption sets held by managers that became self-fulfilling prophecies. **Theory X** captured the perspective of the scientific managers who assumed that it was human nature to hate work and avoid it whenever possible, so coercion, control, discipline, and direction were essential if employees were to be expected to work toward organizational goals. Further, in order to feel secure, employees preferred to be directed, allowing them to avoid taking responsibility for their actions or inactions. **Theory Y** reflected a more evolved perspective, holding that human beings did not necessarily hate work if it was satisfying. It was human nature to take control and personal responsibility when there was personal congruence with organizational goals, so that commitment to organizational objectives was possible.

This attention to motivation, group and intergroup behavior, leadership, power and influence, and the effect of organizational context on individuals were all precursors to some of the later work built from alternative paradigmatic perspectives. In later chapters, it will be clear that the interpretive and radical humanist perspectives, and their attention to meaning in context, owe much to the human relations theorists for what has evolved that is subjective. For now, it is important to recognize that early human relations theorists were decidedly functionalist in their perspective. They recognized the human element in a generalized individualistic way, but for the reason of finding the best way to control and regulate people for productive purposes. As human relations and organizational behavioral theory developed, however, it converged with systems theories that focused more on interdependence and balance. This led to "a belief that rationalism provided an extremely limited and often misleading vision of the 'realities' of organizational life" (Reed, 1996, p. 37). Another major growth spurt in organization theory began developing.

"Modern" Structural Organization Theory

In Chapter 2, we explained why Shafritz and Ott's fourth major perspective is called "modern" structural organization theory. Modern structuralists are theorists who wrote after World War II at the same time that there was a proliferation of human relations writings that influenced their work. Classical organizational theorists were interested in the design structure of organizations and its relationship to production processes, so from that standpoint some of the classical theorists were also structural organizational theorists. Like Fayol, Taylor, Gulick, Weber and others who came before them, modern structural theorists were interested in organizational efficiency based on rationality and the role of rationality in increasing productivity. Their interest in structure was also influenced by neoclassical, human relations, and systems theory developments.

Bolman and Deal (1991) identify the basic assumptions of the structural theoretical perspective:

1. Organizations are rational efforts to accomplish established goals facilitated through rational organizational behavior based on clear rules and authority for control and coordination.
2. There is a "best" structure for every organization based on internal and external conditions.
3. Specialization and division of labor facilitate the achievement of production quality and quantity.
4. Most organizational problems are caused by structural flaws and can be eliminated with a change in structure.

These assumptions fall squarely within the functionalist paradigm, which focuses on finding the best way (the right rules, authority structure, etc.) to solve problems by adapting structure (an objectivist approach). Structural theorists take an interest in what goes on horizontally and vertically in organizations. Vertical (hierarchical levels) and horizontal (between units or departments) differentiation and coordination are the focus of their thinking and organizational research.

Interest in specialization, departmentalization, span of control, and coordination and control of specialized units all reflect historical antecedents in organizational and organizational behavioral research. Newer influences can be seen in the interest in the difference between stable and more dynamic conditions within the organization as well as organizational climate, management systems, and the formal and informal elements of organizational life. Researchers were beginning to realize that normal organizational conditions may not be stable, so the study of organizations' relationship to structure took on new dimensions.

Burns and Stalker (1961) represent how structuralist thinking developed, allowing for the "one best way" or design of an organization to be dependent on certain conditions rather than assuming that organizations are all alike. Their pivotal work at the Tavistock Institute in London resulted in a widely cited book called *The Management of Innovation* in which they identified two types of organizations— mechanistic and organic. The **mechanistic organization** was highly traditional in terms of hierarchy, formal rules and regulations, communication, and decision making. This type of organization was particularly useful in producing inanimate products such as those found in factories. The **organic organization**, on the other hand, was one that functioned in a highly changeable environment requiring staff who could make decisions quickly to adapt to this change, such as in a marketing or service organization. People working in mechanistic organizations were viewed as more secure, whereas those in organic organizations faced more uncertainty. The acknowledgment that different environments called for different structures was ground breaking. It meant that organization structures would need to differ, depending on where that organization fell along the mechanistic to organic continuum.

Following the lead of Burns and Stalker, a number of theorists posed questions about structural differences in organizations. Blau and Scott (1962) asserted that the true structure of an organization could only be understood with a concomitant understanding of the informal values and norms of the organization. Walker and Lorsch (1968) wondered if organizations should be structured according to product or function. Thompson (1967) attempted to capture the essence of complex organizational management of uncertainty by identifying various ways in which units could be coupled (related), further demonstrating the administrative challenges presented by the degree of interdependence among organizational members. In *The Structuring of Organizations*, Mintzberg (1979) masterfully captured, categorized, and synthesized all the theoretical developments to date. His important contribution was to integrate both organization and management theory into a structural representation of the five basic parts of organizations that include: (1) the operating core, (2) the middle line, and (3) the strategic apex supported by the (4) techno structure, and (5) support staff.

The tumultuous nature of the 1960s had its impact on organizations and the research about them. Many theorists from the sixties (through the eighties), whose thinking remained part of the functionalist paradigm, either noted or called for changes in traditional organizational hierarchies. These changes were needed to respond to changes in society, to be able to respond appropriately to rapidly changing environments. Writers such as Bennis (1966), Toffler (1970), Bennis and Slater (1968), and Thayer (1981) in various ways and for various reasons have called for alternative, if not flatter, structures to meet modern challenges. Peter Drucker (1954), best known for his work on developing decision structures such as management by objectives (MBO), in his later work (1988) called for flatter, more information-based organizations. Remaining true to the structuralist traditions, however, one can also find thinkers such as Elliott Jacques (1990) who in "In Praise of Hierarchy" saw bureaucracies as enduring because he believed they are the best way to assure efficiency, while also assuring equity and representativeness in complex structures.

At this stage in theoretical development, as different organizational theories evolved, separating theorists into perspectives or schools of thought became more difficult. Theorists from various perspectives began to incorporate ideas and concepts from others who were writing about organizations, thus blurring the distinctive niches into which their theories might have been categorized. By the time systems theorists were emerging, the modern structuralists and the human relations theorists were influencing systems theory work and vice versa. Where a theorist fits in any classification scheme really depended on which elements were being emphasized at the time of the classification. We think the cross-fertilization of various organizational theories brings excitement and stimulation to the field and reemphasizes the complexity of organizational thought, but trying to keep theories conceptually clean for analysis and categorization becomes quite challenging as the more mutual theoretical influences became the norm. Keeping this complexity in mind, we now turn to systems theory, and remind the reader that there are several branches of systems theory to explore.

Systems Theory

Since Ludwig von Bertalanffy (1951) elaborated general systems theory, organizational researchers have attended to the context in which the organization operates. Based on Bertalanffy and with the aid of emerging quantitative tools, organizational researchers sought to understand the complex relations among organizational and environmental variables. Organizational decision processes and information and control systems were a major focus of analysis. Owing much to Simon's (1957) concepts of bounded rationality and satisficing decisions, cause and effect for optimal solutions were topics of continuing interest.

Weiner (1948), in his classic *Cybernetics*, saw organizations as adaptive, self-regulating systems. Katz and Kahn (1966) saw organizations as open systems and sought to describe and understand the interdependence and interactions between the organization and the environment. Thompson (1967) extended the system notion by envisioning organizations as rational systems with a contingency perspective. He sought to understand and predict effectiveness of organizational action. He believed that optimal decisions are situational because everything is dependent on the relationship between the decision in question and all other elements in the system. The best decision depended on the context of decision making.

The functionalist systems researchers based their work on the assumption that organizations were not static, but multidimensional, complex, always changing entities built on the interaction among the organization and its environment. It is important to note that these researchers recognized that organizations were both social systems and management systems (Shafritz & Ott, 2001). Most researchers looked at inputs, processes, outputs, feedback loops, and the environment to understand and predict continuous internal and external interactions.

Systems theory is not easily located in only one of the paradigmatic perspectives used in this book. Recall that in Chapter 2 we indicated that systems theorists "differ on the kind of system social systems are" (Martin & O'Connor, 1989, p. 54) and that social scientists have used five analogies to depict social systems: mechanical, organismic, morphogenic, factional, and catastrophic (Burrell & Morgan, 1979). Depending on the analogy used, systems theory will be placed in different paradigms. Table 5.2 summarizes the two analogies that are based on functionalist assumptions. We will see the other analogies later when we investigate other paradigmatic perspectives.

The mechanical analogy views social systems as if they were physical machines, derived from physics (Martin & O'Connor, 1989). This is a closed-systems approach that focuses on internal integration. This is how the early structuralists viewed an organization. One can almost hear the early theorists searching for the one best way to make people in organizations work as interchangeable parts and to locate the right structure that will maintain system equilibrium. This approach to systems is definitely in the functionalist paradigm and has been highly criticized for ignoring complexity and the interdependence of organizations and their environments.

The organismic analysis comes from biology and was a reaction to the machine analogy, much like the human relations and modern structuralists reacted to the classical and neoclassical theorists. In this analogy, society is viewed as a biological organism with interrelated parts that are functionally unified. Emerging in the 1940s and 1950s, the organismic analogy developed with advances in biology. Talcott Parsons is credited with having advanced this development in his structural/functionalist approach to systems which dominated theoretical circles between the 1950s and 1960s. "Structural functionalism and its progency, systems theory, provided an 'internalist' focus on organizational design with an 'externalist' concern with environmental uncertainty" (Reed, 1996, p. 37). According to Parsons, social systems had to perform four functions in order to survive: adaptation, goal attainment, integration, and pattern maintenance. In performing these functions, the goal was to seek **homeostasis**, a state of balance in which every part is working together and is integrating with the whole. Focusing attention on the status quo and attempting only incremental change, the organismic systems theory leads to a search for order and consensus. Thus, the organismic analogy also rests

TABLE 5.2 Functionalist Analogies Used by Social Scientists to Depict
Social Systems

Analogy	Description and Principal Tendency
Mechanical	Assumes perfect coordination and integration of parts;
	Assumes that departures from equilibrium result in correct action to return to equilibrium;
	Assumes social systems are like machines;
	Emphasizes order and stability over conflict and change.
Organismic	Assumes high coordination and integration of parts;
	Assumes that departures from homeostasis result in corrective actions to return to homeostasis;
	Assumes society is like a living organism with different organs that cooperate closely to contribute to the survival of the whole;
	Assumes social systems are cohesive because of consensus of citizens, families, communities, etc.;
	Emphasizes order and stability over conflict and change.

Source: From Patricia Yancy Martin and Gerald G. O'Connor, *The Social Work Environment: Open Systems Applications.* Copyright © 1989 by Allyn & Bacon. Reprinted by permission. Adapted from G. Burrell and and G. Morgan, *Sociological Paradigms and Organisational Analysis* (Aldershot, England: Ashgate, 1979), Figure 4.1, p. 67. Used by permission.

on the assumptions of the functionalist paradigm. Martin and O'Connor (1989, p. 54) think that it is unfortunate that open-systems theory "has been used often with an organismic analogy and, as a result, is believed to have limitations that it does not have." This is why you will often hear how conservative or change adverse systems theory is. Persons making this evaluation are referring to the organismic type of systems theory that focuses on maintaining the status quo at all costs. Traditional organizations have often been accused of behaving in this way, of not taking risks, and of focusing on organizational maintenance over client service.

Both mechanical and organismic systems theory are functionalist in perspective. There is an assumption of a reality external to the individual, and knowledge about that reality can be studied with social science methods that allow for generalizability. These approaches to systems theory, combined with structural functionalism, actually were seen to have the potential to depoliticize the decision-making process within organizations. A generation of managers and system designers educated in these brands of systems theory learned to resist conflict, seek consensus, and "aspire to overall control within an increasingly differentiated and complex society" (Reed, 1996, p. 38).

We will return to study the morphogenic, factional, and catastrophic types of open-systems theory in subsequent chapters. At this point, it is important for the reader to realize that just because someone says he or she uses systems theory does not tell the full story. One has to know which type of systems theory is being used and what assumptions are being held. The mechanical and organismic analogies are functionalist in their orientation. But some types of systems theory are radical enough to move toward social change. So many different types of systems theory exist that one can easily become confused.

As we write this part of the chapter, we are smiling because this is where we began our careers. We were taught open systems of the organismic type, when it was believed that order (regulation) was possible if only one could find the right combination of variables and then design the organization accordingly. There was hope that with systems theory one's eyes would open to the orderly pattern of the universe, that social scientists could predict exactly what would happen because they would know how to design the organizations that would work because they would fit within this ordered structure. Soon, however, the limitations of the organismic approach to systems would be clear and the search would continue for theories to deal with the increasing complexity of organizational life.

Shafritz and Ott (2001) categorize contingency, population ecology, and organizational economics with systems theory because these theories are logical extensions of systems theory. Contingency theory is closely related to systems theory because the focus is on actions that are assumed to be dependent on relationships among variables in a particular time frame. Here, everything is situational; therefore, contingency theory has some relativism that makes it akin to systems analogies that fall within other paradigms to be discussed later.

Organizational ecology theorists look at populations or sets of organizations. Organizational economics originated when Ronald H. Coase wrote *The Nature of the Firm* (1937). Observing that price theory alone could not account for organizational behavior, Coase borrowed from the rational framework in assuming that behavior is driven by economics. Economic theories of organization emerged in response to the limitations of classical and neoclassical theories, in order to focus serious attention on resource allocation as a primary influence on behavior. Absent in these theories is an interest in power and conflict (Reed, 1996). They seek ways to maintain consensus and to identify and respond to objective, universal principles, and therefore the theories fit within the functionalist paradigm.

Thus far, we have examined five of the major perspectives on organization theory—classical, neoclassical, human relations and organizational behavior, "modern" structural, and systems theories. As these perspectives have evolved and interacted, it has become increasingly difficult to place entire schools of thought into one paradigm. For example, systems theories, depending on the analogies used to elucidate theoretical assumptions, are based on different paradigmatic assumptions. All dimensions of systems theory are not captured in the functionalist worldview. Figure 5.4 provides a visual location of the theories discussed in this chapter and their placement within the functionalist paradigm. The theory's placement is a commentary on its location on the Burrell and Morgan (1978) objectivist/subjectivist and regulation/change continua.

As we examine each paradigm in subsequent chapters, we will add theories to this figure that fall within the other paradigms. The functionalist paradigm has

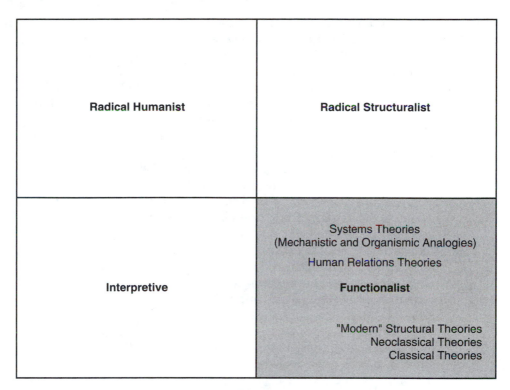

Figure 5.4   Organizational Theories within the Functionalist Paradigm

been the dominant paradigm from the time modern organizations developed. Because of this, theories that fall within other paradigms will be viewed as "alternative," at least by those persons who hold functionalist views. For now, we hope that you have a beginning understanding of what it means when we say that the functionalist paradigm is considered the traditional perspective from which the vast majority of organizational theories have emerged. We hope that you have been able to develop a greater understanding of this paradigmatic perspective because of the organizational theories that fit within it. With this knowledge, you will be much better able to make considered assessments of the usefulness of the theories for your own practice within human service settings.

Costs and Benefits of the Functionalist Paradigm and Its Theories

Not everyone sees bureaucracy and hierarchy as necessary and welcome. Even persons who value them recognize that the level of order and control necessary to maintain the hierarchical standard comes with a price. We now turn to an analysis of the costs and benefits of the functionalist paradigmatic perspective on organizations.

Overall, the functionalist perspective is open to criticism on several grounds that are relevant to understanding organizations. This perspective rests heavily on the ability to operationalize what is of interest for study. This means that what is to be studied must be defined and be made measurable. Such a task is particularly difficult when many aspects of organizational life cannot be "known" at this level, but rather on the tacit or intuitive level. The communication style of the manager may not be totally definable by current standards of measurability, but his or her employees "know" when the manager "means business" even if there is no tool to assess this. Articulating what the employees "know" is next to impossible, but they all can act on that knowledge by attending to business when it is really necessary. Replicating this information for a newcomer is not possible.

The focus of functionalist research is on cause and effect due to the functionalist goal of achieving truth through generalizability. In functionalism, there is no acceptance of the need to understand meaning and its implications. The intent is to reduce uncertainty and difference, working toward consensus. In addition, the attention to determinism and reductionism seems misplaced in an organizational world that has become so complex. This means that making prediction in an individual organization is all but impossible. Finally, in the fast-moving context of the early twenty-first century, the functionalist perspective is not able to deal with the emergent issues of the day. It becomes more and more clear that functionalism rests on a set of assumptions that are increasingly difficult to maintain. Especially when we look at current postpositivist efforts, there are violations of basic paradigmatic assumptions everywhere in order for research to be relevant to the current context of organizational life. Experimental designs are all but nonexistent in organizations; objectivity is not maintained due to lack of randomness in sampling. These are just two small examples of how functionalist assumptions must be violated in today's fast-paced organizations.

Even with these limits and challenges, the theories developed within the assumptions of this paradigm do have strengths. For example, bureaucracy maximizes efficiency. Bureaucractic approaches particularly facilitate the management of greater numbers of tasks in large, complex organizations, allowing for increased productivity. Following the bureaucratic tenets of having only those with the skills do the required job assures quality. This structure continues to be quite acceptable for manufacturing environments, but the vast, impersonal setting of a bureaucracy allows little attention to unique needs of either employees or those being served. Top-down dictates of a hierarchical approach means participants and clients have few rights.

Merton (1952) identified the bureaucratic personality that is derived from this context. The risk of this personality is that the individual becomes more interested in rote rules and procedures than in doing the job as intended. This is a direct result of the technological way employees are understood, as if they are cogs in a wheel. Differentiation and attention to subtleties cannot be addressed either by the theories used to guide practice or by the personality types well suited to the perspective. This results in the potential for exploitation of workers because the bias is toward productivity. This biasing effect may even be more complex. Kelly (1991) asserts that the lack of ability to account for subtleties in goals, decision making, technology, and individual needs creates a male bias in communication and decision-making preferences that has particularly negative effects on women and minorities.

Built on functionalist assumptions, scientific management pays great attention to precision, measurement, and specialization to the detriment of process and meaning. It may be very useful to categorize efforts and to formalize programs, but this does little to promote understanding the human side of service efforts. How do employees feel about the demands of their job descriptions? How do clients relate to the efforts and services rendered? Remember that Taylor's time and motion studies were based on men shoveling pig iron, not workers processing human beings. The potential disconnect should be obvious.

The human relations influence served both to under- and overestimate the importance of social factors in the organization. This theoretical perspective provided a humanizing counterbalance to the formalization of the earlier efforts. Needs and interests of the individual became part of the organizational equation, but with no intention of empowering workers. The attention focused on workers was for the purpose of gaining greater productivity. These efforts did not escape the potential consequence of serving to dehumanize, oppress, and exploit workers because all power and decision making remained at the top of the hierarchy. Attention to personal and social relationships, including networking, continued to disadvantage women and minorities due to their lack of access to powerful networks. Though the human relations school failed to prove a happier worker was more productive, and though it is now recognized that the relationship between worker needs and productivity is much more complex, this major perspective did contribute to the understanding of organizations by showing the importance of teamwork, cooperation, leadership, and positive attention of management.

Systems theory cemented the recognition of the environment as a critical variable in organizations. This recognition is particularly important for human service organizations. Systems attention to organizational survival also opened doors to new understanding of some of the forces behind organizational behavior. Given the variety of analogies on which systems theories are based, the broad flexibility among these approaches may cause confusion to the student of organization. To assure usefulness of a systems perspective for organization practice, the intentions and standpoint of the particular approach must be clear. Only with this clarity can the student or worker know what paradigmatic standards to apply when considering the usefulness of the theory for his or her environment.

Conclusion

Functionalist organizations have a wealth of theories to guide their actions with a long history of dominance in organization practice. It is important to recognize the strengths of the theories and how deeply their cultural assumptions are embedded in their structures.

Classical organization theories showed the benefits of production-related and economic goals and how organizing for productivity through systematic inquiry maximizes production. Neoclassical theories added to the understanding of the complexity of maintaining necessary discipline while organizing for the best productivity. Human relations theories introduced the human needs side of organizing by recognizing necessary elements of viable work contexts in which organizational behavior occurs. Motivation entered the equation for productive purposes. The modern structural organization theory reignited a new interest in organizational efficiency based on rationality, but with a much greater attention to human need. We have examined some aspects of the limits and challenges of these theories and the paradigm within which they are lodged. Functionalist approaches are not sufficient enough to aid in understanding work within the complicated organizations of today and tomorrow. Something more is necessary. But in order for you to understand the degree to which additional perspectives are necessary and useful, more information about the limits of functionalism is needed.

In order to accomplish this, next we turn to mechanisms for understanding the practical aspects of life within the functionalist organization. Having examined the rich and lengthy theoretical background that forms a backdrop for functionalist organizations, let us now investigate the implications for practice in organizations shaped by a functionalist worldview.

CHAPTER

6

Understanding for Practice in Functionalist Organizations

The majority of organizations in which social workers practice have been heavily influenced by functionalist approaches. Yet, it is important to point out that many functionalist organizations are now using language that implies assumptions that are not functionalist at all. For example, the word *empowerment*, drawn from the more radical and critical perspectives in the 1990s, implies that employees will have more freedom to self-actualize on the job. Unfortunately, this language is present when employees in many organizations live in constant fear of being downsized. It is hardly fertile ground for feeling empowered in one's work. Another example is the widespread use of the more subjectively focused term, *client centered*, when many of the outcomes measured in human service programs are predetermined by professionals with minimal client input and without attention to intervening variables beyond the control of the client or the worker. In some organizations, the only thing that makes the measure and the service "client centered" is that they are directed toward clients with the arrogance of professionals who think they know what is best for clients.

It is no wonder, then, that people are confused when they hear language that pertains to a less deterministic perspective spoken in organizations that are steeped in determinism. The language signals changes in perspectives that are rarely born out in the organizational structure or standards of organization practice. Practicing in a functionalist organization in this new century will be fraught with contradictions because the language used may not always reflect the underlying values of these organizations. Instead, they are a reflection of changes in attitudes and assumptions that have not quite permeated traditional assumptions in order to fundamentally change the expectations and the practices in functionalist organizations.

For the foreseeable future, we see functionalist organizations as zones of paradox for social work practitioners. We give the readers permission to heave a sigh of relief in knowing that they can expect to encounter paradox in organization practice, rather than beating themselves up because they can't seem to figure out why words and actions contradict one another. Hopefully, as a result of working with the material in this book, you will be better prepared to understand expectations and perhaps change those and the practice that follows.

We are confident that anyone reading this book will have encountered functionalist organizations because they are a dominant form within the human service planning and delivery system in U.S. society. Even if you have not worked in a human service agency, you will have interacted with persons in functionalist organizations. In this chapter, we focus on what is necessary to understand the practice in functionalist organizations. In similar chapters for each of the remaining paradigms, we will use five questions to guide readers so that they will be able to compare and contrast organizations based on different sets of assumptions. These questions are (1) What are the characteristics of organizations most likely to operate from the assumptions of this paradigm? (2) How does one begin to assess this type of organization? (3) What language is used in these organizations? (4) What approaches to practice are most likely to fit within this type organization? and (5) What are the implications of paradigmatic assumptions for social work leaders in this type organization?

Characteristics of Functionalist Organizations

In Chapter 1 differences between traditional and alternative agencies were presented and compared. Functionalist organizations are traditional and can be distinguished from organizations in the other three paradigms that are considered alternative. One might ask, "Alternative to what?" Essentially, the functionalist paradigm has dominated organizational thought for so long that alternative agencies are literally "alternative" to functionalist organizations. Public, private nonprofit, and private for-profit agencies can be either traditional or alternative in their approaches. Since functionalist organizations are traditional in their approach, in Table 6.1 we return to the characteristics of traditional agencies first introduced in

TABLE 6.1   Characteristics of Traditional (Functionalist) Agencies

Characteristics	Traditional Agencies
Clients	Fund, plan, or deliver socially acceptable programs to socially acceptable clients in need
Funding	Have funding that flows from long-established and multiple sources
Leadership	Have designated administrators and supervisors within a defined structure
Service Delivery	Are part of service delivery structures that are established by agency staff and protocols that have been used over the years
Size	Are typically medium to large in size, given available resources
Staff	Offer staff salaries commensurate with local pay scales
Values	Operationalize dominant opinions, doctrines, and practices

Chapter 1. These characteristics apply to any category of agency operating with traditional, functionalist assumptions.

The characteristics in Table 6.1 reveal a great deal about functionalist organizations. They are typically well-established agencies with much to lose if radical change occurs. Since they have clients who are viewed as worthy of receiving services (or that members of the larger society believe should be served) and predictable funding sources, functionalist organizations generally seek to maintain some sense of security through the status quo. When an organization has resources, it has much more to lose by way of money, status, and power than an alternative agency that may not have gained credibility with powerful environmental forces. Functionalist organizations tend to have been around for a while with an identifiable space in the human service landscape. These organizations wish to preserve and protect their position and therefore will be more conservative or preservative in their decisions and actions.

Functionalist organizations can be of any size, but the large public human service agency that serve thousands of clients is an excellent example. The bureaucratic structure is necessary just to manage the numbers of people, the incredible amount of paperwork, and the demands of a complex political-economy. Functionalist organizations may be well-established, turn-of-the century nonprofit agencies that have long been affiliated with religious groups. They may have begun as alternative agencies when certain population groups needed services, but have developed and grown to respond to community needs. These agencies may still be quite innovative, spinning out new programs as times change, but their size and structural complexity are indicators of their traditional, functionalist nature. They may call themselves advocates, but they are fully aware of how far they can go without alienating a funding source. Thus, they are advocates within boundaries. Functionalist organizations may also be for-profit agencies that have entered the social welfare domain in more recent years, cognizant of the importance of productivity and efficiency—terms well established in business. Functionalist organizations cut across sectors and are a large portion of the human service landscape as it is currently developed.

Within functionalist organizations there are basic assumptions about locus of control and change. From an objectivist perspective, locus of control is external—there is a greater source of truth and knowledge beyond the individual. If people are products of their environments (a functionalist assumption), then functionalist organizations help people adjust to those environments so that their quality of life will be improved. For example, when one goes to a health care clinic, one hopes to have an accurate diagnosis so that successful treatment will follow. In a human service agency that provides counseling, consumers hope to be able to cope better with life's stresses. In these situations, persons are helped to adjust to their circumstances. They have their needs met without major structural upset. Services have been delivered in a socially acceptable manner, a solid *best practices* model. Finding the *best* practices, the *best* fit, and working toward the *best* possible outcomes is what the functionalist organization is all about. A long tradition of looking for *best* ways to enhance organizational effectiveness and efficiency dominates in the functionalist organization.

Given its regulation perspective, the functionalist organization is not designed to seek radical change. These organizations are essentially very conservative. Persons within functionalist organizations can be change agents, but they focus on changes that are controllable and manageable so that harmony can be maintained or restored quickly. If an agency sees that a funding source has changed its service interest, there will be an effort to reconceptualize its service to fit the funding source's new vision. These changes rarely change what service providers do with clients; the change is in the language that describes the services. Changes in functionalist organizations are not intended to alter basic societal structures, but to help people lead quality lives within those structures. The environment in which the organization operates is viewed by functionalists as a set of forces to be controlled as much as possible, so that social order both inside and outside the organization can be maintained or reestablished.

Beginning to Assess the Functionalist Organization

Given functionalist objective and regulation perspectives, Table 6.2 provides a summary of some of the ways in which functionalist organizations approach their work. We have adapted an assessment framework developed by Netting, Kettner, & McMurtry (1998, pp. 277–280) to identify organizational foci and tasks. In Table 6.2 we have incorporated some of the characteristics of traditional functionalist agencies. This same framework of foci and tasks will appear in subsequent chapters as we examine the differing goals of different types of organizations. The table provides an overview of the basic goals of the functionalist organization in important categories one might use to assess an agency. We will briefly expand on each area.

Focus A: Agency-Environment Relationships

Focus A is on agency-environment relationships. We will examine the functionalist organization's view of the environment, particularly elaborating on funding and clients.

Environment. In the previous chapter, Table 5.2 introduced analogies used by social scientists to depict social systems. We pointed out that mechanical and organismic systems analogies fall squarely within the functionalist paradigm. According to organismic systems theory, the organization's goal is to seek homeostasis, a state of balance in which every part is working together and is integrating with the whole. Organismic systems theory guides the functionalist organization as it seeks to focus attention on the status quo and attempts only incremental change in its search for order and consensus. If there is trouble in the environment by way of dissatisfied clients, unmet service demands, or funding sources that are somehow not happy with agency services, the organization listens to the complaint and does what is necessary to assuage the criticism without

TABLE 6.2 Goals of a Functionalist Organization by Task

Focus and Task	Goal
Focus A: Agency-Environment Relationships	
Environment	To recognize that the environment is uncertain and turbulent, and to do whatever possible to control environmental forces.
Funding	To obtain funding that flows from long-established and multiple sources.
Client Populations and Referral Sources	To fund, plan, or deliver socially acceptable programs to socially acceptable clients in need.
Focus B: The Organization	
Mission/Philosophy	To use the best knowledge available to enhance and achieve the highest social order.
Values	To operationalize dominant opinions, doctrines, and practices, focusing on efficiency and effectiveness.
Management and Leadership Style	To designate administrators and supervisors within a defined structure and to work toward consensus (agreement) so that tasks can be logically addressed. Hierarchical communication and decision making are valued.
Organization and Program Structure	To establish clear relationships between organizational members and among units within the organization, and to be part of service delivery structures that are established by agency staff and protocols that have been used over the years.
Programs and Services	To use incremental or gradual change to alter people's status so that they can function best within society.
Personnel Policies and Procedures	To write clear rules and procedures and share them with employees so that they know what to expect and know what is expected of them and to reduce or eliminate conflict within the organization through clear guidelines for resolving problems (e.g., grievance policies, mediation resources, etc.).
Staff	To hire persons who will work in the most efficient and effective manner.
Communication	To develop established protocols, such as organizational charts and information systems, so that expectations about communication are clear.
Products	To create highly factual, quantitative, concrete reports that demonstrate impact.

making major modifications to the agency structure or programming. The functionalist organization is aware of environmental influences, but attempts to control their impacts.

The environment, in the language of systems theory, is looked upon by the functionalist organization as a sea of uncertainty and turbulence. Guiding one's organization through this sea requires active leadership. The task is to maintain as much order within the organization as possible, even as the waves splash and the tide ebbs and flows. The leader must maintain stability at the helm of the agency, responding in ways that do not create monumental change. The functionalist organization interprets the environment as an ever present challenge to be controlled as much as possible. Adjusting to the environment is a survival requirement, but maintaining a semblance of order is the goal. Thus, only incremental change is required, for to truly "rock the boat" would send the agency into greater uncertainty and would upset the status quo.

Martin (2000) does an excellent job of identifying the "major economic, political, social and technological forces in the external environment [that] can play an important role in shaping" administration in social welfare organizations. Beginning with the collapse of communism, he identifies the global economy, national political power, the devolution of social welfare policy, the "graying" of America, the rediscovery of community, the accountability movement, and advances in information technology as powerful environment forces (p. 55). For the contemporary functionalist organization, these forces cannot be ignored and are viewed as both threats and opportunities, depending on how much they may force a change in the position of a particular agency in the human service arena.

Funding.   Functionalist organizations seek to obtain funding that flows from long-established and multiple sources. Stability and predictability are desired. This is expected, given their perspective on the environment. If the environment is viewed as uncertain and if the goal is to keep the agency afloat, then one would want to seek funding from sources that are likely to remain viable. In addition, leaders in functionalist organizations have learned what it takes to survive. For example, leaders know that receiving funds from multiple sources (diversification) will assist in providing a cushion should one source no longer be available. Functionalist organizations of any size will not tend to put all their financial eggs in one basket if they can help it, unlike alternative agencies that might feel fortunate to even locate a funding source for their cause.

Functionalist organizations and their funding sources develop close relationships, and funders actually influence the agency's direction or its programming. Policies and regulations that accompany the receiving of funds will become part of the environmental forces that must constantly be considered. For example, in home health organizations, staff are very cognizant of the potential to be accused of fraud under Medicare. Fear of not following regulations to the letter could actually hamper how much social workers feel they can do for patients. Massive closures of home health agencies in the last decade attest to the realities in which these fears are grounded (Lechich, 2000).

Client Populations and Referral Sources. Just as funding is a critical environmental influence, so are clients. And clients often come to agencies from referral sources—that is, other organizations that have enough confidence in making a referral that a client will be well served. Maintaining a positive public image, then, is critical both to obtaining clients and to ongoing relationships with referral sources.

The functionalist organization typically serves clients who are socially acceptable or that a funding source has found acceptable to serve. This is a practical matter—if clients are socially acceptable, then chances are that public or private charitable dollars will be available to fund services for them. For example, serving children who have terminal cancer will quickly generate funds for a local children's hospice as people overidentify with the vulnerability of these children and the testimonies of their parents. Socially acceptable clients usually do not require personal or social radical change or transformation in order for success to occur. They do not have to first convince the public that they are "worth" serving even before they receive service. Socially acceptable clients will tend to go along with the program more often than persons who are outside the mainstream or feel alienated from society. Socially acceptable clients are likely to be those persons whose values are compatible with those of the organization and its funders.

However, socially acceptable clients may also be persons who have involuntarily been commanded to be served. For example, prisons are functionalist organizations. Clients in prison are anything but socially acceptable, but the larger society supports the building of new prisons and even the taking of lives because prisons perform a socially acceptable function—keeping violent criminals off the streets. Involuntary clients fit within functionalist organizations because its mode of operation is to maintain the status quo—to fit people within the existing structures of society—not to push for radical change. Similarly, functionalist organizations serve clients that society wants to control, such as mothers on welfare who are given limited funds with the stipulation that they must go to work. In this instance, the functionalist organization attempts to coopt mothers to conform to standards established as socially acceptable.

Focus B: The Organization

The functionalist organization is definitely aware of its environment, but it is also exceedingly concerned about the ways in which it operates as an organization. The internal workings of the functionalist organization are influenced by a broad repertoire of theories identified in the previous chapter.

Mission/Philosophy. Building on the belief that the status quo and social order are good things for organizations, the functionalist organization views the social world of the organization as composed of concrete empirical artifacts and relationships that can be identified, studied/measured, and managed through controlled approaches derived from the natural sciences. These methods were first identified by Taylor (1916), who conducted time and motion studies to develop rules and laws to increase productivity or organizational output. Scientific methods continue to be the acceptable way to measure divergence from the ideal or desired state in the organization in order to implement logical plans for reaching those goals.

Mission or philosophical statements are not always easy to decipher because they typically contain lofty words and are written to inspire the reader. Therefore, missions of functionalist organizations may contain words that do not fully fit with basic underlying assumptions. For example, many human service organizations will have the verb *advocate* in their mission statements. Certainly, the functionalist organization will advocate for individual clients to a degree—perhaps getting them signed up for food stamps or bringing their needs to the attention of an appropriate agency—but this type of client or case advocacy does not create major structural change in oppressive systems (Schneider & Lester, 2001). Instead, it is a more conservative approach that seeks to bring clients into the existing service delivery system by changing their status. It is therefore important to read statements of mission and philosophy carefully in light of what the words mean for establishing the standard for acceptable practice within the organizational context.

Values.   In the functionalist organization there is no great need to search for meaning or to spend much time questioning values. Not only would this be a waste of time (highly inefficient) but it would also involve process more than outcome. Products and outcomes are highly valued and if end products are considered effective and efficient, then it is proof in itself that the process worked. This is what is valued.

Remember that the functionalist organization takes an absolutist position. Truth comes from an external source and is not determined by the individual. The functionalist organization operationalizes dominant opinions, doctrines, and practices. This fits with having established funding sources that mirror those same dominant perspectives. What is valued in the agency is what is valued in the society and by the funders at that time. When society saw the woman's place in the home, there was no real effort to prepare and hire women professionals; when societal values shifted to allow women in the world, then organizations began hiring women who would fit within the structures and behavior norms that were already in place. Responsiveness to environmental shifts comes with a serious effort to maintain what exists.

Management and Leadership Style.   The functionalist organization of today is bureaucratic following a Weberian (1946) tradition. Official areas of responsibility for all persons within the organization are stated. These areas are governed by rules and regulations within a hierarchy with levels or gradations of power and authority about organizational processes. The hierarchy is organized either "top down" or "top up" (Gulick, 1937). The organization that has been ordered through a system of subdividing the enterprise under the control and responsibility of a chief executive is top down. Information and directives tend to flow downward. The system may be created in a top-up way by combining individual work units into aggregates that are then subordinated to the chief executive. Information here tends to flow upward, but directives still flow downward. Regardless of the form of the hierarchy, formal means of written communication are used to conduct the business of the organization. Written or understood rules also govern behavior within the organization. Management within the bureaucracy is specialized and trained, so that job performance expectations for management differ from those providing other services within the organization.

Leaders and managers develop job descriptions and organizational charts that provide information on what employees do and how they relate to one another. Clear lines of authority are a goal for such organizations so that valuable time is not lost in trying to figure out who is supposed to do what task. In large organizations the benefits of bureaucratic structure are evident in the way large numbers of employees are coordinated. Time is spent in making roles and relationships clear, with little attention debating how people feel about these roles and relationships. Professional functionalist organizations tend to have undercurrents of tension because professionally educated people do not always conform to expected roles and relationships, no matter how hard managers work to make this happen. In fact, if employees are critical thinkers, they will likely question roles, relationships, rules, and procedures.

Leaders who want to succeed in a functionalist organization will find that there are certain characteristics that are rewarded by functionalists. Figure 6.1 provides a list of characteristics of functionalist social work leaders.

Organization and Program Structure. With goals and processes, the functionalist organization is also absolutist. There is one "best" way of defining the problem and implementing the solution to that problem. The way to achieve problem solution and change is within a context of logical order and maximum control of all elements of the organization. The difficult part is to find that best solution so that a

FIGURE 6.1   Characteristics of Functionalist Social Work Leaders

1. Is comfortable with clearly defined rules, procedures, and directions
2. Seeks consensus among colleagues
3. Sees conflict as something to be reduced
4. Truly appreciates collegiality and mutual respect for organizational goals
5. Is comfortable with maintaining the status quo
6. Likes concrete, measurable artifacts
7. Works toward identifying best practices, and best ways of doing the work
8. Likes having maximum control at work
9. Is viewed by others as "rational" under stress
10. Tolerates process but sees outcomes as most important
11. Is able to separate personal from professional life, believing in the importance of clear boundaries
12. Follows the rules
13. Makes incremental change as needed

formal structure can be designed to support it. In most cases, the solution is organized hierarchically with clear roles and responsibilities.

To serve this aim, the functionalist organization has several structural elements: formality, bureaucracy, and hierarchy. The formal nature of the functionalist
organization is a vestige of the beginnings of social organizing during industrialization and the study of postindustrial organizations. Frederick Taylor (1916) framed
the belief that there is one best way of accomplishing any task, including social organizing. Once the one best solution is discovered, then rules and laws are put into
place to create the formal structure geared to increase output.

Adam Smith (1776) was the first proponent of divided, coordinated work. The
functionalist personality fits the tradition that began with *The Wealth of Nations.*
Functionalists welcome a division of labor and work assignments between management and labor with clear expectations regarding performance, good treatment,
respect, and discipline if the rules are broken. The expectation is that management
does the planning, organizing, staffing, directing, coordinating, reporting, and
budgeting (Gulick, 1937), and labor does as it is told. This division is pragmatic and
acceptable because it is believed to enhance the skills of each. It saves time and
expands creativity in developing best practice methods and technology. All this
serves to increase productive quantity, as the narrow focusing of activities
increases abilities, which in turn increases quality of performance. It is assumed
with this focusing, that workers or managers are much more likely to discover easier methods of achieving objectives. When this occurs, better pay, and, thus, more
satisfied employees will result.

Programs and Services.   In Chapter 1, we introduced different types of programs
and services. Recall that *direct service programs* directly serve clients. *Staff development and training programs* focus on staff, and *support programs* undergird direct service and staff-focused programs. Functionalist organizations may contain all three
types of programs. Regardless of the program type, functionalist programs will be
more concerned about "outcomes," or results, than they will be about the quality of
the process. What will be important about process is that it be efficient.

Program and service goals and objectives require using incremental or gradual change to alter people's status so that they can function best within the larger
society. For example, a program designed for persons with disabilities will attempt
to make clients as proficient as possible, using whatever assistive technology available, for as much independence as possible. Another program targeting welfare
mothers may teach interviewing skills so that the mothers can get jobs. Yet another
program may assist older persons to remain in their own homes. All of these programs are change oriented, but these are not radical or structural changes. Clients
are changed so that their increased abilities will allow them to be a part of, or access,
existing societal resources.

Functionalist organizations generally have programs and services that have
well-defined, measurable objectives. Management and funding sources will expect
this. Program budgeting rather than line item budgeting may be in place. This
allows investigation of each program separately in terms of its revenue sources and

its expenditures. Programs may be viewed as cost centers, with program directors or coordinators responsible for their oversight. This combination of identifiable program objectives and a related budget adds to the stability of the organizational structure, enhances management's ability to discipline the structure, and ensures division of labor and evaluation of productivity.

Personnel Policies, Procedures, and Practices. The formal structure of functionalist organizations includes the deliberate selection of employees and attention to their career development, followed by expectations for increased productivity and subsequent increased pay. Today's functionalist organization operates with formal rules and procedures that govern hiring, firing, training, and motivating workers. Organizations typically have formalized pay scales that are also rule governed.

Handbooks that elaborate policies and procedures are available to employees so that everyone is aware of the rules that govern their working lives within the organization. Whenever a new issue arises, the predisposition in the functionalist organization is to clarify things in writing. The quest for clarity about roles, relationships, and responsibilities are reflected in the vast number of written policies and procedures.

Staff. We suspect that there are functionalist personality types—persons who are more likely to "fit" in functionalist organizations than others. In Chapter 4, we introduced the possibility that the Myers-Briggs personality types can be related to the various paradigms based on their descriptions and defining characteristics. Myers-Briggs personality types ISTJ (introvert, sensing, thinking, judging), ESTJ (extrovert, sensing, thinking, judging), and ESTP (extrovert, sensing, thinking, perceiving) tend to see the world and relate to it from a functionalist point of view. The ISTJ personality is a realist, with great organizing abilities who wants command of facts in order to feel comfortable and capable in an organizational setting. Those with ESTJ personalities need to analyze everything to gain control. Logical order is what brings comfort to this personality type. The ESTP personalities are the most curious of those who approach the world of work from this perspective. This Myers-Briggs type needs to know how objects, events, and people work in order to create logic and provide the analysis of the outer world. It is with this approach that a sense of what is real is achieved and one's life and work experiences make sense.

Given the preferences of these personality types, there are certain aspects of functionalist organizational structure and behavior that are decidedly congruent with their approaches to work. The presence of a clear division of labor, direct communication regarding giving and taking orders, along with incentives directly tied to work performance are important to the behavior and satisfaction of these personalities within functionalist organizations.

A match between personality type and organizational expectations in the functionalist perspective occurs when agreed-upon special skills, knowledge, or behavior is focused on clearly stated organizational production goals. The match deepens when there is belief in the efficacy of specializations regarding training and separate, independent work assignments as a way to be more productive.

Communication.   Formal communication in the functionalist organization is facilitated by having defined, predictable structures. Written rules and procedures are designed to communicate work-related expectations. Job descriptions and organizational charts convey role and relational expectations, whereas flowcharts provide visual images of how work is to be performed, decisions made, and communication accepted. Handouts, memos, websites, and various other methods are used to get this information out to employees.

Communication among employees is facilitated by computerized information systems in most contemporary functionalist organizations. Voice mail, e-mail, cellular phones, palm pilots, and other technological devices are embraced by functionalists as tools to get the work done in as efficient a manner as possible. Managers spend much time looking at ways to promote a more efficient, disciplined operation so that outcomes can be achieved in a more timely, less costly manner. In human service organizations, this means finding ways to enhance and streamline methods of communication among employees, between agencies, and with clients. The result is that clients are expected to take most of the responsibility for their goal achievement as the amount of face time between staff and clients is limited in order to be more efficient. In modern functionalist organizations, accountability regarding service outcomes seems to have shifted from the professional to the service recipient as fewer and fewer professionals are expected to serve more clients in service of agency efficiency goals.

Products.   Products are what organizations produce. They are organizational outputs, and human service outcomes are the quality of life changes that have occurred. Products and outcomes are highly valued in functionalist organizations. The current push for outcome measurement is very compatible with the perspectives held by such organizations.

In designing programs in functionalist organizations, one always starts by defining the problem, for it is the rational, problem-solving process that drives functionalist programs. "The rational approach views the organization as an efficient machine to attain specific goals" (Hasenfeld, 2000, p. 91). Well-designed functionalist programs are ones in which the problem is carefully defined and the causes of the problem are analyzed. A complete search of the literature and relevant studies will reveal what is known about these causes and will then logically lead to decisions about effective interventions. If interventions do not work, it is likely that the problem has been ill defined or that the causes were not well established. Rarely is the linear model of thinking and decision making questioned. There is a generally held assumption that problem definition leads to the identification of problem causation, and intervention is based on the definition and cause. The functionalist organization seeks to link problems to interventions to outcomes. Given a specific problem, the intervention is directed at what is understood to be the problem's cause in order to eliminate (or at least ameliorate) the problem.

In the section that follows, we will examine the major elements of practice in a functionalist organization. Practice, like the organizational structure and behavior, is based on functionalist assumptions that shape what constitutes acceptable practice. The language of practice is congruent with the assumptions.

Practice Language of the Functionalist Organization

Table 6.2 provided a beginning profile for assessment of a functionalist organization. Specific areas were identified that are known to be important in thinking about organizations. We followed with stated goals for each area so that the reader could have descriptive information about a functionalist organization. We see this material as an aid in gathering information about an organization. For us, this data gathering is assessment. No judgment about quality is intended to be part of data gathering. Judgment follows after sufficient information is available.

In recent years, the terms *assessment* and *diagnosis* have been used to approach data gathering about larger systems (organizations and communities) as much as they have been used in direct practice situations. An overview of social work's attention to the terms *assessment* and *diagnosis* may help clarify some of the challenges in the transfer of these concepts from small to larger systems, and will facilitate our examination of practice within functionalist organizations and the others that follow.

The uniqueness of the social work approach to assessment of clients and their problems has been seen as its distinguishing professional characteristic (Kirk, Siporin, & Kutchins, 1989, p. 295). Social work assessment has been described as multifaceted, client-in-situation centered, focused on problems in living, and non-pathological (Miller, 2001). Yet the terms *assessment* and *diagnosis* are often used interchangeably, causing some confusion over what the assessment process is.

The diagnosis/assessment differentiation debate may be at the base of the social work struggle to develop into a full-fledged profession (Rodwell, 1987). Based on early criticism by Abraham Flexner (1915) that social work was not a profession because it was not scientific in its practices, much of the early efforts to characterize social work focused on creating a scientific approach to professional practice by absorbing the medical model of solving patients' problems through study, diagnosis, and treatment. A classic example of the profession's adaptation to the medical view of scientific rigor can be seen in Mary Richmond's work (1917), which she called "social diagnosis." She attempted to demonstrate medical model rigor by using the language of a dominant profession, while simultaneously distinguishing social work diagnosis from medical diagnosis.

Diagnosis comes from Greek and means "to distinguish, discern, to learn to know, perceive" (*Oxford Dictionary*, p. 596). There are, however, discipline-specific definitions of this term. In medicine, *diagnosis* can mean "determination of the nature of a diseased condition; identification of a disease by careful investigation of its symptoms of history." From biology, the meaning is "distinctive characterization and precise terms" (*Oxford Dictionary*, p. 596). In the *NASW Dictionary* (Barker, 1999), *diagnosis* is defined as a "process of identifying a problem (social and mental, as well as medical) and underlying causes and formulating a solution" (p. 127). Barker underscores the strong medical implications of this definition and suggests that there is a preference among social workers for the term *assessment*.

Miller (2001) clearly distinguishes between assessment and diagnosis by stating that assessment and diagnosis are not interchangeable, even though they have been used interchangeably in the profession (see, for example, Goldstein, 1995; Hepworth, Rooney, & Larsen, 1997; Kirk, Siporin, & Kutchins, 1989; Rauch, 1993; Turner, 1994; Woods & Hollis, 2000). She sees assessment as an ongoing, continuous process, in that different tools may be used at different points, given the various roles professionals play. The initial assessment process provides the information for making a diagnosis (i.e., using the *DSM-IV* in clinical practice), which is folded into the ongoing reassessment process. Diagnosis from this perspective is a labeling process for the problems identified as a result of initial assessment and is reformulated as reassessment informs practice.

In the organization literature similar struggles about the distinction between assessment and diagnosis exist, but unlike a definable controversy that impacts direct practice in social work, the struggle in organization practice appears to be simply a question of language usage. Even though some writers recognize that the terms are often used interchangeably (see Lawler, Nadler, & Cammann, 1980; Seashore, Lawler, Mirvis, & Cammann, 1983), others distinguish between the concepts of *assessment* and *diagnosis*. Harrison and Shirom (1999) view assessments as more focused on specific programs or services, whereas diagnosis is designed to be a more systematic look at the entire organization. They point out that one can assess without diagnosing; in other words, one might know there is a problem but have no understanding of its underlying causes. Harrison (1994) suggests that during diagnosis the current state of an organization is compared to a preferred state. The diagnostic study is a search for ways to narrow the gap between the current and the desired state of affairs. However, this label is not static because continuing reassessment refines and shapes diagnoses.

In this book, we borrow from both micro- and macropractice to use the terms *assessment* and *diagnosis* as follows: **Assessment** is a process in which a person or group gathers information about a service, program, or organization. How wide the net is cast will depend on the purpose of the assessment. Some assessments may gather information on a single agency program, whereas others may examine an entire organization. The type of data collected and the method of collection will also depend on the reason one is undertaking an assessment. For functionalists, regardless of the theoretical perspective guiding the assessment methodology, diagnosis cannot be done well without first some elements of assessment occurring. From this perspective, diagnosis is taking assessment data and analyzing it into information that can be used as the basis of identifying problems, resolving issues, or enhancing organizational effectiveness. Assessment involves accurate data gathering or construction. **Diagnosis** occurs when data are understood and translated into information, so that problems and needs are labeled and analyzed.

Following assessment and diagnosis is planning. **Planning** is defined as preparing to resolve problems and address organizational needs. Regardless of the difficulties in distinguishing between diagnosis and assessment, there are commonalities in many of the skills used to perform the tasks of either professional action in large or smaller systems. The performance of these tasks is usually called **incremental change** in functionalist organizations. Professional judgment, information acquisition and processing, and critical thinking are essential skills for effectiveness in all phases of the assessment, diagnosis, planning, and planned change process (see Figure 6.2).

Having examined the use of language for practice and the accompanying debates, we now turn to the specifics in a functionalist organization. As you will see, assessment, diagnosis, planning, and incremental change are viewed as stages used to approach organizational change in most functionalist organizations.

Change in the Functionalist Organization

No matter the type of organization in which one practices, there will always be times when something needs to change. When change agents attempt to change something within the functionalist organization, they will typically follow a non-emotional, rational process. Radical change or strategies that increase conflict are not well tolerated in functionalist organizations. This suggests that assessment, diagnosis, and planning for incremental change will occur through the use of rational decision making with passionate approaches being totally dismissed.

Assessment

In the functionalist organization, assessment is viewed as a rational, beginning attempt to gather data about the organization, its programs, and any situation or problem that needs to change. Initial assessments are first-time, typically quantitative snapshots of a situation, to be followed by periodic reassessments in which the results of changes are identified. Assessment, then, is an ongoing process, important to the functionalist because of the assumption that reality is above and beyond individual intuitive knowledge. Hard and concrete facts are collected because it is important to have as much objective information as possible before diagnosing the organizational or programmatic problem. Information systems that contain statistics on agency performance are important resources in the assessment process.

Given the functionalist's predisposition to standardized measures, tools designed to assess organizations are welcomed. For example, a strategic planning guide that begins with the mission statement, moves to the external environment, identifies best practices, analyzes clients and stakeholders, assesses internal opera-

FIGURE 6.2　Language Used in the Functionalist Organization

Assessment

Diagnosis

Planning

Incremental Change

tions, and develops components of a plan (Austin & Solomon, 2000, p. 346), or a planned change model that begins with assessing all the components of the organization (Netting, Kettner, & McMurtry, 1998), or a management audit that examines all facets of the organization (Lewis, Lewis, Packard, & Souflee, 2001, pp. 331–337) are useful to functionalist organizations. These tools offer the functionalist social work leader a place to begin in looking at what is happening in the organization or program so that a change process can begin.

Program data collected by staff offer another information source for the social work leader who is trying to assess an organization's progress or analyze a situation. Here again, the staff would use instruments that gather concrete facts and figures—highly valuing standardized tools, tested for reliability and validity because they are considered to be as objective as possible. Numbers, not words, are preferred. Programs that fit well within functionalist organizations will tend to keep field notes and qualitative data collection to a minimum because these type data are time consuming to collect and hard to code for translation into computer systems. Progress notes in functionalist programs are written in behaviorally measurable terms so that an objective reviewer unfamiliar with the situation can quickly discern exactly what happened. If judgments are recorded in the assessment or progress note process, they are to be clearly flagged as interpretations so as not to be confused with objective data. Methods selected to gather functionalist assessment information should be well established and acceptable to members of the scientific community. For example, systematic quantitative data collection that can be computer analyzed is highly desirable.

Assessment, then, is a process of gathering data that can be translated by professionals into information and used in determining as objective a diagnosis as possible. It is also very important to use the same tools in order to ask the same questions in subsequent reassessments of the organization or organizational unit. In the assessment and reassessment process, it is important to control relevant stakeholders. Although conflict is inevitable when anyone is assessing a problem situation, the functionalist organization will prefer communication strategies that muffle conflict. For example, organizational change agents will attempt to coopt unwilling stakeholders to be a part of the assessment process so that conflict can be kept to a minimum. Assurances will be made that there is no desire to make radical changes, only to assess the situation so that interventions compatible with the organization can be planned. In reality, who determines what is compatible rests with those in positions of formal organizational power.

Diagnosis

Logically, if accurate and reliable data are gathered, then professional judgment can be used to diagnose or label the organizational problem or situation. Although it is recognized that assessment and diagnosis are ongoing, and will change as things change, there are practical reasons for labeling problems quickly without deep investigation or interpretation. For example, if an organization wants to maintain reimbursement from established funding sources, managers must be certain that all forms are filled out in their entirety before site reviewers from funding and regulatory bodies arrive to monitor files. If an assessment reveals that this is not being done, then the diagnosis may be that the program is out of compliance. Note that in other type organizations, the diagnosis might be that the restrictive policies of a funder might need to be changed to be something more feasible for the organization. This reframing, or reconstruction, of a problem is less likely to occur in functionalist organizations with commitments to following the rules and not "biting the hand that feeds them."

Earlier we elaborated about how diagnosis has traditionally been a medical term, appropriated by social work in the early days of the profession as a method of gaining legitimacy. The term continues to be used today in more clinical social work circles only recently being applied to organizations. Another phrase that historically has implied the labeling or diagnostic process in organizational settings is *problem definition and analysis*. If assessment is a data gathering process, then problem definition and analysis is the process of determining from those data what problem or problems need to be addressed. In the definitional/diagnostic process, analysis occurs because the social work leader in the functionalist organization is trying to examine the potential causes of the problem so that a plan for intervention can be designed.

In macro arenas (organizations and communities), planned change models have dominated the social work literature. For example, in a popular framework for understanding the problem and the target population, the first task is to identify the organizational condition. This is followed by reviewing the literature on the condition, problem, or opportunity; collecting supporting data; identifying relevant historical incidents; identifying barriers to problem resolution; and then determining whether the condition is a problem (Netting, Kettner, & McMurtry, 1998, pp. 98–99). This approach to diagnosis is very systematic and scientific, based on finding the concrete facts that will help in naming the problem and deciding why it exists.

Although assessment can be seen as a broadening exercise, attempting to gather as much knowledge as possible across domains (i.e., financial, physical, mental, social, economic, environmental, functional), diagnosis in the functionalist organization is a focusing or narrowing opportunity. Being able to label a problem or problems and then focus specifically on the accompanying issues makes planning more manageable. It is reductionistic. It reduces what is being considered to its simplest form. In the functional organization, manageability is very important. For example, a diagnosis may require that the organizational process under study be placed on a flowchart so that there is a clear visual representation of what steps are expected. Each step is simplified and connected linearly to the next in a cause/consequence format. Creating flowcharts is an appreciated functionalist tool, grounded in the Taylorist classical tradition because it takes all the chatter from the environment and the data and reduces what is to be done to its simplest form not just for assessment and diagnosis, but also for planning.

Planning

In functionalist organizations, the link between assessment, diagnosis, and planning is critically important. Once a diagnosis has been made, then planning must follow logically from what is known about intervention with organizations that have that diagnosis. If the diagnosis changes, then plans must be revised to reflect different types of interventions that fit with the new diagnosis. Similarly, in the process of reassessment, new data about an organization's situation must be considered in light of current diagnoses. A change in diagnosis will warrant a change in the plan. The inherent logic, and seeming linearity of the process, is based in organismic systems theory.

Planning for change in functionalist organizations is an incremental process. Most changes occur for organizational maintenance rather than fundamental change. The desire for broader-scale, radical change may be entertained by some organizational members who are not satisfied with the conservatism of the functionalist organization, but their voices are expressions of work from a different paradigmatic perspective. What is most often heard in functionalist hallways are statements such as, "If it's not broken, then why fix it?" and "We've tried that before and it didn't work" and "If we're going to make a change, let's be sure we know all the implications of what we are planning." One of the criticisms of functionalists is that by the time they have looked at all the implications, there is little energy left for change, incremental or otherwise.

An excellent program planning model for use in functionalist organizations has been developed by Kettner, Moroney, and Martin (1999). Called an *effectiveness-based approach*, this model begins with problem analysis and needs assessment, then moves to planning, designing, and tracking interventions. Grounded in systems theory, the model is used widely in schools of social work throughout the country to prepare students to design outcome-based programs. Kettner, Moroney, and Martin (1999) explain why their model comes from a functionalist perspective by using three examples. The first example focuses on the political economy as a factor contributing to unemployment. They explain that if the program planner attempted to address capitalism as the cause of unemployment, "proposed solutions would be likely to involve a radical transformation of the existing system or at least its modification. Although the analysis can be theoretically and technically correct, it is unlikely that a planner or administrator at the local level will be in a position to change the system, whether it is a form of capitalism or socialism" (p. 77). They conclude that it is important to recognize these larger systems' problems, but also to accept that they are not within the purview or control of the local human service agency. Therefore, a planner may design a program to provide incentives for unemployed persons within the local community to find jobs, but he or she would be naive to think that the program will tackle capitalism as an oppressive system.

In their statements, Kettner, Moroney, and Martin (1999) explain the distinctive difference between the functionalist organization and the radical structuralist organization (to be elaborated on in Chapters 7 and 8). The functionalist organization is focused on incremental, controllable change so that social order and homeostasis can be established or restored. In the functionalist organization, having knowledge that there are preconditions that set up problems to be addressed does not mean that one has to tackle those preconditions. Not only are they outside the purview of the organization but they are also rife with conflict. The functionalist organization plans programs that are built on consensus, that are designed to address problems that can be controlled, and that move toward establishing or reestablishing a sense of order. Incremental change is seen as the preferred change here. In the next several chapters we will investigate approaches that sees change quite differently.

Incremental Change

In functionalist organizations, interventions need to be logically derived from what was learned in the processes of assessment, diagnosis, and planning. Interventions may take the form of **planned change**, defined as a process of deliberately identifying a problem, analyzing its causes, and carefully determining a strategy to alter the situation according to predetermined outcomes. Planned change interventions, then, are not done haphazardly, spontaneously, or without a great deal of thought.

Since consensus is a core functionalist value, tactics used in planned change interventions are typically conservative—designed to be acceptable to the majority, especially those in positions of power over the organization. For example, some of the early textbooks on change focused on making certain that collaborative or campaign tactics were used before even considering contest tactics (Brager & Holloway, 1978; Resnick & Patti, 1980). Resnick and Patti focused on the importance of working for change from *inside* the organization, not even addressing the concerns of the outside agitator. Their approaches fit well with functionalist organizations because they hold highly compatible basic assumptions. Table 6.3 provides an overview of practice characteristics in functionalist organizations and provides a summary of the discussion in this section. The characteristics can serve to help you understand the established standard of functionalist organization practice.

Implications for the Social Work Leader

Certain aspects of the functionalist perspective are congruent with the values of the social work profession; others present challenges, particularly to its social justice mission. One of the greatest challenges is that this perspective forces a position of ethical absolutism. This means there must be one best way of defining what constitutes the acceptable core values of the profession within organization practice. Further, ethical absolutism means starting with the organization within its own context and perspective. Moving into unique and different ways is impossible, or at least professionally unacceptable, because there is only one true best way of proceeding with all organizations.

Iglehart and Becerra (1995) criticize functionalist approaches to practice because students learn to attempt less conflictual tactics first before moving to more aggressive methods when trying to address larger systems change. They also criti-

TABLE 6.3   **Practice Characteristics in Functionalist Organizations**

Practice Element	Characteristics
Assessment	Systematic data gathering is a first step in planned change within organizations.
	Standardized, quantitative forms, guides, or tools are helpful in the assessment process.
	Assessments provide hard, concrete, objective data that can be used by professionals to diagnose the organizational situation or problem.
	Data collection methods should be consistent.
Diagnosis or Problem Definition & Analysis	Diagnosis flows from objective assessment data.
	With reassessments, diagnoses may change.
	Diagnosis requires consideration of objective data known about identified problems.
Planning	Planning follows logically from diagnosis or problem definition.
	Planning is incremental in its orientation.
	A change in diagnosis will warrant a change in the plan of action.
	In planning, preconditions are recognized, but the goal is to design realistic interventions.
Incremental Change	Interventions may be at the organization or organizational unit level.
	There is a best or better intervention identified.
	Change from within tactics (collaboration and campaign), rather than contest (conflict), are preferred.
	The goal is to change the organization's situation so that homeostasis is reestablished.

cize these approaches for taking "the middle course," avoiding controversy, and supporting determinism (p. 137). Iglehart and Becerra are critical of those practice approaches that avoid addressing larger societal issues. Basically, they are critical of traditional functionalist organizations because aggressive, radical change is purposefully avoided in favor of modifications of the status quo.

On the other hand, some aspects of the functionalist organization are congruent with the social work profession. From bureaucracy, the preference for specialization based on professional training and practice expertise, career orientation, and upward mobility, and valuing abilities on the job more than who one knows all fit well with the concept of professionalism in social work. But the bureaucratic approach is also impersonal and inattentive to the individual in context. Further, the possibility of attention to procedure over effectiveness on the job means that human service workers in a bureaucratic environment might not meet the real needs of those they intend to serve. Instead, because of what is rewarded in a functionalist structure, social workers may move to unthinking compliance with rules rather than critical analysis of the organization's policies and procedures vis-à-vis their clients.

The "scientific" approach supported by theories in this paradigm makes sense in social work service delivery and programming as a means of documenting effects and improving practice. The present focus on accountability and outcome measurement for reimbursement from managed care entities or for financial support by other funding sources may be answered by the rigorous designs of interventions and valid and reliable measures called for by functionalist assumptions. But the fact that most program evaluations produce no significant findings suggests that quantitative measures may not be the only way of knowing what results from a social work intervention.

On the other hand, the influence of a management by objectives (MBO) structure, and the focus on strategic planning that dominated organizational thinking in the late 1900s, makes annual plans an expected part of human service organizations. Functionalist support of outcome measures is good and useful, but the narrow definition of what can be assumed to represent quality results may tend to overlook the process of the intervention. Focus on outputs and outcomes has helped functionalist organizations become more proactive, but this proactivity continues to assume rationality and an ability to control what goes on in an organization. Since there may be other dimensions overlooked in a functionalist perspective, lack of goal achievement may not mean lack of success or incompetence on the part of practitioners. It may only mean that the wrong aspects of the organization are being investigated or that the assumption of rationality among organizational members does not hold.

Being off target for what should have attention in organizational studies is a potential problem in functionalist organizations. This is especially true for organizations favoring a social work values perspective. The social justice target of the profession may suffer in this type organization. For example, in the hierarchical structure of functionalist organizations, women and minorities may be disadvantaged in the expected movement from lower to upper levels of the organization. Given the biases within the structure, many capable people who look and act differently from the traditional administrators of organizations may experience what is known as the "glass ceiling," where the upper reaches of the organization are visible but not attainable. This may be due to some of the negative influences of early human relations theory where power and decisions were always intended to remain at the top, with no empowerment in the ranks, just control for productivity. This leaves the potential for oppression, exploitation, and dehumanization of those in the lower portions of the organization. Even though there is attention to personal and social relations in this approach, women and minorities continue to be disadvantaged in traditional organizations due to lack of access. This leads to exclusion from the important networks that open opportunities for promotion and advancement.

Conclusion

The functionalist organization is committed to the discovery of the one "best" way of conducting assessment and diagnosis to achieve the one "best" way for change. This sets up the expectation that discovery of a generalizable truth is possible and so, too, is control of planning and intervention. When the unexpected happens somewhere in the process, the assumption is that a lack of competence is at the bottom of this absence of control. In actuality, it might be that a theory or paradigm that does not fit is being used to guide the decision-making process around assessment, diagnosis, and planning.

What the organizational leader does gain from functionalist assumptions is valid and reliable instruments to "norm" organizational structure and behavior. The leader gains outcome measurement tools to aid in response to the productivity pressures of outside funders, but this comes with the risk of lack of effectiveness in the outcomes when the significance standard in statistics is used as the only measure of effectiveness. Structural change is not the expectation from this perspective, but cost effectiveness is.

When adopting this perspective for assessment, diagnosis, planning, and incremental change, the social worker loses a view of what is unique to the organization and its members in the organizational environment. Some of the subtle influences regarding processes are not captured in the data collection for decision making. This happens because there is little room for consideration of the more qualitative, affective, intuitive aspects of organizational life due to the rigor expectations that are assumed to be necessary for "knowing."

For the social work leader, there is another serious challenge. This perspective and the theories within it offer no help in assessment, diagnosis, planning, and incremental change in attending to the special opportunities and challenges provided by that which is different from the norm. Further, there is no room for the chaotic and the unexpected that seems to permeate today's organizational life. The presence of chaos or unpredictability is attributed to incompetence in the administration, the program design, the organizational structure, or the personnel, when chaos might instead be the norm for contemporary organizations.

We now turn to a second paradigm: radical structuralism. You will soon see that this paradigm has some assumptions in common with the functionalists. Just as important for social worker, however, are the differences in how change is viewed.

CHAPTER 7

Radical Structuralist Theories about Organizations

This chapter explores the theories and assumptions that create the radical structuralist paradigm in much more detail than was provided in Chapter 4. It also investigates what we are calling radical structuralist organizations. We have chosen to highlight this paradigm next because theories based on a radical structuralist approach to understanding organizations have much in common with the assumptions that create the functionalist paradigm. Radical structuralists, like functionalists, hold assumptions regarding the possibility and desirability of rationality and realism. Within both paradigms, there is a real world "out there" that is logically deducible. However, as you will see, radical structuralists have a very different orientation to change than do their functionalist colleagues.

Description of the radical structuralist paradigm is expanded in this chapter, beginning with basic themes and followed by an elaboration of the assumptions of this perspective. After this thorough paradigmatic grounding, the major organizational and organizational behavior theories that fit within this perspective are identified and discussed. We close the chapter with a critical analysis, so that the reader is left with a perspective of what is gained and what is given up when approaching organizations from a radical structuralist worldview. We then move to Chapter 8, which focuses on the understanding necessary to practice within radical structuralist organizations.

We want to caution the reader that we are referring to the radical structuralist organization as a prototype. Rarely will a "pure" radical structuralist organization be found, though some certainly do exist. Just as in functionalist organizations, radical structuralist organizations may have staff members or contain units that operate under different assumptions from different paradigms. When this happens, staff will encounter paradoxes as differing assumptions clash. Having read this chapter, it is our hope that the reader will understand why radical structuralist assumptions about change may collide with assumptions from other paradigms. We begin with the themes of the radical structuralist paradigm.

Radical Structuralist Themes

Radical structuralists hold assumptions regarding the possibility and desirability of rationality and realism. Although the radical structuralist paradigm is ideologi-

Radical Humanist	Radical Structuralist
Interpretive	Functionalist

cally driven, this perspective also assumes that traditional science should shape organizational study. Here, organizational variables should be carefully defined and operationalized with an expectation of rigor derived from natural science on how one selects samples, collects, and analyzes data. Further, there is the expectation that research will be objective, oriented to prediction and control, so that results can be generalized. This may sound familiar, because both radical structuralists and functionalists are objectivist in their approach. The major departure from functionalism involves the purpose of organizational study. So, in addition to the obvious expectations about controlled procedures for knowing and understanding organizations, there is an expectation that the consequence of knowledge building is change, including radical or revolutionary change.

Though organizational theories in the radical structuralist paradigm are principally positivistic, requiring that propositions be tested or built according to rules of formal logic and based on methods derived from the natural sciences, there is a values sensitivity that also frames organizational studies. Radical structuralists believe that the choice of a value system tends to empower or enfranchise certain persons while disenfranchising and disempowering others. When one takes a position and that position is accepted, the person is empowered, while those holding another position are left without a strong position. They are disenfranchised or disempowered. The role of inquiry into organizations, then, is to determine the gainers and the losers related to the problem selected for study, making any inquiry a political act. It is a political act because the purpose of study from this perspective is to understand the consequences of situations, thus creating transformative knowledge. Knowledge is transformative when participants' awareness has been raised to a level of *true consciousness*. It is with this consciousness that participants (assumed to be oppressed people) will act to transform the situation under investigation in the direction of more empowerment. It is assumed that this transformation can be predicted and controlled because the decisions made are based on true consciousness aimed at liberation.

The methods to achieve true consciousness in the organization are not necessarily as interventionist as those used in the functionalist paradigm to define and control the organization. Basic to radical structuralist research methods is dialogue where participants (sometimes including the researcher) come to a common point of view. Sometimes this is a point of view about the interpretation of traditional organizational research findings; sometimes it is a point of view regarding their common organizational experiences. It is assumed that through a dialetical process in which conflicting views are aired, agreement can occur around the features of the organization under investigation; judgments can be made together about what can and should be altered, thus setting the stage for concerted efforts at transformation. Therefore, beyond the expected elements of natural science rigor that must be exhibited for the research to be considered scientifically sound, there is an additional rigor expectation: Did a transformation result from the research process?

Given the radical structuralist orientation, critical thinking and analytic questioning of arguments and methods within the organization are acceptable sources of knowledge. Theoretical reasoning can come into question, as can the procedures for selecting, collecting, and evaluating traditional empirical data. Everything within the organizational context can be open to scrutiny from this perspective based on the attention to social regulation and unequal distribution of power.

Even though human nature from the radical structuralist perspective is a deterministic product of the environment, there remains human possibility. The recognition that circumstance and the environment shape human nature is mitigated through consciousness raising. There is an assumed power/knowledge connection such that human nature reaches the realm of ultimate possibilities through understanding how boundaries and structures are formed and how they serve to limit. The research participants, through the research process, become cognizant of the elements within the organization that serve to disempower and disenfranchise. There is a development of an understanding about how individuals participate in the creation of oppression both consciously and unconsciously. This understanding comes only through struggle in the face of forces that pervade common sense and become part of the ordinary way of seeing the world (Angus, 1992). It is difficult to see past common practices to their real, if not intended, effects. Struggles will ensue as intended and unintended consequences are highlighted To work for conditions in which critical reflection is fostered as part of the organizing process also requires a struggle. It is assumed that there are forces at work to retain the dominant order as a universal and unalterable existence. For radical structuralists, it is only through the struggle that the advantaged will be forced to engage in the full range of options for consideration so that all, including the marginalized and disadvantaged, can reach their potential in the organization.

In sum, the radical structuralist paradigm holds a commitment to radical change, emancipation, and potentiality. This is assumed to be achievable through an analysis of structural conflict, modes of domination, contradiction, and deprivation. This perspective shares with functionalism realism, positivism, and determinism that produces nomothetic (rule-governed) understanding of the social world. Different from functionalism and related to radical humanism, radical structuralism embraces conflict to generate radical change through crisis.

Assumptions of the Radical
Structuralist Paradigm

Recall that in both Chapters 4 and 5 we reviewed four terms that define objectivism. We repeat this figure (see Figure 7.1) again so that the reader will have a handy reference for review in understanding radical structuralism. We will not repeat the details of what these terms mean, for they are available in earlier chapters Instead, we will focus more on what makes radical structuralist theories very different from functionalist theories.

Radical structuralists see truth as determined by the larger environment, but because the paradigm sits at the intersection of objectivism and radical change, it assumes that having knowledge derived from rigorous study is insufficient unless that knowledge is *used to make change happen*. The radical structuralist rejects being satisfied with knowledge for knowledge's sake in favor of knowledge as a means of consciousness raising and transformational change. The concerns of a radical change perspective are summarized in Figure 7.2.

The radical structuralist paradigm offers a different way to approach organizational studies. Instead of looking at structural and behavioral relationships, the radical structuralist begins with a critical or radical stance that may be oriented toward investigating exploitation, modes of domination, repression, unfairness, uneven power relationships, and the communication and thinking patterns that engender and maintain them. Radical stucturalists are activists who want to overthrow these organizational limits for classes of organizational participants.

This expectation of radical change based on critical analysis represents a challenge to traditional views about organizations and organizational behavior. No more is there authoritative control for disciplined and productive behavior. Revolutionary action is the expectation. It also presents a challenge for research in organizations where structure and control of results are expected at all levels of organizational life. The degree of difficulty, as well as the opportunities that this perspective represent, may be clear by looking at Figure 7.3 in which all assumptions of this paradigm are viewed together.

FIGURE 7.1   Objectivism: Defining Terms

Realism (external)

Positivism (hard, real, tangible)

Determinism (people are products of their environments)

Nomothetic (use methods of natural science to test hypotheses in accord with scientific rigor)

Source: Adapted from G. Burrell and G. Morgan, *Sociological Paradigms and Organisational Analysis* (Aldershot, England: Ashgate, 1979), Figure 1.1, p. 3. Used by permission.

FIGURE 7.2   **Concerns of the Radical Change Perspective**

Radical change

Structural conflict

Modes of domination

Contradiction

Emancipation

Deprivation

Potentiality

Source: Adapted from G. Burrell and G. Morgan, *Sociological Paradigms and Organisational Analysis* (Aldershot, England: Ashgate, 1979), Table 2.2, p. 18. Used by permission.

As you read about the theories highlighted in this chapter, Figure 7.3 provides a reminder of their underlying assumptions. It is also a way of testing the degree to which organizations that you know could fit within this paradigm.

Radical Structuralist Organizational Theories

For further grounding in this paradigmatic perspective, we will now investigate the major organizational and organizational behavioral theories that can be placed within this paradigm, given their assumptions about organizational structure and organizational life. Although few organizational theorists have yet identified with this perspective, those who do hold these views are part of a broader critical tradition. This tradition includes philosophers who have challenged the status quo and

FIGURE 7.3   **Assumptions of the Radical Structuralist Paradigm**

From the Objectivist Perspective
1. Reality is above and beyond individual knowledge.
2. Knowledge about social reality is hard and concrete.
3. People are products of their environments; they are shaped.
4. Natural science methods can be applied to the study and understanding of social reality.

From the Radical Change Perspective
5. Society is characterized by deep-seated structural conflict, modes of domination, and even contradiction.
6. Knowledge for change and action should be the goal.
7. Conflict, rather than consensus, is important.

Source: Adapted from Burrell and Morgan (1979, Chapter 1).

supported those who are marginalized so they are no longer voiceless. The work from this position is in response to social conditions of domination and is motivated by a desire to provide mechanisms for a more inclusive dialogue and dialectic that is assumed to produce a radically different future for all. The assumption is that a presentation of a different perspective, and the resultant disruption of the current dominant discourse, open the way for contested or subjugated knowledge to serve as a medium for the creation of societies and organizations free from domination (Alvesson & Deetz, 1996). When new voices are allowed to be heard, new ideas create opportunities for a freer structure for organizations and society. The antidomination themes that include advocacy, grassroots activities, and radical reform will become clear as we look at the radical structuralist theories and then move in Chapter 8 to understanding types of organizations and personality types that are compatible with this perspective.

In Chapter 5, we revisited the nine major perspectives on organization theory identified by Shafritz and Ott (2001), five of which were closely tied to the functionalist paradigm. In this chapter, we focus on theories within three perspectives closely tied to the radical structuralist paradigm:

1. Systems theory and population ecology
2. Power and politics organization theory (including the feminist and critical theories that challenge the status quo)
3. Postmodernism

Several ideas seem to pervade the theories of interest here. First, organizations are not considered in isolation, but in relationship to total environmental contexts. Second, these theories are attentive to structure, not just of organizations. They include interest in the configurations of social relationships even at the class level that creates totalities separate and independent of the individual's consciousness of them. Another important idea is that of "contradiction" seen at various levels of organizational structure and behavior. Contradictions include the hope that oppressive structures contain the seeds of their own destruction in a radical sense. Contradictions also exist between various organizational goals and individual needs, in class conflicts, or between technology and humanity. The last idea is "crisis," where change comes through crisis of a political, economic, or emotional nature that serves as a point of transformation from one type of totality, one type of social structure, to another more inclusive one.

We begin our theory discussion with certain types of systems theories. Although systems theory was originally introduced in the functionalist paradigm, there are some schools of systems theory that fit well within the radical structuralist paradigm.

Systems Theory

When we examined systems theory earlier, different analogies used by social scientists to depict social systems were highlighted. For example, mechanical and organismic analogies of systems theory are tied to functionalist assumptions, whereas morphogenic, factional, and catastrophic analogies are based in the radical structuralist paradigm. Table 7.1 provides a reminder of the assumptions in these three versions of open-systems theory. Unlike mechanical and organismic analogies, those within the radical structuralist paradigm focus on the dynamic and changing nature of social systems rather than attempting to deny those dynamics. Conflict is seen as a normal part of an organization located within a complex environment.

Morphogenic means structure change, as opposed to *morphostasis*, which means structure maintaining. A morphogenic approach views systems as capable of change. In actuality, the possibility that an organization will return to a previous state of stability (through morphostasis) is only one of many possible options. The expectation is that as organizations gain more knowledge and experience, they will change their structures, forms, goals, policies, and so on. In doing so, maintaining a steady state equilibrium would indicate that the system has not grown and devel-

TABLE 7.1   Analogies Used by Social Scientists to Depict Social Systems

Analogy	Description and Principal Tendency
Morphogenic	Assumes that social systems change constantly through interaction and exchange with their environment(s);
	Assumes that social systems are highly open;
	Assumes social systems may be orderly and predictable but may also be disorderly and unpredictable;
	Assumes that order may rest on coercion and domination as well as cooperation and consensus
	Places about equal emphasis on conflict and change as on order and stability.
Factional	Assumes that social systems are divided into contentious factions that conflict over goals, priorities, resources and strategies;
	Assumes that the turbulent division of the system into factions is the principal tendency of the system;
	Emphasizes conflict and change over order and stability.
Catastrophic	Assumes that social systems are severely segmented and warring;
	Assumes that little order or predictability exists;
	Assumes that conflict may destroy some component parts;
	Assumes complete reorganization of the system is required if the system is to become less chaotic or conflictual;
	Emphasizes conflict and change over order and stability.

Source: From Patricia Yancy Martin and Gerald G. O'Connor, *The Social Work Environment: Open Systems Applications.* Copyright © 1989 by Allyn & Bacon. Reprinted by permission. Adapted from G. Burrell and G. Morgan, *Sociological Paradigms and Organisational Analysis* (Aldershot, England: Ashgate, 1979), Figure 4.1, p. 67. Used by permission.

oped. Systems theory based on a morphogenic analogy expects interaction with the environment to influence what occurs within the organization so that the organization adjusts and changes accordingly. There is a sense of fluidity that comes from recognizing differences and learning from those differences. New organizational forms will emerge over time, hopefully leading to more highly ordered, complex systems (Martin & O'Connor, 1989).

Whereas a morphogenic analogy works well to explain an organization that has members who are in general agreement about direction and purpose, or at least get along reasonably well, a factional analogy views organizations as being somewhat fragmented among various, somewhat contentious, groups. This lack of cooperation is characterized by internal conflict, complete with contention, domination, competition, and lack of cooperation rather than harmony among members. Given that members change and staff turns over in organizations, a factional analogy may apply at times within systems, depending on the presence of contentiousness. This analogy is also compatible with the morphogenic analogy because both assume that organizations are within ever-changing environments in which conflict and disorder are to be expected. The difference is that in the factional system, conflict among groups is also occurring within the organization (Martin & O'Connor, 1989).

The third analogy is catastrophic and, like the other two analogies, assumes that social systems are in constant change. In this view of organizations, however, internal competition is harsh with severe conflict occurring on an ongoing basis, making all aspects of the system in flux. To survive, reorganization is ongoing. Due to this fluctuation, parts of the system may literally be on the verge of collapse. Again, like the morphogenic and factional analogies, change is a predictable part of the organizational experience (Martin & O'Connor, 1989), but here it is of the catastrophic variety.

These three analogies of systems theory bring organizations beyond a simple view that they are shifting in an environmental sea, attempting to regain stability and homeostatis. Instead, they recognize that organizations and environments are in a constant state of interaction and that organizations have various degrees of stability within. There is no expectation that organizations will remain the same; in fact, the potential for change is the constant. Being able to change may make the difference in whether the organization grows, develops, or survives as a viable entity. Change is a productive way of life in these open systems. Systems theory, as represented by these three radical analogies, does not assume that staying the same and achieving a steady state is desirable.

Population Ecology Theory

Shafritz and Ott (1996) include population ecology theories together with systems theories, since they are both very much based in open-systems theory. Rather than focusing on just one type of organization, population ecology theorists are interested in sets of organizations that are engaged in similar activities, how they interact with the environment, and how they relate to one another.

Concepts of particular interest to these theorists are population dynamics and density dependence. *Population dynamics* reflects the idea that as new organizations are founded, resources are often more difficult to obtain, since these sets of organizations typically depend on similar funding sources. This idea is particularly relevant to human service agencies that often compete with one another for limited dollars. As organizations fail, and if new ones are not founded, then the remaining organizations may be able to obtain needed resources more easily, unless the cause for which they were founded becomes unpopular. Population dynamics postulates that if more new agencies are founded, without others failing, then the density of organizations rises and the competition for resources increases. *Density dependence* is the number of organizations in the population. As more organizations are founded, this may signal increasing legitimacy of the service provided by these organizations in the larger environment. However, with increasing density comes an increase in competition and a potential risk for higher rates of failures within this population of agencies due to lack of resources. Technological developments also influence the founding and failing of sets of organizations. Changes in the political and cultural institutions and shifts in demographics also have an impact on organizational stability (Hasenfeld, 2000, p. 98).

Of interest to population ecologists are macrolevel strategies that influence sets of organizations, such as creating institutional linkages with government agencies that increase the legitimacy of the agencies providing human services. These strategies, unfortunately, are less well developed than the understanding of the consequences to organizations that do not have appropriate coping strategies (Hasenfeld, 2000, p. 99). There are related perspectives developing that may add to the work of population ecologists and may contribute to understanding how organizations interconnect and relate to another within population groups.

Weiner (1990) provides an overview of what he calls "the emerging theory of interorganizational relations [which] has become the very foundation of social welfare and other human service organizations" (p. 12). Growing concern about fragmentation and alienation in service organizations has led to an additional focus in organizational theory development, which includes attention to the organization within its social environment and interorganizational relations. Only some branches of this theoretical development can truly be seen to be radical enough to fit within the radical structuralist paradigm. Those influenced by a Marxian tradition would be interested in how the links between government agencies, corporations, and others ensure the continued dominance of certain powerful groups and capitalist interests even within human service organizations (Mizruchi & Galaskievicz, 1993). The social control element involved in the creation of a complacent working class and a clearly defined deviant population would be of interest. Here, the assumption is that integration and coordination of services is a way to continue the functioning of the current welfare system with more efficiency and less resources, thus maintaining the accepted dominant structure (Morris & Lescohier, 1978). This theoretical perspective draws attention to the political functions of an integrated human service system in order to understand how conflict and crisis will be necessary to overcome the capitalistic market economy's effect on the nature of human service organizations.

A more recent approach to transorganizational theory would posit that traditional management concepts are not acceptable in the postmodern world and especially in organizations linked in nontraditional ways. Of interest are the increased self-government of employees in networks created by interorganizational structures. Employees and managers behave differently when they hold allegiance to a network rather than to a particular organization. Kikert (1993) asserts that facilitative incentives and invitations to perform the work replace hierarchical commands in networks. The network is a "kinder and gentler" environment. In addition, the role of government recedes, allowing deregulation, decentralization, and privatization. Marginalized populations have more voice in these antiauthoritarian and antimodernist organizations. This is because the patriarchal structure serving the interests of men (Wilson, 1996) gives way to a collective environment designed in opposition to bureaucratic domination (Hyde, 1992; Ianello, 1992).

The recognition of constant change in open-systems theory, the potential for factional and catastrophic dynamics, acknowledgment of population ecologies, and the increasing emphasis on transorganizational theory all lead to the development of the next set of theories. Theories of power and politics are steeped in assumptions of constant change and are interested in the dynamic nature of interpersonal and organizational relationships.

Power and Politics Theories

Although power and politics theories represent a more recent development in organizational theory, the concept of power has long been a source of interest and concern. Hardy and Clegg (1996) trace the emergence of two voices—the critical and the rational—in the development of power and politics. The critical voice emanates from an older tradition based in the work of Marx and Weber. Marx's work on class structure viewed organizational life as one in which the interests of workers were subjugated to the control of production by a dominant class. Weber was actually the first writer to take Marx's view to a more complex level of thinking when he focused on power as being tied to *both* ownership and control of production. Ownership was only one facet of power; having the knowledge that allowed one to control production activities was a second form of power. Thus, dominance required both economic power (ownership) and the knowledge to actually do the work (labor power). The second voice (Hardy & Clegg, 1996) emerged from 1950s studies in management. This rational voice asserted that the structures established by organizations represented legitimate power.

For example, Bennis and colleagues (1958) distinguish between the formal organization in which authority was based on one's position and the informal organization in which power came from a number of factors in addition to one's position in the organization. French and Raven (1959) identify reward power, perceived coercive power, legitimate (authority) power, referent power, and expert power, and suggested that different sources of power produce different consequences in the organization. Management studies that focused on the manifestation of both formal and informal power caught on during the 1960s. Managers were instructed to use their formalized power (authority) to control informal power viewed as illegitimate and dysfunctional. Baldridge (1971) studied changes in the balance of power and demonstrated how organizational goals show the official version of who is in power. This power structure was also of interest to Thompson (1967) in his study of the transitory nature of power and the interdependence among units of an organization.

This led Pfeffer (1981) and others to see power as a structural issue. Power was viewed as a result of a division of labor and professional specialization. Those who have the expertise to complete critical tasks hold organizational power. Organizational authority through an established organizational hierarchy then becomes only one of many sources of power. Allen and Porter (1983) identify downward power (hierarchical) as only one type, along with lateral and upward power. Other sources of power that reflect the consequence of multiple coalitions within organizations were identified as control of resources (including information and skills), access to power, coalition membership, and credibility. Cohen and March's study of universities (1974) revealed a very modern concept called *organized anarchies* to describe the confused power present in universities based on ambiguity of power, purpose, experience, and what constitutes success. All of these theorists saw power and politics as fundamental concepts for understanding behavior in organizations. They represent the rational voice that framed power from a functionalist perspective.

The critical voice, based on the Marxist/Weberian tradition, held assumptions of the radical structuralist paradigm. "The Marxist/Weberian tradition equated power with the structures by which certain interests were dominated; while the management theorists defined power as those actions that fell outside the legitimized structures, and which threatened organizational goals" (Hardy & Clegg, 1996, p. 626). In this chapter, we are interested in the critical voice of power and politics because it is this view that fits with a radical structuralist perspective.

Of great curiosity to theorists who viewed power and politics as oppressive to various groups was why these groups seemed relatively passive in organizations (Hardy & Clegg, 1996). Some writers suggested that groups were passive because they were satisfied. Others recognized that access to political and organizational structures and their decision-making processes might be so impermeable that interests and grievances might remain unarticulated (Hardy & Clegg, 1996). From this standpoint, groups were not necessarily passive; they just couldn't break through organizational and societal barriers to make their voices heard. The possibility emerged that key decisions might be made by less visible leaders to whom workers did not have access in their organizations. Studies of power began to focus on why issues were suppressed, conflict was not evident, and how people might be manipulated into compliance. It was possible that dominant classes actually controlled reality by defining and thus creating it in their own way (Clegg & Hardy, 1996).

Mann (1986) introduced the concept of *organizational outflanking,* a process used by those in dominance to gain consent and subordination of organizational members. Instead of viewing the oppressed as in denial and the elite as outwitting the masses, Mann theorized that outflanking occurs because the oppressed do not have access to or know the rules. Their affiliations are with others who have little power, and by being ignorant of organizational rules and procedures, their affiliations do not gain them a collective strength. If an individual does not know the manner in which decisions are made and if he or she does not associate with decision makers, then that individual and those with whom he or she associates have little impact on decision making. This situation creates a sense of futility when considering resistance as an alternative to the current situation. In fact, the gain one might achieve from advocating for change would require too much energy to make it worthwhile. Organizational members become self-monitoring and self-controlling. They are outflanked. Outflanking may occur when people are unaware of the rules, but it may also occur when they know the rules but do not have the emotional energy to challenge them. Interestingly, while the critical power and politics theorists were concerned with the oppressive nature of outflanking in keeping with radical structuralism, power and politics theorists in the rational/functionalist tradition were seeking ways to set up barriers to control others based on what they were learning about outflanking.

When organizational theorists began dealing with power and politics, they were strongly reacting to structural and systems theories based on functionalist assumptions in which organizations were considered to be rational. Rationality meant that organizations would have agreed-upon goals around which there was consensus. However, once power and politics theorists acknowledged that consensus was rarely present and that there was often conflict and competition among members and units within organizations, work became more radical. To fully appreciate power also required understanding dominance, control, and oppression within the organization. Rationality was replaced by passion.

Power and politics theorists are open to criticism because they represent less than 30 years of focused attention with less empirical grounding than other theories discussed thus far. Even so, as they are moving beyond the older definition of **power**—"the ability to get things done the way one wants them done…[the] latent ability to influence people" (Shafritz & Ott, 1996, p. 354)—those holding the radical structuralist perspective no longer assume that the organization's primary purpose is to accomplish organizational goals. There is a rejection of the idea that organizational goals are determined and designed by those in charge and measured only for effectiveness and efficiency, restraining personal issues in favor of organizational needs. Power and politics theories reject the notion that power is vested in formal authority. Instead, there is a complex system of individuals and coalitions with interests, benefits, values, perspectives, and perceptions that act in competition for organizational resources and enter into conflict to acquire influence. Behaviors and decisions are recognized not as rational but as the result of influence. This influence is necessary for use in competition and conflict to shape decisions. The coalitions and the individuals within them hold organizational power, but the power and the coalitions are always shifting and so are the behaviors and decisions that result.

We have chosen to place the political economy perspective within the power and politics school of thought. Zald (1970) defines this perspective as "the study of the interplay of power, the goals of power-wielders, and productive exchange systems" (p. 233). Focus on an organization's political economy includes looking at how the management of power and of resource acquisition and distribution occurs, and then seeing how these two systems interrelate. The organization is an arena in which various groups, external and internal to the agency, compete to optimize available resources. The political economy perspective has been used in extensive research on human service organizations—their development, maintenance, and destruction (Hasenfeld, 2000, p. 96).

From a radical structuralist perspective, power has been viewed as a tool of domination, and resistance to power is seen as a way to gain emancipation. Much of the work in this area is still highly theoretical, with little by way of specific practice models. Hardy and Clegg (1996) caution us to be wary of any theory that poses as *the* theory of power. Power can be viewed in many ways; therefore, any general theories of power at this stage in development are more likely to be some group's or individual's attempt to define all situations from one biased standpoint.

Although Shafritz and Ott (2001) do not elaborate on feminist and critical theories, we believe that some dimensions of each are appropriate to include here under the power and politics radical structuralist perspective. Both theoretical approaches also emanate from the Marxian tradition. We will briefly highlight important elements of each, then turn to the postmodern theories that are also highly influenced by the critical voice.

Feminist Theory

The recognition of the relevance of gender within the workplace did not occur until the 1970s when scholars began to reassess previous studies in light of their total neglect of gender. Until then, power and politics theorists were men who studied men in organizations. Hardy and Clegg (1996) contend that the gender bias in organizational studies was yet another way that male dominance permeated the workplace. The sheer force of theory that formed organizational ideology for decades had ignored gender, and power and politics.

Certain branches of feminist theory fit more comfortably in a more radical change approach to understanding organizing against dominance than other approaches. Liberal feminist theory, with its roots in the liberal political tradition, advocated for *reforming* organizations instead of *transforming* organizations, as advocated by radical feminist theory. Similar to the two rational and critical voices identified earlier in the power and politics perspective, liberal feminists took a reasoned perspective that sought to gain access to existing organizations and to incorporate women into these agencies as full and equal participants following traditional rules of behavior. This approach did not require a transformation of the social and political system because all that was called for was an opening for women. The approach was functionalist in its view.

The majority of the organizational literature beginning in the 1960s reflected a liberal feminist approach and focused on women in management. Liberal feminist theory acknowledges conflict and tension within organizations, but with a focus on how women who do reach managerial positions are "rendered structurally powerless" (Kanter, 1987, p. 354). Early work on women's roles in organizations was conducted by Rosabeth Moss Kanter (Millman & Kanter, 1975; Kanter, 1977), whose case studies were the first serious examination of women's numbers, status, and opportunities in the workplace. Kanter (1979) looked at powerlessness in organizations and found that first-line women supervisors, staff professionals, and top executives exhibited a great sense of powerlessness. She also found that dominance, control, and oppression are more likely to result from a lack of sense of power within the organization and that women managers experience special types of power failures. Therefore, she called a sense of powerlessness more a problem for organizations than power itself. Janet Wolff (1977) examined women's roles in organizations and how they related to more general societal roles for women. Her work was expanded by Gutek and Cohen (1982), who coined the term **sex-role spillover**, defined as carrying socially defined gender-based roles into the workplace. None of these theorists sought to move much beyond definition of the problem for women within organizations. There was no call for radical change nor for alternative ways of understanding a woman's perspective in organizations. Therefore, it is important to recognize that just because a theory is feminist in its orientation does not necessarily place it within the radical structuralist paradigm.

Calás and Smircich (1996) use the terms *radical feminist theory* and *alternative organizations* for feminist approaches that fit within the radical structuralist paradigm (p. 227). Taking subordination of women as a fundamental organizing principle of patriarchal society, radical feminist theorists call for organizational and institutional transformation rather than individual change. A woman should not necessarily change her behavior; instead, the organization should change to make way for a woman's way of communicating and decision making. Since radical feminism is *woman centered*, these theorists envision alternative, often separatist, organizations in which women are not subordinated to men. Rejecting functionalist assumptions grounded in regulation and control, radical feminists spurn male forms of power, seeking to create *womanspace* through alternative organizations designed to meet women's nurturing and collaborating needs. In the 1970s, case studies of feminist organizations sought to identify how they would be different from traditional hierarchies. For example, Koen's (1984) study of three feminist businesses identified five elements indicative of feminist values: participatory decision making; rotating leadership; flexible, interactive job designs; equitable distribution of income; and political and interpersonal accountability. Studies such as these are seldom seen in the mainstream management literature, since they often seek to change strongly held values in traditional organizational structures (Martin, 1990). Whereas liberal feminist functionalist approaches take a how-to-succeed-in-organizations perspective, radical feminist theorists attempt to view the world of work from a woman's vision, placing women in the center of the analysis in order to create radically different organizations (Calás & Smircich, 1996, p. 229). Other radical feminist theorists, including those developing Marxist and Socialist feminist theories, also are grouped within the radical structuralist paradigm. All focus on gender inequality and the demand for major structural transformation in organizations.

Critical Theories

Any discussion of power and politics would not be complete without an examination of how critical theorists have influenced the study of organizations. Coming from Marxist thought, in which organizations are viewed as instruments of the dominant class, many critical theorists (see, for example, Beechey & Donald, 1985; Bourdieu, 1977; Dreyfus & Rabinow, 1983; Giddens, 1987; Habermas, 1971, 1984, 1987; Mannheim, 1936; Williams, 1977) are concerned with the ways in which social, cultural, and economic conditions produce a type of selectivity in the processes and structures of organizations. Skepticism follows anything that is accepted as the norm or the socially accepted convention because they constitute social practices derived from power and domination. Critical organizational research is designed to challenge everything accepted as standard in order to unmask the dominant perspectives and establish the arena of conflict. Conflict is created in order to dislodge the natural state. Order indicates domination and suppressed conflicts.

In order to achieve real consideration of the organizational status quo, various perspectives must be allowed voice in addition to the dominant view. When various perspectives are present, conflict is inevitable, but this conflict is believed to be necessary in order to achieve a full picture more amenable to fundamental change. Insight and praxis are of central concern; knowledge or consciousness inevitably leads to change but an antimanagement stance is not always necessary. According to Alvesson and Deetz (1996), "Contributions include input to reflection on career choices, intellectual resources for counteracting totalitarian tendencies in managerially controlled corporate socialization, and stimulation for incorporating a broader set of criteria and consideration in decision-making—especially in cases where profit and growth do not clearly compete with other ends or where uncertainty exists regarding the profit outcomes of various alternative means and strategies" (p. 199). At least for some theorists, full overthrow of the administrative structure is not necessary in order to amend the consequences of organizational oppression.

Generally speaking, critical theorists have paid more attention to the societal issues of unequal power and subsequent oppression, but institutions that engender lack of equality are also of interest. Use of critical theory to guide organizational and management studies is still relatively new, emerging in the late 1970s and early 1980s. In many cases, critical theory has been linked to postmodern theory (see Alvesson & Deetz, 1996, for a good description of similarities and differences).

As the name implies, critical theory generally takes a critical stance on contemporary society. To find new and different responses to the changes that have led to new social conditions, scholars such as Alvesson (1993), Benson (1977), Deetz and Kersten (1983), Fischer and Sirianni (1984), Frost (1980), and Willmott (1993) have looked at the size of organizations, technology, globalization, the nature of work, professionalization, stagnant economies, ecological problems, and generalized turbulence. Human service organizations are of particular interest to critical theorists because these agencies are viewed as buffers between capitalists and the working classes, providing services that keep deviants from challenging the capitalist system (Hasenfeld, 2000, p. 105). The goal of critical theory is to create societies and workplaces free from oppression and domination. These theorists see an environment where all people have equal opportunity to contribute to meeting societal needs. Progressive development is the ideal.

Of particular interest to organizational scholars is how technology and rationality are protecting dominant interests. Modernity is a focus of inquiry because it, too, in its resultant science, industrialization, communication, and information technologies presents problems that include the danger of domination. The rise of modernity has created new conflicts. Critical organizational theorists have focused on "the skewing and closure of the historical discourse through reification, universalization of sectional interests, domination of instrumental reasoning, and hegemony" (Alvesson & Deetz, 1996, p. 195). They hope to "recover a rational process through understanding social/historical/political constructionism, a broader conception of rationality, inclusion of more groups in social determination, and overcoming systematically distorted communication" (p. 195).

With the critique of domination, sometimes called *ideological critiques,* the hope is that all stakeholders will come to enlightened understanding that can result in "communicative action" (Alvesson & Deetz, 1996, p. 199) leading to institutional reform. This can occur through research that focuses on organizations' relationships to the larger society, domination and distortion, politics, and identifiable disenfranchised groups. What is hoped is that morally driven discourse will result in action with direction and orchestration provided by the theoretical framework, but when all else fails, the power resulting from knowledge can lead to resistance or revolution, resulting in transformation of the social order. Critical theorists are very explicit about the purpose of their research—to make organizations communities of authentic dialogue rather than instruments of domination (Handler, 1990). These theorists have greatly influenced postmodern theory development.

Postmodern Theories

Postmodern theorists continue their interest in the marginalized and disadvantaged, and see the organizational world as anything but natural, rational, or neutral. These theorists look at conflicts as opportunities to reconsider and question the social order. Postmodern theories are the most esoteric of the theories examined thus far, and without the clarification provided by the critical theorists, they might not have had much relevance or provided much direction for organizational structure or behavior. In addition, as with a few of the other theories discussed in this text, at least one branch of the postmodernists will be found in another paradigm—radical humanism. Those postmodern theories, more attune to the subjective in domination, will be discussed in a later chapter on the radical humanist perspective. Here, we focus on those taking a more generalized or class-based view of organizational reality.

Postmodern theories are hard to delimit since many different philosophical approaches have been labeled "postmodern." Postmodern organizational work began in the late 1980s with the work of Smircich and Calás (1987) and Cooper and

Burrell (1988). Guided by philosophers who focused on concepts such as fragmentation, textuality, and resistance and growing out of the social mood, the historical period, and the major social and organizational changes that were occurring, postmodern theories represent a different philosophical approach to understanding organizations and behavior within them. A major postmodern theme is that culture is a source of control in organizations because "it objectifies the values, norms, and knowledge of those in power; and . . . perpetuates patterns of dominance" (Hasenfeld, 2000, p. 102). **Deconstruction**, then, is a way of demonstrating just how artificial these values, norms, and knowledge are. The exercise of deconstruction also reveals how the concept of rationality is socially constructed. What seems reasonable depends on the historical moment.

Featherstone (1988), Hassard and Parker (1993), Kellner (1988), and Parker (1992) are a few scholars who have investigated the power/knowledge connection, the role of expertise in systems that oppress or dominate. Their investigations also include the role of the media and information technology in the contemporary world of modern organizations. Like critical theorists, postmodern scholars challenge the status quo and support those without voice, but this is accomplished through research efforts that take apart language in order to understand its relationship to the theoretical, political, and affective dimensions that have created it. This deep understanding is important in order to look deeply at current organizations so that they can be rethought. Theorists are interested in identifying what goes into the production and sustaining domination in organizations. They are interested in identifying and understanding systematically distorted communication that tends to subjugate others (see Knights & Willmott, 1989; Linstead, 1993).

Postmodernists see power as achieved in discursive formation; power is a social construction. They are interested in studying how social institutions organize around language, reasoning, and specific practices that create power and domination. Research is intended to challenge the guiding organizational assumptions, meanings, and relationships in order to move beyond the current constructions. This is accomplished through investigation of texts, deconstruction, and the use of words instead of just numbers as a way to extend the understanding of empirical research. Rather than the revolutionary reform envisioned by the critical theorists, postmodern theorists propose that persons step back and explore feelings heretofore unknown. Many postmodernists can be placed in the radical structuralist paradigm because they would agree that there is a higher social order somewhere in the universe (objectivist). They would also strongly agree that the functionalists have claimed to know what that objectivism is, have named it, and have imposed it on others. Consistent with the radical structuralist paradigm, postmodernism seeks transformational change so that a dominant group does not impose their defined reality on others.

To summarize, note that as theories have become more complex, so have the divisions and alternative views within the various schools of thought. In systems theory, there are five analogies, two of which are built on functionalist assumptions and three of which can be placed in the radical structuralist paradigm. Beginning with power and politics, there are multiple divisions and controversies among theorists who disagree over how theoretical knowledge should be used. For example, management theorists coming from a rational approach study power and politics as something to use in order to control subordinates and remain in the functionalist paradigm. On the other hand, power and politics theorists coming from a critical Weberian and Marxian perspective seek to understand organizational power so that members will be empowered and so that social change can occur. They are radical structuralists. Similarly, radical feminist theories share the quest for social change. Liberal feminist voices advocating for rationality in the ways of making room for women remain with the functionalist paradigm, whereas those voices rising from a critical perspective fit with assumptions in the radical structuralist paradigm. Figure 7.4 provides a visual distribution of the theories discussed in this chapter. Their placement within the radical structuralist paradigm reflects their similarities and differences related to assumptions held in other perspectives.

Costs and Benefits of the Radical Structuralist Perspective and Its Theories

The critical theories presented here serve a very important function to those from other perspectives. They are seriously and rigorously critical of the status quo. Use of these theories to guide understandings of organizational structures, formalized

	Postmodern Theories Power and Politics —Radical Feminist Theories —Critical Theories
Radical Humanist	**Radical Structuralist** Systems Theories (morphogenic, factional, and catastrophic analogies) Population Ecology and Transorganizational Theories
Interpretive	**Functionalist**

FIGURE 7.4   **Organizational Theories within the Radical Structuralist Paradigm**

programs, and their impact in communities helps to target the collective social conscience of the organization to avoid rationalization and cooptation in service of job security and satisfaction. Though revolution may not be the preferred outcome of situations assessed and understood through critical theories, feminist theories, and postmodern theories, they do serve to help the manager and staff consider situations from a very unforgiving lens.

Radical structuralists want sweeping, nonincremental changes to the fundamental structure and belief systems within society. Organizational researchers from this perspective want the same for organizational life and they develop theories in service of these goals. However, most Americans prefer individual merit and individual achievement to class action. The American culture is more likely to support efforts aimed at individual changes instead of sweeping class-based changes. Preference goes to evolution over revolution in the North American ideology. No matter what the impact of social problem definition, most leaders, workers, and clients in human service systems will prefer order and control over chaos to achieve change. They will prefer incrementalism, with all its costs, to revolution, with all its unknowns. It is from this U.S. cultural perspective of pragmatic individualism that radical structuralism will receive most of its criticism.

Regardless of the intellectual attractiveness of the theories presented here, especially for those with a well-hewn social conscience, the practice that results from these theories may not be acceptable to the current context of organizational life. Although the theories will aid in the understanding of the experience within postmodern organizational structure, even when taken together, the possibilities of this worldview predominating in organizational life is unrealistic. Few organizational leaders will risk the consequences, intended or otherwise, of an outright assault on the social structure in order to achieve change within or outside the organization. This will particularly be the case as an organization ages and gains legitimacy within its environment. The radical structuralist organization of the past may become the functionalist organization of the future as forces toward conservatism from funding sources trump idealism. Brilliant's (2000) analysis of women's fundraising organizations illustrates this point. She concludes that in politically conservative climates, it becomes harder for social movement organizations to maintain their cohesion as "larger organizational members become institutionalized philanthropies, whereas small funds continue to struggle to obtain minimal resources. . . . The network's continuation as a social movement may depend on both new skills (such as marketing) and the renewed continuation of a changing leadership to the old passions of the movement's founding mothers" (p. 567). The delicate balance between maintaining passion for social change and surviving as an organization represents a tension between radical structuralist passion and functionalist rationality that is not easily resolved.

Conclusion

In this chapter, we introduced theorists who focus on the same general concepts (e.g., power) but who disagree over basic assumptions. For example, systems theory was introduced in Chapter 5 because two of its analogies were strongly functionalist. In this chapter, we have examined three analogies that fit within a more radical structuralist paradigm. Similarly, theorists interested in power can be in different paradigms, depending on how they choose to view and use their concepts. Rational management theorists, acting from a functionalist perspective, want to understand power so that managers can use their knowledge to keep others in their respective places. Conversely, radical structuralist paradigm power and politics theorists who come from a domination and oppression stance will view the study of power in organizations as a means of understanding how to raise the voices of the powerless. Feminist theories run a parallel course in that liberal feminists (functionalists) study organizations in an attempt to make women fit within existing structures, whereas radical feminists (radical structuralists) come from a set of differing assumptions about change and fundamental transformation in order to find space for women in organizations.

Critical theorists have provided a foundation for much of what is known about radical structuralism and have given power and politics, feminist, and postmodern theorists valuable understandings on which to build. However, all critical or postmodern theorists do not necessarily fit within one paradigm. Beginning with this chapter and throughout the remainder of the book, we will often examine categories of theories that hold views so different that they fall within different paradigms. We hope that this does not confuse the reader, but raises one's interest and extends one's ability for critical thinking and analysis, for it reflects the complexity of the current organizational world and the theoretical developments aimed at understanding them.

The next chapter examines the radical structuralist organization. It is time to see how the theories in this chapter can be used to understand the work and standards of practice of organizations that come from a radical structuralist perspective. We will seek to understand their particular view in order to see the implications for the radical structuralist organization that advocates for, plans, and delivers human services.

Understanding for Practice in Radical Structuralist Organizations

Having read about the theories that are based in a radical structuralist paradigm, it should be expected that radical structuralist organizations are more dedicated to making much broader changes, to upsetting the status quo, than their functionalist counterparts. If there is a basic philosophical difference between these two types of organizations, it is their attitude toward change. Functionalist organizations plan and provide human services that facilitate incremental change and attempt to keep a lid on conflict, whereas radical structuralist organizations face conflict head-on, raising consciousness about needs that are not being met, and making conflict manifest in order to shake things up enough to allow for fundamental change.

Like functionalist organizations, radical structuralist organizations recognize that concrete empirical artifacts and relationships can be identified and studied through scientific methods. However, both types of organizations use the results of these studies differently. Whereas a functionalist organization uses study findings to work toward gradual interventions, radical structuralist organizations seize study findings to mobilize a critical mass of people to advocate for transformative change. This transformation, depending on the problem identified, can be focused internally or externally to the organization.

It is important to recognize that radical structuralist organizations may be developed by many different groups that come together for causes as diverse as there are groups to sponsor them. Cause-driven people are committed people, dedicated to making a difference, often in a dramatic way. Thus, cause-driven organizations bring together collectivities of people who have strongly held beliefs; otherwise, they would not care enough to form, develop, and continue to participate in the time-consuming activities necessary to operate the radical structuralist organization. Passion and commitment are propellants in these organizations. Keep in mind that the causes of these type organizations can vary greatly and represent many different political ideologies, philosophies, and values. The Religious Right, the Southern Poverty Law Center, the National Association for the Advancement of Colored People (NAACP), the Ku Klux Klan (KKK), and the Center for Human Rights Education could be said to hold radical structuralist assumptions— all these groups want to change the status quo, all are very familiar with conflict, and all have definite notions about external truths that need to be vigorously pursued and changed. Obviously, these diverse organizations are not advocating on behalf of the same people, and some are even in extreme opposition to one another.

Although there are fewer "pure" radical structuralist organizations than functionalist organizations, the language of radical structuralism is very familiar to social workers. Principles such as social justice and fairness that call for changes that address the oppression of diverse groups and for advocate empowerment are common in professional social work jargon. These concepts are often embraced by persons working in functionalist organizations, resulting in disillusionment and frustration when employees recognize that the assumptions undergirding these organizations and practice within them do not support the more radical change the social justice rhetoric envisions. We think the advocacy focus of social work is much more congruent with the radical structuralist organization.

This chapter looks at ways to understand practice in radical structuralist organizations. We return to the five questions originally introduced in Chapter 6 to guide the reader: (1) What are the characteristics of organizations most likely to operate from the assumptions of this paradigm? (2) How does one begin to assess this type of organization? (3) What language is used in these organizations? (4) What approaches to practice are most likely to fit within this type organization? and (5) What are the implications of paradigmatic assumptions for social work leaders in this type organization?

Characteristics of Radical Structuralist Organizations

Just as readers will have encountered functionalist organizations in their daily lives, we are certain that readers are familiar with radical structuralist organizations. Even if you have not worked in such an organization, you will likely have received mailings from or heard about the work of radical structuralist organizations. Since these organizations are not "shrinking violets," the fact that you have heard their names or seen their ads or heard about their activities means that they are doing their job of lifting the voice of the voiceless. However, witnessing what radical structuralist organizations do is not the same as working in these organizations.

This section explores the characteristics of radical structuralist organizations. Such organizations may share some traditional characteristics in their structures and ways of operating with functionalist organizations, but for the most part they are considered alternative agencies. Recall in Chapter 1 that we identified differences between traditional and alternative agencies, and that public, private nonprofit, and private for-profit agencies can be alternative in their approaches. Table 8.1 provides a listing of the characteristics of alternative agencies as originally introduced with a comparison to the radical structuralist approach.

The comparison of characteristics reveals a great deal about radical structuralist organizations. They are formed to meet needs that are often not recognized by the larger society, and their clients are persons whose needs are not being met by functionalist organizations. Their advocacy orientation makes them vulnerable in seeking funding, for funders will have to feel comfortable with, and be willing to

**TABLE 8.1 Characteristics of Alternative Agencies:
The Radical Structuralist Organization**

Characteristics	Alternative Agencies	Radical Structuralist Organization
Clients	Are formed to advocate for or deliver services to groups whose needs are not being met by other agencies	Will focus efforts on *cause advocacy*, which is more targeted toward social change at the class level
Funding	Do not have well-established funding sources, which poses a risk to agency survival	Will need to find funding sources that support cause-oriented change
Leadership	Typically are inspired by a charismatic individual who mobilizes volunteers and paid staff to action	Will seek inspirational leaders who have vision and can lead others toward transformational goals based on universal truths
Service Delivery	Establishes service delivery approaches, using client participation and evolving protocols	Will engage high client participation in instrumental tasks, moving people toward social change
Size	Are typically small, given available resources	Will typically be small organizations committed to radical change
Staff	Are heavily dependent on volunteers and staff who will work for less than other agencies pay	Will heavily depend on volunteers and staff who are committed to and passionate about making social change, and are not afraid of conflict
Values	Have guiding values and ideologies that run counter to dominant opinions, doctrines, and practices	Runs counter to ideologies related to incremental change, accepting of persons who face conflict head-on

support, the cause-oriented approach taken by the organization. Their use of volunteers and the type of internal leadership required set them apart from their functionalist counterparts. Although they may work closely in coalitions and alliances with more traditional agencies, their methods will definitely stand out as more radical. There may even be times when traditional agencies use their radical structuralist colleagues to make changes that they feel they cannot make. The more conservative, functionalist organizations tend to be more allied with more conservative groups or be hampered by rules and regulations regarding the degree to which advocacy can be undertaken. People within functionalist organizations who have the same vision of necessary change will choose to have the radical structuralist organization stand in the forefront of articulating problems and seeking needed changes rather than risk losing established funding sources. We have seen functionalist organizations go so far as to provide the needed data or other information to radical structuralists in order to facilitate their activities, while still maintaining their own less radical position in the community.

Radical structuralist organizations will likely be smaller in size than functionalist organizations because their radical approaches and resource limitations may limit their ability to grow. On the other hand, there are radical structuralist organizations at the national level that actually grow to have millions of dollars in funding because they have established credibility about the needs for which they advocate. For example, large associations that are cause-oriented groups advocating for their constituencies may have been originally grounded in radical structuralist assumptions. The American Association of Retired Persons (AARP), for example, advocates for the needs of older citizens and could be seen as attempting to lay the groundwork for elder empowerment. Its network of chapters throughout the country attest to the incredible cadre of members who belong to this association, and its lobbyists are active in advocating for or against proposed bills before the Congress. Compare AARP to those radical structuralist organizations at the grassroots level that are struggling to survive in local communities, and one can readily see how incredibly diverse these organizations can be. Also, given the way in which AARP has developed, one could argue that its original radical structuralist orientation may have been muted by a distinctive functionalist perspective as it has moved into the mainstream of power in more recent years.

Working in a radical structuralist organization requires management of basic underlying assumptions about locus of control and change. From an objectivist perspective, locus of control is external—there is a greater source of truth and knowledge beyond the individual. These collective or universal truths become the rallying cry of radical structuralists. The radical structuralist organization uses these external truths as guides in raising awareness and consciousness. In a way, radical structuralists are proselytizers—they are attempting to convert others to their way of thinking, to seeing the truths that they hold dear. For example, the National Citizens Coalition on Nursing Home Reform (NCCNHR) was established as a nonprofit membership organization in 1975 to spread the message that quality care in America's long-term care facilities must be a top national priority. This group emerged out of concerns over the conditions in America's nursing homes and the need to protect vulnerable older residents who are invisible to the larger society. The advocacy role of NCCNHR, combined with the work of many committed volunteers throughout the country, have influenced changes in federal legislation. Its newsletter, *Quality Care Advocate,* serves as a vehicle to raise consciousness about conditions in long-term care facilities and changes that need to occur. If you are unfamiliar with NCCNHR, we suspect you have heard of groups such as Prevent Child Abuse America, Greenpeace, Mothers Against Drunk Driving (MADD), or Common Cause. These advocacy organizations are firmly in the radical structuralist tradition.

Given its radical change perspective, the radical structuralist organization seeks transformative change that not only affects the organization itself but has an impact on the community and even the larger society. Therefore, when one works within a radical structuralist organization, one has no choice but to become part of a transformational process. O'Donnell and Karanja (2000) define *transformation* as

> the process by which people come to understand their own internal spirit and strength in order to develop alternative visions of their community.... *Transformative community practice* seeks to change: (1) how individual people see themselves, developing deeper understanding of who they are and what they can accomplish; (2) how they see themselves in relationship to others in the community, building a collective identity and senses of common purpose and efficacy; and (3) how people outside the community view the community and its people. (pp. 75–76).

Note that radical structuralists are collectivists, building a common identity among people. They seek transformative change for the collective, not the individual alone.

Beginning to Assess the Radical Structuralist Organization

Given radical structuralist objectives and radical change perspectives, Table 8.2 provides a summary of some of the ways in which radical structuralist organizations approach their work. The foci and tasks in Table 8.2 are those introduced in Chapter 6, but the goals of the organization will have changed to reflect a very different orientation. The table provides an overview of the basic goals of the radical structuralist organization in important categories one might use to assess the degree to which an agency fits a radical structuralist perspective. We will briefly expand on each area.

Focus A: Agency-Environment Relationships

A radical structuralist agency operates within the broader context of its work. The community or environmental context is the location of both positive and negative sanctions that get played out in all dimensions of service. To understand this, we will examine the radical structuralist organization's view of the environment, elaborating on funding and clients.

Environment. In the previous chapter, Table 7.1 reintroduced three systems analogies (morphogenic, factional, and catastrophic) used by social scientists to depict social systems and that fall within the radical structuralist paradigm. Morphogenic systems are in constant interaction with their environments and are highly open. Change and conflict receive equal emphasis. In factional systems, conflict divides

TABLE 8.2   Goals of a Radical Structuralist Organization by Task

Focus and Task	Goal
Focus A: Agency-Environment Relationships	
Environment	To recognize environmental uncertainty as an opportunity to interact with and mobilize diverse forces to benefit the organization's cause.
Funding	To obtain any funding that will support the organization's cause(s).
Client Populations and Referral Sources	To advocate with, rather than for, consumers and to encourage the development of programs that have full community participation.
Focus B: The Organization	
Mission/Philosophy	To use the best knowledge available to enhance and achieve the highest social change for the common good.
Values	To provide avenues for nondominant opinions, doctrines, and practices.
Management and Leadership Style	To establish a participatory, inclusive approach to management and leadership in which dialogue and debate are freely exchanged.
Organization and Program Structure	To allow structure to emerge so that the organization's cause is best facilitated, and to use less bureaucratic, flatter structures whenever possible.
Programs and Services	To develop advocacy-based programs and services designed to change oppressive structures and empower people.
Personnel Policies and Procedures	To focus less on policies and procedures, but more on processes that bring people together in interaction. To embrace conflict when it occurs within the organization and to deal with it.
Staff	To hire persons who will embrace the cause and who have advocacy skills.
Communication	To develop open communication in which the voices of clients, volunteers and staff are equally heard, and to engage in face-to-face exchanges in which conflict is accepted as part of the dialectical process.
Products/Outcomes	To create highly factual, quantitative, concrete reports that demonstrate impact at the macrolevel.

contentious factions as disagreements over goals, priorities, resources, and strategies prevail. The catastrophic analogy focuses on severe fragmentation among groups in which conflict has the potential to threaten the organization's survival or create major shifts. In each, the environment is highly defining for the organization.

Radical structuralist organizations see the environment as a set of forces with which the organization is in constant interaction. Rather than fearing conflict and trying to squelch disagreement, the radical structuralist organization recognizes this instability as presenting opportunities to change existing structures, even to change its own internal structure if needed. This organization listens to its neighbors, encourages criticism and disagreement about its service, and has organizational members who are very visible outside the structure of the organization itself. Guiding this type of organization through the environment requires leaders who are not afraid of conflict and who see the organization as developing over time. The leader is not threatened by how this development may actually move the organization to a new and different place. In fact, the concept of maintaining organizational homeostatis would be seen as somewhat of a cop-out, in which organizational change goals are displaced by keeping things the same. The status quo is of no interest to this organization except in how to change it.

The radical structuralist organization views *change as normal*, even useful. This is a great departure from traditional views of agency-environment relationships in which the *normal* organization seeks stability and equilibrium amid environmental uncertainty. The social movement type of organization would not be adverse to radical internal change, sometimes called *organizational transformation,* which implies a "profound reformulation of not only the organization's mission, structure, and management, but also fundamental changes in the basic social, political, and cultural aspects of the organization" (Leifer, 1989, p. 900). Normalizing change, even embracing it as a continuous menu of new options, is exhilarating to the radical structuralist.

Funding. Radical structuralist organizations often have trouble developing and maintaining a stable funding base because they embrace nontraditional, even unpopular, causes. Unless there are funding sources in the larger environment that agree with their mission, they may literally operate on a shoestring budget, with continuing questions about their long-term survival. This may be out of their own fear of cooptation or due to potential funders' fears of agency processes and outcomes. Radical structuralist organizations see little benefit in working to achieve value consensus or consonance with funders, believing instead that their position speaks for itself and should be supported for what it is.

O'Donnell and Karanja (2000) studied Centers for New Horizons, an organization dedicated to work in extremely low-income urban African American communities to empower parents of childhood education programs and to advocate for local residents. Fighting to maintain their radical structuralist orientation, their continual "fear is that we have become a 'vendor' rather than a community partner in providing child and family welfare services" (p. 71). Since its original founding in 1971, Centers for New Horizons has secured public dollars to hire, educate, and promote community residents. However, they point out "so-called minority agencies like ours in extremely low income communities also lack access to unrestricted funds, such as major donor and endowment funds. One organizing training institute, the Southern Empowerment Project, has taken on fund-raising and funding cooperatives as a core organizing strategy; the Project is encouraged that this effort will strengthen the institutional infrastructure for grassroots groups throughout the South" (p. 80).

Such concerns have been reflected in studies of alternative agencies for years (for example, see Brilliant, 2000). Wilkerson (1988) summarizes the findings from a series of case studies of alternative agencies, focusing on the tenuous nature of external funding. Funding sources, Wilkerson contends, follow "front-burner social issues and crises. Governmental, foundation, and corporate-giving programs all have a bent toward a somewhat whimsical nature: When a more attractive or urgent social need attracts their attention or when social themes change—due to politics, economics, or new social threats—the money route can move in a mercurial flow, contributing to the typically short life-span of the alternative human service agency" (p. 124).

Wilkerson's observation raises an important point about working in an alternative agency. If the radical structualist organization is successful in raising the public consciousness, then the novelty of their cause may attract temporary funding interests. However, the fickle nature of funding streams means that working in a radical structuralist organization could mean that one's job (with funding) disappears as suddenly as it appeared if soft monies are not continued or if another cause catches the eye of funders. The volatility of funding, then, is an ongoing issue for agencies that assume a radical structuralist orientation. Working in them may feel very much like a roller coaster ride, invigorating yet somewhat risky and uncertain.

Client Populations and Referral Sources.   Just as funding is a critical input from the environment, so are clients. Traditional referral agencies may see a new radical structural organization as a resource to which they can send clients who have no where else to go. This may sound appropriate at first glance, but this referral process may be seen as a dumping mechanism by the receiving organization. In most cases, the referral will not include a mechanism to pay for services, since, for the most part, these clients' needs will not have reached the public agenda, much less been institutionalized as a societal obligation worthy of funding.

Just as functionalist organizations typically serve clients who are "socially acceptable," because of the clients or the way in which they are served, radical structuralist organizations may be seen at worst as troublemakers or at best as a refreshing approach to an unresolved community or societal problem. Whatever the popularity of the cause, radical structuralist organizations engage clients in a very different way than their functionalist neighbors. First, radical structuralist organizations may be developed by the very persons they are intended to serve. In neophyte organizations, the entire staff may be volunteers, many of whom are drawn to the cause because of their own needs. Second, use of the term *client* may be offensive, and so words such as *member* and *participant* may be used to describe persons who benefit from what the organization does. Third, use of power among members, participants, and staff is different than in traditional organizations in which there may be a clearer demarcation between persons who work in the organization and those who volunteer or receive services. A dialectical approach in communication and problem solving may be used in which various community stakeholders participate on equal footing with persons who are employed by the agency. Inclusion of community members and participants in the decision-making process assures conflict will be inevitable. This inclusionary process is not efficient and may be messy, meaning that the process may not be viewed as sufficiently efficient by those persons with more traditional views of organization practice.

In summary, radical structuralist organizations view funding and clients differently than do their functionalist colleagues. Funding is far less certain, often short-lived, and a continual struggle. Even if funding is obtained, the organization may have to guard against being coopted into more traditional ways of working. Survival is not assured and environmental forces are constantly being scanned for resources. Clients may not be called *clients* at all because *clients* implies that professionals do something *for*, when in the radical structuralist organization doing *with* is the goal. This view of the environment sets a context for examining the organization's internal structure.

Focus B: The Organization

The radical structuralist organization is influenced by theories that are loosely grouped under systems, power and politics, and postmodern perspectives. These theories are reflected in the organization's internal operations.

Mission/Philosophy. The radical structuralist organization has a mission grounded in advocacy, social action, empowerment, and change. Advocacy may take different forms. For example, **case advocacy** occurs when someone persuades others regarding the interest of an individual, whereas cause, legislative, and administrative types of advocacy cast a much wider net, focusing on social conditions that affect many. Schneider and Lester (2001) define **cause advocacy** as "promoting changes in policies and practices affecting all persons in a certain group or class, for example, the disabled, welfare recipients, elderly immigrants, or battered women" (p. 196). Legislative advocacy occurs when persons seek statutory change that will improve the lot of others; administrative advocacy happens when change from within an organization is proposed. Radical structuralist organizations may do all types of advocacy, having units that provide direct service advocacy and others that focus on broader scale change. Some organizations will focus solely on cause and legislative advocacy. The point is that *advocacy* is a word heard frequently in the hallways of these organizations.

Social action, as a philosophical approach to change, "is a collective endeavor to promote a cause or make a progressive change in the face of opposition" (Hardcastle, Wenocur, & Powers, 1997, p. 349). Social action, then, is highly related to advocacy but may go beyond traditional limits, not staying within the boundaries of acceptable (even legal) policies and procedures so common in traditional organizations. Compared with advocacy, social action has a broader goal and emerged out of insurgency movements that championed the cause of the oppressed. Hardcastle, Wenocur, and Powers (1997) identify three change modalities relevant to direct service: (1) ensuring individual rights, (2) public interest advocacy, and (3) transformation. *Ensuring individual rights* includes assuring that persons have what is legally theirs to have. For example, due process rights may involve access to a public hearing. *Public interest advocacy* involves having the opportunity to take part in the civic process, literally having a seat at the table, giving voice to the voiceless. *Transformation* involves structural change and is more concerned with a vision of a greater society than either individual rights and public interest advocacy. Certainly all these change modalities are related, but transformation is the ultimate, visionary cause-oriented approach (pp. 351–352).

Radical structuralist organizations may engage in all three change modalities, depending on their missions. All types of advocacy can be used simultaneously to advance the conditions of invisible population groups. But it is likely that the transformational type of advocacy, providing a vision of a better world, is the best fit with the driven nature of the radical structuralist organization and its mission/philosophy. These organizations hold to an assumption that social structure, including organizational structure, has the potential for oppression and domination, therefore antidomination themes permeate their mission and philosophy.

Values.   Organizational goals and processes can be termed *absolutist* in this paradigm. They are absolutist in the sense that radical structuralists reject false consciousness in favor of true consciousness. *False consciousness* may be a set of values strongly held by dominant interests who are believed to be in error. True consciousness, on the other hand, is determined through critical analysis and dialectical discussion with the stakeholders about the problem(s) under consideration. True consciousness is achieved when there is enough energy to reject the current situation and its accompanying values, create a crisis, and move to structural change at the organizational or societal levels.

For these reasons, the radical structuralist organization does not have so much an identifiable structure as a definable change mission. These organizations will tend to have a social justice focus directed at creating access in a social and/or political economy for those who have been deprived of their human rights, but access comes through conflict. Therefore, organizations whose major activities involve advocacy at any level could be considered radical structuralist if fundamental structural change is their goal *and* if their intention is to create the possibility for that change through serious, sometimes violent, struggle. Actually, this conflict does not necessarily need to be violent, nor does it need to be directed from the outside of the social structure intended for change, but structural dislocation in an extreme form must be seen as desirable. Radical reform must be the goal, whether the organization is involved in legal services, welfare reform, mental health, or health care reform. Evolutionary change would be seen to be too conservative and be rejected in favor of "catastrophic change" (Burrell & Morgan, 1978, p. 359).

Radical structuralists are also absolutist because they believe that there is an external source of truth to be discovered. However, the functionalist version of truth is the false consciousness of the radical structuralist because functionalist truth represents the dominant version of what is real, acceptable, and valued. The radical structuralist is willing to accept that there is a greater external truth, but that truth is often a completely different reality than the truth held by those in power. In their absolutism, radical structuralists may find themselves accused of being fanatics because they tirelessly push for change. They are also somewhat fundamentalist in their orientation on what ultimate truth is all about. Everyone else could be wrong, but they are never wrong about the oppressive nature of structural power.

Not only do radical structuralists search for and identify what they believe to be *real* external truth and universal values, but there can be conflict among radical structuralist organizations when they strongly disagree about what true consciousness is. For example, in response to the rise of the Religious Right and its version of truth, a nonprofit organization called Interfaith Alliance developed to counter the views of the Religious Right. Similarly, the Southern Poverty Law Center developed Klanwatch to monitor the activities of the KKK. As radical structuralist organizations emerge, there will be other radical structuralist organizations created in reaction to the values they are promoting. These value conflicts are predictable due to the vocal nature of these types of organizations.

Management and Leadership Style. Given such a radicalized stance toward change, most formal change-oriented organizations would not fit comfortably within this paradigm. Instead, more nascent, or some would say "angry," grassroots organizations would embrace the radical structuralist paradigmatic assumptions. Rather than naming organizations, it might be easier to identify personalities, groups, or movements that could be considered radical structuralists. Mitch Schneider and Saul Alinsky could be called radical structuralists. The Black Panthers and the radical wing of the Right to Life Movement are also radical structuralists. None share the same methods of organizing or manner of establishing organizational structures. None have similar management or leadership styles. What they do have in common is the desire for change based on consciousness raising of those affected by the identified problem. In order to create the atmosphere conducive to change, they are willing to create crisis, which at times could be violent in nature.

The concept of charismatic leadership is highly relevant to alternative agencies. Often, these organizations have emerged because someone rose to the occasion and others joined the cause. Given this charismatic nature in radical structuralist organizations, Wilkerson contends that the leader is considered "first among equals" and that others follow her or his lead because they admire and believe in this person's ability. "Thus, the dilemma in the non-exercise of implicit role requirements for an executive is dissolved by the power of the leader's real or imputed charm" (1988, p. 125).

It would be naive to assume that a charismatic leader can carry the organizational banner indefinitely. Should the radical structuralist organization survive, eventually leadership will change because people move on to other areas, retire, or die. It can be expected that leadership succession in an organization that has depended on the charisma of a founder/leader will have major adjustments to make when a new person assumes the leadership role. It is not unusual for these transitions to be fraught with intense power and political dynamics as people adjust. For example, in situations in which there are self-appointed heirs, "the dynamics finally become self-centered; and the group fervor that characteristically carries the flow of democracy, enthusiasm, and compliance ultimately breaks. How many minor cracks can be sustained and whether they can be repaired in an alternative human service agency, short of moving to the bureaucratic model, is an intriguing area for more experimentation and investigation" (Wilkerson, 1988, p. 126). Sometimes it seems that during these times of leadership vacuum, the organization will shift to a more conservative posture vis-à-vis goals and services as a way to seek comfort and stability that had formerly been supplied by the charismatic leadership.

Management in these types of organizations actually may be a misnomer. Terms such as *organizer* and *leader*, rather than *manager* are more reflective of the activities. Depending on the size of the organization, there may be no management positions, certainly not in the traditional sense. However, those leaders who want to succeed in radical structuralist organizations will find that certain characteristics are rewarded because of their usefulness to the organization. Figure 8.1 provides a list of characteristics of radical structuralist social work leaders.

Organization and Program Structure. Radical structuralist organizations emerge in defiance of existing service delivery structures that are not meeting the needs of certain groups. Given their contempt, they often try not to replicate organization and program structures that are viewed as instruments of oppression in functionalist organizations. Since most human service agencies are hierarchically

---

FIGURE 8.1   Characteristics of Radical Structuralist Social Work Leaders

1. Questions existing rules, procedures, and directions
2. Actively engages in conflict
3. Can incite conflict when necessary
4. Is comfortable with dialectical interaction
5. Is thick skinned, able to deal with insults
6. Is cause or mission driven
7. Makes no distinction between personal and work life (sees what he or she does as a higher calling)
8. Makes radical change as needed
9. Believes passionately in what he or she does
10. Can be aggressively assertive when necessary
11. Is invigorated and challenged by taking on "the system"
12. Can support cause with factual information
13. Believes there are higher-order truths to be pursued

structured, "those wishing to create empowering organizations must look beyond the status quo to models that show some promise for providing increased consciousness, confidence, and connection to the world interacting with the organization" (Gutierrez & Lewis, 1999, p. 81). These organizations can be viewed as a work in progress, in which member education is paramount, staff and consumer participation in all aspects of organizational life is encouraged, and leaders recognize the importance of an empowered workforce. The actual structure of the organization would be characterized by a flattened hierarchy, flexibility, teamwork, and a shared philosophy that supports the ability for everyone to take risks (Gutierrez & Lewis, 1999, p. 83).

However, radical structuralist organizations face a dilemma when it comes to structuring their organizations. The concepts of flat structures and shared decision-making sound reasonable until leaders try to mobilize the masses for action. There are times when strict protocols, coordinated efforts, and timing of orchestrated procedures are necessary to move change ahead in a timely fashion. In such times, the flexibility and sometimes seemingly chaotic structure of social movement organizations may take a turn closer to their more orderly functionalist counterparts.

Programs and Services. Different types of programs and services were discussed in Chapter 1. Recall that *direct service programs* directly serve clients. *Staff development and training programs* focus on staff, and *support programs* facilitate direct service and staff programs. The radical structuralist organization may contain all three types of programs. For example, a case advocacy approach that defines its direct service programs may be combined with an emphasis on staff development and education. An agency directed toward accessing appropriate community-based services for the persistently mentally ill does so by training staff and volunteers in innovative ways to create services while also educating the public at large about the special needs of this population. However, the organization's "signature program" may be what human service professionals would call a support program—cause advocacy that seeks more radical change. This same agency is known not for its educational pamphlets that they distribute to family members and service providers to educate them, but rather its "signature" is the executive director's quotable quotes that appear in the area newspapers whenever structural inequities and unacceptable services for those challenged with mental illness are uncovered. A functionalist organization serving persons with mental illness would see advocacy programs as supportive of their direct service work; a radical structuralist organization sees its direct service work as supportive of their primary mission—to empower consumers who have mental disorders.

The implementation of empowerment type programs requires the radical structuralist organization to think consciously about how clients or consumers will be involved in every aspect of organizational functioning. Programs will be designed to be more strengths enhancing and responsive than in more traditional systems. In addition, the dialectical process that opens communication for potentially conflicting views will be particularly important to all levels of the organization.

Personnel Policies, Procedures, and Practices.   Radical structuralist organizations arise out of the consciousness of community people who see injustice; thus, personnel policies, procedures, and practices are more likely to be seen as part of the problem, rather than an aid to problem solution. Therefore, a recently established radical structuralist organization will have minimal policies in place and will take pride in not being so formalized. In fact, such technical details may be seen as tools of impending bureaucratic oppression. This makes sense in the early life of an organization where few employees might have little need for policies and procedures, but many of these organizations will never fully formalize in this regard.

When radical structuralist organizations formally incorporate in order to receive funds, then the need for some policies will arise. Primary energy will not be devoted to these administrative or technical details. Even when policies and manuals are developed, everything contained therein will be under constant scrutiny for oppressive or limiting consequences. Rules will always be suspect because if they serve to help one segment of the organization, they may impinge on the liberty and potentiality of another segment.

Staff.   Just as there are functionalist personality types, we think there are radical structuralist personality types—persons who are more likely to excel in radical structuralist organizations. Myers-Briggs personality types who see the world and react to it from a radical structuralist perspective are likely types ISTP (introverted, sensing, thinking, perceiving), ENTP (extroverted, intuitive, thinking, perceiving), and ENTJ (extroverted, intuitive, thinking, judging). The ISTPs, who have a need to understand how the world works and to fix it, in order to make better use of it, would comfortably fit in a radical structuralist organization. The naturally critical stance of ENTPs also places them in a radical structuralist perspective. These personality types have a dialectical relationship to the world around them. Their criticism of ideas and events in order to understand places them in radical structuralism, although they would not necessarily feel the need to take the radical change position of this perspective. However, ENTJs do have a need for action, so the combination of their analytical needs to bring order to things and their penchant for planning strategic action makes this type a good candidate for the radical structuralist world view.

These personality types bring both strengths and challenges to an organization. The mission-driven nature of most human service organizations will draw them to join the work, but their natural approaches to problem solving may present difficulties if they land in traditional, more conservative organizations. These personality types represent the very contradictions that are so much the focus of the radical structuralist perspective. They are drawn toward order, but they are also drawn toward action.

Perhaps, because of these contradictions, even within the most radically forward-looking organization, these personalities may present challenges to persons who are trying to provide leadership. Since staff with these personality types tend to be critically analytical, everything will be analyzed before being accepted. Sometimes the critical analysis will not be balanced in a way to consider costs and benefits, positives and negatives of the phenomena under analysis. This may mean that these personalities can represent very negative organizational energy without receiving support from others for a balanced approach to their questioning and critiquing of ideas.

These personality types comfortably question authority so that the highly hierarchical, bureaucratized organization would not provide a comfortable fit. Rather, the radical structuralist organization that is open to criticism and sees dialogue and dialectic as ways to improve performance and direction would be a more appropriate fit. There is room here for passion and charisma. Confrontation will be a desired strategy, requiring those in leadership positions to respond with equal strength or the necessary organizational rules and procedures will be ignored in favor of more radical action. Unfortunately, for some of the personality types, confrontation may move into aggression. This aggression might also include violence to prove a point or to set the stage for the desired change.

Communication.   Open, frank communication is valued in radical structualist organizations. In the empowered and empowering organization, Gutierrez and Lewis (1999) identify organizational processes for workers with good communication underlying every process. First, they focus on *consciousness*, in which workers are educated about organizational factors, organizational processes are demystified, and there is dialogue about organizational mission. Second, they examine *confidence*, in which skills are built to increase leadership capability, areas of power and control are identified, and professional growth and development is encouraged. Last, they address *connection*, in which teams are developed to make program decisions, bottom-up and top-down approaches are coordinated, and there is ongoing evaluation of the change process. These processes to empower workers can form an intentional and ongoing communication network that describes what should happen in radical structuralist organizations. Instead of workers, members, volunteers, participants, or consumers feeling left out and wishing for communication from designated leaders, the radical structuralist organization's cultural norm is that there should be no surprises, conflicts should be openly addressed, and everyone should have a voice in decision-making processes.

As Chapter 7 illustrated, a number of theories pertain to radical structuralism, and these theories challenge the status quo. Practicing in a radical structuralist organization is not for persons who are uncomfortable with conflict or want to avoid it altogether. One's practice in this type of organization will be fraught with conflict and will fully engage the practitioner in a constellation of roles that requires constant communication. There will be a healthy irreverence for credentials and titles and an enthusiasm for partnering with consumers. The culture will feel vibrant and alive, with a heavy dose of righteous indignation and moral outrage.

Products/Outcomes.   In radical structuralist organizations, products may take the form of well researched, educational materials used to inform various constituencies about issues and causes. Although direct service programs will have client-centered outcomes that focus on empowerment goals, ultimate outcomes will likely be seen at policy, community, and organizational levels, indicating revolutionary structural changes have occurred in existing systems. Radical structuralist organizations value those products and outcomes that work toward broader, transformational change.

This brings us to the language of practice used in radical structuralist organizations, which will be examined in the section that follows.

Practice Language of the Radical Structuralist Organizations

Table 8.2 provided a beginning profile for assessment of a radical structuralist organization. This description was not intended to provide information to judge or evaluate the organization, because assessment is typically an information gathering process. When we discussed the functionalist organization, we focused on a debate between the use of terms such as *assessment* and *diagnosis.* This debate is irrelevant to the radical structuralist organization. Whereas *assessment* is an acceptable term, *diagnosis* implies a medical, expert, or dominant orientation and will rarely be heard in the hallways of these agencies, even if they provide direct services. Similarly, although *planning* might be used, the term *organizing* is more relevant to the radical structuralist because it implies mobilization. *Social planning* has traditionally been used to mean that experts are in charge, bringing special skills to the design of programs and interventions. Radical structuralists do not use the term *planning* in this way, for it is important to demystify the planning process away from an expert-client dichotomy. Instead, planning is viewed as an all inclusive dialectical process with participant engagement as a cornerstone of the process. In a radical structuralist environment, the term *intervention* may be used, but remember that whatever the intervention is, the goal will be to empower people to transform the organization, community, and society. Note that we are using *collective transformational change* to reflect the more radical language of intervention one finds in radical structuralist organizations.

Figure 8.2 provides a comparison of the practice language used in functionalist and radical structuralist organizations. Note how the language is congruent with the assumptions of each perspective on organizations. Having examined the language of practice, we now turn to the specifics of practice in radical structuralist organizations. As you will see, assessment, problem analysis, organizing, and collective transformational change are viewed as stages used to approach organizational change in most radical structuralist organizations.

Change in the Radical Structuralist Organization

No matter the type of organization in which one practices, there will always be times when something needs to change. When change agents attempt to alter something in the radical structuralist organization, they will typically face the challenge with the same urgency and level of intensity that they devote to external change

FIGURE 8.2   Language Used in Functionalist and Radical Structuralist Organizations

Functionalist Organizations	Radical Structuralist Organizations
Assessment	Assessment
Diagnosis	Problem Analysis
Planning	Organizing
Incremental Change	Collective Transformational Change

efforts. The reason for this intensity is that anything that needs changing in the organization is likely taking attention away from the organizational mission. Radical change and dialectical approaches that increase conflict are well tolerated in these organizations because these methods are already part of the organization's norms. Therefore, assessment, problem analysis, and organizing will be in the context of conflict for change.

Assessment

Assessment is critically important in radical structuralist organizations because, like functionalist organizations, they want to gather as much objective knowledge as possible about the situation at hand. Initial assessment of an organizational situation or problem that needs to change is usually approached with less finesse and diplomacy than it would be approached by functionalists. It is, however, approached with the same kind of objectivist logic. Given the culture of the radical structuralist organization, there is little need to tread softly or to worry about hurting colleagues' feelings. The focus of what is being assessed will depend on the organization's goals and concerns. What is important to remember is that assessment is an ongoing process, and that in this process, hard and concrete facts are collected. Radical structuralists are very concerned that vast and rigorous information is gathered so that their analysis of the problem can be enhanced. Given their objectivist perspective, radical structuralists are predisposed to standardized measures or established tools that are designed to assess organizations.

Needs assessments that convey the problems of vulnerable population groups are ideal sources of information if the organization is seen as not properly addressing identified needs. Program data collected by committed volunteers and staff is another source of information. When needs assessment data on the local level are not available to address an organizational change or perhaps set a new direction for the organization, radical structuralists will search for quantitative data that indicate gaps in service and document just how oppressed a group is. When primary data sources are not available, organizational leaders can extrapolate from existing studies, use resource inventories to identify gaps in services, and collect and analyze service statistics from community agencies. They may collect primary data by conducting their own survey, and even hold or participate in public forums in order to assess needs of at-risk groups (Kettner, Moroney, & Martin, 1999, pp. 49–64).

Each needs assessment method has its strengths and limitations. For the radical structuralist, needs assessment methods must be critically reviewed to determine inherent biases toward certain population groups. For example, conducting one's own needs assessment survey is costly, but it may be the only way to fully explore the perceived needs of an at-risk population. **Perceived needs** are those that have not come to the attention of service providers, and are therefore invisible in the power domain and ignored in the planning of services. Radical structuralist organizations want to bring these needs to the attention of decision makers, and if their own organization is not meeting those needs, they do not hesitate to prompt leaders, board members, or others about what the organization needs to be doing. There is no tolerance for an organization not following through on its own advocacy mandate.

Those radical structuralist organizations that do provide direct services as part of their mission will collect assessment data for their programs using standardized forms. They are interested in gaining knowledge through the collection of facts and figures. But assessment forms used in traditional agencies may not meet the needs of radical structuralists, since these tools may be insensitive to the very population groups they are championing. Development of tools that are normed to various population groups will be an issue, as will the biases in most existing instruments. When assessment data are collected, the focus will be on the patterns and trends that reveal the need for structural change. The radical structuralist organization will collect those data primarily to use the knowledge gained in the interests of drastic change. They may use the information to make the case that their own organization, programs, and services need to change in order to be sensitive to client needs.

In the assessment process, radical structuralists will include all the relevant stakeholders. In internal change demands in radical structuralist organizations, it will be typical for volunteers and client participants to be a part of the assessment process and recognized as change agents. Change agents will face conflict head-on if there are disagreements about how to begin the assessment process or what data to collect. Given the volatility of the radical structuralist organization, assessments may unapologetically lead to identifying numerous fundamental changes that need to occur within the organization rather than to one specific program or service.

Problem Analysis

With assessment data collected, the radical structuralist views problem analysis as a broadening experience. Rather than trying to prematurely label and narrow, problem analysis becomes a time to engage others in the process, attempting to gain as much new information as possible. Consciousness raising is important in order to avoid false consciousness about what constitutes the problem. Labeling the problem is a group process in which a successful collective commitment to change the organization is as much a goal as the labeling. Thus, the practitioner who does not enjoy the dialectical group process will be miserable in the radical structuralist organization, for the inclusionary nature of practice will continue as the individual engages in problem identifying, organizing, and transforming.

In cause-oriented organizations, there is a need for multiple constituents to own the problem and to be adamant that some action be taken. The importance of working closely together in naming the problem is a bonding experience, and the commitment to the problem definition must be total so that the necessary zeal can be garnered to overcome obstacles and effect fundamental change. Working out differences and dealing with conflict about what are the most urgent needs, problems, or issues in the organization takes time. Every voice must be heard and every participant must be more sophisticated in his or her understanding of the situation; otherwise, the problem analysis is not complete.

Organizing

Mobilization toward a common goal in a radical structuralist organization emerges from the consciousness raising that occurs in assessment and problem identification. Organizing or mobilizing constituents is nothing new to social work. There is a long tradition of community organizing in the profession, and entire casebooks have been written about partnerships among community agencies and multiple constituencies (Nyden, Figert, Shibley, & Burrows, 1997). In the radical structuralist organization, it is assumed that the analyzed problem leads to the need for change in the organization or one of its units because that is the nature of organizations and social problems. Radical structuralist organizations exist in order to tackle the problem by organizing the staff members, participants, volunteers, or others involved so that change can occur.

Fenby's (1991) action model is in keeping with the transformative, empowerment expectations of the radical structuralist organization. The empowerment perspective is also a long time part of the social work tradition (see Levy, 1994; Mondros & Wilson, 1994). Fenby builds her model from a critical approach that moves from the technical aspects of management to mechanisms used to understand the process of action. She identifies the need for deep understanding of underlying values and perceptions on the part of those calling for action in order to advocate appropriately and ethically for desired institutional change. Seeing connections, viewing people holistically, and changing established organizational patterns are elements of the action model understood as "radical action within the patriarchy" (p. 32). In addition, the literature on feminist organizations (for example, Bordt, 1997; Gottlieb, 1992; Hyde, 1992, 2000) and women and power (Odendahl & O'Neil, 1994) go beyond empowerment to provide explicit examples of the link between power and politics theory and feminist theory in organization practice.

The action model asserts that altered power relationships and reallocation of economic and social resources through structural change in social institutions is the goal of social change. This approach continues the tradition of social reform in social work with a primary focus on community organization and development, but it is relevant to organizational development as well. It is also most akin to the radical social work perspective as seen in the work of Bailey and Brake (1975), Galper (1976), and Piven and Cloward (1971). Asserting that economic, political, and social-class stratification is created by and creates structures and institutions that allow some segments of society to suffer while others prosper, the effort is for the organizer, partnering with the oppressed or disadvantaged, to overcome the oppression (Alinsky, 1969; Rothman, 1999). Thus, in radical structuralist organizations, it is not unusual to have staff join with clients to advocate for change in the very organization they helped design to address those changes.

Recognizing injustice, inequity, and exploitation, the idea is to organize the disenfranchised to exert power such that change, by way of concessions from the dominant groups, is extracted. In organizations, dominant groups may take multiple forms—boards of directors, factions, formal or self-designated leaders, and even colleagues who have become comfortable in their positions and have lost sight of the cause. Since resources are scarce and those with resources will not give them up willingly, conflict is inevitable. But it is only through this show of power by way of mass organizing and use of the political process that those with power are forced to share that power. There must be active advocacy, agitation, brokerage, and negotiation to overthrow current institutional arrangements. When the interests of the powerful and the powerless are irreconcilable, harmonious solutions are impossible. Rather, struggle and conflict are inevitable in order to arrive at a new social order. Sometimes this struggle leads to the overthrow of current administration; other times the struggle spawns a totally new organization more appropriately targeted to the desired change. The struggle does not abate until reordering has been accomplished. Interestingly, there is an assumption by some that this new social order will inevitably oppress some segment of society, leading to other waves of dissent, struggle, conflict, and change. It is a cyclical process embedded in consciousness raising and responsive to the intended and unintended consequences of even the most desired change. Therefore, organizing for organizational renewal and change is an ongoing element in radical structuralist organizations.

Collective Transformational Change

Radical structuralists seek logic, given their objectivist assumptions. Therefore, radical structuralists will use the processes of assessment, analysis, and organizing to intervene in what might be called *radicalized planned change*. Instead of an incremental process, collective transformational change will be sought in which planned change processes are intensely used to revolutionize the organization.

Collective transformation in the radical structuralist organization is based on a social action approach that "presupposes the existence of an aggrieved or disadvantaged segment of the population that needs to be organized in order to make demands on the larger community [or organization] for increased resources or equal treatment. . . . This particular approach . . . aims at making fundamental changes . . . including the redistribution of power and resources and gaining access to decision-making for marginal groups" (Rothman, 1995, p. 32). The social action model uses confrontational strategies and tactics such as demonstrating, picketing, striking, marching, boycotting, and even engaging in civil disobedience. This "approach has been widely used by AIDS activists, feminist organizing groups, gay and lesbian organizations, consumer and environmental protection organizations, civil rights and black power groups, and LaRaza and victim rights groups. It has been embraced by the Industrial Areas Foundation and ACORN (Association of Community Organizations for Reform Now) projects, labor unions, including the United Farm workers, and radical political action movements" (Rothman, 1995, p. 32).

Radical structuralist organizations have a history grounded in social action at the turn of the twentieth century and the causes of the 1960s. Today, their interventions are more refined and their adversarial strategies are more sophisticated as public tolerance of disruption has decreased. In an earlier chapter, we introduced different tactics often used in human service organizations—collaboration, campaign, and contest. Campaign and contest tactics are the tactics of choice used by radical structuralist organizations, even within their own organizations. There is little tolerance for neglecting the organization's cause or any of its constituencies.

Table 8.3 provides a summary of the elements of practice characteristics of a radical structuralist organization. It should serve as a summary of the discussion in this section and as a way to assess the degree to which agencies that you know are practicing from a radical structuralist perspective.

Implications of Radical Structuralist Organizations for Social Work Leaders

The nature of this worldview and the theories that are derived from it make the radical structuralist perspective a very dangerous and a very attractive one. It is dangerous because it may be so attractive to those it draws that they may overlook the idea that many others will be repelled by it. This visceral reaction may mean that reasoned analysis of costs and other potentially negative consequences will not be assessed in an even-handed manner in advance. The passion of the perspective may overtake the reason necessary for success and organizations dedicated to a specific "cause" may be seen as having tunnel vision. At the same time, regardless of whatever reasonableness that an approach guided from this perspective may represent, the mere fact that it is designed from such a radical and potentially violent worldview will make some consumers of the thoughts and ideas unable to even consider the perspective out of real fear. This fear may make them overreact to the ideas put forward in the perspective, making reasoned dialogue and analysis impossible.

An organizational leader coming from this perspective will feel much congruence with the values of the social work profession, but paradoxically there will also

TABLE 8.3   **Practice Characteristics in Radical Structuralist Organizations**

Practice Element	Characteristics
Assessment	Systematic data collection is a first step in gathering information about identified issues.
	Standardized, quantitative forms are preferred, although instrument insensitivity to at-risk groups is a concern.
	Assessments provide hard, concrete, objective data to be used by interested parties to analyze the situation or problem.
	Data collection methods should be consistent.
Problem Analysis	Problem analysis flows from objective assessment data.
	With reassessments, analyses may change.
	Analysis requires consideration of objective data known about identified problems.
	Data gathering among all constituencies means engaging in a dialectical process to hear all voices and to achieve consciousness about what constitutes the problem.
Organizing	Mobilizing people for the change is critically important.
	Organizing is very action oriented, inclusive, and fraught with conflict.
Collective Transformational Change	Interventions may be at any level of the organization, but change is framed in the context of the organization's cause.
	Campaign and contest (conflict) tactics are used without reservation if necessary.
	The goal of organizational change is to keep the focus on the advocacy mission, making the organization more viable in its societal transformation.

be challenges to its social justice mission. One of the greatest challenges is the radical structuralist position of ethical absolutism. Once critical consciousness is achieved, there is assumed to be a best way of defining what constitutes the core values of this or any profession. Granted, this best way will be a progressive one, but an absolute one nonetheless. Radical structuralists are fundamentalist in their orientation. In fact, they may be rabid fundamentalists for their cause, failing to see other alternatives. For the mental health advocacy organization, used as an example earlier, there is no way to define what constitutes mental disorders but *their* way; there is no way to serve those with the disorder but *their* way; and the only way to advocate for needed change is head-on and aggressively.

Individualized attention to the person within a particular situation will also present a challenge to the absolutist vision. Each individual is not a unique person, but a member of a certain class of individuals representing either the powerful or the powerless. Understanding and managing complexity regarding individual experiences and motivations becomes a great challenge and mostly beyond the scope of this perspective.

Many aspects of this perspective are congruent with the social work profession. The "scientific" approach to documenting social work service delivery and programming to establish effects and justify changes to improve practices is a plus. In fact, this policy-analytic stance represents one of the most common forms of social work practice found outside the United States. Even so, some aspects of the perspective will be difficult in an essentially conservative profession. For example, radical structuralists eschew organizational structures that tend to impinge on or prevent radical responses to mediate known needs. The manager or worker coming from this perspective may be seen in a traditional organization as a "loose cannon," unable to determine which battle to choose because all battles within the oppressive structure merit waging. The person may be a loose cannon because he or she will not wait for the right time or place for change, preferring to act because no one else will.

This suggests that focus for change action may be difficult. Organizing for change may also be difficult because setting priorities may be impossible. Like the functionalists, assuming rationality and the ability to control what goes on in an organization, the radical structuralist may overlook important dimensions of individual reality in favor of class issues. Overlooking important dimensions of reality because of the focus on quantitatively valid and reliable measures may mean that radical responses become "overkill." In addition, other types of off targeting are also possible. An effort to overcome oppression, exploitation, and dehumanization of one class of individuals may result in yet another class of individuals becoming disadvantaged. Opening opportunities for women and minorities in an organization does not guarantee that a new way of doing business will evolve. Without other important changes, the shift will only represent a different combination of who has power and who does not.

Conclusion

The radical structuralist organization is committed to the alternative "best" way of approaching change. This sets up the expectation that discovery of a generalizable truth is possible and so, too, is control of organizing. When the unexpected happens in the process, this may be seized on as a way to get around traditional approaches to the identified problem. The intent of the radical structuralist is revolution by superimposing a better way to meet identified societal needs.

What the organizational leader gains from radical structuralist assumptions is the creation of new valid and reliable instruments to assess organizational structure and behavior—tools that may be more sensitive to the collective needs of the groups for whom they advocate. The leader gains outcome measurement tools to aid in response to the productivity pressures of outside funders, but this comes with the risk of lack of effectiveness in the outcomes when the significance standard in statistics is used as the only measure of effectiveness. Structural change is the expectation from this perspective and that type of change may be so long coming that measures for funders have come and gone.

When adopting this perspective for assessment, analysis, organizing, and collective transformational change, the social worker loses a view of what is unique to the organization and its members in the organizational environment. Some of the subtle influences regarding processes are not captured in the data collection for decision making. This is true because there is little room for consideration of the more qualitative, affective, intuitive aspects of organizational life due to the rigor expectations that are assumed to be necessary for a critical consciousness.

For the social work leader there is another serious challenge. This perspective and the theories within it offer little help in attending to the special opportunities and challenges provided by that which is different from the norm. Certainly, the radical structuralist seeks to change existing norms, but the assumption that there should be definitive norms remains. In other words, a set of traditional norms may be replaced by a set of nontraditional, but equally rigid, norms and expectations.

We now turn to a third paradigm: interpretive. You will soon see that this paradigm holds assumptions about change and the use of knowledge in common with the functionalists. However, it has a distinctively different perspective on absolutism that distinguishes it from both functionalist and radical structuralist views.

CHAPTER

9 Interpretive Theories about Organizations

In Chapter 4, we introduced the interpretive paradigm, and in this chapter we expand on our original description. We begin by examining themes found in interpretive thinking and the assumptions that flow from this paradigm, resulting in what we are calling interpretive organizations. Following this thorough paradigmatic grounding, the major organizational and organizational behavior theories that can be said to fit within this perspective are identified. We close the chapter with a critical analysis, so that the reader is left with a perspective on what is gained and what is given up when approaching organizations from an interpretive world view. We then move to Chapter 10, which focuses on the understanding necessary for practice in interpretive organizations.

As with the other paradigms, the interpretive organization is a prototype. In day-to-day experiences, it is not always so easy to classify organizations with exact precision. Like organizations based in assumptions from other paradigms that may have staff members and contain units that operate under different assumptions, so may interpretive organizations. When this happens, staff may experience paradoxes as differing assumptions clash. Having read this chapter, it is our hope that the reader will understand why interpretive assumptions about change may collide with those of radical structuralists. It will also be clear that both interpretivists and functionalists seek order and stability, but differ in what they think is necessary and possible. Later it will also be clear why interpretivists and radical structuralists disagree fundamentally around the goals for organizing.

Interpretive Themes

Some of the more modern sociologically or interpretively oriented approaches to understanding organizations are based on assumptions that create the boundaries of the interpretive paradigm. From this perspective, the study of organizations is a mix of rational, serendipitous, and intuitive thinking for both data collection and analysis. This approach is very personal, oriented to process within the organization and interested in *understanding*, rather than controlling organizations or organizational behavior. The assumption is that this very understanding is sufficient for successful organizing. Inquiry from this perspective accepts many ways of know-

Radical Humanist	Radical Structuralist
Interpretive	Functionalist

ing. One can come to know and comprehend the organization from experience, use of the senses, intuition, and conversation, among other ways. In addition, those taking this standpoint hold an interest in the meaningfulness of research findings to both the scholarly and the user communities. Therefore, relevance is a measure of the quality of organizational research. The results need to make sense to those within the organization as well as to the scholars. The focus is on what is unique, although frequently occurring within a certain context. Because the particular context influences what meaning is constructed, it is assumed that the organizational context is central to understanding meaning of any phenomena under investigation in an organization.

For interpretivists, good research represents a rehumanization of the study process in which organizational researchers are human beings dealing with human problems in human ways. Knowledge building is based on the recognition of the gifts of the human instrument—namely, creativity, flexibility, and reflexivity. Language and its interpretation are at the base of the research process because through language comes shared meaning. Therefore, qualitative methods—including observation, participant observation, and various forms of interviewing—are recognized as the most helpful ways to make sense of complex situations. There is an appreciation of both induction and deduction as ways of analysis, along with a recognition of tacit, intuitive knowledge as a rigorous way of coming to an understanding of the views held by those people involved in the situation. From this perspective, truth emerges not as one objective view but as the composite picture of how all those involved think. Observation is shaped by what is observed. Respondents are shaped by their interacting perceptions, expectations about the organizational research, and how the data will be used. What questions are asked and by whom largely determine what the results will be.

In the traditional view of knowledge building, the structural elements of the research design establish objectivity to guard against investigator bias. In interpretivism, objectivity is not expected; therefore, one gets adaptability, insight, and intuitive knowledge. There is no statement about human behavior in organizations being time and context free. There is no certitude—just tentatively held working hypotheses about what is occurring here and now. The most that can be expected as a result of an interpretive process is a statement about characteristics and presumed relationships in this time and this place. What is known is understood to be limited to the organizational context under investigation.

Generalizable theories are of little use in this socially constructed and socially sustained environment. Instead, tentatively held hypotheses or grounded theories, those that are derived from the inquiry itself, are acceptable for the purposes of knowledge building. What is known is held tentatively because it is always changing. Knowledge building occurs within the context of the phenomena under investigation and is aimed at capturing not only the content but also the process of meaning making about the phenomena. The context and its values bound the rules that guide rigorous knowledge building, thus preserving the frames of reference of the participants. Those involved in the research in the context of their organizational practice help to determine what should be researched by whom and what constitutes acceptable results. There is no expectation that results should have meaning to anyone beyond those who participate. No generalizability is called for or expected. Findings may be useful in another time or context, but the responsibility for this determination rests with the consumer of the results—those who hear or read about the research product—not the researchers or research participants.

Assumptions of the Interpretive Paradigm

Unlike both functionalists and radical structuralists, interpretivists see reality as a product of human consciousness. Reality is what a human thinks it is. Interpretivists believe in a subjective, rather than an objective, reality. Subjectivity assumes that the social world exists as an emergent process that is created by the individuals concerned. Reality, then, is not independent of the human mind, but is inextricably linked to individual experience. This makes reality little more than a network of assumptions and intersubjectively shared meanings that are always in flux due to the shaping of multiple individual perspectives. How reality is constructed depends on who is involved in the construction. Rather than the realism of more traditional perspectives, there is a relativist assumption that the world, though ordered, is emergent and always being created intersubjectively. Nothing holds as true across time and context.

Recall that in Chapter 4 four terms that define subjectivism were reviewed. We repeat the figure here so that the reader will have a reference for review (see Figure 9.1). A subjectivist perspective assumes that social reality exists primarily in the human consciousness (a product of one's mind). A subjectivist would say that knowledge about reality is soft, subjective, and natural (antipositivism). Human nature is based in voluntarism; people can be proactive in creating their own realities. Free human beings participate actively in the creating and construction of social reality. Further, to be transmitted and understood, reality must be experienced. One cannot understand without experience. And last, a subjectivist perspective is ideographic, meaning that concern should not be focused on universal

FIGURE 9.1   **Subjectivism: Defining Terms**

Nominalism (in the mind)

Antipositivism (soft, subjective, must be experienced)

Voluntarism (people create their environments)

Ideographic (analyze subjective accounts which one generates by "getting "inside" situations of everyday life)

Source: Adapted from G. Burrell and G. Morgan, *Sociological Paradigms and Organisational Analysis* (Aldershot, England: Ashgate, 1979), Figure 1.1, p. 3. Used by permission.

principles or in an absolutist view. Instead, subjectivists emphasize what is unique and relative to the individual and the ways in which individuals create, change, and interpret the world. This is an insider's view, not the objective view of an outsider.

Since interpretivists see the world subjectively, they do not abide universalism in which there is "one best way." Interpretivists would not agree with functionalists or radical structuralists about the nature of reality. They do not look for universal truths, derived from some external force. Interpretivists look for multiple truths to arise from within people. Therefore, the interpretive organization would be an alternative to traditional ways of thinking because traditional thinking seeks order through locating the best way to do the work of the organization. The interpretive paradigm seeks order but knows that order is socially constructed by those involved and will change over time. What is considered a best way today may no longer be a best way tomorrow.

Interpretivists do seek order, rather than conflict, and this makes them cousins of functionalists. These two paradigms may disagree on how truth is derived, but both interpretivists and functionalists are interested in maintaining order. Like functionalists, interpretivists hold a regulation perspective in which they believe that consensus, social integration, solidarity, needs satisfaction, and actuality are possible and desirable. Figure 9.2 summarizes the concerns of this regulation perspective.

Interpretivists believe in the status quo. However, the status quo will have been constructed through a consensual process very different from a functionalist consensual process. Functionalists gain consensus when members agree on universal principles or assent to the average (those with the most votes win), whereas interpretivists keep refocusing their consensual decisions depending on the current need. The source of truth is found among the members in interaction and is therefore subject to change as new ideas emerge and new members join the organization. Consensus is a process, not a product. It is ongoing so that the process builds solidarity. When individuals are in constant conversation and communication, they become more conversant about the issues under discussion, but they also become

FIGURE 9.2   **Concerns of the Regulation Perspective**

Status quo

Social order

Consensus

Social integration and cohesion

Solidarity

Need satisfaction

Actuality

Source: Adapted from G. Burrell and G. Morgan, *Sociological Paradigms and Organisational Analysis* (Aldershot, England: Ashgate, 1979), Table 2.2, p. 18. Used by permission.

more familiar with those in the conversation. These connections of ideas and people establish the possibility for solidarity, an important element of interpretive stability.

The assumptions of the interpretive paradigm are summarized in Figure 9.3. This figure may serve as a reference to determine the degree to which organizations known to the reader fit within this paradigmatic perspective.

In sum, human nature for the interpretive paradigm involves ultimate possibilities. Human consciousness creates reality through consensus, social integration, and cohesion. Human nature is social. It is within social interaction and solidarity that self-actualization and meaning are created. Truth is what the individual thinks it is, based on personal, subjective experience. Coming to truth is an ongoing process because truth is socially created and recreated. Truth is personally derived or socially constructed. Truth in the organization is a social construct, as well. Inter-

FIGURE 9.3   **Assumptions of the Interpretive Paradigm**

From the Subjectivist Perspective
1. Social reality exists primarily in the human mind.
2. Knowledge about social reality is soft, subjective, and natural.
3. People can be proactive in creating their own realities.
4. Given that individuals create, change, and interpret the world, qualitative approaches to understanding are useful.

From the Regulation Perspective
5. Society is characterized by social order and equilibrium.
6. Knowledge for knowledge's sake is acceptable.
7. Consensus, rather than conflict, is important.

Source: Adapted from Burrell and Morgan (1979, Chapter1).

pretive organizations are intimate organizations. To understand how this intimacy is achieved, let's look at the major organizational theories in this paradigm.

Interpretive Organizational Theories

A number of organizational theories were introduced in previous chapters on functionalism and radical structuralism. These theories tended to seek universal approaches to organization practice and to guide managers toward the best way to achieve goals, encounter the environment, and identify an ideal organizational structure. However, it is important to note that functionalists and radical structuralists are not necessarily naive about subjectivism. Indeed, persons coming from these two paradigms acknowledge that there are differences in the ways people think and in the ways organizations function. However, knowing that there are differences is one thing; embracing them is an entirely different matter. For example, systems theorists recognize the complexity and diversity of organizational environments. To an objectivist, this plurality is something to be controlled. To an interpretivist with a subjectivist focus, this multiplicity of difference is stimulating and interesting, assisting in understanding the organization in context.

Perhaps theories previously introduced could be adapted by interpretivists to enhance their quest for understanding organizations. However, in the 1970s and beyond, the limits of existing theories led to the development of most of the theories that are placed within the parameters of the interpretive paradigm. Since they are relatively new, they are not as well tested or as well developed as some of the more traditional theories that have already been discussed. It should be clear why testing for generalizability is not of interest in this perspective; meaning and meaning making in context is. This lack of traditional testing and the mandate for relevance of what is developed leaves these theories open to criticism, even among interpretivists. Given the objectivist nature of both functionalist and radical structuralist paradigms, interpretive theories are often viewed with disdain since they have not proven to be generalizable through rigorous "scientific" testing, even though most represent insights about organizations that make intuitive sense. Ironically, from an interpretive perspective, if theories attempted to reach this generalizability standard, then this achievement would be contrary to the assumptions of uniqueness and the impossibility of generalization found in the interpretive paradigm. To avoid criticism from traditionalists, interpretivist theoreticians would have to violate the assumptions of the paradigm developed to overcome their own criticisms of traditional ways of understanding organizations.

In previous chapters, we used Shafritz and Ott (2001) as a resource to identify major perspectives in organizational theory. In this chapter, we focus primarily on theories within one of their groupings: organizational culture and sensemaking. Other theoretical perspectives have influenced the development of interpretive theories, but we consider theories of organizational culture and sensemaking to have originated from interpretive assumptions, so they represent the purest examples of this paradigmatic perspective. Organizational culture and sensemaking theories are pivotal in understanding the interpretive organization.

Organizational Culture Theory

Organizational cultural theorists discovered a very different construction of organizational reality by rejecting the methods of traditional organizational research. The units of analysis, the methods, and the approaches undertaken to understand organizations and their cultures were very different from those used in the functionalist quantitative tradition. Borrowing from sociology and anthropology, organizational researchers adapted qualitative research designs and methods to get at the meaning dimension of organizational life. They recognized that inquiry into organizational structure, management information systems, planning processes, market decisions, goals and objectives development, and other areas of focus in the functionalist paradigm will give clues to what the organization is about, but the traditional quantitative methods miss important subtle, unconscious, forgotten elements. Based on their research results, they assert (see for example Van Maanen, 1979, 1983; Van Maanen, Dabbs, & Faulkner, 1982) that to understand the organization's behavior, it is necessary to understand the organization's culture. For these researchers, organizational culture is more easily identified and understood using ethnographic and phenomenological methods rather than standard quantitative methods.

Interest in organizational culture dominated organizational thinking during the 1980s and 1990s. Martin and Frost (1996) metaphorically refer to the struggle among researchers interested in organizational culture as a game of King of the Mountain, in which different theoretical perspectives about cultures vie for control. They categorize three groups of cultural research: (1) the revolutionary vanguard, (2) value engineering and the integration perspective, and (3) the differentiation perspective.

Revolutionary Vanguards. Although the language of culture in organization began to appear in the 1950s, it was mostly used as a way to describe the necessity of socializing the individual into the organization so that he or she would conform to the culture and thus assure better productivity. Books such as *The Changing Culture of the Factory* (Jacques, 1951) and *The Organization Man* (Whyte, 1956) focused on how the individual conformed to corporate life. Not until the 1960s and 1970s did several books begin to pay increased attention to the natural socialization that occurs within organizations and professions. Widely read were books such as *Boys in White* by Becker, Greer, Hughes, and Stauss (1961), which focused on the socialization of students into the medical profession, and Kaufman's *The Forest Ranger* (1960) that studied conformity among remotely stationed rangers in the United States Forest Service.

Early organizational cultural theorists viewed functionalist approaches to organizations as too reliant on rational ways of understanding human behavior.

What was known about organizations was typically based on quantitative analyses, and managers were expected to control numbers rather than to understand people. The emergence of this interpretive approach to understanding organizational culture was filled with hope and expectation as theorists actually advocated for thinking beyond the structural boxes, so common in functionalist thinking, to the humanity of the persons working in the structures. Organizational culture theory gave managers permission and encouragement to examine the human factors often seen as irrelevant in traditional organizations.

The understanding of the mental processes of how organizational participants come to understand organizations is based on a ground-breaking work by Berger and Luckman (1967) who described the cognitive and affective dimensions of what they termed a socially constructed reality. Their work, the basis of the social constructivism and constructionism so popular in direct practice today, was based on their study of the process of organizing. For them, it did not matter whether things were real in and of themselves; it is the perceptions of these things that have impact and are real. Thus, perceptions of the organizational symbols that result from organizational culture became an integral part of organizational culture theory and was called symbolic management.

Shafritz and Ott (2001) list Bolman and Deal's (1997) basic tenets of symbolic management that emerged during the 1970s:

1. The meaning or the interpretation of what is happening in organizations is more important than what actually is happening.
2. Ambiguity and uncertainty, which are prevalent in most organizations, preclude rational problem-solving and decision-making processes.
3. People use symbols to reduce ambiguity and to gain a sense of direction when they are faced with uncertainty. (p. 364)

The culture theories that are congruent with Japanese management and the perceived failures of traditional approaches to organizations began to appear in the 1970s. They represented, and continue to represent, alternative perspectives to traditional organizational theories based on very different assumptions about organizational realities and relationships. These early theorists were interested in understanding how organizational cultures form and change and how culture affects leadership and relationships in establishing organizational directions. As a result, organizations began to be understood in more symbolic ways.

With this vanguard, the struggle among cultural theorists to play King of the Mountain was just beginning (Martin & Frost, 1996, p. 604). There was almost a playfulness among theorists as they focused on new ways of understanding dimensions of organizations that had long been neglected. Martin and Frost categorize these earlier theorists as revolutionary vanguards because they opened the way for others to begin thinking about socialization to organizational culture. This focus on socialization and the impact of existing cultures on workers did not yet include questions about how cultures are formed and change, or how leaders affect culture. In fact, as late as 1987, traditional writers such as Shafritz and Ott (1987) introduced organizational culture in an earlier edition of their book as being countercultural, indicating that this approach to understanding organizations had not yet been accepted as part of mainstream organizational thought.

Value Engineers and Integrationists. Martin and Frost (1996) categorize the next wave of organizational culturalists as value engineers and integrationists. In the early 1980s, more and more popular literature appeared on the topic of organizational culture, and writers declared that a culture could be established by leaders who were in touch with their values or the values one wished to create within the organization. This approach was termed *value engineering* because these theorists assumed that a leader could actually instill her or his own values within the organization.

In attempting to go beyond what earlier theorists had discovered about socialization to an organization's culture, Louis (1980) began to explore what happens when newcomers enter unfamiliar settings. Identifying a number of ways in which newcomers are surprised when they enter cultures, Louis expanded the understanding of the complexity of the transitional process from being an outsider to being inside. This move toward more complex thinking about organizational culture occurred simultaneously with a number of developments in the popular management literature.

When Peters and Waterman published *In Search of Excellence* in 1982, the concept of corporate culture burst into the management literature like a welcomed boost to morale. They promoted a unified corporate culture as the key to organizational success. *Corporate culture* became a buzz word in the popular management literature. Consultants on the development of corporate culture proliferated. Full of practical information on how to develop a unified culture, Peters and Waterman were the first among a barrage of books on how to create and change culture.

In some ways, this energy was built on the popular influence of Ouchi's *Theory Z* (1981), where excellence was seen in organizations that promoted a sense of family. Focus on simplicity and consensus permeated the field. Bored by traditional organizational research, some academicians were enthralled with the possibilities of this approach. The idea of creating a unified culture, without focusing on potential conflicts, was well received, and studies that looked for this consistent, consensual organization-wide cultural experience were labeled as *integration* research (Martin & Frost, 1996, p. 602).

An integrationist perspective fit well with interpretive assumptions. There was a search for consensus, and if conflict did occur, it was seen as a natural transition that occurs when change is about to take place. If an organization was going through a cultural transformation, then some discomfort and uneasiness would naturally need to occur, but the point was to get to a place in which everyone could collaborate within a culture that all parties could embrace. Harmony among members of the culture was the goal. The concept of shared values, vision, and culture revealed an underlying message that organizational members could forge a joint subjective consensus.

Whereas Peters and Waterman's book hit the popular press and influenced both academic and managerial audiences alike, Edgar Schein's 1985 book, *Organi-*

zational Culture and Leadership, offered a more theoretical or academic approach that spelled out the cultural concept in detail. Schein (1992, pp. 9–10) provides a list of concepts used by various writers to allude to culture:

1. "Observed behavioral regularities when people interact," including their language, customs, traditions, and rituals
2. "Group norms" that evolve as standards and values for working together
3. "Espoused values" that people announce as the beliefs that guide what they do
4. "Formal philosophy," the board policies and ideologies that direct the work
5. "Rules of the game," often known as *the ropes*
6. "Climate," the physical layout and how it *feels*
7. "Embedded skills," the ability to pass on competencies to the next generation
8. "Habits of thinking, mental models, and/or linguistic paradigms," as things taught to new members as they are socialized to the organization
9. "Shared meanings," group understandings that develop as they work together
10. "Root metaphors or integrating symbols," the ideas, feelings, images, and even physical layout that represent the group's artifacts.

Schein's point is that all of these concepts reflect aspects of an organization's culture, but that none of them are culture unto themselves. He adds that culture implies two additional elements: *"structural stability* in the group," [and] *"patterning or integration* of the elements into a larger . . . gestalt that ties together the various elements and that lies at a deeper level" (p. 10). The point of view needs to hold together and permeate the perspectives and behaviors of organizational participants.

Schein (1992) defines *organizational culture* as "a pattern of shared basic assumptions that the group learned as it solved its problems of external adaptation and internal integration, that has worked well enough to be considered valid and, therefore, to be taught to new members as the correct way to perceive, think, and feel in relation to those problems" (p. 12). Note that Schein begins with "shared basic assumptions." Yet, one often enters organizations in which those basic assumptions are so ingrained that they are often not even recognized on a conscious level. Have you ever entered an organization and known that you had stepped into another culture in which you did not know "the rules"? Perhaps you had a sense that you said or did something "wrong," but you didn't have a clue about what it was? Chances are that you tripped over a basic unstated assumption that everyone else held as the correct way of behaving in that culture. Note that Schein indicates that these assumptions are *considered valid,* whereas Louis (1980) would call these surprises. Have you ever tried to change an organization and wondered why you met resistance, when the change seemed so logical to you? Perhaps what you considered valid was not what others considered valid. Perhaps the stated norms or rules were not *really* the norms guiding behavior in that organization.

Solving problems of external adaptation and internal integration refer to the ways in which organizational members go about working on their relationship with the larger external environment and dealing with issues internal to the organization. Schein (1992) contends that adapting externally includes gaining a consensus on the following elements:

1. *Mission and strategy*—coming up with a shared understanding of the organization's mission, major task, and manifest and latent functions.
2. *Goals*—using the core mission to develop a consensus around goals.
3. *Means*—figuring out ways to attain the goals (e.g. organizational structure, staffing, incentive systems, power and authority relationships).
4. *Measurement*—establishing criteria to measure how the work is going, including an information system to track effectiveness.
5. *Correction*—identifying remedial or repair strategies to use when goals are not met.

According to Schein, if these five areas are minimally necessary for an organization to structure itself to survive in its environment, then there is great potential for misunderstanding when persons from different backgrounds enter the organization. What if you were from a voluntary organization with a very loose structure in which power and authority relationships were considered unimportant, where people worked as colleagues, and teams worked toward goal achievement with minimal supervision? What would happen when you entered a large public bureaucracy in which authority and power were differently defined and in which teamwork was not encouraged? No matter how much you liked your colleagues, this would be an adjustment to a different culture. Would you become acculturated, meaning you would embrace this new culture? Or might you accommodate, missing the familiar culture from which you had come? Might you even want to change the culture you had entered?

Schein also elucidates the factors required for internal integration of an organization's culture. These include the development of a common language and conceptual categories, group boundaries, power and status dimensions, norms concerning relationships, rewards and punishments, and even ways to explain uncontrollable events (Schein, 1991, p. 66). Schein explains that cultural assumptions provide a filter for how one views the world and that if one is stripped of that filter, anxiety and overload will be experienced. Cultural solutions offer routine answers to what would normally be complex problems. The major reason organizational members resist cultural change is because it challenges deeply held assumptions that stabilize one's world—it questions the status quo. This is why members of a dysfunctional culture might choose to retain current assumptions rather than risk having their cultural roots challenged. Schein also lists three levels of organizational culture, as reflected in Figure 9.4. Identification with artifacts, values, and assumptions allows the group to develop, and group development results in culture. These are also clues about ways an outsider can get to know an organization's culture.

In the theoretical literature, it was Schein's work that revealed the necessity of identifying the assumptions that leaders bring to an organization. He contended that it is those assumptions that will help identify how acceptable change occurs within an organization. Kilmann and colleagues (1985) and other writers also rec-

FIGURE 9.4   Levels of Organizational Culture

Level 1: Artifacts
— Most visible level of the culture
— The organization's constructed physical and social environment
— Use of physical space
— Output of group
— Written and spoken language
— Metaphors used
— Artistic productions
— Members' behavior

Level 2: Values
— Cognitively transformed into a belief when holding that value works
— Ultimately some values will be transformed into assumptions
— "Espoused values" are what people say they believe, but they don't always act in accordance with them; this would be a separation of culture from behavior

Level 3: Basic Underlying Assumptions
— So taken for granted that one finds little variation in a unit
— Theories-in-use
— Often hard to assess whether we are dealing with organizational culture or
  ■ professional culture
  ■ disciplinary culture
  ■ regional variations
  ■ ethnicity
  ■ gender

Source: Adapted from Schein (1992, Chapter 2).

ognized that values, beliefs, assumptions, perceptions, norms, and artifacts in organizations are the forces behind organizational activities and change. In fact, organizational culture is the social dynamic that moves people; culture is the behind-the-scenes, yet motivating, theme that adds guidance and meaning for actions within an organization. These internal actions are dependent on the patterns of assumptions held by those in the organization. Those assumptions are linked to what worked in the past. They are not necessarily a conscious part of the current organizational ethos, but remain forceful even when the organizational context changes. The culture tends to remain an underlying force, unquestioned, universally accepted, and not open to critical analysis. The culture remains the unquestioned reasons for what is done; it controls behavior. Unlike what has been asserted in other theories, it is not personal preferences, nor formal rules, authority, or norms of rational behavior that control organizational behavior. Instead, it is cultural norms, values, beliefs, and assumptions that maintain the status quo in the interpretive organization. Context is everything.

It is very important to recognize that functionalists wanting to know how to manipulate and persuade employees also embraced the more popularized version of the corporate culture discussion. The discussion was attractive because it facilitated employees embracing a common point of view so that productivity could increase. The functionalists' language may have been interpretive, but the use of culture was anything but a subjectivist appreciation of difference. Instead, managers looked for ways to change existing cultures and to engineer (or reengineer) values for the organization's benefit. For example, managers couched their desires for change in terms such as *empowerment* of employees and *team work* when they were unwilling to relinquish control over decision making. Persons with no intent of relinquishing control can appeal to a sense of group identity and espouse norms of inclusiveness. Such uses of organizational culture to place one's own values over the values of others is anything but interpretive in its intent. One could say that such a manager is a functionalist in interpretive clothing.

An example of the functionalist usurping of an interpretive concept can be found in Shafritz and Ott (2001), who devote a chapter in their book on classics of organizational theory to what they call the organizational culture reform movements. These are viewed as "a concession to readers and reviewers who repeatedly asked us to include articles that are representative of the current trends in management or organization. The 'reform movements' that are represented here share a common theme—the centrality of organizational culture" (p. 425). Included in this chapter is the work of Dr. W. Edwards Deming, the Total Quality Management (TQM) Movement, Japanese management concepts such as the Z Organization, Peters and Water's Excellence Movement, Senge's work on the learning organization, Al Gore's report on reinventing government, and the whole concept of reengineering. We refer the reader to this particular chapter in Shafritz and Ott or to the incredible amount of literature on how to change organizational culture that can be seen on the bookshelves of any management library. But beware of the underlying assumptions in most of these works. The language is interpretivist, but the goals are often functionalist. For the most part, these movements have been focused on applying the concept of organizational culture with the purpose of providing prescriptive techniques for managers and leaders whose better understanding of organizational culture could then be used to control and change the organization. This is not interpretive paradigm organizational thinking.

Differentiators. Within interpretivist thought, as excitement about organizational culture and the proliferation of integration research grew, another group of scholars were working independently on similar concepts. They agreed that traditional organizational theory and research was uncreative and dull. Some of these scholars were qualitative researchers who were relieved finally to see interest develop in more than quantitative methods. Others were persons who had been on the fringe of organizational research, convinced that something new had to happen in understanding organizations and hoping to capture new ways of thinking that would go beyond traditional ways of knowing.

Like integration studies, differentiation studies focused on topics such as values, symbolism, meaning, and emotion—topics neglected in traditional organizational research. However, differentiators did not limit their focus to the informal, interactional, esthetic aspects of culture. They advocated for a more holistic view in which formal practice and structural aspects of organizations were considered, as well.

Reacting to the value engineers and integrationists, some differentiators faced the challenges of conflict head-on, believing that a good organizational study could not ignore the complexities of deep-rooted conflict, inconsistencies, and differences in interpretation among cultural members. Given their predisposition to focus on conflict and inconsistences, differentionists draw heavily from Marxist/critical theory and take a more critical than interpretive perspective. Having less concern about consensus than their interpretive colleagues, organizational cultural theorists and researchers who come from a differentiation perspective eventually became more aligned with the assumptions of the radical humanist paradigm. Therefore, when we summarize the placement of organizational theories within the interpretive paradigm later in this chapter, we will place organizational culture differentiators very close to the line between the two paradigms.

Sensemaking Theory

Closely related and highly compatible with organizational culture theory is sensemaking theory. The idea of sensemaking in organizations developed when Roethlisberger and Dickson (1939) suggested that an organization's environment could be understood based on the meaning that employees attach to objects or events. More modern thoughts about sensemaking are concerned with language and symbols as well as understanding.

Historically, sensemaking theory emerged form the legacy of Festinger's (1957) cognitive dissonance theory. This theory holds that explanations of events are often based on a retrospective, rather circular thinking, instead of a linear process based on linear logic. For example, when a person chooses among mutually exclusive alternatives, he or she will have to live with his or her choice. Since most such choices have negative as well as positive consequences, the person may experience anxiety or feel agitated. This is dissonance. To reduce dissonance, the person will quickly focus on the negative features of the alternatives he or she did not take, while simultaneously playing up the positive traits of the selected option. Retrospectively, the person alters the meaning of his or her decision or action and changes the meaning of the other possible options, thus constructing a plausible story that makes "sense" and helps to reduce the dissonance and explain the "rightness" of the choice.

Some feminist scholars on organization can be placed in the interpretive paradigm for their contributions to sensemaking theories. The feminist theorists in the interpretivist perspective are those who focus on how gender affects culture and leadership. Calás and Smircich (1996) categorize feminist theories and their contribution to organizational studies as liberal, radical, psychoanalytic, Marxist, socialist, poststructuralist, and third world/(post)colonial (p. 220). The liberal and socialist traditions fit with interpretive assumptions, although Calás and Smircich would argue that the liberal feminist tradition is functionalist in orientation.

Because liberal feminists tend to use quantitative methods, they might be considered functionalists, but because they base their work on interpretive assumptions regarding meaning making for women in organizations, they are very much within the interpretive paradigm. Many of these feminist organizational scholars (see, for example, Davies, 1975; Hearn & Parkin, 1987; Kelly, 1991) assert that male control of organizations has been accomplished by the use of a male lens to understand organizations. It is the feminist perspective, with questions in the woman's voice, that show organizations are not gender neutral and that research and theories used to understand organizational structure and behavior are also not gender neutral.

Gherardi (1995) brings culture and gender together for sensemaking by arguing that "organizational cultures differ according to their gender regimes and, consequently, according to the social patternings that they give to gender citizenship. . . . How gender is 'done' in an organization is a crucial cultural phenomenon; and how it can be 'done' differently is a challenge to all those who work for organizations " (pp. 3–4). She further asserts, "In a gender regime which systematically devalues everything connected with the female, the organization can never become democratic, whatever affirmative action it may introduce, and whatever equal opportunity legislation may be promulgated" (p. 9). It is from the socialist feminists that the intersections of gender, race, class, and sexuality have been highlighted (see Acker, 1990, 1994; Collins, 1990; Lugones & Spelman, 1983) to expand sensemaking about organizations.

Without necessarily adopting a gender lens, the mental processes used to make sense of organizational environments are central to sensemaking theory. For example, conscious thought in understanding and coping with organizations is the focus of the work of Louis (1980) and features change, contrast, and surprise for newcomers to organizations. Her research on retrospective accounts to explain organizational surprises indicates that "newcomers often attach meanings to action, events, and surprises in the new setting using interpretation schemes developed through their experiences in other settings. Based on these, "inappropriate and dysfunctional interpretations may be produced" (p. 450). From this research came a call for practices that facilitate sensemaking, including research techniques that produce relevant and useful information for the context in which the research is undertaken.

Gareth Morgan (1986) provided more clarity about the symbolic aspects of making sense of organizations in his *Images of Organizations*. In 1997, Morgan published a second edition, the first version of which had sold extremely well because it touched a chord with readers attempting to define and understand organizations. Morgan demystified what was often seen as "a kind of magical power to understand and transform the situations [successful managers and problem solvers] encounter" (p. 3). His premise was "that all theories of organization and management are based on implicit images or metaphors that lead us to see, understand, and manage organizations in distinctive yet practical ways" (p. 4). Defining *metaphors* as "attempt[s] to understand one element of experience in terms of another" (p. 4), he proceeded to elaborate on the metaphorical images most frequently used when people try to define and understand organizations. Morgan's list of metaphors are:

- Organizations as machines
- Organizations at organisms
- Organizations as brains
- Organizations as cultures
- Organizations as political systems
- Organizations as psychic prisons
- Organizations as flux and transformation
- Organizations as domination

Morgan details each metaphor, identifies theories that reflect each metaphor, and examines the strengths and limitations of each. Morgan's metaphors highlight certain interpretations of the organization. For example, if one encounters organizations as prisons, then he or she will act within the organization as if it were a prison. Morgan goes beyond connecting the metaphor to understanding and behavior by saying that the metaphor can also be used as an instrument of change. Metaphorically imagining an organization as different from what it is can be the first step to changing the character and culture of the organization. Since the ways in which individuals read organizations are distinctive, but also only partial pictures, the metaphor can be used as a device for expanding conversations within the organization. Understanding each other's use of metaphor is to understand each other's way of thinking and seeing the organizational world. This is a step to understanding the complex, ambiguous, and paradoxical world of the organization. For Morgan, metaphorical thinking presents new ways of approaching and solving organizational problems.

As another mechanism for sensemaking and problem solving, Starbuck and Milliken (1988) focus on how individuals place stimuli into some kind of framework. Sackman (1993) was interested in the mechanisms organizational members use to attribute meaning to events in order to understand the "standards and rules for perceiving, interpreting, believing and acting that are typically used in cultural settings" (p. 33). These scholars of sensemaking in organizations are interested in how individuals organize information structurally, comprehend information, compensate for surprise, construct meaning, and interact with others in the organization in pursuit of mutual understanding.

Weick (1995), who recognizes the instability of organizational contexts and the real challenges in providing "relevant and reliable" information, sees sensemaking as less about discovery and more about invention. Because as an interpretivist, there is no reality "out there," but only that which can be constructed in the mind, to engage in sensemaking is to construct, filter, frame, and create that which can act as fact (Turner, 1987). Weick embraces the ambiguity and uncertainty of organizational life. He sees sensemaking as the way to take advantage of the situation and has identified its seven properties:

1. *Identity.* As individuals name, describe, and analyze organizations, they rethink their understandings based on their changing experiences and their effects on sense of self. Therefore, "making sense" of an organization is tied to

a person's identity, and understandings about that organization change as the person grows and develops.

2. *Retrospection.* Understanding organizations is based on "lived" experience because people make sense of what happens after they have experienced reality. According to Weick, "Students of sensemaking find forecasting, contingency planning, strategic planning and other magical probes into the future wasteful and misleading if they are decoupled from reflective action and history" (p. 30).

3. *Enactment.* Organizations are understood in the context of the actions that are possible within them. Action in organizations—such as enacting policies, writing rules, setting time lines, organizing space, establishing categories, and changing the environment in numerous ways—give meaning to the organization and life within it.

4. *Social.* The actions that occur in organizations are interactive, people working with people. Shared experiences and processes do not always mean agreement or shared understanding, but there is shared history. How a person is socialized, and the groups to whom one looks for feedback, will influence what a person does and thinks about in organizational life.

5. *Ongoing.* Weick contends "that sensemaking never starts [because] people are always in the middle of things, which become things" (p. 43). Connecting events, seeing how things fit with the past, and even puzzling over interruptions to routines are ongoing. People's interests and experiences continue to change, and therefore understanding the organization itself is ongoing.

6. *Extracted cues.* Extracted cues are pieces of information from which people draw implications about organizations. What a person makes of an extracted cue depends first on themselves and their lived experience and then on context, both in terms of what cue is extracted and in how it is interpreted.

7. *Plausibility.* Sensemaking does not require that people in organizations know the "truth." In fact, they piece together extracted cues, so that they know enough to do current projects acceptably. This means that "sufficiency and plausibility take precedence over accuracy" (p. 62).

Weick (1995) sees both organizations and sensemaking as "cut from the same cloth" because to organize is to "impose order, counteract deviations, simplify, and connect, and the same holds true when people try to make sense" (p. 82). In summarizing his approach to sensemaking in organizations, he sees it as necessary to understand ideologies, paradigms, theories of action, traditions, and stories because their content pervades organizations and colors interpretations. All of these are in play all of the time. Moments of meaning occur when any two of the paradigms, theories, and so on become connected in a meaningful way. Those meanings vary as a function of the content and the connection. Thus, there is no such thing as a fixed meaning for the content resources of sensemaking, but simply because the meanings of content shift is no reason to ignore content and focus just on the process of connecting. Sensemaking, after all, is about the world. And what is being asserted about that world is found in the labels and categories implied by frames. These words express and interpret; these words include and exclude; these words matter (p. 132).

The concepts of organizational culture and sensemaking are grounded in the interpretive paradigm. These theories are designed to recognize subjectivity and to focus on interactions within the organization. Figure 9.5 provides a summary of where these theories can be placed within the interpretive paradigm.

Costs and Benefits of the Interpretive Paradigm and Its Theories

The antipositivistic, antideterministic stance of the interpretive paradigm is troublesome to many who think that humans are not as free and undetermined as interpretivists assert they are (see Reed, 1993; Thompson, 1993). In addition, the move from realism to relativism that is a logical consequence of this paradigm's assumptions is unacceptable to those who believe in immutable truth. But most of the criticism about organizational research derived from this perspective is due to its subjectivist, insider perspective. It is not generalizable, and therefore not useful to

Radical Humanist	Radical Structuralist
Organizational Culture Diffusionists **Interpretive** Organizational Culture Revolutionary Vanguard Organizational Culture Integrationists Sensemaking Theory	**Functionalist**

FIGURE 9.5   **Organizational Theories within the Interpretive Paradigm**

the traditional scientific community. Preferences for language-based research that relies on qualitative methods and is attentive to various perspectives makes it impossible to escape the criticism of the traditionalist researcher whose scientific standards include randomization, objectivity, and other controls for generalizability. To date, the alternative approaches to research rigor proposed in a variety of methodologies developed from this perspective (see Lincoln & Guba, 1985; Rodwell, 1998) have yet to receive acceptance in the more powerful traditional scientific community, though respect and acceptance is growing with scholars from other paradigmatic perspectives.

As with any criticism of qualitative methods, qualitative interpretive research in organizations is not efficient. Though research based on the language and the thinking of the participants provides a certain richness and attention to subtleties and is responsive to the complexity of modern organizational environments, it is not produced without great costs. Interpretive organizational research takes much more time in the process of data collection and data analysis. Overall, the research is more expensive. The answers that are provided via the research product are not as "clean" and precise as those produced in traditional research, even if they do provide more visceral meaning to the consumers of the research results.

On the other hand, research participants benefit more noticeably in interpretive research because of the change in power of the inquirer. Research "subjects" become inquiry "participants" who help to shape the process and evaluate the quality of the product. Since there is recognition that the participants own their data and have their own perspective on the phenomena under investigation, the power differential between the research and the researched is changed. Participants have a say in the process and by virtue of this involvement, unintended consequences, both positive and negative, accrue to all involved. The research is never easy and the researcher is never really in charge once the research has begun. This suggests that much less control of the research process is possible so that those organizations that cannot risk negative findings will not have the capacity to accept inquiry processes that can emerge in surprising ways.

As far as we can tell, Theory Z (Ouchi, 1980), a pure framework for an interpretivist organization, has not been fully implemented within an organization in the United States. Perhaps the communal, all-encompassing nature of the approach is not technologically appropriate in a culture that has such respect for individuality. On the other hand, perhaps the time necessary to introduce such a dramatic departure from a traditional hierarchical bureaucracy has rarely been afforded organizations choosing to experiment with the approach. However, many of the elements of a Theory Z approach have found their way into the organizational excellence literature popularized by Peters and Waterman (1982). The same is true for most of the organizational culture and sensemaking theoretical work with the focus on recognizing and working with diversity.

Each of these approaches offers interesting insights into the processes involved in developing policies, practices, and organizational structures that can benefit both the organization and the individuals within them. These theories do not provide an "easy fix" for organizations wanting quality and efficiency while also addressing the human side of the enterprise. None can provide the "one best" approach, no matter how much managers and employees wish that were possible. In fact, many of these theories will provide more questions than answers. Further, the answers that are produced will be unsettling because they will underscore how much more is needed to achieve both political and economic wisdom within organizations.

Conclusion

The theories that are based on the interpretive paradigm are in their youth, developmentally. They have opened up new ways of viewing organizations that were not even considered appropriate, much less central to organizational thinking, by early theorists. Depending on the use of theoretical concepts, or on the school of thought within a theoretical category, theories in one paradigm have influenced theory development in others. In the interpretive paradigm, the focus has shifted to the way in which meaning and culture develop among diverse organizational players.

With this shift has come the recognition that there exists no one "best" way of doing organizational practice. Instead, the "best" that is possible is what makes sense and works for the here and now. No quest for certainty persists in this paradigm. It is replaced with an acceptance of complexity, ambiguity, and uncertainty. But along with this tenuousness comes a depth of understanding and local knowledge that provides its own security and solace within organizational life. The search for perfection has been replaced with pragmatics. It is enough to know what works now.

We next turn to the interpretive organization, the prototype of the interpretive paradigm. It is time to see how the themes and theories in this chapter can be translated into the work of understanding organizations in order to practice within an interpretive perspective.

CHAPTER 10

Understanding for Practice in Interpretive Organizations

Interpretive organizations are interested in maintaining a status quo that has been established through ongoing collaboration and consensus-building processes. Like the functionalist organization, incremental change and minimal conflict is acceptable in interpretive organizations. Both types of organizations are seekers of a status quo, but they go about determining the nature of that status quo in different ways. Whereas functionalists believe there is a best way that forms *the* status quo and is guided by universal truths, interpretivists accept a more fluid status quo. Given this fluidity, the status quo is simply what is agreed upon today. This will shift and change as new ideas and thoughts emerge and as a new consensus is established; thus, the interpretivist status quo evolves as an ongoing process.

It is important to recognize that interpretive organizations may be developed by different groups that come together because there is a need to *understand* a situation or set of circumstances that has been neglected by other organizations. The intent is to increase awareness, to promote collaboration, and to enhance apprehension. The concept of a *think tank* is interpretive in that these organizations emerge so that scholars and practitioners can engage in dialogue and begin to understand complex situations. The think tank is particularly interpretive when multiple perspectives are garnered to create a consensus. Think tanks may be affiliated with or used to promote different political agendas (a more functionalist or radical structuralist notion), but for those who come together to seek more understanding, the process of thinking things through is highly interpretive. Similarly, some professional associations formed to increase knowledge about specific groups of people may also be interpretivist. For example, the Gerontological Society of America is an association of persons interested in studying and understanding aging, whereas the Child Welfare League of America is dedicated to increasing providers' awareness and competence about services to children. Organizations created by study commissions or designed to educate clients and staff about complicated problems and issues can be interpretivist in their orientation.

Although think tanks and associations are dedicated to promoting awareness and understanding, and typically stop short of delivering direct services, there are interpretive organizations that do plan and deliver human services. These organizations are those that promote client awareness and understanding, seeing knowledge as a way to empower clients. Instead of seeking broad social change (cause advocacy), these organizations seek to provide case advocacy in that they encourage clients to fully participate and work with staff toward the goal of deep understanding for personal change. An example of this type of organization would be a freestanding hospice that uses a team of professionals and paraprofessionals to work with families and patients. Such an organization would be dedicated to preparing families and patients for the dying process, providing staff to assist clients as they seek meaning in their final months, weeks, and days. This meaning making is an interpretivist experience, in that each patient's journey will be highly individualized and the staff will have to be flexible in encouraging the patient's meaning to emerge rather than imposing their own views. This fluid, evolving experience engages staff, families, and patients in a customized process since each person is unique, and both staff and clients will construct their own personal stories of what is happening. Awareness and understanding are encouraged and supported, with meaning being tied to the process, since death is the ultimate outcome.

Freestanding hospice organizations are interpretive in their approach, as are hospice programs that are housed in larger health care networks. In the latter case, when interpretive programs are placed within functionalist organizations, staff will encounter contradictions bordering on paradox. While the larger system may be stressing outcome measurement and efficiency, hospice staff will be highly focused on processes that may be perceived as anything but efficient. Both goals are being held at the same time. In this example, a hospice team dedicated to making joint visits is using interpretive techniques—gathering persons with different perspectives together to make their best joint decision about patient care. Seen as highly inefficient and labor intensive to tie up so many professionals simultaneously, a functionalist might suggest that joint visits are too costly and should be limited. To the interpretivist, making fewer joint visits would mean that the importance of multiple viewpoints and expertise would be reduced and thus less collaboration and meaning making would occur. Indeed, interpretivists are concerned with the meaningfulness and civility of the process because it is understood that the network of relationships within the process actually create meaning.

This chapter focuses on what is needed to understand practice in interpretive organizations. We return to the five questions originally introduced in Chapter 6 to guide the reader: (1) What are the characteristics of organizations most likely to operate from the assumptions of this paradigm? (2) How does one begin to assess this type of organization? (3) What language is used in these organizations? (4) What approaches to practice are most likely to fit within this type organization? and (5) What are the implications of paradigmatic assumptions for social work leaders in this type organization?

Characteristics of Interpretive Organizations

Unlike both functionalist and radical structuralist organizations that are devoted to finding objective external truths, interpretive organizations are open to different ways of understanding that emerge in context. However, before one assumes that interpretive organizations have nothing in common with radical structuralist organizations, it is important to recognize that both are considered alternative agencies. Neither is a dominant form of organizational life. Interpretive and radical structuralist organizations are quite different types of alternative organizations, but nonetheless they suffer some of the same consequences of not being mainstream, functionalist agencies. Table 10.1 summarizes the characteristics of alternative agencies presented previously, but this time we have included a comparison with the interpretive organization. We encourage you to look at the differences in this comparison, and to return to the similar comparison for radical structuralist organizations (Table 8.1) in order to begin to determine for yourself their similarities and differences.

TABLE 10.1   Characteristics of Alternative Agencies: The Interpretive Organization

Characteristics	Alternative Agencies	Interpretive Organizations
Clients	Are formed to advocate for or deliver services to groups whose needs are not being met by other agencies	Will deliver *case* advocacy, which is more individually focused
Funding	Do not have well-established funding sources, which poses a risk to agency survival	Will need to find funding sources that focus on research about or understanding about problems or on collaboration
Leadership	Typically are inspired by a charismatic individual who mobilizes volunteers and paid staff to action	Will seek collaborative, process-oriented leaders who work well with persons who have diverse views and can build consensus
Service Delivery	Establish service delivery approaches, using client participation and evolving protocols	Will engage client participation designed to enhance understanding of problems
Size	Are typically small, given available resources	Will typically be small agencies or units within larger agencies
Staff	Are heavily dependent on volunteers and staff who will work for less than other agencies pay	Will be highly inclusive of volunteers and staff, attending to the importance of process
Values	Have guiding values and ideologies that run counter to dominant opinions, doctrines, and practices	Run counter to ideologies of objectivism (external truth), accepting of alternative opinions and practices, and multiple values

The characteristics in Table 10.1 reveal a great deal about interpretive organizations. They are formed to help clients whose needs are not being met by other organizations or society at large. Their case advocacy, which is highly attendant to process, makes the organization vulnerable in seeking funding, for funders will have to recognize and respect the importance of meaning making at a time when outcome measurement dominates. The way in which interpretivists include and use volunteers and the type of leadership required set them apart from their radical structuralist and functionalist counterparts. Although the organization may work closely in coalitions and alliances with more traditional agencies, its methods will be much more focused on collaboration and consensus building, and it will be time consuming, as the interpretive organization listens to multiple perspectives on every issue. For functionalists and radical structuralists who believe in established universal truths, their interpretivist colleagues will be seen as somewhat tiresome and inefficient.

As alternative organizations, both interpretive and radical structuralist organizations have similar issues, but they are dealt with differently because they are grounded in different assumptions. For example, both type organizations will advocate for clients who are not served by traditional agencies, but advocacy will be done differently. The interpretive organization will seek to engage clients in a collaborative process with staff to better understand their problems, whereas radical structuralists are never satisfied with "just" understanding problems. Instead, radical structuralists do not rest until the societal structure that contributes to the problem has been changed and the voice of the client is understood from an **etic** (outsider's) perspective, not **emic** (insider's) perspective. Interpretivists might be viewed by radical structuralists as being somewhat wishy-washy and tedious because they examine every aspect of a problem and seek multiple perspectives to enhance understanding. The radical structuralist finds this process frustrating—in fact, disempowering—because it takes much too much time, leads to individual rather than class or collective change, and does not ultimately result in transformational societal change. On the other hand, the interpretivist is frustrated with the impatience and lack of insight demonstrated by the radical structuralist who is seen as racing forward without adequate understandings. Actually, the two paradigms have something to offer one another. The in-depth understandings about social problems spawned by interpretivists can actually be fuel for social change if used by radical structuralists, should they decide to respect one another's different assumptions.

Interpretive organizations will likely be smaller in size than functionalist organizations because their approaches and resource limitations may limit their ability to grow. They may choose to maintain a certain size in order to assure that all stakeholders have a voice in the construction of the agency and the services provided. On the other hand, some interpretive organizations at the national level actually grow quite large because they are seen as ongoing, developing sources of knowledge about issues that are constantly changing. For example, the Urban Institute in Washington, D.C., produces policy briefs, occasional papers, state reports, and highlights of state reports on various social welfare policies. They maintain a databank of all 50 states and the District of Columbia in areas including income security; health; child well-being; demographic, fiscal, and political conditions; and social services. They make this information available to multiple users, including researchers, journalists, policymakers, citizens, and community groups. Their intent is to provide information and to make the views of various parties accessible.

Another example is the Association for Research on Nonprofit Organizations and Voluntary Action (ARNOVA), an international group of scholars and practitioners dedicated to understanding voluntarism and the nonprofit sector. Bringing together members at annual conferences, increased understandings of the third or voluntary sector is enhanced as varying perspectives are presented based on the latest research. The Urban Institute and ARNOVA do not advocate for a particular viewpoint, as would radical structuralist organizations. Instead, they are interpretive organizations that seek to promote and increase knowledge, understanding, and awareness—constantly seeking new perspectives and different views so that the understanding of complex issues can be enhanced.

We are sure that readers have encountered interpretive organizations in their daily lives, even though they may not have classified them as such. Even if you have not practiced in such an organization, you will likely have received mailings from or heard about the work interpretive organizations do because they are bent on increasing awareness and understanding. Whether their focus is a particular problem (e.g., domestic violence), a disease (e.g., Alzheimer's disease), or a group (e.g., welfare recipients), these organizations often make appeals for money to support their research or programs.

Beginning to Assess the Interpretive Organization

Basic underlying assumptions about locus of control and change in an interpretive organization differ from what has been seen so far. Given its regulation perspective, the interpretive organization is not designed to seek radical change. Like functionalists, persons in interpretive organizations can be change agents, but they focus on changes that are controllable and manageable so that harmony can be restored or maintained. One could say that their cultures are steeped in a standard of civility. Change is not intended to alter basic structures, but to help people understand and find meaning in their situations within existing structures. The interpretive organization exemplifies in many ways the learning organization as described by Peter Senge (1990): "At the heart of the learning organization is a shift of mind from seeing ourselves as separate from the world to connected to the world, from seeing problems as caused by someone or something 'out there' to seeing how our own actions create the problems we experience. A learning organization is a place where people are continually discovering how they create their reality. And how they can change it" (pp. 12–13). Therefore, the environment in which the organization operates is viewed by interpretivists as a set of forces to be understood as much as possible so that social order can be reestablished through incremental change that comes from learning.

Given interpretive and regulation perspectives, Table 10.2 provides a summary of some of the ways in which interpretivists approach their work. The foci and tasks in Table 10.2 are the same as that introduced in previous practice chapters, but the goals of the organization will have changed to reflect a very different orientation. The table provides an overview of the basic goals of the interpretive organization in important categories one might use to assess an agency to determine the degree of its interpretive focus. We will now briefly expand on each area.

Focus A: Agency-Environment Relationships

We will examine the interpretive organization's context-dominated view of the environment, elaborating particularly on funding and clients.

Environment.   The interpretive organization recognizes the importance of the environment as part of the broader context in which it operates. There is an appreciation of and a need for information from diverse opinions, perspectives, and values to influence the organization for meaningful practice. Rather than trying to ignore or control the environment like functionalist organizations, interpretive organizations welcome the diversity of opinions represented by environmental forces and recognize that the environment has everything to do with their structuring for success. Rather than engendering conflict within the environment like radical structuralists, the interpretive organization seeks to be inclusive and to encourage participation from diverse groups and persons entering the organization from the larger environment while at the same time managing conflict as consensus emerges about the structure and focus of the organization.

In the interpretive organization, the environment is seen as a critically important context or backdrop against which the organization assesses its daily work. For interpretivists, context is everything. It is within context that the interpretive organization creates a consensual organizational culture and makes sense out of processes, problems, and issues of concern. The environment, then, serves as a resource for new information and knowledge that assists with organizational meaning making. As new information and knowledge is gained, the organization is open to considering new ways of thinking and recreating meaning for doing the work. Interpretivists are not fearful of environmental turbulence and change, for this is just reflective of the highly subjective nature of their world. But unlike radical structuralists, they are not bent on embracing conflict to influence structural change. Environmental information in the form of conflict, then, is more grist for the mill in understanding complex situations, not necessarily something to be seized with the intent of making broad-scale change. The interpretive organization is more likely to organize a hearing about an issue than participate in the planning of a march about the same issue.

Funding.   Interpretive organizations may have trouble developing and maintaining a stable funding base because they can be seen as inwardly focused, and as not responsive to the pace required by the funding sources. This is generally true be-

TABLE 10.2   Goals of the Interpretive Organization by Task

Focus and Task	Goal
Focus A: Agency-Environment Relationships	
Environment	To try to understand the complexity of the environment and to use this understanding to set a meaningful context.
Funding	To obtain any funding that will support the organization's search for knowledge, understanding, and meaning.
Client Populations and Referral Sources	To include clients, referral sources, staff, and others in a collaborative process so that programs will be as respectful of diversity as possible.
Focus B: The Organization	
Mission/Philosophy	To seek the best knowledge available to enhance awareness and understanding in providing meaningful information and programming, while recognizing complexity at all levels of society.
Values	To provide avenues for both nondominant and dominant opinions, doctrines, and practices so that inclusion is maximized.
Management and Leadership Style	To establish a participatory, relationship-focused approach to management and leadership in which dialogue is freely exchanged in as collaborative and civil a manner as possible.
Organization and Program Structure	To allow structure to emerge so that the learning process is best facilitated, and to use less bureaucratic, flatter structures whenever possible to facilitate a network of relationships.
Programs and Services	To develop educational and human service programs that assist participants in understanding complex issues by increasing consciousness to the degree that understanding leads to more meaningful living.
Personnel Policies and Procedures	To focus less on policies and procedures, but more on processes that bring people together in interaction. To seek harmony when conflict occurs within the organization.
Staff	To hire multicultural staff who respect differences, can tolerate process, and who are dedicated to self-awareness and ongoing development.
Communication	To develop open communication in which the voices of clients, volunteers, and staff are equally heard and respected, and to engage in direct exchanges in which consensus is the goal among diverse perspectives.
Products	To create in-depth, qualitative narratives and reports that seek to increase knowledge and understanding of alternative options.

cause the quest for meaning cannot be rushed. Their predisposition to understand everything holistically, carried to an extreme, may become tedious and tiresome to funding sources. Funders that seek clearly defined outcomes and definitive deadlines will not appreciate interpretive work efforts, sometimes rejecting this type organization as not well organized or well run. On the other hand, for funding sources devoted to generating new knowledge, and not quite as focused on immediate applicability, an interpretive organization can be a dream come true. For the funding source interested in creative expression and free thinking, or understanding new or old problems in new ways, an interpretive organization can be a perfect match.

Wilkerson (1988) found that funding can be "whimsical" given rapidly changing societal themes (p. 124). When new problems arise in which there has been no research done or in which there is little information on the topic, and when the problem becomes politically "hot," an interpretive organization may actually be created to generate knowledge and understanding about the subject. The whimsy that Wilkerson identified can occur when understanding has advanced and funding is then diverted to other hot topics. The smart interpretive organization will have a group of creative people who can explore diverse issues and will be able to convince other funding sources to continue to fund them as collaborators as new issues emerge. If the funding source is seeking creative understandings and participating service recipients, the interpretive organization will be a good resource.

Client Populations and Referral Sources.   Since interpretive organizations are based on principles of inclusiveness and collaboration, staff in these organizations view clients and referral sources as colleagues. A collaborative, consensus-building approach will be used in which various community stakeholders, including service recipients, participate on equal footing with persons who are employed by the agency. Client populations served by interpretive organizations will represent diverse groups. These organizations will provide services to persons not always served by traditional agencies and may name their clients something like *participants* to emphasize the inclusive nature of their work.

Even though radical structuralist organizations include various stakeholders in their processes, there is a big difference between that approach and the one employed by interpretivists. Whereas radical structuralists embrace conflict, even encourage conflict, interpretivists seek consensus through less conflictual means. When conflict does occur, interpretivists seek to use the conflict to increase the collaborative effort toward understanding, not toward revolutionary change.

In summary, interpretivists view funding and clients as resources from the environment, representing diverse interests. Funding is far less certain than it is for functionalist organizations. Because the process of organizing and service providing is fluid, the funding is often short lived and tends to be a continual struggle. Survival is not assured, and environmental forces are constantly being scanned for resources. Clients may not be called *clients* at all because the word implies that professionals do something *for*, when in the interpretive organization doing *with* is the goal. This view of the resource environment sets a context for examining the organization's internal structure.

Focus B: The Organization

The interpretive organization's structure and process is influenced by theories that are mostly grouped under organizational culture and sensemaking perspectives. These theories are reflected in the organization's internal operations.

Mission/Philosophy.   The interpretive organization seeks knowledge to enhance awareness and understanding in providing meaningful information and programming, regardless of the chosen topic. Since it is not satisfied with simplistic answers, dominant methods, or one way of knowing, this organization's philosophy is very open and accepting of diversity. In fact, if there is any organization that is particularly sensitive to dealing with multiculturalism and diversity, it is the interpretive organization. Everyone's opinion is valued and hearing every voice is important. Structures are established to ensure this.

The interpretive philosophy is that people need complete understandings of issues, problems, and concerns from the point of view of all those with a stake in order to make informed choices. Every choice is a value-laden decision and there is perhaps a better choice at one time that will not necessarily remain the better choice when things change. Being flexible and collaborating with others allows new choices, understandings, and meanings to emerge. This means that the agency's mission today may not be the same in two or five years because situations in the context change, requiring the organization to change in order to assure its relevance in problem solving.

Values.   Interpretive organizations are grounded in subjectivism, which takes a relativist stance on values. This position is very different from functionalist and radical structuralist orientations in which there is an assumption of ultimate truth and unchanging, universal absolute values. Instead, interpretivists are very open to situational ethics in which choices made in one situation may actually change in light of new information or a shift in the scenario. Being relativists, interpretivists believe that principles change, values change with time, there are multiple truths, and there are multiple ways of knowing and doing.

Therefore, interpretive organizations are particularly sensitive to two principles in the NASW Code of Ethics: dignity and worth of the person, and the importance of human relationships. Since these organizations respect difference, they value each individual and the individual's opinions, thoughts, and contributions. Also, because these organizations seek to establish a status quo, they are particularly attentive to human relationships and the importance of connectedness. How people feel about the work context and the process of receiving help will be important. Central to work will be a genuine respect for the perspective of each individual because that person is an expert in his or her own experience. Managing the consequences of such fundamental and closely held differences is important in these organizations.

Management and Leadership Style.   Management within a more collaborative organization will not have the same "feel" as management within a more bureaucratic, hierarchical structure because managers will manage for difference instead of managing to control difference. Though managers may be as specialized and educated as their more functionalist counterparts, what is rewarded within the interpretive organization requires that managers conduct their business very differently. In fact, *management* may be a misnomer in this alternative agency, just as it was for radical structuralists. Whereas radical structuralist organizations typically call their managers *leaders* and *organizers,* interpretive organizations likely use terms such as *coordinators, facilitators,* or *team leaders.*

Leadership is exercised, but this leadership is of a facilitative and connected nature. A strong standard of civility and respect exists among organizational members. For example, coordinators will still need to make hard decisions that govern employees' lives inside the organization, but they will make special efforts to make sure that employees understand the process and the results and feel that they have been sufficiently involved in the decision-making process. Senge (1990) referred to this type of leadership as building a shared vision: "The practice of shared vision involves the skills of unearthing shared 'pictures of the future' that foster genuine commitment and enrollment rather than compliance. In mastering this discipline, leaders learn the counter productiveness of trying to dictate a vision, no matter how heartfelt" (p. 9).

Interpretive managers attend to the meaning of the work and the organization. They are attuned to the affective dimension of the work life. They respond to the individual human needs of employees beyond the bounds of the organization. Karen Boes Oman, a winner of the *Working Women* 2000 Entrepreneurial Excellence Award for Best Employer, says, "It's the lazy approach to management. If you ask people what they want and give it to them, they stay with you" (cited in Wiesendanger, 2000, p. 60). This means that more than only "official" business will be conducted within the interpretive organization as long as it does not inhibit the work of the organization. This also means that the boundaries between management and workers, between real life and work life, can become blurred. The interpretive organization will have a more intimate culture than a more traditional organization. This intimacy suggests that organizational norms include expectations that there will be connections among employees and more engagement in one another's lives. Figure 10.1 provides a list of characteristics of interpretive social work leaders that would be most attune to an interpretive organization.

Organization and Program Structure. Not being certain that organizations really exist in anything other than a conceptual sense (in the minds of the stakeholders), it should not be surprising that organizational structure is not of utmost importance in the interpretive organization. Instead, the process of organizing the work and the perspectives of those who are involved in this organizing are of interest. Much more attention is placed on understanding the individuals who gather together in the organization, because through this comes an understanding of the organization itself. It does not matter so much who is in charge or who is called accountable, what matters is that all participants have a space to offer their opinions and a responsibility to exercise their expertise for the good of the whole effort.

FIGURE 10.1   Characteristics of Interpretive Social Work Leaders

1. Is comfortable with ambiguity, uncertainty, and new and emerging ideas
2. Thinks hearing all perspectives is important
3. Sees the status quo and order as something worth establishing
4. Truly appreciates diversity
5. Tolerates differing opinions well
6. Is predisposed toward creativity
7. Has a strong curiosity
8. Is satisfied with spending time on understanding, meaning-making activities, without having to use what is learned to make broad-scale change
9. Is willing to fully participate in organizational life
10. Enjoys people and has strong interpersonal skills
11. Plays with others, is a team player
12. Desires to be a lifelong learner
13. Examines situations from many different directions and is willing to be persuaded to change one's mind
14. Tolerates process and delayed closure well
15. Respects people for their strengths and is open to hearing their ideas

Most interpretive organizations will be more informal than bureaucratic and hierarchical in their structure. There is an attention to order, but that order is more likely based on the personalities and the preferences of the participants and their perceptions of need than on any vision of "ideal" structure. Attention is consistently focused on how organizational participants feel about the social world of the organization. Attention, then, will be based on concrete empirical artifacts alone. Workload and salary structure, though important, are not the only elements considered in job satisfaction and performance. In fact, intuitive and ephemeral thoughts are considered acceptable to include in decision making about how to structure work or proceed toward organizational goals. Does the structure of the process feel right to all involved? If not, why not?

Programs and Services.   In Chapter 1, we introduced different types of programs and services. Recall that *direct service programs* directly serve clients, *staff development and training programs* focus on staff, and *support programs* undergird direct service and staff programs. Interpretive organizations may contain all three types of programs, but they will look very different than the same type programs offered in radical structuralist or functionalist organizations because their purposes are different.

When direct service programs are provided, they will focus on empowering clients through personal awareness and understanding, so clients can gain meaning in life in order to respond to problems and challenges. Interpretive programs are particularly sensitive to assisting persons in finding meaning in unsolvable situations in which they must learn to adjust and in redefining or reframing problems so that understanding can occur. The therapies used in interpretivist programs are intended to enhance insight, such as those services provided in victim assistance programs or women's shelters.

Perhaps the signature program for an Interpretive Organization is its staff development and training programs because interpretive organizations are intent on developing staff and educating others to understand complex issues and to seek meaning through their professional and personal development. In this organization, special emphasis is placed on drawing from the strengths of diversity.

Interpretive organizations offer support programs, particularly in the area of research and development. The broader outcomes of these programs are to disseminate new ways of thinking that are of interest to varied audiences. Note that these organizations are satisfied to distribute this information without using it themselves to make large-scale change, even though their radical structuralist colleagues might seize upon their findings to use for their own change purposes.

Personnel Policies and Procedures.   Since they focus on informal organization, interpretive organizations will tend to be constructed as collaboratives or collectives and will rely heavily on teams and teamwork to accomplish the business of the organization. Today's interpretive organization, while influenced by the laws and policies that have been derived from a more functionalist perspective, will choose a looser model to guide hiring, firing, training, and motivating workers. Rules will govern how these processes work, but these rules will always be open to interpretation and discussion by everyone in the organization. Rather than being closely tethered to a policy manual, flexibility is assumed to be the way to keep employees over the long term.

Staff.   This attention to personal connection is what places four of the Myers-Briggs personality types within the interpretive perspective on organizations. Introverted, sensing, feeling, perceiving (ISFP) personalities, with their quiet but deep-felt connections to others, along with extroverted, sensing, feeling, perceiving (ESFP) personalities and their interest in activities and relationships have interpretive assumptions about organizational settings. In addition, abiding interest in gaining deep understanding places introverted, intuitive, thinking, perceiving (INTP) types within this paradigm because of their sensemaking need. The extroverted, intuitive, feeling, perceiving (ENFP) personality type also is congruent with interpretive paradigmatic assumptions. Their attention to the world of possibilities, deep concern for others, and general curiosity places them comfortably within this worldview. Sensemaking for all these personality types can be achieved in connection with others. Given its preferences for connectedness, many aspects of the interpretive organization are congruent with these personality types' approaches to and expectations of work and the work setting. Rules and procedures are only acceptable when they make sense for the current situation and the current needs and resources of the context. Alternative decisions should be acceptable given different situations and contexts. What rules do exist should be developed in collaboration with all those responsible for their implementation in order for the rules to have meaning and to be fair.

Mindless paperwork being done in isolation merely because accountability requires it will be a challenge for these personalities because of their need for meaningfulness and collaborative connections in the work environment. Attention to the affective dimension of the work environment and the management of personnel will be essential to their work satisfaction and tenure within an organization. Those with an interpretive approach to organizational and work expectations will not necessarily follow those in authority without question. Instead, they will require an understanding of directives and their consequences, thus making it appear that they question authority. More than that, they require collaboration for their comfort in organizational life. They like working with others.

Skills and expertise for the requirements of the work activity will be important. Respect for competence will be present, but work in teams where strengths are combined to overcome a variety of weaknesses will be preferred over independence, specialization, and separate work assignments. Division of labor will have less meaning and there will be an expectation that each person's voice will be heard and considered in management decisions regarding staffing, directing, coordinating, and other organizational activities. Connections with the work at hand on all levels will be seen to be the way to accomplish more productivity, more quality, and more satisfaction. Pay is less important than collaborative work culture for those with interpretive expectations for organizations.

Communication. Organizational goals are based on consensus, where all participants are expected to have a voice and an appropriate influence regarding the organization. This does not necessarily mean that all will have equal voice. It does mean that all voices are respected for their standpoint vis-à-vis the organization. Given the value of communication across stakeholding groups, the goals and processes of the interpretive organization are relativist. What should happen or what should be constructed as goals will depend on all the unique dimensions of the organization in its context. There is a pragmatic attention to what works for now.

If there are lines of communication within the interpretive organization, they will be loose and fuzzy. Rigid structures in which individuals have to communicate along chains of command do not fit. In fact, communication that freely occurs among all participants serves the organization's purpose of hearing multiple perspectives and of learning from others.

Products. Interpretive organizations are more focused on process than they are on products. However, this does not mean that they do not produce products and even outcomes, only that they value the means taken to achieve them as much as they do the ends achieved. The products and outcomes in interpretive organizations are different from those in functionalist and radical structuralist organizations, and are often viewed with some disdain by their colleagues in these other paradigms. For example, a valued product for an interpretive organization would be a narrative analysis that uses critical thinking and multiple perspectives to fully articulate an understanding of a highly complex problem. This report would likely present options and their implications, rather than recommendations for a specific way of solving the defined problem preferred by a functionalist or radical structuralist.

Similarly, outcomes for human service programs delivered in interpretive organizations are often seen as too soft, difficult to measure, or only reflecting how people feel, rather than what they can do differently as a result of program intervention. For example, a battered women's shelter may seek to empower women by raising their consciousness and enhancing their feelings of self-worth. Viewed as a meaningful outcome by interpretivists, functionalists would ask, "But what about the needed skills to get them into the societal mainstream?" Radical structuralists would retort, "But what about *changing* the societal structures that oppress women?" In other words, interpretive outcomes are often viewed as being only immediate outcomes from which intermediate and ultimate outcomes must emerge.

Yet, the products and outcomes of interpretive organizations are highly thoughtful, time-consuming endeavors that contribute to meaning in the lives of all participants. One danger in the interpretive organization is that staff will be so engaged in meaning making that client outcomes become secondary. We have witnessed interpretive organizations in which the staff felt so good about the culture that had developed that it was difficult to distinguish whose needs the staff were there to serve—their own or those of their clients.

Having assessed the organization, it is equally important to know the language used within the interpretive organization and the way that language guides one's practice. The next section identifies language differences between paradigms, then focuses on interpretive language and its practice implications.

Practice Language of the Interpretive Organization

The interpretive perspective assumes no such thing as a "best" way of conducting organizational assessment and diagnosis to achieve the best or ideal change. Instead, there is a pragmatic expectation that constructing what will work to solve problems can occur through consensus within the organizational community. The idea is that all involved start from where they are. The challenge of assessment and problem analysis, then, is to identify all starting points and then enter into a conversation about how to cope with the situation at hand. Therefore, from the interpretive perspective, assessment and analysis do not so much consist of finding the best plan for change, but rather creating the opportunity for meaningful change. Through conversation, participants come to greater clarity about the situation and the possibilities. With that, change energy develops. In previous chapters, we introduced practice language used in functionalist and radical structuralist organizations to describe organization practice. In Figure 10.2, we compare the use of language for practice in each type organization thus far.

Assessment is a common term used across the three paradigms. In fact, we have just used this term in the previous section to examine the variables encountered in organizational life. Note that problem analysis is typically used in radical structuralist organizations, even though the use of diagnosis (with a medical con-

FIGURE 10.2 Language Differences across Three Paradigms

Functionalist Organization	Radical Structuralist Organization	Interpretive Organization
Assessment	Assessment	Assessment
Diagnosis	Problem Analysis	Understanding
Planning	Organizing	Collaborating
Incremental Change	Collective Transformational Change	Sensemaking

notation) is still very prevalent in functionalist organizations. However, problem analysis takes a much different turn in interpretive organizations because the process of analyzing is so central to the organization's philosophy. Since interpretive organizations may be less prone to label situations, we use the term *understanding* to describe the process used to fully analyze a situation. *Collaborating* is a more interpretive term than *planning* or *organizing,* and *sensemaking* is interpretive language that implies a very different way of looking at organizational processes and products as meaningful. We will use this language to guide our exploration of what it is like to practice in an interpretive organization.

Attempting to Change the Interpretive Organization

No matter what type of organization in which one practices, there will be times when something needs to change. When change agents attempt to alter something in the interpretive organization, they will typically take on the challenge with the same standard of civility and collaboration that they use in their daily work. Civility and respect toward colleagues are established principles in the interpretive culture. We now turn to the approach one might take to change in this type organization.

Assessment

In the interpretive organization, assessment is an ongoing process that is viewed as only one snapshot in time. Since the organization is always evolving, reassessment must be a continual process, for what is believed to be true about the organization one day can be different tomorrow. The culture of the organization is committed to hearing the voices of all participants, and when new information arises, adjustments may be made if everyone thinks that it is a good idea. There is flexibility, fluidity, and a natural evolutionary process going on within these organizations. Since the changes being made are not radical or revolutionary, the status quo is maintained, but minor adjustments and accommodations are a natural continuous occurrence. No rules are made in stone because there are no absolutes.

Members of an interpretive organization find assessing organizational culture to be very congruent with the philosophy of the organization. In fact, as we have already seen, organizational culture theories are congruent with the assumptions of the interpretive paradigm. To understand the organization from this perspective is to look at the elements identified by organizational culture theorists to guide one's assessment. Elements for dealing with the larger environment are mission and strategy, goals, means, measurement, and correction. These elements could be framed in questions that would guide one's understanding of the organization:

- How does the organization develop shared understandings of the mission and the tasks to be done?
- How does the organization's core mission contribute to consensus around goals?
- How are goals attained in this organization?
- What criteria are used to measure goal achievement?
- What repair or remedial strategies are used to make adjustments when goals are not achieved? (Schein, 1992, p. 52)

Similarly, questions pertaining to internal integration of the organization's culture follow:

- What common language and conceptual categories are used?
- Who is a part and who is not a part of this organization?
- How do members get, maintain and lose power in this organization?
- How are appropriate peer relationships defined?
- What is valued and what is not valued in this organization?
- How do members make unexplainable situations meaningful? (Schein, 1992, p. 66)

And, last, one's organizational assessment could include a look at the levels of culture:

- What are the artifacts of this organization (e.g., physical space, group output, artistic expressions, products, members' behaviors, etc.)?
- What values are espoused within this organization?
- What are the underlying assumptions within this organization?
- Do the artifacts and values fit with the underlying assumptions?

Assessing the interpretive organization, then, requires attention to elements not always valued or even seen as very important in traditional organizations.

Having assessed the organization's culture, it will be helpful to examine the implications of this culture on the use of assessment within the organization's programs. For example, in the functionalist and radical structuralist organization, assessment of clients, organizations, and communities requires systematic quantitative data collection that can be easily translated into numbers and analyzed statistically. The interpretive organization's subjective nature values very different types of assessment tools and strategies. Since interpretive organizations typically focus on complex problems and issues in contexts that are not well understood, the use of qualitative assessment procedures will be highly valued because they provide depth and flexibility. Tools may not be available that focus on the problems addressed in interpretive organizations because context is considered to be everything, thus standardization or the use of established instruments are viewed as barriers when in depth responses are desired. If the context is essential to understanding the problem, then a tool that has been shaped to capture generalizable variables will not be able to capture the unique situation at hand. Tools emerge from the context and the experience. Instead of a standardized instrument to guide the work, questions are asked of participants that they think are important to know. Therefore, the results are informative to them because the answers are to their own questions.

Understanding

In the interpretive organization, problem analysis is much more difficult than it would be in functionalist and radical structuralist organizations because of the belief that nothing is static, but always in process. Organizations with objectivist perspectives focus on universal truths, and champions of that position guard against goal displacement, whereas interpretive organizations are prone to switch goals if that is the group consensus. Therefore, analyzing the problem in an interpretive organization requires a great deal of patience and a dedication to diversity. On the other hand, colleagues will be ready participants in analyzing an organizational problem since interpretive personality types naturally engage in ongoing dialogue and analysis. If a problem arises in an interpretive organization, one will have no trouble finding willing colleagues to participate in the collaborative process of analyzing the situation.

The difficulty encountered by practitioners in interpretive organizations is that problem analysis can take a long time. Since the culture tolerates ongoing collaboration and dialogue, people may enjoy the process of trying to understand all the nuances of an organizational problem so much that nobody gets around to do anything about it. The process-oriented nature of these organizations, which values examining every possibility, can actually make achieving consensus difficult. A prime example is a university faculty. Working with faculty members is often described as "herding cats," with persons who are very functionalist in their orientation frustrated with the amount of effort it takes to get to any decision. However, if one looked at universities as a prime site of interpretivists, then one could relax and realize that the assumptions valued by faculty members do not make for efficiency. In fact, the value placed on careful analysis of every issue is a value to be admired in this setting because complex issues are being treated in complex ways.

Programmatically, interpretive organizations must at least temporarily settle on certain opportunities or problems in order to do their work. However, their programs will be highly creative and the curiosity of staff will likely produce some findings formerly unanticipated. Breakthroughs are likely to occur in interpretive organizations because staff members are open to new unexpected possibilities. How often have stories of major findings been reported as accidents when in fact they were the coming together of previously disconnected items in a new way? To the interpretive organization, this is hardly an accident—it is the nature of subjective reality.

Collaborating

Whereas planning and organizing are trademarks of functionalist and radical structuralist organizations, *collaborating* is the term often heard in interpretive hallways. According to Hess and Mullen (1996), "to collaborate is to labor together" (p. 5). Wheatley and Kellner-Rogers (1996) frame collaboration differently—as actually playing together, since they view life as creative and "intent on discovering what's possible" (p. 20). Regardless of how one frames the collaborative process, it has been the subject of much dialogue in recent years (Ede & Lunsford, 1990; Foreman, 1992; Jacobsen, 1998; O'Connor & Netting, 1999). Macduff and Netting (2000) defined the *collaborative process* as when "two or more persons work and play together to achieve some result or create some product in which they are jointly invested, about which they care enough to pool their strengths" (p. 48). These persons may be from the same or different fields, disciplines, and/or professions. In interpretive organizations, practitioners, clients, volunteers, and others dialogue so that whatever is decided will be based on the strengths of multiple perspectives. Connecting multiple players can result in demystifying the process so that professionals and clients alike contribute to cogenerative learning (Greenwood & Levin, 1998).

Since collaboration is the hallmark of interpretive organizations, if one wants to change this type of organization then one must be prepared to work with others in the change process. Bulldozing a change through (even if one has authority) or imposing one's moral stance on another is not well received in interpretive organizations. The norm and expected behavior must be steeped in a willingness to listen to all sides of an issue and to be prepared to change one's own view given persuasive evidence of an alternative. In other words, the problem one may have originally defined may be reconstructed a number of times in the collaboration process, since the heart of this organization is to fully understand the concerns expressed.

Similarly, when one develops programs within this organization, methods used in working with others will be highly collaborative, typically involving persons from diverse perspectives, backgrounds, and even disciplines. Teamwork, particularly true interdisciplinary teaming, is likely to be used in interpretive organizations. Programs will be designed to be highly inclusive of consumers so that their voices and opinions are genuinely respected and heard.

Sensemaking

Phrases such as "this makes sense" and "that is meaningful" are appropriate to use in interpretive organizations. Whereas functionalist organizations seek efficient interventions and radical structuralist organizations are bent on social transformation, interpretive organizations are dedicated to making sense of situations. Therefore, if one collaborates on changing this type of organization, one must work with others to be sure the change makes sense to all involved. This takes time. As theorists note, this does not necessarily mean that sensemaking will occur in a linear fashion. In fact, as Weick (1995) notes, sensemaking may be retrospective and plausibility may take precedence over accuracy. In other words, people have to feel comfortable with the change, mull it over, rethink their original positions, and pay particular attention to the social cues. One can expect one's proposed change to be studied in depth with multiple opinions offered along the way. We have often seen interpretive sensemaking processes occurring in functionalist organizations and the fit is deadly. Functionalists get frustrated, tired, angry, and even obstinate in these situations when interpretivists are only trying to participate in and own the process. When functionalists say, "I don't have any idea what just happened in there," or "I would have never guessed that that decision would result from this meeting," they have typically been engaged in an interpretive process and didn't like it.

Just as sensemaking forms the process by which practice in an interpretive organization occurs, it also forms the nucleus of how interpretive programs work. After assessing, understanding, and collaborating, interpretive programs are designed to engage consumers with staff in a joint process of making sense of difficult situations, finding meaning in their lives, or working toward a more in-depth understanding of their conditions. If one believes, as interpretivists do, that self-actualization involves sensemaking and understanding, one could actually argue that their programs meet higher-order needs moving beyond survival to self-actualization.

Since interpretive organizations do not hold to positivist goals about objective knowledge or truth, plans must be held tentatively, keeping alternative approaches alive as possibilities. A current example of this idea is the parallel planning now in vogue in public child welfare. If the plan for a child placed out of the home is to return the child home, then all service efforts are designed to overcome the problems that led to the child's removal. At the same time, however, other planning for adoptive placement is also being undertaken, just in case the family cannot reclaim the child. The idea is that the best interest of the child should be served and both ways might work, so both plans should be evolved. Similar to this example where children, families (biological, foster, and adoptive), workers, and other service personnel must participate, all participants in interpretive work need to be engaged in constructing the reality of the desired change. The ethics involved in assessing, understanding, collaborating, and sensemaking for change are meant to design changes so that all stakeholders are given a fair chance. The measure of success becomes: Was the problem as constructed solved as desired without oppressing one another?

Table 10.3 provides an overview of practice characteristics in interpretive organizations and provides a summary of the discussion in this section. You may use this as a way to determine if organizations with which you are familiar support interpretive organization practice.

Implications of Interpretive Organizations for Social Work Leaders

The interpretive perspective offers more value congruence than conflicts for the social work profession. At the same time that it is professionally congruent, this paradigm also presents many challenges for the social work organizational leader who is charged with the responsibility of managing the organization, its employees, and its services with as much efficiency as efficacy. This perspective provides

TABLE 10.3   Practice Characteristics in Interpretive Organizations

Practice Element	Characteristics
Assessment	Attention to hearing multiple perspectives from diverse groups and persons is critical to information gathering.
	Collection of word data is as important as collection of numeric data.
	Use of open-ended questions and emerging instruments is useful, given the need to develop deep understandings in context.
	Reassessment is a continual and ongoing process.
Understanding	Subjective needs assessment data are shared with all constituencies.
	Analysis is viewed as a broadening process, with efforts made to avoid premature narrowing down of what is known.
Collaborating	Involvement of all parties is highly valued.
	Collaborative process is seen as meaningful unto itself.
	Hearing all perspectives and views is encouraged.
	Consensus building is the goal.
Sensemaking	Sensemaking may occur at any level, but the primary focus is typically at the individual and organizational levels.
	Change-from-within tactics (collaboration and campaign) rather than contest (conflict) are preferred.
	The goal is to make changes that become the new status quo and are owned by everyone.

an ability to start where the individual is, but it also limits an ability to know for sure that what is being planned or implemented is "right."

A great challenge in the contemporary context is that outcome measures have limited meaning in an interpretive perspective. Of interest is what the client thinks, even though other stakeholders will be considered. The lack of a "right" answer reverberates with the values of the profession: service, social justice, dignity and worth of the person, importance of human relationships, integrity, and competence. This perspective actually operationalizes the notion of "person-in-environment." What is ethical and effective depends on the various elements of the person within a specific context. In the interpretive frame of reference, the determination of an acceptable level of professional performance regarding each value will ever remain a work in progress. The determination of each within the organization will depend on the time and context of the decision. The service should be delivered, and what can be determined to be socially just must be context dependent and therefore unique to the situations of all involved. The same is true regarding the assurance of dignity and worth of the person, the importance of human relationships, integrity, and competence. Each must be assiduously determined within the time and context of the situation, which absolutely requires well-honed critical thinking skills of all within the organization.

The assumptions of the interpretive perspective on organizations are also congruent with social work attention to diversity and multiculturalism. In fact, this perspective can help to operationalize multicultural practice because it forces attention to, and respect for, multiple voices. The approach will not be simple. The answer will not be clear, but the process will result in the complexity necessary for real recognition of diversity without oppression. It also assures that the organization will never be stuck in political correctness because there will never be certainty about what the best approach to diversity and multiculturalism should be. This suggests a difficult challenge, fraught with frustration and other surprising issues, but the relativist stance of the perspective allows for pragmatic modification whenever necessary. When the challenge appears too difficult to guarantee consideration of the voices of the myriad of perspectives, something can change.

Professional ethics from this relativist perspective will be difficult to determine. But in exchange for lack of certainty there is great flexibility to probe for deep understandings of all perspectives and an opportunity for powerful targeting of organizational activities. Women and minorities who are represented in both the service-providing and the service-receiving populations will be less disadvantaged than in several other organizational perspectives due to the access provided and required for the presence and consideration of all voices.

Conclusion

The interpretive organization is committed to discovery and understanding. This sets up the expectation that discovery of a generalizable truth is not possible, nor does the understanding process result in a final truth. Change will occur as new persons interact intersubjectively within these organizations, and that is to be expected and valued. When the unexpected happens somewhere in the process, then the assumption is that this is how the world works now. Interpretivists live well with ambiguity, not assuming that anyone is in control—there are only fleeting images of being in control for the time being.

What the organizational leader gains from interpretivist assumptions is a commitment from colleagues to work through the process of change and to continue to work in teaming relationships with one another. The leader recognizes that there will be pressures from more traditional funding sources or other agencies to use standardized approaches and tools to aid in response to the call for productivity. Yet, productivity is defined very differently in interpretive organizations, for making sense and making meaning are seen as valuable unto themselves. They are empowering to all participants. Persons who want more concrete products may view these soft "outcomes" with disdain.

When adopting this perspective for assessing understanding, collaborating, and sensemaking, the social worker gains a view of what is unique to the organization and its members in the organizational environment. Subtle influences regarding processes are captured in the data collection for decision making. This is because there is room for consideration of the more qualitative, affective, intuitive aspects of organizational life.

For the social work leader, this perspective and the theories within it offer great help in assessing understanding, collaborating, and sensemaking in attending to the special opportunities and challenges provided by that which is different from the norm. Further, there is room for the chaotic and the unexpected that seem to permeate today's organizational life. The uncontrolled or uncontrollable presence, often attributed to incompetence in the dominant world, is seen in interpretive organizations as normal chaos in contemporary organizations that leaves space for much creativity.

We now turn to the fourth and final paradigm—radical humanism—the least well defined worldview. You will soon see that this paradigm has some assumptions in common with interpretivists, but when it comes to the way in which change is viewed, radical humanists part company with the interpretive paradigm.

CHAPTER 11

Radical Humanist Theories about Organizations

In Chapter 4, we introduced the radical humanist paradigm, but in this chapter, we deepen our original description. We begin by examining themes found in radical humanist thinking and the assumptions that flow from this paradigm, resulting in radical humanist organizations. Following this thorough paradigmatic grounding, the major organizational and organizational behavior frameworks that fit within this perspective are identified. Notice that we use the concept of *framework* here because a radical humanist perspective actually takes an antitheoretical approach to knowledge building in its rejection of traditional structures and processes for knowing. The chapter closes with a critical analysis, so that the reader is left with a good picture of what is gained and what is given up when approaching organizations from a radical humanist view. We then move to Chapter 12, which focuses on understanding the dimensions of working and practicing within radical humanist organizations.

At this stage in the history of organizational development, there probably is no "pure" radical humanist organization, though more and more organizations may be moving in that direction. Think of this discussion, then, as detailing the radical humanist organization prototype. Like organizations based in assumptions from other paradigms, radical humanist organizations may contain staff members that operate under different assumptions. When this happens, staff will encounter paradoxes as differing assumptions collide. What is the most likely scenario is that employees holding radical humanist assumptions will find themselves in organizations based on other paradigmatic assumptions, rather than the reverse. Either way, at the conclusion of the chapter, it is our hope that the reader will understand why radical humanist assumptions will fundamentally collide with those of functionalists. It will also be clear that both radical humanists and radical structuralists seek transformational change, but differ in how they go about it. Similarly, radical humanists have subjectivism in common with interpretivists, but the two paradigms part company in how one approaches change.

Radical Humanist Themes

The most radical approaches to understanding organizations are based on the assumptions of the radical humanist paradigm. It is from this perspective that the

Radical Humanist	**Radical Structuralist**
Interpretive	**Functionalist**

most experimental (and some would say most outlandish) efforts are undertaken to reconcile the challenges and the opportunities of modern technology and an emerging world economy into a manageable work life in a complex social structure. It is also from this perspective that the study of organizations is most likely to take on a metaphysical aspect and that the impact on and the role of the individual in organizational life takes center stage. Sharing with the interpretive perspective, there is a recognition that useful study of organizations must be a mix of the rational, the serendipitous, and the intuitive as individuals make sense of the processes and the accepted practices of organizational life. Though the assumptions of radical humanism also require a certain degree of rigor to produce acceptable results, there is an explicit recognition of multiple ways of knowing and understanding. The artistic, the spiritual, and the "other" are included as viable sources of knowledge about organizational life. What an individual feels, senses, or intuits is acceptable information from which to work. From this perspective, *all* the ways the human instrument processes and creates knowing are recognized as mechanisms that allow individual consciousness to reach its full potential.

Interestingly and most paradoxically, this recognition of multiple ways of knowing, including the spiritual and the artistic, may have brought philosophy of science full circle. The natural sciences evolved as a way to refute, overcome, or otherwise eliminate "lesser" ways of knowing the world. The early empiricists chose hard facts over the "magical thinking" of religion, art, and philosophy to build a sensible world. Now, the radical humanists return to pre-Vienna Circle scholarly thinking in ways that accept all sensible sources as potentially rigorous ways of knowing, especially from a subjectivist, individualistic standpoint. (For those wishing to read more about the history and politics of philosophy of science, see Diesing, 1991).

In radical humanist thinking, objectivity is not expected, but instead the full use of intuition, tacit knowledge and the insights derived from them are desired dimensions of rigorous knowledge building. Instead of generalization, individual consciousness raising is the expected result of inquiry. The true measure of an acceptable level of rigor is if the individual, as a result of the organizational inquiry process, is released from the constraints that hamper personal human development related to the area being investigated. Individual change must be associated with organizational inquiry guided by this perspective in order for the research to reach its expected standard of quality. Personal transformation is the goal of research.

This very different way of understanding organizational behavior and organizational structure presents interesting opportunities to explore the unexplored in organizational life, but its differences presents great challenges in a traditional scientific community. At the completion of this chapter, the degrees of opportunities and challenges for organizational work from this perspective should be clear. To accomplish this, we will look at the assumptions undergirding the perspective in a bit more detail. We will also explore the liberty and individualism themes that are important to this approach to organization. The issues involved in the developing concept of the virtual organization will also be of interest in this paradigm.

Assumptions of the Radical Humanist Paradigm

Radical humanists see reality as the result of individual consciousness. Reality is created due to active individual participation in the construction of social reality. The assumption is that no universal laws exist. Instead, there is the unique and the particular, so that knowledge becomes soft, subjective, and even spiritual. Knowledge to be knowledge must be experienced. Therefore, it is believed that human nature is free and proactive. Humans have a central role in the creation of reality. They are self-directing and self-correcting.

Figure 11.1 reintroduces the concept of subjectivism one last time. Recall that interpretivists believe in subjectivism, as well. A subjectivist perspective was elaborated in Chapter 9. In brief, radical humanists are subjectivists because they do not abide universalism in which there is "one best way." Multiple truths are viewed as arising from within people. Radical humanists are open to alternative ways of thinking, believing what is considered a best way today may no longer be a best way tomorrow.

FIGURE 11.1   Subjectivism: Defining Terms

Nominalism (in the mind)

Antipositivism (soft, subjective, must be experienced)

Voluntarism (people create their environments)

Ideographic (analyze subjective accounts which one generates by "getting inside" situations of everyday life)

Source: Adapted from G. Burrell and G. Morgan, *Sociological Paradigms and Organisational Analysis* (Aldershot, England: Ashgate, 1979), Figure 1.1, p. 3. Used by permission.

Radical humanists and interpretivists part company in how they view change. It is with this change perspective that the association with radical structuralists is most apparent. Like radical structuralists, radical humanists are change oriented. Figure 11.2 summarizes their radical change perspectives.

Individualism and what is necessary to reach personal potential is a central notion in radical humanism. Personal self-interest and involvement in the types of organizational change necessary to assure personal actualization are important in this paradigm. The expectation of radical change, based on critical analysis for personal gains, represents a challenge to traditional views about organizations and organizational behavior. Because the very idea of organizing into a structure subsumes the individual into something that is greater, this alternative perspective questions the basic foundation upon which classical organizing is built. It also presents a challenge for research in organizations where structure and control of results are expected at all levels of organizational life. Because this perspective honors individual autonomy above all else, aggregate research becomes irrelevant. What is important is a very personal view of organizing and structuring for results that have personal, rather than organizational, meaning. The degree of difficulty in all these aspects, as well as the opportunities that this perspective represent, will become clear as we take a thorough look at all of the assumptions of the radical humanist paradigm.

Taken altogether, the assumptions of this paradigm are summarized in Figure 11.3. As you read about the theories highlighted in this chapter, Figure 11.3 may be a useful reminder of their underlying assumptions.

Given its subjectivist perspective, the radical humanist paradigm does not limit knowledge building to just operationalizable, empirical data. Philosophy, history, arts, and social practices are also seen to be basic to knowledge building (Guba, 1990). The perspective becomes radicalized by means of its association with radical change. The focus of organizational research is structural conflict and modes of domination. The goal is to uncover contradictions and in doing so to provide avenues for emancipation (an emancipation that is much more active than

---

FIGURE 11.2   Concerns of the Radical Change Perspective

Radical change

Structural conflict

Modes of domination

Contradiction

Emancipation

Deprivation

Potentiality

Source: Adapted from G. Burrell and G. Morgan, *Sociological Paradigms and Organisational Analysis* (Aldershot, England: Ashgate, 1979), Table 2.2, p. 18. Used by permission.

FIGURE 11.3   **Assumptions of the Radical Structuralist Paradigm**

From the Subjectivist Perspective
1. Social reality exists primarily in the human mind.
2. Knowledge about social reality is soft, subjective, and natural.
3. People can be proactive in creating their own realities.
4. Given that individuals create, change, and interpret the world, qualitative approaches to understanding are useful.

From the Radical Change Perspective
5. Society is characterized by deep-seated structural conflict, modes of domination, and even contradiction.
6. Knowledge for change and action should be the goal.
7. Conflict, rather than consensus, is important.

Source: Adapted from Burrell and Morgan (1979, Chapter 1).

what was seen in the interpretive paradigm). Of interest to radical humanists is understanding deprivation and oppression in order to allow for consciousness raising and empowerment. It is assumed that with an understanding of the forces and processes in modes of domination, individual potentiality can be uncovered and tapped for true personal fulfillment in organizational life.

Unlike radical structuralists who seek change that moves the organization closer to universal goals and principles, radical humanists seek change so that individuals can be emancipated from domination. And in this case, a major instrument of domination is suspected to be traditional organizational structures, rules, and procedures. Since there are no universal goals and truths, the premise of this emancipation is that each person may come to different conclusions about reality. Imagine, then, how this translates into organization practice—everyone will have a different construction of organizational reality, and because of this and the inherent need to assure individual self-interest, conflict over competing realities will be ongoing. Unlike radical structuralists, there is no demand to move toward collective change or to mobilize groups. Change and mobilization occur in radical humanism for individuals, and these changes are just as urgent since individual oppression can not be tolerated.

Organizational research from this perspective is actually an invitation to discourse. There is no imposition of authoritative interpretations about the phenomenon under investigation. Instead, the effort is to create reflexive interpretation where language and personal reality are connected. Since the basic assumption of the paradigm is that language constructs that which is social, this perspective is also characterized by a certain skepticism about truth claims. "Truth" becomes relative to the language and context that constructs it, so no construction is privileged over another. This makes judgment difficult. But because of the belief in the potentiality of human consciousness, the focus is on perception about language and conceptual insight that can result from various sources, including individual intuition.

Also because of the trust in and focus on the individual, this perspective can be against institutions that reflect or require sameness and seek consensus. This perspective rejects uniform rules and procedures, standardization of any kind, including such things as dress codes that constrain or impede individuality and individual potentiality. Many of the frameworks considered part of this paradigm are constructed to deny privilege and power in bureaucracy. Authority over the individual robs the individual of liberty, and liberty of the individual is the desired state within organizations. Keeping these assumptions in mind, we now turn to the emerging theories that have developed the radical humanist paradigm.

Radical Humanist Organizational Theories

The frameworks included in this theoretical consideration of radical humanist organizations share three basic themes: (1) the importance and possibilities of the individual and self-creation, (2) the call to freedom to create the self as one chooses, and (3) organizations manifest various modes of social domination and therefore are oppressive entities working against individual liberty. These themes are grounded in subjectivist assumptions that value difference, combined with assumptions about the importance of radical change or departure from structures that limit by their oppression.

Some of the frameworks presented here see self-creation and freedom as only being possible through conflict. For example, later in this chapter you will see that Morgan (1997) uses the metaphor of "the ugly face" to describe organizations as instruments of domination in which multiple oppressions occur. When the organization is seen as an instrument of domination, conflict is inevitable. Other theorists see subjective radical change as being more poetic or playful, "exploring possibilities of meaning in a world which is also all the time exploring possibilities" (Wheatley & Kellner-Rogers, 1996, p. 49). Some radical humanists will focus more on conflict and others will focus more on play; both coexist in this paradigm. While traditional ways of thinking might imply that conflict and play cannot coexist, a radical humanist might explore how, through the juxtaposition of intense conflict and the joy of play, people can "find" themselves and thus be transformed.

Radical humanist theories are revolutionary. Living with ambiguity, dealing with paradox, and even questioning the entire concept of organization is relevant here. There are no universals or grand theories in radical humanism. In a way, radical humanists react against all the other paradigms on issues of principle. Functionalists and radical structuralists are viewed as attempting to place their agendas on others. Their assumptions that they have the "best" way, that there are "best" approaches, and that there are universal truths frustrate radical humanists. Although interpretivists are open to subjectivity, their inertia frustrates radical humanists. Being open to subjectivity and difference is one thing, moving to do something about it is entirely another. There is no room for satisfaction with the status quo in radical humanist thinking.

In previous chapters, we used Shafritz and Ott (1996) as a resource to identify major perspectives in organizational theory. In this chapter, we focus primarily on theories within two of the same groupings that we introduced in Chapter 7 on radical structuralism:

- Power and Politics Organization Theory
  —Feminist Theories
  —Critical Theories
- Postmodernism

Since radical humanists seek change, power and politics theories are relevant here. Because the postmodernist critical stance tends to focus on oppression and domination, it has had a tremendous influence on radical humanism. However, it is important to understand that there are different schools of critical thought within each of these theoretical categories. Theorists coming from a radical humanist perspective will be focused on subjectivism and individualized oppression, as opposed to theorists coming from a more radical structuralist, objectivist orientation that call for universal or class-based changes directed toward a more just society.

Power and Politics Theory

When we discussed radical structuralism, we introduced the concept of power and the emergence of two voices—the critical and the rational voices. Radical humanists have been influenced by the critical voice that emanates from the early work of Marx and Weber, and cannot relate in any way to the rational voice that sees power as a threat that must be controlled. Radical humanists seek to understand, use, or oppose power so individuals can be liberated. They use theoretical understandings from writers on power and politics, but use them in different ways than do their radical structuralist colleagues. Whereas radical structuralists use power and politics theories to organize collectives or classes of people for social change, radical humanists see organizing for social change as an attempt to oppress groups of people with different but still oppressive sets of truths. The alternative, "liberating" truth replaces established truths with new and potentially oppressive truths. Radical humanists are antifunctionalist and antistructuralist, objecting to those who have new truths with which to push their agendas. Instead, radical humanists are open to many ways of going about individually based change. Group organizing is not acceptable. In short, radical humanists may not even form organizations with agreed upon goals because their hope is that individuals will be free to self-determine in their work life. When they do form organizations, it is not with the intent to corral or control people; it is with the intent of liberating people to achieve their highest potential.

Power and politics theorists with radical humanist perspectives no longer assume that the organization's primary purpose is to accomplish organizational goals. There is a rejection of the idea that organizational goals are determined and designed by those in charge and measured only for effectiveness and efficiency with personal issues restrained in favor of organizational needs. They reject the notion that power is vested in formal authority. Instead, there is a complex system of individuals and coalitions with interests, benefits, values, perspectives, and perceptions that act in competition for organizational resources and enter into conflict to acquire personal or professional influence. There is recognition that behaviors and decisions are not rational, but the result of influence. This influence is necessary for use in successful competition and conflict.

Morgan's metaphor of "the ugly face" fits well within this power and politics school of thought. Morgan contends that tracing the development of this metaphor takes one back to ancient peoples. For example, he refers to organizing to build the pyramids and to the great sacrifices of human life that accompanied the achievement of these large constructions. For some organizational theorists, this paradox of organizational achievement paired with exploitation of individuals has been a continual feature of organizational life throughout the centuries. Pursuit of the goals of a few through the labor of many is one mode of social domination that has been the focus of radical theorists such as Marx, Weber, and Michels.

Weber was concerned with the role of bureaucracy as a form of social domination. For Weber, "the process of bureaucratization presented a very great threat to the freedom of the human spirit and the values of liberal democracy, because those in control have a means of subordinating" (Morgan, 1997, pp. 304–305). The very process of rationalization, giving reason to setting limits, in an organization is understood as oppressive. Similarly, Michels, a French sociologist, coined the phrase "iron law of oligarchy" to describe how groups of people are controlled by the desires of formal leaders. His studies of supposedly democratic organizations revealed that democracy was little more than window dressing. Michels's ideas, combined with Weber's, resonated with the works of Marx (before Engles's influence), who focused on domination and oppression of the less powerful and ways to move to individual liberation from this domination. In more recent years, radical theorists attempting to understand domination have built on these ideas, continuing to explore the multiple processes of domination and exploitation (Morgan, 1997). For example, Hearn and Parkin (1993) focus on organizations as multiple oppressors, emphasizing the complexity of domination modes and the depth of exploitation often perpetrated in organizations.

Understanding power and politics creates the infrastructure of the critical voice in radical humanism. We can now turn to feminist theory and critical theory to deepen the understanding of the issues of power and oppression in organizations.

Feminist Theory.   In previous chapters, we recognized that there are many different types of feminist theories (Calás & Smircich, 1996). Depending on the assumptions held by various theorists, feminist theory can fall within any of the four paradigms. Feminist theory that assumes a radical humanist perspective is what Calás and Smircich call third world/(post)colonial theorizations. This type of feminist theory goes beyond Western thought, questioning the dichotomy of male/female and any generalizations about gender and gender relations. Third world theorists "hold in common a fundamental suspicion of 'gender' as a stable and sufficient analytical lens that can be applied unproblematically across cultures and histories" (Calás & Smircich, 1996, p. 238). Recognizing the subjectivity of terms and the oppressive nature of Western thought, theorists in this tradition question themselves and others who attempt to deconstruct Western concepts. They argue that this very deconstruction is value laden because there is always danger of replacing one dominant construction with another that is equally oppressive.

Third world/(post)colonial theories raise many questions that illustrate some of the problems faced by radical humanists. How does one move from being part of the dominant culture in a way that does not replace one way of thinking with another? How does one challenge traditional assumptions without simply replacing them with new assumptions that, in being accepted, will become the oppressive, traditional assumptions of tomorrow? How does one respect difference to the point of recognizing individuality, rather than creating a romantic view of emerging nations and perspectives? How does an organization allow those differences to exist without having to organize or control them?

Feminist theory, then, has certainly had an influence on radical humanist organizations but not because of traditional Western feminism. As scholars from around the world publish their work on women-in-development in Western publications, the third world/(post)colonial approaches to feminist theory are emerging in the United States in greater detail. Work examining nongovernmental organizations (NGOs) in third world countries is a space where this type of feminist thinking is beginning to appear (Calás & Smircich, 1996). It is this scholarship that has influenced the conceptualization of practice in the radical humanist organization by suggesting that subjugated knowledge—knowledge held by the powerless individual—must be allowed a voice in order to fundamentally transform the ways of organizing worldwide.

Critical Theory.   As with some types of feminist theory, the more individualized perspectives of critical theory fit comfortably in the radical humanist paradigm. These more subjectivist critical theorists find fertile ground for criticism of management and organizations based on what they see as a decline in the effectiveness of and disillusionment with modern assumptions about organizations and their practices. They also participate in the attack on the modernist (positivist or functionalist) tradition. They criticize the individual or personal negative consequences of the size of organizations, the rapid implementation of communication and technology, globalization, the nature of work, and turbulence in the marketplace, among other aspects of current organizational life. Critical theorists see a crisis in organizations. Rejecting much of the current organizational discussion that no one can control or be controlled, the critical theorist taking a radical humanist perspective rejects the current situation on the basis of personal costs. The current state is unacceptable for humanity. The option is a shift in organizational thinking and behavior in order to be attentive to power consequences and individual needs. More attention must be given to employees, or modern organizations are doomed (Alvesson & Deetz, 1996).

Many of the early radical humanist critical theorists (see, for example, Benson, 1977; Burrell & Morgan, 1979; Deetz & Kersten, 1983; Fischer & Sirianni, 1984) began their discourse with a criticism of organizational cultural theories that attempt to engineer (or reengineer) personal/professional values. The alternative provided was a focus on collaboration in order to achieve organizational goals. More recent theorists (see Alvesson, 1993; Willmott, 1993) see new social conditions with important individual impact requiring a different analysis for a different comprehension in order to achieve significant changes in the way people organize. Many call for organic, adhocratic organizations (Parker, 1993; Thompson, 1993) as a way to overcome the personal exploitation, repression, and unfairness of modern organizations.

Following a central notion of power, the radical humanist critical theorists investigate exploitation, repression, unfairness, asymmetrical power, distorted communication, and false consciousness. Attention to false consciousness about power and the results of power is important because of the assumption that there are power relationships in knowledge creation. What gets declared as "acceptable" knowledge in organizations is due to the power of those asking the questions and interpreting the results. The critical theorists move closer to personal experience in organizations. Their attention is on the intersubjective, the interconnections among those who staff organizations, and how people, realities, and social relations are constructed under conditions of power and conflict. The goal is to encounter and then deconstruct the contradictions and suppression of conflict that exist in the dominant discourse. The attempt is to identify that which prevents honest personal expression of needs and thoughts in organizational life. The goal in the process is to open the personal intellectual space for autonomy through reason (Alvesson & Deetz, 1996). Work from this perspective highlights the negative implications of arbitrary authority and subordination by technological rationality that only protects the dominant group interest to the detriment of the individual's personhood. The needs of the powerful organization are superceded by the needs of the people who comprise the organization. It is their needs to be highlighted as organizations move toward achieving their intent.

Critical theories focus on current social and organizational conditions and seek to uncover the costs of modernity that technology cannot fix. In fact, from this perspective, technology may participate in some of the problem creation. These theorists want to eliminate the mistaken or false consciousness that is attached to the myth of modernism—the myth that what is modern is by definition better with better results for the individual. An identification of false consciousness can begin a personal and organizational reconstruction of understanding of the current reality that allows inclusion of multiple considerations from all stakeholders. Multiple points of view serve to overcome systematic distortions in communication that occur as a result of the domination of one perspective. In the process, this reconstruction offers an understanding and critique of domination so that the degree to which the individual is an active participant in his or her own subjugation is made clear. It is assumed that from this new consciousness a more moral and therefore enlightened discourse will ensue, where all organizational participants will provide equal contribution to the future of a changed organization offering more liberty and freedom for all to reach their potential.

In the radical humanist paradigm, critical theorists seek discourse so that all voices can be heard and so that individual perspectives can be articulated and respected. This allows individual discourse participants to self-transform beyond the constrictions of dominant systems. Competent, thinking individuals will become "smarter" about the situations illuminated in the discourse in order to come to their own personal conclusions free from subtle or not-so-subtle pressures to take a particular position. The discourse process, by its very nature, supports variation in ways of coming to an understanding and determining the personal consequence of that understanding. Individualism and individual liberation is the driving force in this type of action guided by critical theory. Collective thought or action is not of interest; personal enlightenment and transformation is.

Radical humanist critical theorists are very explicit about the purpose of their research—to make organizations communities of authentic dialogue among empowered individuals rather than instruments of personal domination (Handler, 1990). As the reader will see in the next section, these theorists have greatly influenced postmodern theory development.

Postmodern Theory

As with critical theory, the more subjectivist aspects of postmodernism also fit comfortably with radical humanism. However, as emphasized in our earlier discussion of postmodernism from the radical structuralist perspective, remember that there is no clear consensus about exactly what constitutes postmodern theory (Hassard, 1993). Postmodern theorists from this paradigm react to cultural changes by deconstructing organizational orthodoxy. Just because "We have always done it this way" or because it is the "rule" is no reason to shy away from revisiting practices and procedures. New situations (or even well-known, old situations) must be investigated for their consequences to the individual. Currently, the radical humanist postmodern focus is on the individual experience of participating in the information age and maintaining personal and professional boundaries when confronted by the anarchy, fragmentation, and inconsistencies in organizations and society. The approach rejects the unidimensional relation between forms of representation, such as words and images, and the objective world in favor of "the rules grounded in practices which precede subjectivity" (Power, 1992, p. 111). All postmodern theorists recognize subjectivity, but radical humanists reach out to embrace it to the point of personalization.

Most postmodernists recognize that the traditional social and economic structures that have evolved since the industrial revolution are now fragmented. What has developed is a diverse, almost indefinable network, held together by information technology and postmodernist sensibility (Lash & Urry, 1987). This has created a sense of uneasiness for organizations as they are forced to abandon the modern and become what some have called "actors in a play" (Lyotard & Thibaud, 1985). The basis of the play is language. Language becomes the game of organizing. It is in flux. In fact, meaning is constantly slipping so that it is never stabilized into unchanging terms. This focus becomes radical humanist in orientation when personal experience with language becomes the focus. What is the consequence of a personal understanding of the message? What does that have to do with a person's role to be "played" in organization? What are the personal consequences of learning the language, learning the rules?

It is through the language game that the various discourses emanate, and it is through language and discourse that critical analysis becomes possible. Critical analysis permits the central notions of postmodern subjectivist thought to appear. This critical stance allows organizational members to be suspicious about intellectual assumptions (Lawson, 1985) and to engage in **reflexivity**, which is the ability of the human mind to turn back on itself and know that it is knowing (Platt, 1989). This process allows deconstruction to occur, thus identifying the real, the language, and the universe divorced from language. It is from this self-reflection that the person becomes cognizant of the "games" and the personal consequences of those games. With this information, then, the person is prepared to change the language, the communication patterns, and the game in favor of his or her own empowerment.

A postmodern approach to the individual within organizations suggests that knowledge cannot be characterized with any prestige, nor can it be separated from everyday life. Knowledge, then, is "more or less" knowledge, interesting to the individual, and no more. For the individual within organizational life, the expectation of linear "progress" or even the progress narrative is rejected. Linearity precludes many voices, so linear progress is rejected in order to allow for the possibility of multiple alternative voices in the discourse. Further, there is no assumption of rationality in the discourse in order to capture the wisdom and power of the nonrational and the surprise of the irrational. Once an individual recognizes that his or her own perceptions of the situation within the organization have merit—in fact, they are just as meritorious as any other perspective—personal permission to enter the conversation is likely. Once in the conversation, because it is a very personal one, progress related to the object of focus will occur simply because energy is directed in that way. But the expectation of linear achievement of goals is eliminated because there is no "if . . . then" linearity in the conversation or work process. Results emerge almost serendipitously as a result of the multiple perspectives, honest conversations, and consciousness raising that have ensued.

Raising suppressed voices is important to postmodernists, and finding ways to demarginalize these voices is critically important to radical humanists in order to achieve individual transformational change. Farmer (1998) suggests that there are three aspects of demarginalizing what is unconscious in organizations. First, administrators have to accept that the unconscious is an important aspect of organizational life that has been trivialized by rational thinkers. Psychological considerations are not peripheral, but are actually very much tied to what happens in organizations and in helping one understand why things happen. Second, once the unconscious is recognized, it is important to accept the interpretations that emerge from repressed thoughts. Third, dismantling the oppressive mechanisms within the organization that keep the unconscious suppressed must occur. "Because language and speech are intersubjective, so the unconscious is transpersonal" (Farmer, 1998, p. 69).

Because of the paradigmatic assumptions, the radical humanist postmodernist is really unconcerned about theory construction at the institutional level. In fact, it is rejected as not useful. Instead, the focus is on individual power and how individuals become empowered through coordinated action. Managers no longer control fate. The power is in the social interdependence that is unique to each organizational relationship of each person. This is the transpersonal aspect of understanding, devoid of theories that bind the organization to prescribed avenues of analysis and performance.

Postmodernists challenge the concept of grand narratives; history becomes individual histories, and professionals represent only their own construction of what they should do in their discipline. The concept of a professional is called into question and the privileged position of persons in positions of authority for whatever reason is questioned. Organizationally, managers, administrators, and persons with formal power fall off their pedestals and are subject to scrutiny. No longer do the cloaks of professionalism or disciplinary lines allow one to hide behind illusions of expertise. There is no more of "do it my way because I know what is best." Diversity becomes relevant—with all the differences that this implies. The more information from more standpoints, the richer the potential, even in the chaos and cacophony of opinions. Strengths are based in individuals rather than in silos of oppressive professionalism.

Antiadministration. Since postmodernists reject established notions about organizations, it is important to consider what would happen if one tried to view an organization from a different, nonrational perspective. Antiadministration approaches are such examples. Just as rational approaches attempted to prescribe how one might begin to perform administratively in an organization using rational thought and linear decision making, antiadministration begins to develop circular or nonrational strategies for organizing. Antiadministration is the most complete current description about what a nonrational radical humanist organization might be like.

Antiadministration is the embodiment of the rejection of bureaucratic technology and technocratic rationality seen in most postmodern thought (see Arendt, 1998; Heidegger, 1977; Marcuse, 1991; Oakeshott, 1962). It demonstrates the same antipathy to bureaucracy as postmodernism, but it differs in its solution in organizations. The solution is a type of self-conscious practice that is hoped to produce relevance for all stakeholders in the organization. Those taking an antiadministration view see facts as social constructs, such that the facts are changing as the context changes. In recognizing the complexity of current organizations, this position calls for a serious exploration of bureaucracy and its internal functioning and relationships to other societal features. From this position, it is also necessary to explore the place and functioning of this complexity in the lives of individuals as bio-psycho-socio-spiritual entities (Farmer, 1999, p. 304). The human side of the organizational enterprise must take central stage in the discourse. With this attention to the individual humanity in organization comes a recognition that the societal/contextual factors to be considered will include the political, legal, economic, psychological, sociological, biological, cultural, and spiritual.

There is no simple way to grapple with the personal and organizational together. Understanding and managing this complexity requires a personal self-consciousness of those within organizations built on assumptions of contingency (planning for the chance or possible event), plurality (there is no single dominant answer or truth), and arbitrariness (meaning depends on the roles and relationships in the context). In other words, a personal understanding of organizations requires assumptions that anything might happen because anything might be true because everything depends on everything else.

From this there is a recognition that not only is bureaucracy not possible but it is also not desirable. In its antipathy toward bureaucracy, an antiadministrative goal is avoidance of marginalization. It is against hierarchy because hierarchy serves to marginalize participants. Antiadministration holds an emphasis on achieving human liberty with demarginalized groups, types of reason, and language. Giving preference to certain groups (or types of thought or certain language) marginalizes not only the preferred group but all others. This same marginalization happens against alternative ways of thinking, ways of communication, or ways of capturing meaning.

The alternative to bureaucracy is a type of play that allows the use of reflexive (reflective) language. Play results in a playful framing and reframing of the situation where multiple perspectives are entertained. "What ifs" are considered so that not just the scientific answer gets precedence, but also the aesthetic aspects of imagination comes from the margins into the organizational investigation and analysis. The organization becomes antiadministration to the degree that measures of organizational success other than efficiency are considered. This opens the opportunity for social justice, liberation, and the public good to become part of the consideration of organizational quality. Farmer (1999) calls this a process of transcending self-interest (p. 316).

Antiadministration offers an alternative to hierarchy and bureaucracy[1] by suggesting a more interpretive process of organizing that promotes and values understanding in organizations in a way that all are equal even though their positions differ. This change in the way of organizing is based on dialogue where knowledge is seen as valuable and true for those who recognize it as such. There is a shared commitment to the work and a shared commitment to create shared language. The idea is to facilitate an engagement in the organizing process by all stakeholders who know that the process is always changing but is essential to the effort and to personal self-actualization. The process of organizing and including is built on care and respect where participants are humble, hopeful, and trusting that all will contribute to the search for possibilities in the organization. This requires comfort with multiplicity, with conflict, and with the creation of many options to select for the next stage of the organization. Through the search for options, it is hoped that liberation and empowerment of all will be achieved.

The practice of antiadministration (Farmer, 1995, 1998, 1999) is based on several simple principles. First, there should be hesitancy in decision making. Work should be tentative, slow, intentional, interpersonal, and adaptive. This means no "quick fixes." It should be skeptical with a real resistance to finding a final, true answer. If it feels like the "right" answer, try the opposite alternative as well. Work should be collaborative in that decision making should connect all stakeholders in a tentative process. It should be incremental with an enthusiastic engagement of "muddling through," including much recycling and various iterations to a contingent finding. This decision should be full of "it depends" so that the value of the interaction of all stakeholders and all perspectives is respected over efficient, quick action.

Second, the process should be based on **alterity** that moves knowing the "other" at a distance to a real relationship with the "other." Alterity removes objective engagement with others in the organization and replaces objectivity with real, subjective, personal connections. The stakeholders in an antiadministration framework overcome distance by valuing each individual's self-identity. The "other" is different but not distant. In this difference, meaning making is promoted so that what different people bring to the organization can really be part of the process. Difference presents opportunity for personal growth. Growth happens as all stakeholders are compelled to understand and find meaning in the difference. No discourse, no way of being, thinking or doing takes precedence over another. Difference, then, is the medium of the discussion, rather than being marginalized through a dominant discourse regarding the way it "is" or "should be."

Finally, the practice of antiadministration counts on imagination over instrumental rationality for the work. Instead of deductive, linear thinking that limits options, this approach calls for a spontaneous, open, creative, uncertain, ambiguous, reflexive stance. Divergent thinking is preferred over convergent thinking. This makes room for play, games, dance, and song and the creation of different metaphors for work and organizations. This divergence, developed without a need for consensus, along with an embracing of conflict, is what makes this approach radical humanist. Games are encouraged to exist in the sense that the rules for the organizational structure and organizational behavior are expected to be made up as needed. Each who wishes to play is included, no person is seen to be the first or best authority, each game is different, and each time there is a need a different person may go first or take the lead in creating the structure and the rules of operation. If the secretary has the best idea about how to help clients access service, test the idea by trying to recruit recipients, and if it works, no one will see this as inappropriate or surprising. This type of playfulness ("He had an idea that worked, now let's use it until it does not work any more") should generate options, alternatives, and ideas that have not yet been imagined to respond to the as yet inexperienced in postmodern organizations. Instead of the familiar organizational chart with many symbols of hierarchy and power, the antiadministration organizational design may more closely resemble a tic-tac-toe game where players and places change depending on the perceived need.

Figure 11.4 shows the theories discussed in this chapter and their placement within the radical humanist paradigm. Notice that their placement is a reflection of commonalties with assumptions from neighboring paradigms.

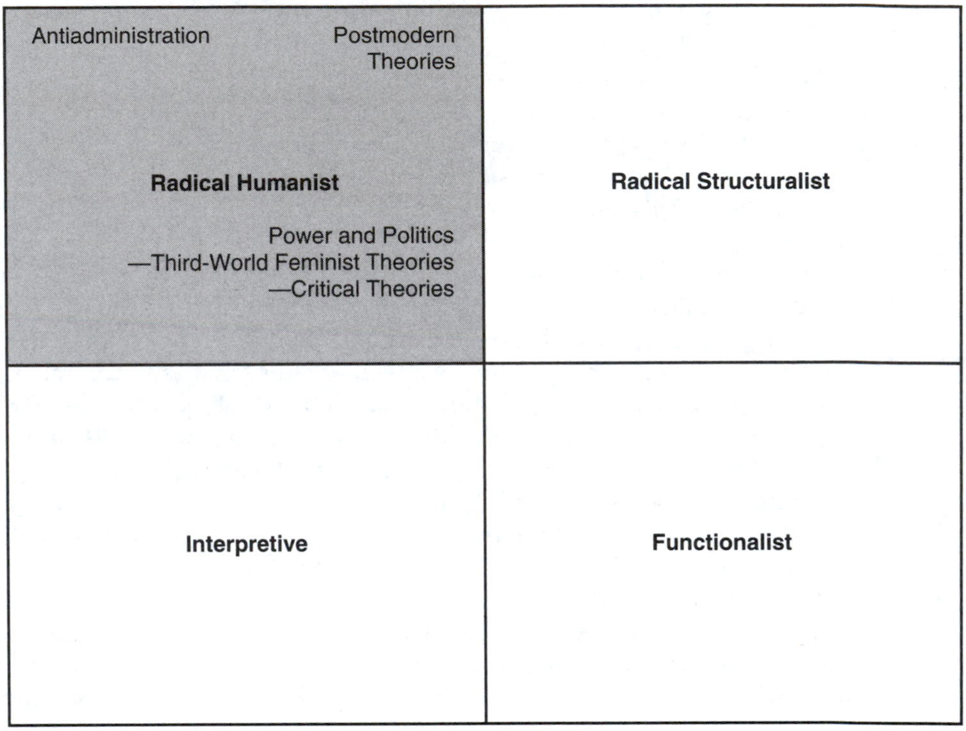

FIGURE 11.4   Organizational Theories within the Radical Humanist Paradigm

Costs and Benefits of the Radical Humanist Perspective and Its Theories

The greatest costs and the greatest benefits of the radical humanist perspective come from its position against traditional theoretical frameworks and the assumptions upon which they are built. Radical humanists make every idea worthy of consideration, but also make it very difficult to test ideas using any commonly agreed upon standard or manner of testing. Having a context tied so heavily to different personalities who determine what has merit makes any judgment according to commonly agreed upon standards impossible. The only thing that can be measured is whether the individuals participating in the process are more aware of the elements and complexity of the focus of their inquiry. Are they smarter for having participated? Are they more able to effect changes in desired directions? Are they more free? Can they more easily reach their human potential? The challenge is to determine when one *really* knows the answers to these very fundamental questions because *really* knowing the answers (and the relevant questions) will change over time and context.

From a philosophical perspective, does this consciousness and liberty mean more satisfaction in the work environment and more personal happiness? At some level, many of the postmodern thinkers would hope that this is the result of all the desired conscious analysis, but perhaps satisfaction and happiness are not natural by-products of empowerment. From a metaphysical perspective, what is needed for consciousness raising in order to escape the constraints of structural limits may not produce happiness. Instead, what may be produced is a transcendent empowerment regarding the full role of the individual in organization and society. This requires taking personal power and personal responsibility for the context of work and assuring that the context is structured to support all human potential. This sounds like very hard work and work that may require commitment and responsibility beyond what is normally found in one's work life.

Perhaps this also means that the separation between work and the rest of life becomes less definable. For those who enjoy the challenges of the work organization, this may be a pleasant, seamless existence. For those who need real boundaries between work and the rest of life, the demands of work from a radical humanist perspective may be too costly and too intrusive.

Clearly, the critical and analytic demands of thoughtful life within organizations working from the radical humanist perspective could be exhausting to some. In addition, the antipositivistic and antideterministic stance of the paradigm will be a source of great discomfort for those who really must work from the assumption of an immutable truth and a determined human existence. A wish for certainty and a rejection of subjectivity will cause some to reject out of hand both the uncontrolled nature of the radical humanist organizational process and the nongeneralizable insiders' views of organizational reality. Since those taking a traditional view of knowledge and organizing see nothing rigorous or useful in the radical humanist view, much criticism will accrue from traditional researchers, administrators, or leaders. What might be worse, no criticism will be forthcoming because what is produced from this perspective is not seen to be even worthy of critical assessment. There will probably be great criticism of the preferred qualitative aspects of radical humanist research designs. But because other ways of knowing, including art and religion, can be brought to the inquiry process and product, many will question the worth of the effort and reject the results as irrelevant to knowledge building.

On the other hand, the philosophical perspective of radical humanism creates an adequate space for play. Playing with ideas about organizations, how they do work and should work in the future, and how human nature fits into this work is absolutely possible here. The power of ideas and the power of people shift in such ways that all can benefit from the exchange of ideas. Granted, there is little control of the research or work process, and there exists much need to trust others and the emergence of process and product. But individuals committed to achieving the goals of the organization of which they are members will have a great chance of recognizing and being recognized for the contributions made. This makes experiencing organizing and the organization profoundly unlike what is found in many organizational structures today.

Conclusion

The theories touched on in this chapter have one thing in common—they question everything. Theorists holding radical humanist assumptions are reacting against dominant ways of thinking that oppress individuals in countless ways. This "anti" stance poses somewhat of a dilemma in that some feminist, critical, and postmodern theorists are too quickly written off by persons from other paradigms for railing against *what is* rather than offering viable options for how things *could be*. But that is just the point. Determining what is a viable option is a judgment call and is usually based on what dominant thinkers believe to be acceptable. It is little wonder that dialogue stops and stalemate ensues when alternative thinkers want each individual to have a space for their own personal approach. Unfortunately, at this stage of the development of this paradigm, even the concept of antiadministration implies *what it is not*, rather than *what is*.

The radical humanist paradigm is foreign to current forms of organizational life in the United States. It may be the rare person who can comprehend what it would be like to practice in an organization that espouses a completely different set of assumptions and values than previously encountered for centuries in North American organizational life. However, we contend that the vast majority of people in the Western world understand radical humanism more than they know. The focus on individualism over the collective good, the right to free speech, and a host of other factors taken for granted in U.S. society fit quite well with radical humanist thought.

If radical humanists are individualists, then the individualism in U.S. society would seem to fit within this paradigm. However, most people were schooled to accept as "truth" that organizations are collections of people who come together for a purpose and work toward common goals. Therefore, individualism within organizations historically was defined as a problem or as a nonrational act, appropriate for one's personal life but something to give up (at least partially) in one's organizational life. Ironically, radical humanists would suggest that individualism within organizations is actually a desirable condition. Not only would bringing one's sense of self into an organization be a way to strengthen the organization but it would also be compatible with the way in which employees have been socialized to seek individual self-fulfillment. Certainly, radical humanism offers provocative possibilities currently being tested in some cutting-edge, high-tech organizations.

Next, we examine the radical humanist organization, the prototype of the radical humanist paradigm. It is time to see how the theories in this chapter can be translated into understanding human service practice in organizations that come from a radical humanist perspective.

ENDNOTE

1. We are indebted to Jon Singletary for his work in synthesizing the work of Farmer and bringing it to social work administrative practice.

CHAPTER 12

Understanding for Practice in Radical Humanist Organizations

The most radical or postmodern approaches to designing organizations are based on the assumptions of the radical humanist paradigm. But it is also interesting to note that much of the language in the traditional and popular organizational literature sounds very compatible with radical humanism. Words such as *empowerment*, *transpersonalism*, and *organizational spirit*, and concepts such as *transformational leadership*, *leading with soul*, and an assortment of other rather spiritual and artistic terms and phrases are sprinkled throughout the current management literature. We caution the reader about such terminology. Often, the language of radical humanism is used wittingly or unwittingly to engage employees in organizations that are still based on dominant modes of thinking. Therefore, one has to be very careful to look beyond the language used and into the behaviors and attitudes within the organization to determine if the organization is indeed based on assumptions of the radical humanist paradigm.

In the radical humanist organization, there will be a passion for individual transformation. Such organizations will recognize and respect diversity, but they will also not be satisfied until they have made changes that will fully liberate individuals from oppression. Participants in radical humanist organizations will not necessarily concern themselves with consensus building, but rather will embrace conflict and difference in order to empower individuals. Empowering individuals will take different forms, since no two people are alike. Radical humanists do not hold deterministic assumptions about universal principles or values. In fact, they will strive for creative innovation that takes people to places where they may not have been before and even where others fear to go. If one seeks comfort in well-defined structures, universal values, and certainty, the radical humanist organization could well be one's worse nightmare.

Radical humanist organizations will be loose collections of people who are open to individual differences. Rather than coming together for a joint purpose, there may not be consensus about one organizational goal. There may be multiple goals. In fact, organizational goals may be constantly shifting as new ideas emerge, if there are organizational goals at all. A group of practitioners may come together in order to share creative energy, but they may not agree on intervention methods, accountability standards, or ethical positions, but feel that their practice with people in pain is improved because of their association with other service professionals also wishing to provide their own best possible practice. The intent is to find ways to increase individuals' abilities to be, to self-actuate, to create, to perform, or to do whatever the person desires to be or do.

For example, the concept of self-help is based in radical humanist assumptions. In an organization dedicated to self-help activities, there is an assumption that every individual will have to determine what is a quality-of-life experience for her or him. Granted, some of the same methods may be used across people, but each person will have a carefully customized plan for achieving his or her individual desires and growth, with every person changing at his or her own pace and unique way. Persons join self-help groups for very personal reasons, having unique needs from those of other members. Change in each person's life, even among others having had a similar experience, will be very different from what other persons experience. The radical humanist organization is an incubator for individual transformation.

At this time in organizational development, few fully formed radical humanist organizations can be identified. Close to this organizational prototype are the new, fast-paced, high-technology organizations with structures that exist only in the minds of their founders and whose employees work wherever they want, whenever they want, as long as there is electricity and a computer with sufficient capacity. The central notion of information and the need for its free flow defines such organizations. What is not yet clear is how other types of organizations with other types of goals, including service ones, can be constructed within this vision of work.

Perhaps the structure of a loosely affiliated number of social workers who form a private practice group may have elements of a radical humanist perspective. Assuming that the empowerment of individual therapists to do their own best work with clients is their intent, rather than collaboration and community among therapists, a private practice group could be viewed as a radical humanist organization. Therapists could share the same building, even the same office space, yet rarely see one another. Their basic needs could be handled by a management firm that attends to independent, autonomous individuals who rent space within the facility. Tasks pertaining to mail sorting and delivery, answering phones, and building management is purely a contractual arrangement in which individual private agents go about their business without a sense of being part of a community or collective. Similar to artists' studios where each person rents a space and seeks personal transformation through his or her medium of choice, the individualism of private practice could potentially fit within the radical humanist paradigm.

This chapter focuses on what it is like to practice in radical humanist organizations. We return to the five questions originally introduced in Chapter 6 to guide the reader: (1) What are the characteristics of organizations most likely to operate from the assumptions of this paradigm? (2) How does one begin to assess this type of organization? (3) What language is used in these organizations? (4) What approaches to practice are most likely to fit within this type organization? and (5) What are the implications of paradigmatic assumptions for social work leaders in this type organization?

Characteristics of Radical Humanist Organizations

Radical humanist organizations are considered alternative agencies to traditional, functionalist organizations. More than that, because they hold nothing in common, the radical humanist organization can be conceived as the exact opposite of functionalist organizations. Radical humanists' openness to diversity and their high desire for change opposes their functionalist colleagues. If there is an alternative agency that is seen as "on the fringe" by functionalists, it would be the radical humanist organization. Radical humanists would be seen as turning the functionalist organization upside down because they do not organize in any way that would be understandable from a functionalist perspective. Everything held as "true" for the functionalist would be questioned by the radical humanist, in the same spirit of the earlier discussion of the antiadministration framework. On the other hand, like interpretivists, radical humanists are open to diversity and context. Like radical structuralists, radical humanists are focused on change and are open to conflict. These linkages suggest that the paradigm, though departing fundamentally from traditional ways of doing the business of organizing, still maintains elements in common with paradigms that developed over the last half of the twentieth century.

In previous chapters, we have presented the characteristics of alternative agencies and we continue that pattern here. This time, Table 12.1 summarizes the already familiar characteristics of alternative agencies, adding commentary on how radical humanist organizations fit with these characteristics.

Radical humanist organizations are alternative agencies, but they are so different from other organizations that the very terminology used to describe their characteristics may be a loose fit. For example, the term *clients* will rarely be used in these organizations because *client* as a concept implies a power imbalance in which a professional has expertise. In radical humanist organizations, professional lines are no longer drawn since radical humanists respect everyone's experience and a "client" is considered the expert in his or her own life. Professionals are not held on pedestals, so clients can benefit from their insights. Instead, each person has expertise based on his or her subjective experience and professionals and clients mutually benefit from their respective expertise. *Leadership* is another word that fits uneasily into radical humanist language. For radical humanists, leadership is a shared concept, one in which people take turns as designated leaders, but in which there are not permanent lines drawn between leaders and followers. There is a preference to use each person's competence and strengths as needs emerge. *Service delivery* as a term sits uneasily in the language of the radical humanist as well. *Service delivery* implies that something will be given to someone. In instances of individual transformation, service is not "delivered" as much as one attains the knowledge or skills to be able to empower oneself. It is not delivered or given to that person; instead, the person accesses what is necessary. Similarly, the concept of *size* is somewhat irrelevant since radical humanist organizations are not in the business of worrying about size and expansion. Whatever is necessary is what is

**TABLE 12.1   Characteristics of Alternative Agencies:
The Radical Humanist Organization**

Characteristics	Alternative Agencies	Radical Humanist Organizations
Clients	Are formed to advocate for or deliver services to groups whose needs are not being met by other agencies	Will focus efforts on cause advocacy, with an emphasis on individual transformation
Funding	Do not have well-established funding sources, which poses a risk to agency survival	Will need to locate funding sources that are interested in individual change and alternative perspectives; may have to focus on persons who can pay
Leadership	Typically are inspired by a charismatic individual who mobilizes volunteers and paid staff to action	Will see all persons as having potential to inspire and lead, finding charisma in more than one individual—a kind of strengths perspective
Service Delivery	Establish service delivery approaches, using client participation and evolving protocols	Involves members in their own delivery of services so that individual needs remain paramount
Size	Are typically small, given available resources	Will typically be small, resisting attempts to formally structure
Staff	Are heavily dependent on volunteers and staff who will work for less than other agencies pay	Relies heavily on paraprofessionals, volunteers, and other service recipients
Values	Have guiding values and ideologies that run counter to dominant opinions, doctrines, and practices	Runs counter to ideologies related to objectivism (external truth), accepting of alternative opinions and practices, focusing on individual empowerment and social justice

expected to develop. In other words, when one looks at the concepts typically used to characterize even other alternative agencies, the radical humanist organization does not fit. It is an alternative to the alternatives!

Recognizing the degree to which language constructs reality, assessing the radical humanist organization is somewhat difficult because there is a tendency to use words (e.g., *assessment*) that have a different meaning in each paradigm. We now turn to "assessing" these organizations with the caveat that special attention to the importance of thinking about terminology and language has just begun.

Assessing the Radical Humanist Organization

There are basic underlying assumptions about locus of control and change in a radical humanist organization. It is designed to seek radical change. Radical change is intended to transform individuals, and although individual transformation may lead to broader social change, this is only a residual of personal, individual transformation. Radical humanists, then, will not be spending time mobilizing groups of people toward joint goals. When these organizations deal with groups, each member of the group will be expected to unapologetically have or develop his or her own personal agenda.

Table 12.2 provides a summary of some of the ways in which radical humanists approach their work. The foci and tasks of Table 12.2 are the same as introduced in previous practice chapters, but the goals of the organization have changed to reflect a very different orientation. The table provides an overview of the basic goals of the radical humanist organization in important categories one might use to understand an agency. We will now briefly expand on each area.

Focus A: Agency-Environment Relationships

We will examine the radical humanist organization's view of how the environment is central to the work and the individuals doing the work, elaborating particularly on funding and clients.

Environment. The radical humanist organization recognizes the environment as part of the broader context in which it operates. The organization and environment are viewed as mutually influential as diverse opinions, perspectives, and values interact. The organization embraces environmental forces that represent a diversity of opinions, recognizing that diversity can create oppression that stultifies human potential. Radical humanists do not always worry about seeking ways to build consensus among differing opinions. Instead, they are intent on addressing issues of oppression that affect organizational participants so that everyone has a chance to be everything they can be.

In fact, the radical humanist organization is so connected to the environment that its boundaries are typically far more porous than agencies with other paradig-

TABLE 12.2   Goals of the Radical Humanist Organization by Task

Focus and Task	Goal
Focus A: Agency-Environment Relationships	
Environment	To see the environment as a source of invigorating differences and unlimited subjectivities, once liberation from limits is achieved.
Funding	To seek financial resources that give individuals as much control as possible.
Client Populations and Referral Sources	To open one's doors to individuals from all walks of life, embracing diversity.
Focus B: The Organization	
Mission/Philosophy	To seek individual transformation.
Values	To inspire ultimate self-determination for all persons, thus respecting that every person will self-determine in his or her own unique way.
Management and Leadership Style	To alternate and even share leadership roles among members in as informal a way as possible with the goal being individual transformation.
Organization and Program Structure	To develop minimal structure so that changes can easily be made in an ongoing manner without impinging on the individuals inside the structure.
Programs and Services	To create opportunities for people to grow and develop individually.
Personnel Policies and Procedures	To establish minimal rules, procedures, and protocols so that freedom is engendered.
Staff	To engage persons in a creative process, thus seeking persons who are conscious, self-directed, and committed.
Communication	To use the latest in information technology to enhance connections among people, while also honoring all methods, means, and mediums of communication.
Products	To transform individuals.

matic assumptions. Such an organization might have clients that also deliver service or service providers who are also recipients of service. What is important is doing what is necessary to access the resources to reach personal potential, defined differently by everyone associated with the organization. Since diversity is embraced and differences are expected, there is little need to shield the agency against environmental forces or to control what is inevitably uncontrollable. The concept of the environment as a turbulent source of unexpected conditions to be feared is foreign to the radical humanist. Instead, the environment is exciting and stimulating, for it brings unlimited possibilities for liberation. The biggest problem the environment imposes on radical humanists is that there is such an explosion of knowledge that one can never fully attend to the rapid swirl of information amid unlimited possibilities. Thus, there is heavy reliance on discourse and dialectic to gather multiple ideas about meaning and implications of current conditions.

Funding.   Radical humanist organizations may have difficulty developing and maintaining a stable funding base because they are seen as too threatening to the status quo or too "loopy" to be defined and controlled for accountability. Stable funders may appear to participants to have too much power in the organization. Beyond this, though, the creativity and innovation that permeates radical humanist organizations suggest traditional ways of thinking about funding do not always fit well here, nor are they necessary. The idea of an organization receiving United Way dollars or government grants and contracts does not even compute here because these funding sources would not be able to identify with radical humanist approaches in which outcome measurement is not seen as relevant. Perhaps some private foundations with quirky leaders who are enamored with postmodernist thought might consider funding such organizations, but even they might be a little concerned about how to monitor organizational activities for accountability.

Funding, then, for the radical humanist organization may be as individualistic as the agency's mission. For example, persons who participate might pay for what they receive, in much the same way as in a for-profit business, or someone might sponsor another person by donating money for a scholarship for services. The radical humanist organization is a place in which individual entrepreneurs could flourish, if they could also maintain a focus on individual rights and responsibilities. Just as private donations, endowments, personal fees, and other private monies fund innovative, traditional companies, the radical humanist organization could find its support in those arenas. Consider that radical humanist organizations fit very well into free-market economies where freedom and individualism reigns and everyone is encouraged to "do their own thing." In fact, funding patterns in radical humanist organizations could make them very much a part of free-market enterprise, especially because of the recognition and inclusion of politics in the organizational and individual consciousness.

Client Populations and Referral Sources.   In the radical humanist organization, renewed consciousness reveals that organizing is a process rather than an object. The organization is always in the process of organizing rather than staying within some defined picture of what it must be. Therefore, engaging clients and referral sources in the organizing process is critical. Accessing the resources, information, or people to engage in the service process is the role of all organizational participants. This inclusive shift in perspective allows a new way of thinking about the stakeholders in the organization so that they become self-organizing. Clients are not so much *clients* as they are *members* or *participants.* Radical humanists will see clients and referral sources as participants in the work of the organization and will be highly inclusive in their approach.

Stakeholders in the radical humanist organization will be seekers of service or knowledge who emerge from the larger environment. They will be encouraged to represent as much difference as one can imagine. In this organization, participants will not feel they have to conform, but will engage in experiences in which they actually self-transform. Thus, the very concept of referral sources may be difficult to comprehend in the radical humanist organization because there may not be other radical humanist organizations available within the community to which to refer participants. Instead, there may be a loose network of groups and opportunities that look very different from traditional service delivery systems. What is necessary will be constructed by the individuals needing the service, which is a very different approach to human potential development. It grows from within the individuals with need instead of being delivered from without, so monetary funding may be less necessary than human resources for human service delivery.

In summary, radical humanists view funding and participants as resources from the environment, representing diverse interests. Funding patterns may look very much like those of innovative for-profits that are dependent on private sources of support. Or they might not look like any configuration yet seen in human services. Clients may not be called *clients* at all because *clients* implies that professionals do something *for* someone in need, when radical humanist organizations attempt to support individualization and growth among all concerned. This view of the environment sets a context for examining the organization's internal structure (or lack thereof).

Focus B: The Organization

The radical humanist organization is influenced by frameworks that are grouped under power and politics as well as postmodernist perspectives. These are reflected in the organization's internal operations.

Mission/Philosophy. The mission of the radical humanist organization is to establish a platform from which individuals can self-transform within arenas where power and politics do not always support such transformation. There is an assumption that the societal context and its institutions are oppressive. Radical humanists engage in meaning and sensemaking, but they do not stop with this enhanced understanding. Their philosophy is that one will take this new meaning and sensemaking and use it to make individual changes against personal oppression. There is acceptance that this is not always easy, particularly when one has been oppressed in multiple ways. In human services, this might mean helping a victim of domestic violence recognize her right not to be violated, not through therapy but through discussions with others who have been abusers, victims, and therapists. The goal would be for this woman to find her own way not just to safety but to a sense of power such that she would never allow personal victimization in the future.

Embracing diversity and opening the possibility for mutual engagement requires that organizational members hear multiple views. Members will often be in conflict when views clash. However, the expectation is that conflict is a healthy part of the creative process. Its purpose is for clarity, not to oppress or to "win." Through conflict, clarity is derived and strength for making change can happen. Participants can actually find this creative endeavor playful: "It requires a new way of being in the world. It requires being in the world without fear. Being in the world with play and creativity. Seeking after what's possible. Being willing to learn and to be surprised" (Wheatley & Kellner-Rogers, 1996, p. 5). This playfulness seems counterintuitive, given the serious and incredible oppressions many participants face or have experienced. Part of the agency's philosophy is seeing the nature of what is or has been in a completely different way and pushing for change in as unusual and creative a way as possible. There is a hopeful energy in this work.

Values. The radical humanist organization is grounded in subjectivism, which takes a relativist stance on values. Radical humanists are very open to situational ethics in which choices made in one situation may change in light of new information or a shift in the scenario. Being relativists, radical humanists believe that principles and values change with time, that there are multiple truths, and that there are numerous ways of knowing and doing that can lead to useful results.

True consciousness, true understanding of the personal implications of the work and work life, is an important element of radical humanist organizational quality standards. All the dimensions in the organization that might constrain individual fulfillment or potential are targets for elimination because of the belief that the best work and the best effects can be achieved when individual organization members are not constrained by anything that might inhibit personal development. Rules and procedures will not be present in any objective way. Instead, decisions about what needs to be done now will be determined by those involved now. Liberty, then, is a central value within the organization. The idea is to transcend structures, bonds, or limits that exist in traditional organizations. There is a belief that existing social patterns hamper development, so questioning the status quo is not only expected but it is also demanded in order that true liberty of all can be achieved through honest dialogue.

Management and Leadership Style. Management is almost a misnomer in the radical humanist organization. Terms such as *coordinators*, *facilitators*, and even *team leaders* may better describe these organizational roles. Leadership is completely reconceptualized from traditional notions of leaders and followers. Everyone is considered to carry elements of leadership within radical humanist organizations. In a sense, each person is his or her own leader since individualism is so valued.

In the radical humanist organization, needed structures, patterns of behavior, and processes for accomplishing goals are designed as individuals come to know what they need in order to do their work. Through dialogue among participants, agreement is achieved about what makes sense. Behaviors and relationships, especially related to support and trust built on excellent communication, emerge from the process of doing the work. All this is useful but temporary. The conditions of work are the focus of the designated leader. It is his or her role to assure the support of necessary structures. Freedom, not conformity and compliance, is the vision. Individual responsibility where people do for themselves what has been done to them in other organizations in the past becomes the focus of all members of the organization. Think about work teams where each person is secure in his or her own skills and talents and all of the team together have constructed a vision about where they want to go and then go about the business of getting there with what seems from the outside to be unlimited energy and creativity. This is the type of "leaderlessness" seen in the radical humanist organization. The organization becomes a virtually leaderless organization because all who are part of it are leading it to creative consequences because people are supported for who they really are. This sets up a productive context for both stability and personal discovery.

In a radical humanist organization, each individual needs to work at his or her maximum pace or level of creativity. Having said that, management, in fact, has little to manage other than information. This is because few employees are present to be managed and few decisions will rest with a single individual. The expectation is that all employees within their levels of competence will participate in all portions of the life of the organization. Just as no piece of communication should take precedence over another, no privilege is given to a particular individual within any existing organizational structure. The idea of "the buck stops here" has no meaning within the radical humanist organization because both the authority and the accountability rest with all who have a stake in the particular organizational undertaking. All are held accountable by all who participate in the organizational dialogue and the organizational life.

In service organizations, rather than having a full-scale radical humanist organization in the current human service environment, it will be more likely that some of the spirit of the radical humanist perspective will be operationalized in smaller units of an organization by midlevel organizational leaders who can promote and facilitate the vision on a smaller scale. At a minimum, this would include instituting a collaborative leadership style noted for collaborative decision making (see O'Connor & Netting, 1999) in which conflict is faced squarely when it arises and even encouraged as an element of creative thinking. This would also mean selection of employees who wish to have a great degree of liberty, autonomy, and individual responsibility within their work lives. This would include employees who are stable enough to agree to disagree.

Figure 12.1 provides a list of the characteristics of radical humanist social work leaders. See how these characteristics vary from those of previous paradigms.

Organization and Program Structure.   Not being certain that organizations really exist in anything other than a conceptual sense, radical humanist organizations do not recognize organizational structure as really important. Instead, the process of organizing the work and the perspectives of those who are involved in this organizing are of interest. This informal mode of organizing means that the nature of the organization evolves as new ideas or needs emerge. How things are struc-

FIGURE 12.1   Characteristics of Radical Humanist Social Work Leaders

1. Is comfortable with ambiguity, uncertainty, and new and emerging ideas
2. Thinks that hearing all perspectives is important
3. Sees conflict as inevitable when all perspectives are heard
4. Truly appreciates and acts on diversity
5. Tolerates differing opinions well
6. Is predisposed toward creativity and innovation
7. Has strong curiosity and passion for change
8. Is not satisfied with just understanding and meaning making, but is committed to turning what is discovered into action
9. Maintains one's sense of individualism within organizational life
10. Is self-directed
11. Is able to examine situations from many different directions and will argue passionately for a cause
12. Tolerates process, as long as radical change is the goal
13. Sees self-transformation of individuals as a desired state

tured today might change as situations and needs change tomorrow. Although radical humanists are concerned with how participants feel about the social world of the organization, they are equally concerned with how they use these feelings and meanings to advance the cause of individual change. Thus, the structure may change not for productivity's sake but because personal needs demand it.

Along with the surprisingly rapid development of the high-technology industry and the astonishing changes in everyday life brought about by the Internet, the structure and feel of the radical humanist organization is just beginning to emerge. At its most understandable in traditional organizational terms, the radical humanist organization is a loosely coupled entity where information is the organizing element. At its most radical, it demonstrates no measurable organizational structure, while at the same time also producing a desired product that results from concerted efforts of its members. These organizations may not have the same time and space orientation of more traditional organizations. People do not need to be working at the same time or in the same location in order for organizational goals to be attained. Through the help of telecommunications, members of organizations can maintain their own work rhythms, working while others sleep or working where others play, as long as the desired product is produced or the desired goal is attained. Think of a therapeutic service offered on the Internet. Therapists are located all over the world and the service is available at all times and in all parts of the world. What is being described is the emerging virtual organization where individuals are connected and organized via information technology—and nothing more.

Whether as a full organization or as a unit in a larger organization, a radical humanist approach requires the recognition of and the choice to live in the paradoxes of modern life. One of the major paradoxes of the radical humanist organization is that in the face of complexity, this type of organization seeks to think simply about how to organize human activities. Instead of being drawn to more complexity, participants in the radical humanist organization find more delightful ways of organizing their programs and services. Philosophy, poetics, novels, and spiritual teachings enter the dialogue as means of exploring what can be possible in the new organization. Team meetings might have poetry readings on a subject related to the work as a means of focusing all participants in a useful direction. This would be chosen over the presentation of a recipe for performance presented by those in charge. At the base of this thinking are new images of organizations and new incentives for the organization of human endeavor. This approach to organization calls for the questioning of, if not the breaking of, old habits, by investigating and questioning the beliefs about people, life, and the world that underlie them. It is this thinking and the resulting consciousness that is the essential ingredient for the construction of a different understanding of how to organize. If the radical humanist organization ever becomes the "traditional" organization of the future, it will be totally unrecognizable to those with only functionalist organizational experience.

Programs and Services.   In Chapter 1, we introduced different types of programs and services. Recall that *direct service programs* directly serve clients, *staff development and training programs* focus on staff, and *support programs* undergird direct service and staff programs. Radical humanist organizations may contain all three types of programs, but they will look very different from the same type of programs offered in other organizations.

Programs and services in radical humanist organizations focus as much on the experience as they would on final results, primarily because nothing is considered "final." The concept of *end products* or *outcomes* do not translate well in radical humanist organizations because things continually change, even change itself. But more important is that requiring certain outcomes as a measure of success is in itself a type of oppression. Therefore, radical humanist programs and services may not be appreciated by traditionalists who seek control, closure, or finality in their programming.

Programs and services are designed to be highly flexible—so flexible that they may not be "designed" as we commonly understand the process. Instead, they will be encouraged to emerge. They are intended to incorporate participants in every aspect of their own transformation as much as possible, in order to counter oppression and to seek customized approaches to change. In this way, two persons will not go through a radical humanist program in exactly the same way, nor will they experience exactly the same changes. This is likely the case in traditional programs also, but it is not recognized, is not accepted, or is hidden because achieving client conformity is valued. This nonstandardized way of programming is valued in the radical humanist organization because it is assumed to enhance growth and development, creating opportunities for unexpected possibilities. To traditionalists, this nonstandardized approach is nonscientific, if not irresponsible and unethical.

Personnel Policies and Procedures.   Personnel policies and procedures are not very important in the radical humanist organization. Certainly, some guidelines must be established legally for the organization to operate in a predominantly functionalist environment, but these procedures are kept to a minimum. In fact, procedure can be oppressive, and each person will have his or her own understanding of what any procedure means. Therefore, basic guidelines exist so that the organization will be able to function in the larger environment, but these will not be the focus of the organization or its members. Keeping things simple procedurally is a must, so that the complexity of understanding and change can be the focus.

Staff.   Six of the Myers-Briggs personality types fit within the radical humanist paradigm. The personality types that fit comfortably within the radical humanist worldview are those who are or aspire to be most individually autonomous: ISFJs, ESFJs, INFJs, ENFJs, INFPs, and INTJs. Introverted, sensing, feeling, judging types (ISFJs), with their sense of personal responsibility and their valuing of respect for oneself and others, are compatible with this perspective. Extroverted, sensing, feeling, judging types (ESFJs), who embrace a very different way into individuality, are also placed in this paradigm. These individuals derive their knowledge from their own sense experience and hold to a rather radical standard of intense caring and responsibility about people and their individual experiences. Introverted, intuitive, feeling, judging types (INFJs)—with their preference for the internal, subjective world of possibilities, ideas, and symbols—are radical humanists. This is true, too, for extroverted, intuitive, feeling, judging types (ENFJs), who use personal intuition to guide them when confronting the new, the unknown, and the possible. Introverted, intuitive, feeling, perceiving types (INFPs) have a personal intensity and caring about ideas, projects, or anything seen as important. This places them both subjectively and radically in this paradigm because of their interest and concern for human potential. In addition, introverted, intuitive, thinking, judging types (INTJs) are included here because of their concern for the inner or subjective world of possibilities and their intensity toward making their conscious visions into realities.

Notice that the largest numbers of Myers-Briggs personality types are located in this paradigm. This would suggest that the largest number of employees in any organization would approach the organization and overlay their own expectations from this perspective, regardless of the orientation of the organization. For the manager in a radical humanist organization, this means identifying the problem and simply getting out of the way as the members of the organization mobilize to take action to right that which is wrong. The challenge is to facilitate a common understanding of the problem and an understanding of that which can be associated with its existence. Employees with this worldview will be ethical relativists, seeing what is deemed "right" as being imbedded in the context. Multiple experiences with the reality will result in multiple constructions of the reality, its meaning, and what should be done about it.

Managing the consequences of the need to view all experiences and all goals from an individualistic lens will be a challenge. Coming to consensus or at least achieving the appropriate level of consciousness among all stakeholders to the question will require strength of character, great communication skills, and implicit trust in the potential of the individuals involved. The task of creating a culture to support this may be the responsibility of organizational administrators, but all the stakeholders must be helped to share the vision. This may become a challenge when the stakeholders do not share time or space.

If the organization is one with these radical humanist cultural norms, but peopled by individuals who do not share this vision or expectations for organizational life, the challenges for managers and other radical humanists within the organization will be great. Those who approach problem solving more linearly or empirically will question the call to action by those with shared radical humanist vision. Those from a more traditional worldview will find it hard to join the dialectical processes. They will tend to doubt the goals and procedures that result. They may be seen to be obstructionists to the organization and its members. Though teamwork is not necessarily expected in this very individualist view of organization, participation in the organizational dialogue is demanded. The independence/dependence paradox operant in these organizations may not make sense to those who do not share the radical humanist vision.

Communication.   Giving and receiving accurate information at the right time becomes the currency of the radical humanist organization, whether its structure resembles a traditional, alternative, or virtual configuration. Without the free flow of information, not only will the organization fail to meet its goals but it will also fail to exist. Information in all its forms becomes the context or the framework of the radical humanist organization.

The individualized subjective view of the organization, its expectations, and its potentiality must be an important part of this communication. No organization really exists outside the individual consciousness, so presenting that consciousness in some linguistic form is essential for the work of the organization to proceed. The conversation or dialogue could move to dialectic as misconceptions and politics become part of the communication among organization members. Some would say that dialectic and even stronger conflict is inevitable due to the limits currently existing with communication. The full potential of the radical humanist organization will be limited in reaching its more spiritual or holistic goals for organizational members until a transcendent communication modality is developed (perhaps in the form of a "mind meld," as seen in the old *Star Trek* television series). This is because individuals have uneven levels of skills in moving intuition into propositional, or word, forms. Also, individuals have varying levels of consciousness and varying levels of commitment and capacity to reach the existential goals of radical humanist organizations.

Given the openness of the radical humanist organization, conflict among divergent forces, opinions, ideas, and information is inevitable. Fortunately, radical humanists expect conflict, feel comfortable with conflict, and do not always feel the need to make things right collaboratively. Since conflict is a part of life, there are times in which people will simply agree to disagree and go their separate ways within the organization or in the larger environment. When this happens, it is without feeling they must have closure or needing to be sure no one's feelings are hurt. Feelings will be hurt, an inevitable result of embracing subjectivity and change, but consciousness will be raised, which is more important.

Products. Radical humanist organizations are more focused on process than products or outcomes. Therefore, persons in other paradigms may not value the products of these organizations. Yet, the concepts of radical personal transformation, self-actualization, spiritual wholeness, and an assortment of other related terms signal for many people the ultimate in meaning and growth.

Whereas interpretivists may delight in greater meanings and understandings nurtured through intense collaboration, radical humanists want to take those meanings and understandings and use them to make radical individual or personal change. The radical change that is expected will be individualized because radical humanists recognize that every person is unique. Therefore, a self-help group within a radical humanist organization may take participants to new ways of living, more centered lives, more spiritually complete lives, more artistic lives, more balanced lives so that they will become transformers of their selves within the context of the larger environment. To persons who need products that are easy to measure, using standardized tools, radical humanists will be seen as soft, subjective, and somewhat esoteric, perhaps even a bit crazy.

Practice Language of the Radical Humanist Organization

The radical humanist perspective assumes no such thing as a "best" way of approaching organizational change. Radical humanists will work to solve problems by engaging multiple persons with diverse views in an effort to understand what the problem is. Radical humanists are concerned with moving the process beyond simply understanding and taking those understandings to make individual change occur. They welcome contention and conflict, expecting to have intense dialectical interactions as a normal part of a conscious organizational life. Radical humanists are not satisfied with personal incremental change.

FIGURE 12.2   Language Differences across Four Paradigms

Functionalist Organization	Radical Structuralist Organization	Interpretive Organization	Radical Humanist Organization
Assessment	Assessment	Assessment	Assessment
Diagnosis	Problem Analysis	Understanding	Discovery
Planning	Organizing	Collaborating	Innovating
Incremental Change	Collective Transformational Change	Sensemaking	Empowering Individuals

In previous chapters, we introduced language used in other paradigms to describe organization practice. In Figure 12.2, we show the use of language in organizations built on the assumptions of all four of the paradigms.

Assessment implies that there are facts to collect and concrete data to gather in order to begin thinking about a situation, even if that assessment represents only a snapshot in time. What follows is a close look at assessment in a radical humanist organization. The process may not be understood as "assessment" in any of the other paradigms.

Assessment

For the radical humanist, there is no expectation that assessment will happen in a formalized way using standardized tools. The process is viewed as only one of an unlimited number of ways to understand a situation, condition, or problem. In fact, standardized tools may be subtle instruments of oppression that hinder individual understanding of the institutional setting because standardized tools ask the questions that those in power want answered, not necessarily what an individual worker needs to know in order to perform. Radical humanists also assume that even after organizational participants have started to take one approach to assessment, it is just as likely that they will change course in the process as they discover other viable approaches. To assess from this perspective requires organizational members to be constantly vigilante, open to new possibilities, and keenly aware of what appear to be "flukes" and even mistakes that can offer incredible insights. Radical humanists are critical thinkers who are not afraid of ambiguity and ambivalence. Assessment may be a starting point from which stakeholders begin. Where it emerges will be anything but linear in its progression.

In the radical humanist organization, assessment is a continuous process because the organization is always evolving. Since diverse ideas and opinions are constantly circulating, assessment is tricky business. Nothing stays the same from day to day, even hour to hour. Therefore, radical humanists are open to surprise, even playful in their assessing. No idea is too frivolous or trivial to consider in examining a situation within the organization. People are heard to exclaim, "Well, just when I thought I had seen everything!" or "I've never seen that happen before" or "I've never even thought of this that way!" In radical humanist organizations, these exclamations are not made in fear, but are cries of surprise (and even joy). Unusual and creative thoughts about agency conditions are sought. Since radical individual change is a goal, radical ideas about what is going on and how to proceed are welcomed.

Wheatley and Kellner-Rogers (1996) describe the process of assessment as a form of emergence:

> What do we do with surprise? What do we do with a world which cannot be known until it is in the process of discovering itself? It requires constant awareness, being present, being vigilant for the newly visible. We need to notice things we weren't looking for, things we didn't know would be important, influences we hadn't thought of, behaviors we couldn't predict.... An emergent world welcomes us in as conscious participants and surprises us with discovery. (p. 75)

Although Wheatley and Kellner-Rogers frame this process as somewhat playful, members of the radical humanist organization are used to and expect conflict. There is no need to soft pedal or underplay what is discovered in the assessment process, even when the processes raise emotional feelings and political eyebrows. Assessing their organization, radical humanists may borrow from the differentiators in organizational culture theory, those independent scholars who think that traditional organizational theory and research is uncreative and dull. Recall that some of these scholars are qualitative researchers or persons considered on the fringe of organizational research. They focus on topics such as values, symbolism, meaning, and emotion—topics neglected in traditional organizational research. They face conflict head-on, believing that a good organizational study must uncover the complexities of deep-rooted conflict, inconsistencies, and differences in interpretation among cultural members in order for the process to have individual and/or organizational transformational merit.

These differentiators are helpful in guiding the radical humanist through the assessment process. Radical humanists understand that there will be as many social constructions of the organization as there are people in that organization. They are attentive to differing ways of knowing about their organization. The purpose of assessment is to find out what the situation is so that it can change for the individual. The process is to bring people together to figure out what needs to be worked on, and once there is some sense of what needs to change, the discovery process has already begun.

Discovery

Subjectivists engage in discovery with a strong belief in the value of emergence—a process in which unexpected ideas and new information will be constantly appearing and interacting with what is already "known." Unexpected understandings (the "aha" experience) result. Emergence takes a much different turn in radical humanist organizations because the process of discovery is so central to the organization's philosophy of considering multiple subjectivities. There is little narrowing down for problem analysis because radical humanists do not necessarily assume there is even a problem to be analyzed. Their discovery process could reveal conditions and opportunities that have not yet been defined as problems by the larger society, just for individuals.

Discovery in the radical humanist organization is a totally inclusive process in which everyone's experience and any knowledge held by anyone about a particular situation entered into the process. Rather than stopping with analysis and renewed understanding of the situation, participants argue and disagree among themselves in order to come up with ways in which change can occur. The intent of these participants is to remove barriers or constraints that would liberate persons to do their work in a more powerful and fulfilling way. Radical humanists take the understandings that emerge from discovery and push hard for transformational change.

If there is a need to sort out why people in the neighborhood are not participating in the activities of the local activity center, discovery will not be limited to asking for answers to this question. Those employed by the agency might be asking themselves this question, and then, out of the various answers that might emerge, the agency might decide first to ask the neighbors around the agency what they think about the service and why people might not want to come. They might also be asked what might get them to go there or whether there might be another way of delivering activities. Former clients would be contacted and asked about their experiences, but also about what they thought the agency ought to do to get other individuals involved. All this information together would be shared with all having a stake in the services in order to determine what might be the ways of being available to all the individuals in the neighborhood as well as assuring that the employees are satisfied with themselves and the services they are rendering.

Innovating

Radical humanists are creative. However, one can be creative without fully engaging in radical change. Innovative people are the ones who take creativity and use it for change. The trademark of radical humanist organizations is creativity *and* innovation. When change needs to occur within the organization, radical humanists seize the opportunity to innovate. Their innovation will be based on what they learned in the processes of assessment and discovery. Innovation will not be sacrificed on the altar of civility among colleagues in these organizations. In fact, engaging in innovative change in radical humanist organizations will involve contentiousness and playfulness side by side, depending on how much conflict the proposed change engenders. Of particular importance will be the desire to think outside the box and then to act accordingly for individual purposes.

In the same neighborhood center, the idea of closing the formalized services and developing moveable activities that could go from block to block might be a consideration resulting from the discovery of why the organization is not serving sufficient clients. This might upset those clients that had continued to value what was offered. It might upset employees who had their pat way of relating to clients. It might offer a nightmare of logistics to those responsible for that aspect of the organization. Feelings might be hurt in the process or people might express their dissatisfaction or fear related to such a radical change, but after many hours of conversation and argument, it becomes clear that each block could be transformed with the neighborliness that might evolve from neighbors interacting with neighbors. Less fear of each other and of the location would be the result of a mobile unit moving from block to block. This is real innovation.

Individual Transformation

The individual transformational process is one in which subjectivist traits are extremely important as individuals attempt to make sense of what needs to change. In radical humanist organizations, participants must move beyond current oppressions and find ways to liberate themselves from those restrictions that have hampered their personal evolution. The organization composed of more highly evolved individuals will be changed because its participants will look on it differently, thus causing new cultural norms to emerge.

In the neighborhoods mentioned earlier, both the service providers and the participants may be changed as a result of the renovation in service delivery. Neighbors connect with neighbors. Employees may grow to know their neighborhood. People might agree to participate with each other in many ways. Some people will take responsibility for organizing activities for those who are homebound; others will respect the wishes of those who do not want to be involved but need to overcome social isolation by developing telephone trees. All participants could become less fearful in the neighborhood because they know who is there. Those who looked scary before will now be appreciated for what they brought to the life on the block. Individuals who live in this neighborhood will begin to feel safer, more empowered, and more in control of their own lives. Individual transformation can occur.

In order to summarize the specifics of practice within a radical humanist organization, Table 12.3 provides an overview of their specific practice characteristics.

TABLE 12.3   Practice Characteristics of Radical Humanist Organizations

Practice Element	Characteristics
Assessment	Attention to hearing multiple perspectives from diverse groups and persons is critical to information gathering.
	Collection of word data is more important than collection of numeric data because of meaning making and dialectic possibilities.
	Use of dialectical and honest dialogue is needed to develop deep understandings—hermeneutic circles may be used.
	Reassessment is a central, continual, and ongoing process.
	Participants trust emergence in order to evolve to the right questions.
Discovery	Subjective needs assessment data are shared with all constituencies for the purpose of consciousness raising.
	Discovery is viewed as a broadening process, with efforts made to avoid narrowing down of what is known.
Innovating	Involvement of all stakeholders is critical.
	Conflict is faced as inevitable and important to the creative process.
	Honest communication can be playful, contentious, or otherwise because of respect and acceptance of difference.
Individual Transformation	Transformation occurs for all participants.
	Contest (conflict) tactics are preferred.
	The goal is to liberate individuals.

It should serve as a synopsis for assessing the degree to which an organization is practicing from a radical humanist perspective.

Implications of Radical Humanist Organizations for Social Work Leaders

For a profession that claims attention to the individual within his or her context in order to help the individual navigate more effectively, there could be no better fit between the goals of the profession and the assumptions of the radical humanist perspective. However, regardless of the progressive rhetoric, history would suggest that social work is a much more traditional and conservative profession than many social workers would like to believe. Therefore, although radical humanism has a great deal of congruence with the values and practice principles of the profession as elucidated in the NASW Code of Ethics, the practical consequences of this congruence create problems for the profession of social work that we see as reactive, rather than proactive, regarding human needs.

The radical demands of this perspective mean that change must come to the individual as a result of the work. Not only is the social worker held to the standard of helping the individual to help himself or herself but also to be changed personally as a result of the interaction. This requires a level of introspection and honesty that is rarely found in a profession filled with individuals whose goals are to be seen as professional experts. Radical humanists do not bow to professional experts. In fact, they question the nature of professional identity and the false dichotomy of the expert-client.

On the other hand, this perspective gives ample room and guidance for recognizing, respecting, and relishing difference. We see this perspective as the most amenable to a multicultural lens. Unfortunately, because of its very responsiveness to difference and respect for individuality in the construction of meaning and subsequent behaviors, those requiring specific steps to assure good practice will be frustrated by the lack of traditional theoretical guidance. A shift in expectations will be necessary in order to get the most of what the paradigm and the frameworks within it have to offer for diversity and complex practice.

This radical humanist paradigm provides the context for more questions than answers, and more discomfort than surety. To be ethical will require serious thought and complex considerations. The ethical relativity that is present here is a relativity that has no functional tether other than the measure of whether transcendent change has occurred as a result of the work. The real measure of ethical performance, then, is emergent, both during and after the process. And since the process is always in process, there is an aspect of "never knowing" that comes with any consideration of social work professional ethics from a radical humanist perspective. Further, due to the nature of the assumptions of the paradigm, there is no hope that more clarity will emerge as the dimensions of the paradigm develop in the future. Therefore, social work professionals working from this perspective must have astutely developed human instruments to guide their practice. And they must practice with those who are similarly evolved in order to assure ethical performance within the organization.

The current practice arena that is constructed of service delivery systems (or nonsystems) responsible for brokered care will be both a particular challenge and an opportunity for practice from this perspective. Barriers can be broken down between agencies when leadership is assumed by social workers operating from the social work professional ethical perspective. Their voices in the service context are essential to prepare the way for social work leaders to exhibit a strong presence in the evolving virtual service organization and other helping services that will be developed and delivered in the future through advanced technological means.

Conclusion

The radical humanist organization is committed to discovery and understanding. Radical humanists want to use new understandings to enact individual, transformational change. They do not believe that there is a "best" way for change. For them, there is no possibility of a generalizable truth, nor does the understanding process result in a final truth. Change will occur as individuals interact intersubjectively within these organizations, and that is to be expected and valued. When the unexpected happens somewhere in the process, then the assumption is that this is how the world works, unexpectedly and serendipitously. Radical humanists live well with ambiguity, not assuming that anyone is in control. There are only fleeting images of being in control, for the time being.

What the organizational leader gains from radical humanist assumptions is a commitment from colleagues to work through the process of change and to continue to work in a passionate manner toward subsequent personal changes. The leader recognizes that pressures from more traditional funding sources or other agencies will be to use standardized approaches and tools to aid in response to the call for productivity. Yet, productivity is defined very differently here, for meaning and sensemaking are seen as essential to fundamental personal change. In radical humanist organizations, there is a commitment to make meaning and use it to empower individuals in ways never imagined. Persons who want more concrete products or who are fearful of the unknown may view these "outcomes" with disdain.

When adopting this perspective for assessment, discovery, innovating, and individual empowerment, the social worker gains a view of what is unique to the organization and its members in the organizational environment. Subtle influences regarding processes are captured in the data collection for decision making. This is true because there is room for consideration of the more qualitative, affective, intuitive aspects of the individual perspective on organizational life. For the social work leader, this paradigm and the theories within it offer great help in attending to the special opportunities and challenges provided by that which is different from the norm. Further, there is room for the chaotic and the unexpected that seems to permeate today's organizational life. The presence of chaos and the appearance of the unexpected, often attributed to incompetence in the dominant world, is seen in radical humanist organizations as normal organizational life, full of unlimited possibilities.

This is the last of a series of chapters that have focused on specific paradigms, the theories derived from them, and the practice implications in four types of organizations. Now it is time to integrate all these differences, because individuals and organizations from different paradigms interact daily in organizational life. The next chapter examines the importance of being able to practice multiparadigmatically so that social workers can fully actualize their leadership skills in diverse, contemporary organizations.

CHAPTER

13 Multiparadigmatic Practice

By now you may know what paradigm you prefer. It is probably the place where you feel most comfortable or it may be the one you think best serves your professional goals. We hope that by now you realize that wherever you land does not mean that this is the "best" paradigm or that you should expect others to prefer the same set of assumptions or worldview. When we analyze our own professional growth, we recognize that people do not necessarily stay in the same paradigm at every life stage. The important, central element in multiparadigmatic practice is being aware of one's current paradigmatic standpoint. Self-awareness requires knowing where you prefer to be and why you feel most comfortable there. This sets the stage for beginning organization practice.

Knowing your preferred fit is important for understanding why certain people or events may cause a person to overreact, become angry, or feel threatened or hurt. Individuals have times in organizational life in which they find themselves reacting quickly or feeling strongly about an issue, an event, or an interpersonal interaction. This may not come from profound psychological sources; it may be a viewpoint clash. Understanding paradigmatic perspectives is another aid to being aware of why a person responds in a particular way and what might be the basis of the reactions.

Understanding paradigmatic perspectives is also an excellent framework for engaging in the type of advanced critical thinking that was discussed in Chapter 3. Recall that leadership requires self-awareness and critical thinking. In Chapter 3, we introduced various levels of awareness: preconscious, simple conscious, reflective, reflexive, social constructive, critical reflectivity, and contextual awareness (Kondrat, 1999). The ability to engage in the intellectual flexibility that comes with critical reflectivity and contextual awareness is necessary for multiparadigmatic thinking and is the mark of a skilled organizational leader.

Each of the four paradigms has different assumptions, and a person trying to operate within more than one paradigm simultaneously is a living contradiction. Attempting to meet contradictory expectations in understanding and performance is a setup for paradox. The alternative is the ability to move to different paradigms at different times, depending on the situation or need. This requires practicing stretches in thinking to assume the perspectives of other paradigms. When it is not your "home" paradigm, effective understanding or action in a "foreign" paradigm requires a great deal of work in translation, much like moving comfortably in another culture or language. Effective action is more difficult because the assumptions from another paradigm are not as "natural" or familiar.

To manage this challenge, some people consciously or unconsciously may locate their "comfort zone" paradigm, then search for an organization that is based on those same assumptions. This option provides great comfort, but closes many options for creativity and discovery. If any reader has come to the conclusion that this is the preferred way to manage the complexities touched on in this book, we want to be clear that this is not what we are suggesting. Certainly, there will be people who do work in their preferred paradigmatic organizations, but with or without paradigmatic match between an individual and his or her organizational setting, there will always be circumstances requiring cross-paradigm engagement. People or units within an organization or even an entire organizational culture will embrace a set of assumptions different from yours. Navigating those differences requires multiparadigmatic practice. Practicing multiparadigmatically requires the ability to think and work within paradigms that are not one's preferred, recognizing where others are coming from, knowing how assumptions vary, and being able to cross over into the language, assumptions, and expectations of another paradigm.

This chapter begins by briefly reexamining organizational theory across paradigms, comparing and contrasting various approaches, followed by focusing on how multiparadigmatic practice is a critical part of working in a changing human services landscape. Next, the primary focus will be comparing and contrasting the four types of organizations that grow from differing paradigms, examining the strengths and challenges of each. Last, we examine what this critical analysis means for social work leaders.

Organization Theory Revisited

In previous chapters, we introduced organizational theories that fit within each of the four paradigms. Figure 13.1 provides an overview of all these theories and where we have located them within the confines of each paradigmatic perspective. Note that location within the paradigm gives an indication about the "purity" of the theoretical perspective. The purest representatives of each perspective are closer to the outside corners of each quadrant and those being most related to other paradigmatic perspectives are closer to the lines that determine paradigmatic boundaries.

The functionalist paradigm contains early organizational theories that dominated the way in which the first organizational developers understood how one led, managed, and worked within organizations. The classical, neoclassical, modern structural theorists and early human relations and systems theorists were functionalist in their assumptions. In fact, organizational theories in the first half of the 1900s were reflective of the assumptions of their time. It was assumed that there were best ways to structure organizations and if one could find that best way, then accepted truths about division of labor, human interaction, systems functioning, and a host of other traits would prevail. Since most of these theories were based on a closed-systems perspective, one did not have to consider the larger environmen-

Antiadministration Postmodern Theories **Radical Humanist** Power and Politics —Third-World Feminist Theories —Critical Theories	Postmodern Theories Power and Politics —Radical Feminist Theories —Critical Theories **Radical Structuralist** Systems Theories (morphogenic, factional, and catastrophic analogies) Population Ecology and Transorganizational Theories
Organizational Culture Diffusionists **Interpretive** Organizational Culture Revolutionary Vanguard Organizational Culture Integrationists Sensemaking Theory	Systems Theories (Mechanistic and Organismic Analogies) Human Relations Theories **Functionalist** "Modern" Structural Theories Neoclassical Theories Classical Theories

FIGURE 13.1 Organizational Theories within the Four Paradigms

tal context of the organization. One could focus instead on determining how to structure and work within the organization, ignoring environmental forces such as power and politics. In the early days of the industrial revolution, when the modern organization was developing, this thinking was sufficient to guide organizational decision makers in solving the problems at hand.

Even when open-systems theories became the dominant way of viewing organizations, some theoreticians continued to guard the organization from the consideration of environmental forces, as witnessed by mechanical and organismic analogies. These systems theorists understood the environment as a force that worked against maintaining the organization's equilibrium. They believed the environment could be bounded and controlled as part of the perfect structure.

As the need was recognized, there were also open-systems analogies that embraced the interaction between organizations and their environments that viewed the environment as providing opportunities. These latter ways of theorizing about organizations as in morphogenic, factional, and catastrophic analogies not only considered the existence of conflict but, in some cases, they actually embraced it as a useful way to change larger structures. With organizations developing and becoming more sophisticated and complex, more complex thinking was necessary to respond to the needs of the times. Radical structuralist systems theorists began to see conflict as inevitable. Systems were constantly changing; there was turbulence among diverse groups within systems and this was not necessarily something to be avoided. Instead of believing that systems always sought equilibrium and it was only the environment that was turbulent, these newer theorists did not need to reduce conflict; instead, the dynamics within organizations served as an incubator for change. This position opened thinking for power and politics theorists to articulate the assumptions of radical structuralists by acknowledging these powerful dynamics and multiple constituencies within organizations and their environments.

The theories that emerge from both the functionalist and the radical structuralist paradigms have something very important in common: objectivism. Objectivism accepts definite, concrete truths. People may disagree about what those truths are, but the goal of both paradigms is to identify or convince others of the superiority of the universal truths one embraces. The theories in these two paradigms, then, are steeped in a desire to point organizations and their managers toward the best way to achieve goals and the best structures to keep the organization focused. For functionalists, that way is the established standard of the status quo. For radical structuralists, it is the *new* best way that is a morally superior approach able to recognize the voices of oppressed persons so that oppression can cease through radical, fundamental change.

The search for order and universalism does suggest that functionalists and radical structuralists are naive about subjectivism (a basic assumption held by the other two paradigms). Indeed, functionalists and radical structuralists acknowledge that there are differences in the ways people think and in the ways organizations function. Functionalists are often so aware of differences in the environment that they may dedicate their efforts to shielding their organizations from the uncertain and turbulent factors created by difference or by making attempts to quash difference within the organization. Radical structuralists, aware of the larger environment, spend a good deal of time trying to persuade others to join their vision. From both perspectives, knowing that there are differences is one thing; embracing those differences is an entirely different matter. Both functionalists and radical structuralists believe in the truths they embrace. They want people who bring different views to the organization to accept their way of thinking.

The challenge of managing differences within systems unleashed systems theorists. Open-systems theory established the consideration of the importance of context for organizations, and contingency theory cemented the recognition that the best way for planning and structuring within an organization will depend on what is happening both inside and outside the organization. Organizational ecology brought research precision to the organizational decision-making enterprise.

However, theorizing then began to get complicated because those using the system, contingency, and population ecology theories to guide their work in organizations started branching out beyond a unitary perspective to answer the challenges of a rapidly changing organizational environment. Now, looking back, it is clear that these theories began taking the standpoint of a variety of paradigms, while still remaining connected to a particular theory label. For this reason, clarity about the assumptions underlying the research and decision making that results is essential in order to judge the usefulness and rigor of the research process and product for application in a particular organization. If, for example, systems theory is used interpretively, then generalizability beyond the current time and context is a virtual impossibility. If a manager requires answers that go across time and locality, then that manager will be frustrated by what open-systems, contingency, or population ecology theories can produce from an interpretive standpoint. If, on the other hand, those theories are used to provide a deep understanding of current environmental considerations from a more radical structuralist perspective in order to suggest survival strategies for now and not beyond, then the product will be very useful for the manager.

All this change in theoretical thinking and the emergence of new schools of organizational thought did not mean that early theories were thrown out. In fact, sometimes researchers coming from different assumptions used elements of earlier theories to rethink organizations. Recognition increased about just how complex organizations are and how difficult it is to understand organizations. Postmodern theorists, working in reaction to theoretical history, influenced all the alternative views of organizations in various ways, beginning with radical structuralists and moving to the more subjectivist interpretivists and radical humanists. *Complex, diverse, multicultural, pluralistic,* and many other terms began to be used in describing organizations. These were terms that assumed difference—something traditional organizational theorists had been less inclined to recognize.

It is logical that the next phase of organizational theory development would introduce schools of thought such as sensemaking and organizational culture. Early theorists in this interpretive tradition were viewed as countercultural, somewhat interesting but not in line with previous schools of organizational thought. Something important was happening regarding understanding organizations, though. The interpretivist perspective began to have influence in the direction of more traditional thinkers. The search for excellence movement revealed nuances in how leaders influenced culture. Popular, traditional management literature adopted new, softer language referring to organizations as "dancing giants" and using terms such as *empowerment* and *leading with the spirit.* The floodgates were open and the interpretive language penetrated even the functionalist organization. The problem this created was that even though interpretive language was increasingly used in functionalist organizations, basic, underlying assumptions had not changed. Understanding paradox in organizations became even more essential because what was done and how one talked about it began to seem like parallel processes fraught with potential for mistake, misunderstanding, and bad feelings.

Bad feelings may, in fact, be the basis of the most modern theoretical developments from the radical humanist paradigm. Theories here seek to unhinge, implode, or otherwise decommission traditional ways of doing business in organizations. Starting with the deconstruction of the postmodernists and moving through the consciousness-raising efforts of the critical theorists who are listening to women's voices and assessing power and politics that disenfranchise, ideas are developing to again rethink the way people organize to achieve goals. Antiadministration is the most recent example developed as a way to honor and enhance the payoff of difference.

In general, most organizational theories recognize that there are differences among organizations, structures, and people. How one addresses the elements of difference is the point of departure. For example, recognizing the plurality of interests in the environment is very important regardless of perspective. To a subjectivist, this multiplicity of difference is stimulating and interesting, assisting one in understanding the organization. To an objectivist, this plurality is something to be controlled. To a subjectivist, establishing a quality circle is a method of getting workers to share their diverse views and to come to a collective and most certainly richer consensus. To an objectivist, quality circles can be used to allow people to feel they have had their say, but then to guide and even maneuver them in working toward the best way or universal truth.

In summary, besides understanding the real differences in perspectives created by theories using differing paradigmatic lenses, it is also important to realize that thinkers are using elements of various theories from different paradigms to fashion theoretical guidance for completely different reasons. Much more precision in thought is now necessary to get the full measure of the theoretical implications of paradigms for organizations and the behavior within them. Without this, use of theories to guide practice will be more than just confusing; it might be damaging to good decision making.

The Changing Organizational Landscape

We began this book with a chapter on the changing organizational landscape. At that time, we introduced three types of programs often planned for and/or provided in organizations dedicated to human needs: direct service, staff development and training, and support. By now, we hope that the reader recognizes that these programs will look different if they are under the auspices of organizations coming from varying paradigmatic assumptions.

How Programs Differ

In the functionalist organization, direct service programs will be highly organized and designed with outcome measurement in mind. Given its predisposition to maintain the status quo, the functionalist organization will usually not attempt to solve societywide, large-scale problems, focusing instead on meeting immediate human needs. Staff development and training programs may be heavily focused on training for specific skills, such as filling out forms accurately or following established practice protocols. Support programs, such as advocacy efforts, will be primarily focused on case or client advocacy, which might emphasize the importance of getting a client his or her benefits.

In the radical structuralist organization, direct service programs will also be highly organized and outcome focused, but identified outcomes will be more radical or far-reaching than those of a functionalist organization. Beyond meeting immediate client needs, larger-scale programs designed to bring about community or even societal changes are expected. Staff development and training programs may be designed to assist volunteers, paraprofessionals, staff, and consumers, first, in understanding the "problem(s)" and, then, in community organizing, campaign development, and mobilizing resources. Radical structuralists may look at functionalist programs with disdain, indicating that they are not concerned enough with change on a broader scale and that their programs are just band-aids. In fact, support programs such as advocacy efforts may actually be the defining programs of many radical structuralist organizations, since their emphasis is on collective change.

In the interpretive organization, direct service programs will be much more subjective or affective, focusing on the importance of clients and staff relationships and in understanding themselves and others. These programs may be very reflective, thoughtful, and insightful, viewing all parties as colearners in the process of collaborative program implementation. Staff development and training programs in these organizations may focus on the development of critical thinking skills, learning new collective human service approaches and methods, such as cooperative decision making, and emphasizing staff development over training. Staff development for improved personal and professional development will be a signature program for interpretivists, but the goal of this development is connection and relationship building for greater understanding. Interpretivists will look with some antipathy at functionalists who seem more concerned about training for precision than for meaning. They will also look at radical structuralists as somewhat obsessed with change to the exclusion of understanding. Therefore, support programs in an interpretive organization may take the form of research or education units designed to enhance the efforts of members who want to understand fully the context and concepts of problems.

In the radical humanist organization, direct service programs are typically constructed as self-help or empowerment programs, seeking to create opportunities for individuals to grow and develop beyond where they are now. Staff development and training may be provided, but on a very individualistic basis, such as encouraging organizational members to seek their own sources of new knowledge across a range of disciplines. Since everyone's learning is unique, there will be little desire to corral people into training events. Self-paced learning is preferred and now very possible in the virtual training platforms of cyberspace. But regardless of the medium, developing a mechanism for individual, life-long learning is preferred. To this end, support programs may be loosely established to offer participants opportunities to identify and secure what they need to move toward individual empowerment through their own learning to speak to power. Essentially, the programs of the radical humanist organization are nontraditional in every aspect, with the goal to free the human spirit to achieve a higher level of being. Radical humanists may mock the rigid, protocol-oriented, rule-bound programs developed by functionalists as being irrelevant for human development. They could scoff at the radical structuralist organization's need to form collective goals in their change efforts for lack of attention to the individual. They would push interpretivists to use their new understandings to effect change, particularly at the individual level.

Organizations in all four paradigms may have all types of programs (direct service, staff development and training, and support), but they will differ in how they are designed and what will be emphasized. They will differ regarding what programs are preferred or even seen as useful and relevant. Also, regardless of paradigm, some organizations may devote themselves to only one program and be highly specialized; others will not. For example, a functionalist organization might be a government planning agency dedicated to the planning of human service programs that serves as a pass-through for funding to provider organizations with no efforts in advocacy and little expectations regarding staff development. A radical structuralist organization may be a social movement organization or a grassroots organization dedicated to programming in a highly specialized, cause-oriented fashion that would require approximately equal attention to programming, staff development, and advocacy. An interpretive organization may be a research institute on social problems that finds depth and understanding about the very problems other agencies will try to resolve. In this organization, there would be no real direct service, but attention to staff development and advocacy by way of dissemination of findings would be central to their efforts. A radical humanist organization could be a self-improvement organization, running groups and retreats that focus on spiritual growth. Programming and staff enrichment would be central, with little effort expended in the direction of advocacy as it is commonly defined. The point is that the preferred manner of intervention will be guided by the worldview and assumptions that the organization may have about the "best" way to solve individual and societal problems.

So, with each "best" way, some things are gained and others are lost. Here are just a few of the most obvious considerations. The functionalist organization works in favor of the status quo and stability over the chaos and uncertainty in change, sometimes missing opportunities to make real societal differences. In doing so, attention is generally given to the collective or average information, overlooking the individual or the unique, and missing opportunities to make individual differences. Focusing on the greatest good for the greatest number, radical structuralist organizations tend to take an "in-your-face" approach to problem identification and solution at a class-based level. The tensions created with this approach will create "aha" moments in certain segments of the population, but will be threatening or distasteful to those who do not appreciate or cannot comfortably engage in confrontation. This might lose potential collaborators. While focusing on large-scale change, like the functionalist organization, the radical structuralist organization overlooks the unique needs and abilities of the individual in favor of mass issues and actions, potentially leaving the individual behind.

The interpretive organization is so engrossed in the effort to understand multiple perspectives and multiple connections in any given problem that change efforts may be overlooked in favor of further investigation. Though deep, individual meaning is addressed and collaborative efforts are encouraged, so much attention may be paid to the relational process that product may not appear. When products do appear, statements such as "additional study is needed" usually accompany them. Finally, the radical humanist organization, while helping members and service recipients to identify and overcome the powerful institutional and societal influences that serve to impede growth, their "anti" position may also serve to impede joint action toward a common good. With the rejection of traditional ways and means of organizing, nothing but personal "naval gazing" may be accomplished.

Now, we leave it to you to consider other more subtle challenges and opportunities of organization practice grounded in each particular cluster of assumptions provided by paradigmatic perspectives. Given the boundaries of each paradigm, what else might enhance or limit the work on improving the human condition? Think about this in preparation for the analysis of the differences and similarities that will accrue when considering the kinds and types of organizational relationships that will grow out of different worldviews. Next, we will focus on these differences as they influence the role and structure of human service organizations. In order to clarify the real complexity the different paradigms produce, we now turn to the consequences of differing perspectives in organizational relationships.

Organizational Relationships

Just as programs vary within organizations, so will organizational relationships vary, whether they are public, nonprofit, or for profit. Over their life course, organizations seek, maintain, and even sever relationships and allegiances. Earlier, we categorized these relationships as (1) associations, (2) ideological relationships (including religious or faith communities, ethnic communities, feminist communities), (3) franchises, and (4) host relationships. Paradigmatic perspective also influences preferences regarding preferred organizational relationships.

Functionalist organizations will comfortably choose relationships in any of these categories. This is not difficult to understand, since most of these forms of organizational connection grew out of the history of traditional organizational development. For example, membership associations, such as the American Association of Homes and Services for the Aged (AAHSA), are formed to provide technical assistance and the latest information for their member organizations. Functionalist organizations with names such as Catholic Charities or United Methodist Services dot the human service landscape, receiving both public and private dollars to provide their programs. These faith-based affiliates are typically functionalist in their orientation, having deep cultural roots in their faith and local communities. Liberal feminist organizations are typically functionalist in their orientation, attempting to get women into the mainstream, rather than trying to fully change existing organizations. Franchises such as Planned Parenthood deliver services in a functionalist, more bureaucratic manner than more radical feminist health organizations in the radical structuralist tradition. Host relationships, such as hospitals that house case management or social service units, are highly functionalist in their orientation.

Radical structuralist organizations have relationships with groups that are more change oriented than are functionalist organizations, so the choices to create formal relationships are more related to the purpose of the relationship than the particular structure. Associations such as the National Association of Social Workers strive to be more radical structuralist in their orientation, lobbying for change and taking positions on social issues. Membership organizations such as Klan Watch, Amnesty International, and Greenpeace are radical structuralists, seeking to change the status quo through massive, collective campaign and contest strategies. Radical structuralist organizations affiliate with groups devoted to change, such as nontraditional religious, ethnic, and radical feminist communities. Franchises such as Prevent Child Abuse America are radical structuralist in their orientation because they are built around assumptions that massive change must occur. Host relationships often are problematic for radical structuralists, when they find themselves locked within more conservative, functionalist systems. When this happens, radical structuralist units or individuals are seen as house radicals or mavericks, always questioning or even ignoring host agency rules, procedures, and protocols.

Interpretive organizations will also choose organizational relationships based on what can be produced rather than the particular structure of the organizational relationship. Interpretivists will most likely be drawn to relationships represented by membership organizations devoted to higher levels of understanding and collaboration. For example, the Association for Research on Nonprofit Organizations and Voluntary Action (ARNOVA) is devoted to scholarship and professional development. Interpretive organizations may be think tanks affiliated with liberal or conservative groups studying issues and advancing understanding. They may be the research or education arm of religious, feminist, or ethnic groups. Interpretive organizations may be part of franchises as long as the franchise holds a quest for understanding and meaning as its major focus and allows relational issues to be part of general considerations. Interpretive programs typically fit well within host organizations because they are formed to promote understanding and, by design, may be somewhat different from other units, but collaborative enough to prevent negative friction. For example, a large state agency may be highly functionalist, but there may be a team of researchers hidden within its bowels that spends its time studying social trends and changes. This unit could be interpretive in its orientation if all views of the problem are encouraged and if the goal is understanding through collaborative teamwork.

Radical humanist organizations are least likely to have highly structured relationships with other organizations because the concept of the collective is the antithesis of their underlying assumptions. Since radical humanists believe in individualism and in questioning administration, these organizations would tend to loosely affiliate, if they affiliate at all. They would rarely be parts of associations or franchises because they do not seek subservience, consensus, or sameness, but rather independence and diversity carried to its extreme.

The human service landscape, then, is a mixture of functionalist, radical structuralist, interpretive, and radical humanist organizations. Public agencies will typically be functionalist, given their vast size. However, there are public alternative agencies residing in other paradigms, and there are public agencies that contain units representing alternative perspectives. Nonprofit agencies will be in all four paradigms, with older, more traditional agencies more likely being functionalist. But traditional nonprofits can spawn alternative organizations in different paradigms, as new organizations arise to respond to emerging needs in a community. Similarly, for-profit agencies can exist in any of the paradigms because a profit motive rests well in all paradigms. In short, one has to be very careful not to label organizations by their sectoral affiliation because public *and* private agencies can exist in each paradigm. It is also important to remember that, just like the individual, one organization may be in different paradigms at different stages of organizational development.

The task in understanding organizational relationships is to be able to assess where individual agencies are in terms of their guiding assumptions and perspectives, what their affiliations are, and what this means to practice inside of or in collaboration with that organization. The agency choice to associate, affiliate, or become part of a franchise or to allow other kinds of host relationships is based on differing assumptions about what is best for the organizations and the clients they serve. We hope you recognize the importance of understanding sectoral and relational elements of the organization in the context of the paradigmatic perspectives. Besides providing important information about performance expectations of those acting within the organization, knowing the perspective of the organization will help to identify characteristic possibilities and resource potential of agencies within the human service system. In addition, this information is important in clarifying expectations between organizations that are seeking to establish a formal relationship. Relationship failures can be largely prevented, and the benefits of creating organizational relationships will be enhanced when differing expectations are made clear.

Comparing and Contrasting Organizational Goals

Just as theories are derived from paradigmatic perspective, organizational goals are related to the theories within these perspectives. Differing expectations can be made most clear at the organizational goal level. This section will compare organizational goals and show the differences that accrue when practice is guided by different paradigmatic and theoretical assumptions. Table 13.1 takes each of the goals that were identified earlier for organizations operating from each paradigm and places them side by side. This should provide a quick guide for understanding differing practice expectations. But we have a further interest in effective multiparadigmatic practice. In multiparadigmatic practice, one needs to know and to understand the differences across organizations—but one also must be able to accomplish very different activities toward differing goals, depending on the underlying assumptions and expectations of the organization.

TABLE 13.1 Comparing Organizational Goals across Paradigms

Focus and Task	Functionalist Goal	Radical Structuralist Goal
Environment	To recognize that the environment is uncertain and turbulent, and to do whatever possible to control environmental forces.	To recognize environmental uncertainty as an opportunity to interact with and mobilize diverse forces to benefit the organization's cause.
Funding	To obtain funding that flows from long-established and multiple sources.	To obtain any funding that will support the organization's cause(s).
Client Populations and Referral Sources	To fund, plan, or deliver socially acceptable programs to socially acceptable clients in need.	To advocate with, rather than for, consumers and to encourage the development of programs that have full community participation.
Mission/ Philosophy	To use the best knowledge available to enhance and achieve the highest social order.	To use the best knowledge available to enhance and achieve the highest social change for the common good.
Values	To operationalize dominant opinions, doctrines, and practices, focusing on efficiency and effectiveness.	To provide avenues for nondominant opinions, doctrines, and practices.
Management and Leadership Style	To designate administrators and supervisors within a defined structure and to work toward consensus (agreement) so that tasks can be logically addressed. Hierarchical communication and decision making are valued.	To establish a participatory, inclusive approach to management and leadership in which dialogue and debate are freely exchanged.
Organization and Program Structure	To establish clear relationships between organizational members and among units within the organization, and to be part of service delivery structures that are established by agency staff and protocols that have been used over the years.	To allow structure to emerge so that the organization's cause is best facilitated, and to use less bureaucratic, flatter structures whenever possible.
Programs and Services	To use incremental or gradual change to alter people's status so that they can function best within society.	To develop advocacy-based programs and services designed to change oppressive structures and empower people.
Personnel Policies and Procedures	To write clear rules and procedures and share them with employees so that they know what to expect and know what is expected of them and to reduce or eliminate conflict within the organization through clear guidelines for resolving problems (e.g., grievance policies, mediation resources, etc.).	To focus less on policies and procedures, but more on processes that bring people together in interaction. To embrace conflict when it occurs within the organization and to deal with it.
Staff	To hire persons who will work in the most efficient and effective manner.	To hire persons who will embrace the cause and who have advocacy skills.
Communication	To develop established protocols such as organizational charts and information systems so that expectations about communication are clear.	To develop open communication in which the voices of clients, volunteers, and staff are equally heard, and to engage in face-to-face exchanges in which conflict is accepted as part of the dialectical process.
Products	To create highly factual, quantitative, concrete reports that demonstrate impact.	To create highly factual, quantitative, concrete reports that demonstrate impact at the macro-level.

TABLE 13.1 Continued

Interpretive Goal	Radical Humanist Goal
To try to understand the complexity of the environment and to use this understanding to set a meaningful context.	To see the environment as a source of invigorating differences and unlimited subjectivities, once liberation from limits is achieved.
To obtain any funding that will support the organization's search for knowledge, understanding, and meaning.	To seek financial resources that give individuals as much control as possible.
To include clients, referral sources, staff, and others in a collaborative process so that programs will be as respectful of diversity as possible.	To open one's doors to individuals from all walks of life, embracing diversity.
To seek the best knowledge available to enhance awareness and understanding in providing meaningful information and programming, while recognizing complexity at all levels of society.	To seek individual transformation.
To provide avenues for both nondominant and dominant opinions, doctrines, and practices so that inclusion is maximized.	To inspire ultimate self-determination for all persons, thus respecting that every person will self-determinate in his or her own unique way.
To establish a participatory, relationship-focused approach to management and leadership in which dialogue is freely exchanged in as collaborative and civil a manner as possible.	To alternate and even share leadership roles among members in as informal a way as possible with the goal being individual transformation.
To allow structure to emerge so that the learning process is best facilitated, and to use less bureaucratic, flatter structures whenever possible to facilitate a network of relationships.	To develop minimal structure so that changes can easily be made in an ongoing manner without impinging on the individuals inside the structure.
To develop educational and human service programs that assist participants in understanding complex issues by increasing consciousness to the degree that understanding leads to more meaningful living.	To create opportunities for people to grow and develop individually.
To focus less on policies and procedures, but more on processes that bring people together in interaction. To seek harmony when conflict occurs within the organization.	To establish minimal rules, procedures, and protocols so that freedom is engendered.
To hire multicultural staff who respect differences, can tolerate process, and who are dedicated to self-awareness and ongoing development.	To engage persons in a creative process, thus seeking persons who are conscientious, self-directed, and committed.
To develop open communication in which the voices of clients, volunteers, and staff are equally heard and respected, and to engage in direct exchanges in which consensus is the goal among diverse perspectives.	To use the latest in information technology to enhance connections among people, while also honoring all methods, means, and mediums of communication.
To create in depth, qualitative narratives and reports that seek to increase knowledge and understanding of alternative options.	To transform individuals.

To fully understand the consequences of the differences in organizational goals across paradigms, it is necessary to compare and contrast each goal by the major foci and tasks of organizations. It is important to recognize the implications of the differences revealed, but an analysis in such detail is beyond the scope of this chapter. However, we think it is of such importance that we have provided an example of how this analysis could be accomplished. Our intention is to provide an analytic model so that the reader using the model can get a taste of the insights such an analysis will provide. We have selected two important foci, environment and programs and services, to illustrate differences across the four organizational types. After studying our analysis of the two, we challenge you to complete the analysis in order to provide for yourself a full picture of differences. Take another look at the challenges and opportunities presented by the differing perspectives.

First, let's examine how organizations from different worldviews engage the environment. For the functionalist organization, the environment is an uncertain and turbulent sea of forces to be controlled as much as possible, whereas the radical structuralist organization seeks to seize or create that uncertainty and mobilize diverse forces for change. Both organizations attempt to control environmental forces, but in different ways: for the functionalists, it is control to maintain order; for the radical structuralists, it is to create chaos within which major change becomes possible. The interpretive organization wants to understand environmental complexity, seeing this complexity as a way to achieve higher understanding and meaning. Without the environmental context, there would be no meaning. The radical humanist organization, on the other hand, goes beyond understanding context and sees the environment as a source of invigorating differences into which the human spirit can soar to new heights if escape from environmental limits is achieved.

Think about the implications for practice posed by these four views of an organization's environment. Functionalist practitioners may be fearful of an uncontrolled environment, almost shielding themselves and their organizations from uncertain forces. Maintaining calm within the organization, feeling that the organization is a refuge from the storm, and making peace within the organization may take precedence. Radical structuralists may actually bring environmental influences into the organization, challenging themselves and others to harness those forces for change against the status quo. Interpretivists will be content to process the nuances of environmental context, seeking new ideas and perspectives with an eye to the importance of what they are learning and what it all might mean for the organization. Radical humanists likely agree with their radical structuralist colleagues on the importance of environmental forces, but they will use these forces in very different ways. Radical structuralists will seek collective change, spurred by environmental opportunities, whereas radial humanists will seek individual transformation.

The same degree of difference is apparent when one examines another of the organizational goals in Table 13.1: programs and services. Functionalists are incrementalists who think that people must be helped to adapt, adjust, and be accommodating to the larger society in order to function in it. Thus, their programs will not look toward large-scale reformation, but rather just small changes within the individual or society. Radical structuralists see no usefulness in accommodation to the status quo, preferring a strategy that forces fundamental changes in institutional or societal structures in order to meet group needs. Interpretivists work at achieving incremental change through understanding, believing that with consciousness raising and collaboration, opportunities for change will emerge. Further, all will be better off because change will be the result of consensus. Radical humanists focus on individual resistance to adaptation, adjustment, and accommodation. Societal structures should be forced to change in order to meet individual needs, but if individual accommodations are not certain, the individual can be helped to transcend the limits of society in order to achieve a much more evolved state.

So it is that programming across organizations will be planned and delivered very differently, even when they focus on the same population group. A good example of how these differences in program philosophy get operationalized in practice would be through the creation of an English language program for recent immigrants. Functionalists would design the program for participants to acquire language and cultural skills as quickly as possible in order to replace old practices and languages. Assimilation would be the goal. Radical structuralists would see the functionalist program as only a temporary fix, possibly designed to deny one's culture of origin and to get immigrants to disappear into the melting pot. As an alternative, their language program would first seek to organize immigrants to stand up for their language rights. Although English as a second language might be desirable, the primary goal of services would be to form a collective in which the participants in the program could become empowered as a group and recognized as a viable community.

Interpretivists might develop a language program that would educate staff to become multicultural and multilingual. The goal would be understanding the subtleties of language and the meaning attached to words so that the staff could better collaborate with recent immigrants from the immigrants' perspectives. English language acquisition would emerge from this educational process, but the service would be a consciousness-raising experience for all involved, one in which all participants were learners. Radical humanists would focus on the individual immigrant and his or her empowerment, even resisting the learning of English and certainly never encouraging the loss of one's first language in the process of socialization to this country. Radical humanists would create programs that were highly individualistic and customized to the needs of the individual immigrant rather than lumping recent immigrants into a collective category.

The structure of practice changes in each paradigm, just as the organizational structure and expected behavior changes depending on the paradigm. What makes multiparadigmatic practice most challenging and exciting is not simply understanding the implications of these structural differences, but acquiring the language that would allow one to understand practice within these differences. The next section completes our comparing and contrasting of organizational implications by looking at the language of practice in each paradigm and how the actions derived from that language produce real differences in the business of organization practice.

Characteristics of Practice in Organizations in Different Paradigms

Multiparadigmatic practice implies that one can recognize the differences across organizations and actually learn to work with organizations in paradigms very different from one's own. Meeting organizations where they are and understanding the goals they have is required if one is going to practice effectively. Direct practitioners know this; it is now essential that organization practitioners know this as well. Just as in direct practice, the language one uses to describe the behaviors of organization practice is basic to what is considered effective practice. The most important aspect of social work leadership involving multiparadigmatic organizational practice is knowing the language of desired practice and what is required to practice acceptably. For this, one must recognize and understand the differences in how language is used across organizations in different paradigms. Figure 13.2 provides a view of how language varies. The next section compares and contrasts implications for practice in human service organizations where the goal is understanding a problem and doing something about its elimination.

We will now briefly examine the characteristics of different paradigms in a series of tables constructed for comparative purposes. We start with assessment because all paradigms embrace information gathering as an acceptable starting point for practice within an organization. This is followed by a consideration of problem identification, which is conceived differently in each paradigm. We then move to practice considerations, conceptualizing the change process and the results, which also provide marked differences with interesting challenges and opportunities.

Assessment

From Figure 13.2 we see that regardless of paradigm, organizations engage in assessment. Whereas functionalist organizations and radical structuralist organizations appreciate hard, concrete, objective data in assessment, interpretive organi-

Figure 13.2   Language Used across Organizations in Different Paradigms

Functionalist Organizations	Radical Structuralist Organizations	Interpretive Organizations	Radical Humanist Organizations
Assessment	Assessment	Assessment	Assessment
Diagnosis	Problem Analysis	Understanding	Discovery
Planning	Organizing	Collaborating	Innovating
Incremental Change	Collective Transformational Change	Sensemaking	Empowering Individuals

zations and radical humanist organizations prefer more qualitative approaches to data collection. Word data in these latter two types are more important than numbers because members of these organizations are subjectivists, preferring word data for its ability to get close to the meaning of what is being assessed in context and from the perspectives of the individuals involved. For the organizational practitioner, knowing what data are respected determines what credible information will inform what can be heard as part of the assessment process. Knowing what is preferred in an organization can make the difference in whether the practitioner is considered competent in the assessment process.

Table 13.2 provides an overview of how assessment itself is viewed in different organizations. In addition to the preferred method of collecting information, the practitioner must also know how assessment is performed, what the goals of that assessment are, and how assessment data will be used in an organization. For example, the functionalist organization will engage in organizational assessment using standardized instruments to produce objective data believed to provide a

TABLE 13.2   Characteristics of Assessment across Paradigms

Functionalist Characteristics	Radical Structuralist Characteristics	Interpretive Characteristics	Radical Humanist Characteristics
—Systematic data gathering is a first step in planned change within organizations. —Standardized, quantitative forms, guides, or tools are helpful in the assessment process. —Assessments provide hard, concrete, objective data that can be used by professionals to diagnose the organizational situation or problem. —Data collection methods should be consistent.	—Systematic data collection is a first step in gathering information about identified issues. —Standardized, quantitative forms are preferred, although instrument insensitivity to at-risk groups is a concern. —Assessments provide hard, concrete, objective data to be used by interested parties to analyze the situation or problem. —Data collection methods should be consistent.	—Attention to hearing multiple perspectives from diverse groups and persons is critical to information gathering. —Collection of word data is as important as collection of numeric data. —Use of open-ended questions and emerging instruments is useful, given the need to develop deep understandings in context. —Reassessment is a continual and ongoing process.	—Attention to hearing multiple perspectives from diverse groups and persons is critical to information gathering. — Collection of word data is more important than collection of numeric data because of meaning making and dialectic possibilities. —Use of dialectical and honest dialogue is needed to develop deep understandings—hermeneutic circles may be used. —Reassessment is a central, continual, and ongoing process. —Participants trust emergence in order to evolve the right questions

clean, clear, generalizable view of the situation or problem. The assessment is geared to detailing what is to be changed or solved in ways found generally useful in responding to this problem or situation in other times or places. In a radical structuralist organization, assessments will also be highly quantitative and will utilize roughly the same processes for data gathering and analysis. Likewise, the goal will be to obtain objective facts about a situation, but the information that results will be used differently. Radical, rather than incremental, change is desired, so the language of the assessment may contain words to provoke action rather than maintain the status quo.

An interpretive organization highly regards words to clarify the multiple perspectives that should be considered when coming to understand the depth and scope of a situation. Since there is attention to the role of context in shaping meaning, very little attention will be paid to instrumentation or information that has emerged from other organizational settings. That information or data collection tool may not resonate with the particulars of the case at hand, so only that which is seen as useful for understanding among those with a stake in the assessment will be included. Interpretivist assessment has as its goal greater organizational understandings, so the process of assessment is as important as the assessment product. Radical humanist organizations are also partial to word data, but expect a data collection process that is more conflict oriented. Dialectical processes are seen as the way to come to a more sophisticated criticism and understanding of the situation under assessment. Only through the challenges of dialectics can the individual be relieved of false consciousness vis-à-vis the situation and come to grips with what will be necessary to achieve a personal radical departure from the current situation.

Although assessment from all paradigms is a systematic undertaking, certain data and processes are preferred in each. These have great implications for both the process and the product of the assessment. Functionalist organizations value valid and reliable instruments to collect quantitative data for statistical analysis to compare the current situation against general rules that have been developed in other organizational settings. This assessment process offers precision, but may underemphasize the particulars of the situation being assessed. Radical Structuralist organizations see assessment as the first step to radical change. Even though quantitative data are analyzed to produce generalizable information, the goal of the assessment requires selective attention in the results that require change, leaving little room to consider anything that needs no changing. Interpretive organizations attend to the perspectives of all those with a stake in whatever is being assessed. Although the goal is to come to a consensus about the situation, the process of collecting, reducing, analyzing, and making sense out of complex word data may mean that full assessment is never completed before action is required. Radical humanist organizations focus on the impact of the assessment process and product on the individual participants in the assessment. Through the criticism created by a dialectical process, all participants will come to understand that which must be transformed to assure a more acceptable individual status, but this limits collective potential.

Problem Identification

From the assessment discussion, one can see that the goals of assessment differ across paradigms. The shifting of the goals of assessment also calls for language shifts across paradigms. Table 13.3 illustrates these shifts. Terms such as *diagnosis* are less often heard in the hallways of alternative organizations. Although functionalists often use *diagnosis* or *problem identification and analysis* interchangeably, radical structuralists will rarely use the word *diagnosis.* The term implies a very individualistic focus and a medical labeling process. This is exactly what radical structuralists will be attempting to change for groups that have been so labeled. Interpretivists may use terms such as *problem analysis,* but would typically describe what they do as a result of an assessment as *understanding.* Radical humanists, attempting to transcend to a higher level of individual development, may use words such as *discovery* to describe that process after assessment. Whatever it is called, organizations will typically have preferred methods and approaches for identifying problems.

Problems will be seen differently by each organizational type because of the differences in reasons for and methods of assessment. Since functionalists use quantitative data and seek to categorize findings, the concept of labeling and diagnosing is a logical fit. Whereas radical structuralists seek to use objective data to

TABLE 13.3   Characteristics of Problem Identification across Paradigms

Functionalist Characteristics *(Diagnosis or Problem Definition and Analysis)*	Radical Structuralist Characteristics *(Problem Analysis)*	Interpretive Characteristics *(Understanding)*	Radical Humanist Characteristics *(Discovery)*
—Diagnosis flows from objective assessment data. —With reassessments, diagnoses may change. —Diagnosis requires consideration of objective data known about identified problems.	—Problem analysis flows from objective assessment data. —With reassessments, analyses may change. —Analysis requires consideration of objective data known about identified problems. —Data gathering among all constituencies means engaging in a dialectical process to hear all voices and to achieve consciousness about what constitutes the problem.	—Subjective needs assessment data are shared with all constituencies. —Analysis is viewed as a broadening process, with efforts made to avoid premature narrowing down of what is known.	—Subjective needs assessment data are shared with all constituencies for the purpose of consciousness raising. —Discovery is viewed as a broadening process, with efforts made to avoid narrowing down of what is known.

make change occur, they will engage constituencies in the problem identification process so that there is joint ownership of the analysis. Interpretivists will enjoy the understanding process in which problems are identified and will feel very comfortable in continuing to collect more information from multiple sources, engaging in an ongoing dialogue that brings new deep meaning to and a complex understanding of the problem. The process may be somewhat prolonged, due to having assessed the problem with far more than quantitative information. Radical humanists will seek subjective information, as well as look for ways to use what is learned in problem identification to radicalize individual consciousness regarding needed change.

Taken paradigmatically, diagnosis requires a narrow label that, if incorrect, can serve to stigmatize the situation and off target the change intervention. Problem analysis flowing from objective data rests on narrowly construed definitions of what constitutes useful information. Since change is sought in all human service organizations, the analysis may overlook that which merits preservation. On the other hand, understanding has no real ending point, so the assessment process may never conclude. Analysis provides a broadening, not a narrowing, of perspective, so a clear vision of the next steps may never emerge because assessment and reassessment are so compelling. Discovery is an individualistic consciousness-raising experience that will have great power with each person involved, but that will have little chance of resulting in collective change action.

Conceptualizing the Change Process

How the problem gets defined has everything to do with how change is envisioned within the organization. Table 13.4 provides an overview of how the change process is conceptualized across paradigms. Again, note how the language shifts as different organizations describe what this process should entail. Functionalist organizations diagnose a problem and plan for an incremental change process. Radical structuralist organizations engage in problem analysis as a precursor to organizing for fundamental change. Interpretive organizations, through a network of relationships, come to an understanding of a problem or situation and then engage in a collaborative change effort. Radical humanists make personal discoveries through assessment and innovate for personal transformation.

Although the familiar term *planning* will be used by functionalist organizations, the planning concept is not foreign to the other perspectives. The idea of a systematic thoughtfulness about making things different may require the use of the term *planning* in any one of the other paradigms. However, there are other terms that seem more compatible with alternative assumptions. Radical structuralists are often *community organizers* rather than *technical planners.* For them, *organizing* implies a mobilization of resources rather than an expert-client relationship. Interpretivists, as collaborators, seek *consensus* and not *organizing for a cause.* Radical humanists are individual innovators. Whereas *planning* and *collaborating* are more status-quo–oriented concepts, *organizing* and *innovating* imply conflict-ladened change.

TABLE 13.4 Characteristics of Conceptualizing Change across Paradigms

Functionalist Characteristics *(Planning)*	Radical Structuralist Characteristics *(Organizing)*	Interpretive Characteristics *(Collaborating)*	Radical Humanist Characteristics *(Innovating)*
—Planning follows logically from diagnosis or problem definition. —Planning is incremental in its orientation. —A change in diagnosis will warrant a change in the plan of action. —In planning, preconditions are recognized, but the goal is to design realistic interventions.	—Mobilizing people for the change is critically important. —Organizing is very action oriented, inclusive, and fraught with conflict.	—Involvement of all parties is highly valued. —Collaborative process is seen as meaningful unto itself. —Hearing all perspectives and views is encouraged. —Consensus building is the goal.	—Involvement of all stakeholders is critical. —Conflict is faced as inevitable and important to the creative process. —Honest communication can be playful, contentious, or otherwise because of respect and acceptance of difference.

The methods used to "plan" in these organizations will be different, just as the goals of the process will vary. Practicing multiparadigmatically requires, then, the full range of data collection, analysis methodologies, and various interpersonal skill packages ranging from personal introspection, through collaboration, to contest. Conceptualizing the change process in each paradigm will require selecting and planning the implementation of the appropriate techniques required by the situation and the organizational aims. These decisions must be made within the context of what may be gained and lost from each standpoint.

Functionalist organizations will require logical connections between the problem diagnosis and the plan of action. This logic will not allow for serendipity or surprising developments along the way. The radical structuralist organization expects movement from problem analysis to mobilization, using action and conflict management and enhancement skills. But since the emphasis is more on revolution than evolution, existing strengths within may be overpowered by the need for change. The change-directed understanding of the interpretive organization requires collaborative involvement skills of all with a stake in the change action. Efforts to build consensus may be so resource depleting that the desired change will never occur. Radical humanists are so individualistic and against organizing for anything, even change, that the personal discoveries resulting from assessment and the innovative ideas that grow from the process may never come to fruition at an organizational level.

The Result

Assessment, problem identification, and conceptualizing the change process are used by effective organizations to make a difference. Making a difference usually suggests that change occurs. Each paradigm envisions the results of the change effort differently. Table 13.5 provides characteristics of results across paradigms.

Functionalists see change as incremental, attempting to approach the situation systematically, with the goal to reestablish equilibrium as quickly as possible. Similarly, interpretivists are not seeking widespread change. Their organizations are attempting to make sense out of what has been assessed and identified, with a goal of moving toward a new more effective status quo. Functionalists would be sure that the majority agrees and complies, whereas interpretivists want the status quo to be owned by everyone. Functionalists see incremental change as desired. Interpretivists see sensemaking as desired.

Radical structuralists seek collective transformation, being very dissatisfied with "what is" because of what is not. Their goal is to advocate for societal or collective change affecting classes of individuals. Radical humanists are just as adamant about transformational change, but their goal is to liberate individuals rather than large groups. Collective versus individual transformation is the change choice that differentiates these paradigms.

The way in which each organization assesses, identifies problems, and plans leads to its view of the process of change and change itself. For example, a functionalist planner who seeks objective facts would have difficulty relating to a radical humanist who not only eschews facts but embraces conflict. Both would reject the

TABLE 13.5   Characteristics of Results across Paradigms

Functionalist Characteristics *(Incremental Change)*	Radical Structuralist Characteristics *(Collective Transformational Change)*	Interpretive Characteristics *(Sensemaking)*	Radical Humanist Characteristics *(Individual Transformation)*
—Interventions may be at the organizational or organizational unit level. —There is a best or better intervention identified. —Change-from-within tactics (collaboration and campaign), rather than context (conflict), are preferred. —The goal is to change the organization's situation so that homeostasis is reestablished.	—Interventions may be at any level of the organization, but change is framed in the context of the organization's cause. —Campaign and contest (conflict) tactics are used without reservation if necessary. —The goal of organizational change is to keep the focus on the advocacy mission, making the organization more viable in its societal transformation.	—Sensemaking may occur at any level, but the primary focus is typically at the individual and organizational levels. —Change-from-within tactics (collaboration and campaign) rather than contest (conflict) are preferred. —The goal is to make changes that become the new status quo and are owned by everyone.	—Transformation occurs for all participants. —Contest (conflict) tactics are preferred. —The goal is to liberate individuals.

position of the other perspective: The functionalist would see the radical humanist as engaged in art or spirituality, not organizational planning, whereas the radical humanist would see the functionalist planner as wrong-headed, asking the wrong questions for the wrong reasons.

A radical structuralist would see radical humanists as missing an opportunity to transform society by focusing on individuals one at a time. Interpretivists and functionalists may not feel comfortable with their radical colleagues who seem demanding and contentious. Radical humanists and structuralists may feel their functionalist and interpretive colleagues are much too conservative in how they approach change. Functionalists elect small forward steps for change without the chances for the drama of revolution. Radical structuralists choose campaign and contest to produce major departures from the current status quo. Functionalists and interpretivists would suggest that the adrenaline of passion could take precedence over the stability of reason. Interpretivists want collaboration and conversation over high drama, leading to comfortable new versions of the status quo. Radical humanists get unstuck and unorganized, producing liberated individuals who have no real link to the collective.

Multiparadigmatic Leaders

By now, we hope you have a personal sense of what all this multiparadigmatic analysis means to you as an organizationally based practicing social worker. You have probably been able to locate organizations with which you are familiar within the different paradigms. You may even have found organizations where the rhetoric is in one paradigm and the expected behavior falls in another. Perhaps you have had difficulty identifying an overarching paradigm for an agency because each unit in the organization seems to have a different orientation. What you have identified are some of the ways organizations of today can be paradoxical, holding apparently contradictory notions at the same time. An organization may be understood to be dysfunctional, difficult to understand, inconsistent, or confusing, when it may just be paradoxical, having certain characteristics that fit within one paradigm but others that fit within another. When this happens, organizational members do not have clear directions about expected behavior. Our effort in this book has been to demonstrate the difficulties when such lack of clarity persists. Our intent has been also to normalize the experience so that the social work practitioner can look outward into the organizational assumptions instead of inward into his or her own competencies in order to get clarity about the locus of the problem.

We also hope by now that you are able to articulate the differences between paradigms, identifying the ways in which organizations may vary and why, in order to aid in organizational assessment. Details of the paradigms are particularly important to understanding organizational structure. For example, a highly bureaucratic structure fits well with the functionalist paradigm, whereas a loosely affiliated grassroots organization may fit well with radical structuralism. The highly bureaucratic grassroots functionalist organization would never be able to accomplish its organizational goals because it would take too much time to get permission to react. A large, loosely structured, public radical humanist organization would have major difficulties achieving its goals with the requisite level of accountability because no one would be in charge to orchestrate action and to implement organizational discipline.

The paradigm and the organizational structure have much to do with expected human behavior within the organization. It is here that personality match with an organization is first evident. Functionalist organizations may feel more ordered for some organizational members and possibly more oppressive to others. The functionalist organization may be more familiar, even if it is oppressive, whereas radical structuralist organizations may be more uncomfortable because of their aggressiveness and fast-paced nature. Interpretive organizations may be comfortably friendly or too personally invasive, depending on one's expectations. Radical humanist organizations may support individual autonomy or become isolating impediments to real work. These elements do not necessarily represent dysfunction either on the part of the organization or its members. They represent real differences with real implications.

It is the effective social work organizational leader who can quickly identify what is expected in the work environment and compare that to what is needed to meet human needs. Table 13.6 provides a comparative view of the role of the social work leader in organizations in differing paradigms.

Each role represents a personality and skill package interaction. Think about which you prefer. Then think about the other three paradigms and their characteristics within those perspectives. How do you think you could work with people from other paradigms? Meeting people where they are is a basic tenet of direct service, but it is also basic to organization practice in which you may have to meet entire organizational cultures or units that hold assumptions different from your own. The point of this analysis is answering the question: Can another way of proceeding based on another perspective serve our social work goals and values better?

By now, you will have had the opportunity to examine the strengths and limitations of each paradigm, probably identifying with one more than others. It is our hope that you will have located your preferred set of assumptions. You should give yourself permission to *start* from there. Our challenge to you is not to forsake who you are, but to learn to be multiparadigmatic or multicultural in your approach. Leaders are conscious of their preferences and they are able to cross boundaries to work with others who do not share their preferences. They do this in order to accomplish needed organizational goals.

Practitioners of today cannot afford to be bound to one paradigm. Too much information and too many creative opportunities are available outside one paradigm. Human potential and organizational potential rests within each perspective. Risks and challenges also abound within each. It is the role of the multiparadigmatic practitioner to unlock that potential and to manage the risk through critical analysis of what will work best in each situation. Crossing the borders into other paradigms is our one hope, so that we join the forces of difference to confront what

Table 13.6   Characteristics of Social Work Leaders across Paradigms

Functionalist Leaders	Radical Structuralist Leaders	Interpretive Leaders	Radical Humanist Leaders
—Is comfortable with clearly defined rules, procedures, and directions —Seeks consensus among colleagues —Sees conflict as something to be reduced —Truly appreciates collegiality and mutual respect for organizational goals —Is comfortable with maintaining the status quo —Likes concrete, measurable artifacts —Works toward identifying best practices, best ways of doing the work —Likes having maximum control at work —Is viewed by others as "rational" under stress —Tolerates process but sees outcomes as most important —Is able to separate personal from professional life, believing in the importance of clear boundaries —Follows the rules —Makes incremental change as needed	—Questions existing rules, procedures, and directions —Actively engages in conflict —Can incite conflict when necessary —Is comfortable with dialectical interaction —Is thick skinned, able to deal with insults —Is cause or mission driven —Makes no distinction between personal and work life (sees what he or she does as a higher calling) —Makes radical change as needed —Believes passionately in what he or she does —Can be aggressively assertive when necessary —Is invigorated and challenged by taking on "the system" —Can support cause with factual information —Believes there are higher-order truths to be pursued.	—Is comfortable with ambiguity, uncertainty, and new and emerging ideas —Thinks hearing all perspectives is important —Sees the status quo and order as something worth establishing —Truly appreciates diversity —Tolerates differing opinions well —Is predisposed toward creativity —Has a strong curiosity —Is satisfied with spending time on understanding, meaning-making activities, without having to use what is learned to make broad-scale change —Is willing to fully participate in organizational life —Enjoys people and has strong interpersonal skills —Plays with others, is a team player —Desires to be a lifelong learner —Examines situations from many different directions and is willing to be persuaded to change one's mind —Tolerates process and delayed closure well —Respects people for their strengths and is open to hearing new ideas	—Is comfortable with ambiguity, uncertainty, and new and emerging ideas —Thinks that hearing all perspectives is important —Sees conflict as inevitable when all perspectives are heard —Truly appreciates and acts on diversity —Tolerates differing opinions well —Is predisposed toward creativity and innovation —Has a strong curiosity and passion for change —Is not satisfied with just understanding and meaning making, but is committed to turning what is discovered into action —Maintains one's sense of individualism within organizational life —Is self directed —Is able to examine situations from many different directions and will argue passionately for a cause —Tolerates process, as long as radical change is the goal —Sees self-transformation of individuals as a desired state

until now have appeared to be intractable social problems at the local, national, and international levels.

We wish you well as you begin your great adventure into social work leadership in organization practice. Our hope is that this book has given you some resources to construct a career of taking advantage of opportunities, recognizing risks, and embracing the advantages of difference. Have the courage to take your place and think differently about how to organize human service activities. Explore the possibilities of new designs and arrangements, but don't forget to continue to examine your beliefs, because it is at the belief level that true change originates. Enjoy a lively adventure!

GLOSSARY

absolutists: Persons who believe that basic principles do not change and that there are overriding universal values that will withstand the test of time and are in fact "God given."

advocacy: "The exclusive and mutual representation of a client(s) or a cause in a forum attempting to systematically influence decision making in an unjust or unresponsive system (s)" (Schneider & Lester, 2001, p. 65).

affiliations: Formal and informal connections made by organizations with other groups that are aligned with their values or ideology. These connections add to the cultural identity of the organization and to their public visibility.

alterity: The process of moving from knowing the "other" at a distance to developing a real relationship with the "other."

alternative social agencies: Organizations formed to address social needs of specific population groups that are not being addressed adequately by other human service agencies. They can develop through public or private efforts

antipositivism: The view that knowledge about reality is soft, subjective, and natural.

assessment: A process in which a person or group gathers information about a service, program, or organization. How wide the net is cast will depend on the purpose of the assessment. Some assessments may gather information on a single agency program, whereas others may examine an entire organization. The type of data collected and the method of collection will also depend on the reason one is undertaking an assessment.

bounded rationality: A concept that recognizes no matter how much information individuals collect, they will always have to make decisions within limits.

campaign tactics: Approaches to change that are seen as middle ground between collaboration and contest, and in which one has to be highly persuasive and skilled in political maneuvering, bargaining, and negotiation. Campaign tactics are typically used when the target is open to change, but needs to be convinced.

case or client advocacy: Assuring that "services provided to clients are both relevant to the prob-

lem and available within the community" (Schneider & Lester, 2001, p. 152).

cause advocacy: "Promoting changes in policies and practices affecting all persons in a certain group or class, for example, the disabled, welfare recipients, elderly immigrants, or battered women" (Schneider & Lester, 2001, p. 196).

collaborative tactics: Approaches to change characterized by open communication in which people are willing to engage in problem-solving for change.

contest tactics: Approaches to change in which participants are in conflict and unwilling to compromise and in which the violation of social and legal norms could occur.

critical thinking: "Involves a careful appraisal of claims, a fair-minded consideration of alternative views, and a willingness to change your mind in light of evidence that refutes a cherished position" (Gibbs & Gambrill, 1996, p. 23).

cultural fit: "The degree of alignment between two or more cultural configurations" (Cox, 1994, p. 170).

culture groups: Persons who espouse different shared norms, values, and traditions from those of other groups.

deconstruction: A way of demonstrating just how artificial values, norms, and knowledge are. The exercise of deconstruction also reveals how the concept of rationality is socially constructed. What seems reasonable depends on the historical moment.

determinism: The belief that reality shapes action and perception.

diagnosis: Occurs when data are understood and translated into information, so that problems and needs are labeled and analyzed.

direct service program: Programs that assist clients, usually attempting to make their situations better in some way.

diversity: Differences that represent fundamental and instrumental variations. Organization diversity includes elements such as structure, type, affiliation, and location. Group diversity includes gender, race, nationality, sexual orientation, culture, and discipline. Individuals also reflect diversity within groups, including differences represented and covered by the Americans with Disabilities Act or the Age Discrimination Act. These multiple, and often overlapping, aspects of diversity are related to organizational behaviors and outcomes.

emic: Proving an insider's perspective.

epistemology: Assumptions related to what can be known and how scientists can be expected to come to know it.

ethnic agency: An organization affiliated with a particular ethnic group, having the following characteristics: (1) serving primarily ethnic clients, (2) predominately staffed by persons who have the same ethnicity as the clients served, (3) having a majority of its board from the ethnic group served, (4) having an ethnic community and/or ethnic power structure to support it, (5) integrating ethnic content into its programs, (6) desiring to strengthen the family as a primary goal, and (7) maintaining an ideology that promotes ethnic identity and participation in the decision-making process (Jenkins, 1980).

etic: Providing an outsider's perspective.

fallacies: Mistakes in thinking that take skill to spot. Fallacies may occur when (1) the premises do not support the conclusion, (2) broad generalizations are applied too liberally, (3) facts and positions are misrepresented, and (4) emotional appeals are not grounded in facts.

feminist organization: Agencies defined as meeting "any of the following criteria: (1) has a feminist ideology; (2) has feminist guiding values; (3) has feminist goals; (4) produces feminist outcomes; (5) was founded during the women's movement as part of the women's movement (including one or more of its submovements, e.g., the feminist self-help health movement [or] the violence against women movement)" (Martin, 1990, p. 815).

for-profit organizations: Businesses that are part of the commercial or market economy. They pay taxes, have boards of directors who generally are compensated, and they may have investors or stockholders who can benefit financially from the organization's profits.

franchise: Organizations that conform to a particular approach to doing business with permission from a national or regional group. Although nonprofit agencies may not think of themselves as franchises, there are numerous long-estab-

lished exemplars, including Goodwill Industries, Planned Parenthood, Prevent Child Abuse America, and the Alzheimer's Association.

fraud: Intentional deception and misrepresentation.

functionalist paradigm: A perspective that assumes the social world is composed of relatively concrete empirical artifacts and relationships that can be identified, studied, and measured through approaches derived from the natural sciences.

Gantt chart: Bar graphs illustrating who is supposed to do what task at what time. Originally developed during World War I by H. L. Gantt to track ammunition.

goal displacement: Occurs when an organization moves in a different direction from its original purpose, without planning to do so.

grassroots associations (gas): One type of voluntary association that is focused on the local community. Smith (1999) defines GAs as "locally based, significantly autonomous, volunteer-run, formal nonprofit groups that manifest significant voluntary altruism as a group; they use the associational form of organization and thus have an official membership of volunteers who perform all or nearly all of the work done in and by the nonprofits" (p. 443).

homeostasis: In systems theory, a state of balance in which every part is working together and is integrating with the whole.

host organizations: Large agencies that deliver human services or employ social workers as part of what they do, but whose primary purpose is not the delivery of human services.

ideographic: Having the nature of a graphic symbol that represents an object or idea, rather than a word used for the same purpose.

idiographic: Descriptions or interpretations that are unique to the individual, and that capture what is individually distinctive.

incremental change: A change that is finite, not sweeping or revolutionary, allowing partial growth in the desired location.

interpretive paradigm: A perspective informed by a concern to understand the world as it is at the level of subjective experience, within the realm of individual consciousness and subjectivity, and from the frame of the participant, as opposed to the observer of action. It sees the social world as an emergent social process that is created by the individuals concerned. Reality is little more than a network of assumptions and intersubjectively shared meanings that hold only as meaning is shared.

intervention: Action taken to change an organization or an organizational unit.

leadership: An attitude about responsibilities in an organization based on professional skills and a set of values that compel an individual to act. Leadership may come from any organizational member, regardless of the formal authority and power structure in that organization.

managing diversity: Planning and implementing organizational systems and practices to manage people so that the potential advantages of diversity are maximized while minimizing its potential disadvantages.

market sector: Broadly viewed as "the economy," the commercial, the business, or the for-profit sector.

mechanistic organizations: Organizations that are highly traditional in terms of hierarchy, formal rules and regulations, communication, and decision-making. This type organization is particularly useful in producing inanimate products (Burns & Stalker, 1961).

metaphors: Using one element of experience to explain another. An example would be comparing organizations to machines.

minority practice: "The art and science of developing a helping relationship with an individual, family, group, and/or community whose distinctive physical or cultural characteristics and discriminatory experiences require approaches that are sensitive to ethnic or cultural environments" (Lum, 1996, p. 6).

morphogenesis: A change in structure.

morphostasis: Maintaining structure.

multicultural organization: Agencies in which the majority of organizational participants hold distinctly different group affiliations of cultural significance. Multicultural organizations can be diverse in four ways: (1) the clients they serve, (2) the staff and volunteers they use, (3) their own corporate culture and subcultures, and (4) how they vary from other agencies.

multiparadigmatic practice: Being able to identify assumptions in use within an organization and then use one's critical thinking and practice skills to move in and out of different ways of thinking (paradigms).

nominalism: The belief that human reality exists within the mind.

nomothetic: The view that natural science methods can be applied to the study and understanding of social reality.

nonprofit organizations: Agencies referred to as nongovernmental, third sector, voluntary, charitable, or tax exempt. They have uncompensated, voluntary boards of directors who cannot benefit financially from the organization's profits. Any profit made must be reinvested in the organization. Nonprofit voluntary agencies are more bureaucratically structured than voluntary associations and are "governed by an elected board of directors, employing professional or volunteer staff to provide continuing social service to a continuing clientele in the community" (Kramer, 1981, p. 9).

objectivist perspective: The view that people are shaped by reality as products of their environment and that knowledge is hard and concrete.

ontology: Perspective on the nature of reality. Is it above and beyond individual knowledge or is it based on individual consciousness without regard to the outside world?

organic organizations: Organizations that function in highly changeable environments, requiring staff who can make decisions quicky in adapting to change (Burns & Stalker, 1961).

organization: "Social unit[s] with some particular purpose" (Shafritz & Ott, 1996, p. 1).

organization practice: Working and surviving in organizational arenas by making changes that address the needs of multiple stakeholders and constituencies and reflect a strong grounding in professional values, critical thinking, and self-awareness.

organizational culture: "A pattern of shared basic assumptions that the group learned as it solved its problems of external adaptation and internal integration, that has worked well enough to be considered valid and, therefore, to be taught to new members as the correct way to perceive, think, and feel in relation to those problems" (Schein, 1992, p. 12).

paradigm: A worldview that contains a set of deep-seated assumptions that are so much a part of the person that it is hard to step back and even know what those assumptions are. Paradigms, then, are the basic assumptions that order a person's world regarding what is and what can be discovered.

perceived needs: Those needs that have not yet come to the attention of service providers, but are identified by those persons in need. They remain invisible and ignored in the planning of services.

planned change: A process of deliberately identifying a problem, analyzing its causes, and carefully determining a strategy to alter the situation according to predetermined outcomes.

planning: Preparing to resolve problems and address organizational needs.

positivism: The assumption that knowledge about social reality is hard and concrete.

power: The ability to influence others.

principles: Standards for action related to values.

private agencies: A broad category of organizations, including those that are called nonprofit and for-profit.

programs: "Pre-arranged sets of activities designed to achieve a set of goals and objectives" (Netting, Kettner, & McMurtry, 1998, p. 300). **Direct service programs** focus on clients. **Staff development and training programs** target staff, the intention being that because staff will have additional knowledge and skills they will be able to do better direct service provision. **Support programs** are designed to assist direct service or staff development and training programs.

propaganda strategies: When someone tries to persuade or convince another person to come over to his or her way of thinking.

pseudoscience: Occurs when claims are couched in scientific language, but these claims are not substantiated by word or number data.

public or governmental agencies: Organizations mandated by law at some level of government, established through a local, state, or federal system with the purpose of that agency contained in legal statutes. Examples of public agencies are local, state or federal departments of human or social services, health, education, and aging.

public sector: The governmental or state portion of the economy.

purchase of service contracting (POSC): Public subsidies or private agencies, sometimes called federalism by contract or private federalism, occurs when public agencies engage organizations from other sectors to actually deliver government funded services.

quackery: Pertains to the promotion of unproven, even harmful, claims.

quasi-nongovernmental organizations (QUANGOS): Private, nonprofit incorporations largely financed by government, created by government initiative, and serving an important public purpose (Pifer, 1983). The Community Action Agency that emerged out of the 1960s War on Poverty was a QUANGO.

radical change perspective: Focuses on deep-seated structural conflict and modes of domination and contradiction. Assumes that reality is conflict ridden, if not chaotic.

radical humanist paradigm: A highly individualist perspective that respects differences and engages conflict in the interest of individual transformation.

radical structuralist paradigm: A perspective that assumes the social world is composed of relatively concrete empirical artifacts and relationships that can be identified, studied, and measured through approaches derived from the natural sciences. The results of this study and measurement should be used to transform conditions for oppressed populations.

realism: The assumption that reality is above and beyond individual knowledge.

reflexivity: The ability of the human mind to turn back on itself and therefore know that it is knowing.

regulation perspective: Held by persons who embrace the status quo, and seek consensus rather than focusing on conflict. Assumes that society is characterized by social order and equilibrium.

relativists: Persons who believe there are multiple truths because "ethical standards depend on cultural practices, political climate, contemporary norms and moral standards, and other contextual considerations" (Reamer, 1995, p. 48).

religious affiliates: Social service organizations that publicly acknowledge a relationship with a religious group or faith community. Typically, they are separately incorporated as nonprofit organizations and have names such as Lutheran Social Ministries, Catholic Charities, and United Methodist Homes.

satisficing decision making: Decisions made without all possible information necessary for a fully considered decision.

service: A service is a specific intervention, a combination of which may comprise a program. For example, a service could be counseling or receiving a mobile meal. Both are human services for they directly impact clients.

sex-role spillover: Carrying socially defined gender-based roles into the workplace.

social work perspective: A view that recognizes the worth of the individual and individual strengths and potentialities within the context of community rights and responsibilities.

solipsism: The assertion that there exists no independent reality outside of the mind.

staff development and training programs: Programs that focus on staff, the intention being that because staff will have additional knowledge and skills, they will be able to do better direct service provision.

subjectivist perspective: Assumes that social reality exists primarily in the human consciousness (a product of one's mind).

support programs: Program; organizational-, or community-based programs with the intention being that their activities are processes that will lead to higher-quality programming.

theory x: The assumptions held by managers that it is human nature to hate work and to avoid it whenever possible. Therefore, coercion, control, discipline, and direction are essential if employees are expected to work toward organizational goals.

theory y: The assumptions held by managers that it is human nature to take control and personal responsibility for their work. Therefore, one can assume that employees will be self directed and motivated.

third party government: Salamon (1987) coined this term to refer to what happens when private organizations are used as agents of the public sector. Purchase of service contracting is an example of this concept in action.

third sector: A term used to describe the voluntary or nonprofit portion of the economy.

traditional social agencies: Organizations that deliver socially acceptable programs to socially acceptable clients in need. Funding and community sanction flow from long-established patterns of acceptance of the need to serve clients in the ways that are chosen by these agencies. These agencies practice in very conventional ways, operationalizing local opinions, doctrines, and practices as demonstrated in who is served and how services are rendered.

umbrella associations: "Nonprofit associations whose members are themselves nonprofit organizations." It is estimated that one out of every five nonprofit organizations belongs to an umbrella association (Young, 2001, p. 290).

values: Dimensions of a profession held in high esteem.

verstehen: A concept used by Gadamer to describe the results of hermeneutics, which should be agreement or understanding through critical controlled interpretation.

voluntarism: The belief that people can be proactive in creating their own realities.

voluntary associations: Membership organizations in which persons come together for a specific purpose. They may be highly formalized or informal grassroots oriented.

REFERENCES

Acker, J. (1990). Hierarchies, jobs, bodies: A theory of gendered organizations. *Gender and Society, 4*(2), 139–158.

Acker, J. (1992). Gendering organizational theory. In A. J. Mills & P. Tancred (Eds.), *Gendering organizational analysis* (pp. 248–260). Newbury Park, CA: Sage.

Acker, J. (1994). The gender regime of Swedish banks. *Scandinavian Journal of Management, 10*(2), 117–130.

Aldrich, H. E. (1979). *Organizations and environments.* Englewood Cliffs, NJ: Prentice-Hall.

Aldrich, H. E., & Pfeffer, J. (1976). Environments of organizations. In A. Inkeles, J. Coleman, & N. Smelser (Eds.), *Annual review of sociology* (Vol. 2, pp. 79–105). Palo Alto, CA: Annual Reviews.

Alexander, J., Nank, R., & Stivers, C. (1998). Implications of welfare reform: Do nonprofit survival strategies threaten civil society? *Nonprofit and Voluntary Sector Quarterly, 28,* 452–475.

Alinsky, S. (1969). *Reveille for radicals.* New York: Vintage.

Alinsky, S. (1971). *Rules for radicals: A practice primer for realistic radicals.* New York: Vintage.

Allen, R. W., & Porter, L. W. (1983). *Organizational influence processes.* Glenview, IL: Scott, Foresman.

Alvesson, M. (1993). *Cultural perspectives on organizations.* Cambridge: Cambridge University Press.

Alvesson, M., & Deetz, S. (1996). Critical theory and postmodernism approaches to organizational studies. In S. R. Clegg, C. Hardy, & W. R. Nord (Eds.), *Handbook of organization studies* (pp. 191–213). London: Sage.

Angus, I. (1992). The politics of common sense: Articulation theory and critical communication studies. In S. Deetz (Ed.), *Communication yearbook 15* (pp. 535–570). Newbury Park, CA: Sage.

Arendt, H. (1998). *The human condition.* Chicago: University of Chicago Press.

Argyris, C. (1970). *Intervention theory and method.* Reading, MA: Addison-Wesley.

Auslander, G. K. (1996). Outcome evaluation in host organizations: A research agenda. *Administration in Social Work, 20*(2), 15–27.

Austin, M. J., & Solomon, J. R. (2000). Managing the planning process. In R. J. Patti (Ed.), *The handbook of social welfare management* (pp. 341–359). Thousand Oaks, CA: Sage.

Axinn, J., & Stern, M. J. (2001). *Social wefare: A history of the American response to need* (5th ed.). Boston: Allyn and Bacon.

Bailey, D., & Koney, K. M. (2000). *Creating and maintaining strategic alliances: From affiliations to consolidations.* Thousand Oaks, CA: Sage.

Bailey, R., (1976). *Radicals in urban politics: The Alinsky approach.* Chicago: University of Chicago Press.

Bailey, R., & Brake, M. (Eds.). (1975). *Radical social work.* London: Edward Arnold.

Baldridge, J. V. (1971). *Power and conflict in the university.* New York: Wiley.

Bales, F. (1954). In conference. *Harvard Business Review, 32*(2), 44–50.

Bargal, D. (2000). The manager as leader. In R. Patti (Ed.), *The handbook of social welfare management* (pp. 303–319). Thousand Oaks, CA: Sage.

Barker, R. L. (1995). *The social work dictionary.* Washington, DC: The National Association of Social Workers.

Barker, R. L. (1999). *The social work dictionary.* Washington, DC: The National Association of Social Workers.

Barnard, C. I. (1938, 1968). *The functions of the executive.* Cambridge, MA: Harvard University Press.

Becker, H. S., Greer, B., Hughes, E. C., & Stauss, A. L. (1961). *The boys in white: Student culture in medical school.* Chicago: University of Chicago Press.

Beechey, V., & Donald, J. (1985). *Subjectivity and social relations.* Philadelphia: Opa University Press, Milton Keyes.

Bennis, W. G. (1966). *Changing organizations.* New York: McGraw-Hill.

Bennis, W. G., Berkowitz, N., Affinito, M., & Malone, M. (1958). Authority, power and the ability to influence. *Human Relations, 11*(2), 143–156.

Bennis, W. G., & Slater, P. E. (1968). *The temporary society.* New York: Harper and Row.

Benson, J. K. (1977). The interorganizational network as a political economy. *Administrative Science Quarterly, 20.*

Benson, J. K. (1977). Organizations: A dialectical view. *Administrative Science Quarterly, 22*(1), 1–22.

Berger, P. L., & Luckman, T. (1967). *Social construction of reality.* Garden City, NY: Doubleday Anchor.

Bertalanffy, L. von. (1951). General systems theory: A new approach to unity of science. *Human Biology, 23*, 303–361.

Billis, D. (1993). *Organizing public and voluntary agencies.* London: Routledge.

Blake, R. R., & Mouton, J. S. (1978). *The new managerial grid.* Houston: Gulf Publishing.

Blau, P. M., & Scott, W. R. (1962). *Formal organizations.* San Francisco: Chandler.

Bolman, L. G., & Deal, T. D. (1991). *Reframing organizations: Artistry, choice, and leadership.* San Francisco: Jossey-Bass.

Bolman, L. G., & Deal T. (1997). *Reframing organizations: Artistry, choice, and leadership.* 2nd ed. San Francisco: Jossey-Bass.

Bordt, R. L. (1997). How alternative ideas become institutions: The case of feminist collectives. *Nonprofit and Voluntary Sector Quarterly, 26*(2), 132–155.

Bourdieu, P. (1977). *Outline of a theory of practice.* Cambridge: Cambridge University Press.

Bowers, D., & Seashore, S. (1966). Predicting organizational effectiveness with a four-factor theory of leadership. *Administrative Science Quarterly, 11,* 238–263.

Brager, G., & Holloway, S. (1978). *Changing human service organizations: Politics and practice.* New York: The Free Press.

Brager, G., & Specht, H. (1973). *Community organizing.* New York: Columbia University Press.

Briggs Myers, I., & McCaulley, M. (1985). *Manual: A guide to the development and use of the Myers-Briggs type indicator* (2nd ed.). Palo Alto, CA: Consulting Psychologist Press.

Briggs Myers, I., & Myers, P. (1995). *Gifts differing: Understanding personality type* (2nd ed.). Palo Alto, CA: Davies-Black Publishing.

Brilliant, E. L. (2000). Women's gain: Fund-raising and fund allocation as an evolving social movement strategy. *Nonprofit and Voluntary Sector Quarterly, 39,* 554–570.

Brody, R. (2000). *Effectively managing human service organizations* (2nd ed.). Thousand Oaks, CA: Sage.

Brown, L. D., & Moore, M. H. (2001). Accountability, stategy and international nongovermental organizations. *Nonprofit and Voluntary Sector Quarterly, 30*(3), 569–587.

Burns, J. (1978). *Leadership.* New York: Harper and Row.

Burns, T., & Stalker, G. M. (1961). *The management of innovation.* London: Tavistock Publications.

Burrell, G., & Morgan, G. (1979). *Sociological paradigms and organisational analysis.* London: Heinemann.

Calás, M., & Smircich, L. (1992). Rewriting gender into organisational theorizing: Directions from feminist theorizing. In M. Reed & M. Hughes (Eds.), *Rethinking organization: New directions in organization theory and analysis.* London: Sage.

Calás, M. B., & Smircich, L. (1996). From "the woman's" point of view: Feminist approaches to organization studies. In S. R. Clegg, C. Hardy, & W. R. Nord (Eds.), *Handbook of organization studies* (pp. 218–257). London: Sage.

Clegg, S. R., Hardy, C., & Nord, W. R. (1996). *The handbook of organization studies.* London: Sage.

Cnaan, R. A. (1999). *The newer deal: Social work and religion in partnership.* New York: Columbia University Press.

Coase, R. H. (1937). The nature of the firm. *Economica, New Series, IV,* 386–405.

Cohen, M. D., & March, J. G. (1974). *Leadership and ambiguity: The American college president.* New York: McGraw-Hill.

Collins, P. H. (1990). *Black feminist thought.* New York: Routledge.

Cooper, R., & Burrell, G. (1988). Modernism, postmodernism, and organizational analysis: An Introduction. *Organization Studies, 9,* 99–112.

Cortes, M. (1998). Counting Latino nonprofits: A new strategy for finding data. *Nonprofit and Voluntary Sector Quarterly, 27,* 437–458.

Cox, T., Jr. (1993). *Cultural diversity in organizations: Theory, research & practice.* San Francisco: Berrett-Koehler Publishers.

Dalton, M. (1950, June). Conflicts between staff and line managerial officers. *American Sociological Review,* 342–352.

Daly, A. (Ed.). (1998). *Workplace diversity issues and perspectives.* Washington, DC: National Association of Social Workers.

Davies, R. (1975). *Women and work.* London: Arrow.

Deetz, S., & Kersten, A. (1983). Critical models of interpretative research. In L. Putnam & M. Pacanowsky (Eds.), *Communication and organizations.* Beverly Hills: Sage.

Denarest, L. (1997). *Looking at type in the workplace.* Gainesville, FL: Center for the Applications of Psychological Type.

DePoy, E., Hartman, A., & Haslett, D. (1999). Critical action research: A model for social work knowing. *Social Work, 4,* 560–569.

Devore, W., & Schlesinger, E. G. (1991). *Ethnic-sensitive social work practice* (3rd ed.). New York: Macmillan.

Diesing, P. (1991). *How does social science work? Reflections on practice.* Pittsburgh: University of Pittsburgh.

Donaldson, L. (1996). The normal science of structural contingency theory. In S. R. Clegg, C. Hardy, & W. R. Nord (Eds.), *Handbook of organization studies* (pp. 57–76). London: Sage.

Dreyfus, H., & Rabinow, P. (1983). *Michel Foucault: Beyond structuralism and hermeneutics* (2nd ed.). Chicago: University of Chicago Press.

Drucker, P. F. (1954). *The practice of management.* New York: Harper.

Drucker, P. F. (1988, January-February). The coming of the new organization. *Harvard Business Review, 45*–53.

Ede, L., & Lunsford, A. (1990). *Singular texts: Plural authors: Perspectives on collaborative writing.* Carbondale: Southern Illinois University Press.

Ellor, J. W., Netting, F. E., & Thibault, J. M. (1999). *Religious and spiritual aspects of human service practice.* Columbia: University of South Carolina Press.

Etzioni, A. (1961). *A comparative analysis of complex organizations.* New York: Free Press of Glencoe.

Etzioni, A. (1964). *Modern organizations.* Englewood Cliffs, NJ: Prentice-Hall.

Etzioni, A. (1975). *Comparative analysis of complex organizations: On power, involvement, and their correlates.* New York: Free Press.

Executive Office of the President and Office of Management and the Budget. (1987). *Standard industrial classification manual.* Washington, DC: Office of Management and Budget.

Ezell, M. (2001). *Advocacy in the human services.* Belmont, CA: Brooks/Cole.

Ezell, M., & Patti, R. J. (1990). State human service agencies: Structure and organization. *Social Service Review, 64,* 23–45.

Falck, H. S. (1988). *Social work the membership perspective.* New York: Springer.

Farazmand, A. (Ed.). (1994). *Modern organizations: Administrative theory in contemporary society.* Westport, CT: Praeger.

Farmer, J. D. (1995). *The language of public administration: Bureaucracy, modernity and postmodernity.* Tuscaloosa: University of Alabama Press.

Farmer, J. D. (Ed.). (1998). *Papers on the art of anti-administration.* Burke, VA: Chatelaine Press.

Farmer, J. D. (1999). Public administration discourse: A matter of style? *Administration & Society, 31*(3), 299–320.

Farmer, R. L. (1999). Scenes from the unconscious. *Public Voices, 3*(1), 67–81.

Fayol, H. (1949). *General and industrial management* (C. Storrs, trans.). London: Pitman. (Original work published 1916).

Feldman, M. S. (1989). *Order without design.* Stanford, CA: Stanford University Press.

Fellin, P. (1995). *The community and the social worker* (2nd ed.). Itasca, IL: F. E. Peacock.

Fenby, B. (1991). Feminist theory, critical theory, and management's romance with the technical. *Affilia, 6*(1), 20–37.

Featherstone, M. (Ed.). (1988). *Postmodernism.* Newbury Park, CA: Sage.

Festinger, L. A. (1957). *Theory of cognitive dissonance.* New York: Harper & Row.

Fiedler, F. E. (1967). *A theory of leadership effectiveness.* New York: McGraw-Hill.

Figueira-McDonough, J., Netting, F. E., & Nichols-Casebolt, A. (Eds.). (1998). *The role of gender in practice knowledge: Reclaiming half the human experience.* New York: Garland.

Fischer, F., & Sirianni, C. (Eds.). (1984). *Critical studies in organization and bureaucracy.* Philadelphia: Temple University Press.

Flexner, A. (1915). Is social work a profession? In *Proceedings of the 42nd National Conference of Charities and Corrections* (pp. 576–590). Fort Wayne, IN: Fort Wayne Printing Co.

Follet, M. P. (1926). The giving of orders. In G. Lindzey (Ed.), *Handbook of social psychology, Volume II: Special fields and applications* (pp. 1104–1123). Reading, MA: Addison-Wesley.

Foreman, J. (1992). *New visions of collaborative writing.* Hanover, NH: Boynton/Cook.

Foreman, K. (1999). Evolving global structures and the challenges facing international relief and development organizations. *Nonprofit Voluntary Sector Quarterly, 28,* 178–197.

Fox, C., & Miller, H. (1995). *Postmodern public administration: Toward discourse.* Thousand Oaks, CA: Sage.

French, J., & Raven, B. (1959). The bases of social power. In D. P. Cartwright (Ed.), *Studies in social power* (pp. 150–167). Ann Arbor: Institute for Social Research, University of Michigan.

Frost, P. J. (1980). Toward a radical framework for practicing organization science. *Academy of Management Review, 5,* 501–507.

Galper, J. (1976). Introduction to radical theory and practice in social work education: Social polity. *Journal of Education in Social Work, 12,* 3–9.

Gherardi, S. (1995). *Gender, symbolism and organizational cultures.* London: Sage.

Gibbs, L., & Gambrill, E. (1996). *Critical thinking for social workers: A workbook.* Thousand Oaks, CA: Pine Forge Press.

Gibbs, L., & Gambrill, E. (1999). *Critical thinking for social workers: A workbook* (2nd ed). Thousand Oaks, CA: Pine Forge Press.

Giddens, A. (1987). *Central problems in social theory.* London: Macmillan.

Goldstein, E. G. (1995). *Ego psychology and social work practice* (2nd ed.). New York: Free Press.

Gottlieb, N. (1992). Empowerment, political analyses, and services for women. In Y. Hasenfeld (Ed.), *Human services as complex organizations* (pp. 301–319). Newbury Park, CA: Sage.

Greenwood, D. J., & Levin, M. (1998). *Introduction to action research: Social research for social change.* Thousand Oaks, CA: Sage.

Guba, E. (Ed.). (1990). *The paradigm dialog.* Newbury Park, CA: Sage.

Guerra-Pearson, F. (1998). Organization forms and architectural space: Building meaning in charitable organizations in New York City, 1770–1920. *Nonprofit and Voluntary Sector Quarterly, 27,* 459–487.

Gulick, L. (1937). Notes on the theory of organization. In L. Gulick & L. Urwick (Eds.), *Papers on the science of administration* (pp. 3–13). New York: Institute of Public Administration.

Gutek, B. A., & Cohen, A. (1982). Sex ratios, sex role spillover, and sex at work: A comparison of men's and women's experiences. *Human Relations, 40*(2), 97–115.

Gutierrez, L. M., & Lewis, E. A. (1999). *Empowering women of color.* New York: Columbia University.

Habermas, J. (1971). *Knowledge and human interests* (J. Shapiro, trans.). London: Heinemann.

Habermas, J. (1984). *The theory of communicative action, Vol. 1: Reason and the rationalization of society* (T. McCarthy, trans.). Boston: Beacon.

Habermas, J. (1987). The philosophical discourse of modernity: Twelve lectures (Frederick Laurence, trans.). Cambridge, MA: MIT Press.

Hall, P. D. (1987). A historical overview of the nonprofit sector. In W. W. Powell (Ed.), *The nonprofit sector: A research handbook* (pp. 3–26). New Haven, CT: Yale University Press.

Handler, J. F. (1990). *Law and the search for community.* Philadelphia: University of Pennsylvania Press.

Hannan, M. T., & Freeman, J. (1977). The population ecology of organizations. *American Journal of Sociology, 82,* 929–964.

Hansmann, H. B. (1981). Reforming nonprofit corporation law. *University of Pennsylvania Law Review, 129*(3), 500–563.

Hardcastle, D. A., Wenocur, S., & Powers, P. R. (1997). *Community practice: Theories and skills for social workers.* New York: Oxford University Press.

Hardy, C., & Clegg, S. R. (1996). Some dare call it power. In S. R. Clegg, C. Hardy, & W. R. Nord (Eds.), *Handbook of organization studies* (pp. 622–641). London: Sage.

Harper, K. V., & Lantz J. (1996). *Cross-cultural practice: Social work with diverse populations.* Chicago: Lyceum.

Harris, M. (1998). Doing it their way: Organizational challenges for voluntary associations. *Nonprofit and Voluntary Sector Quarterly, 27,* 144–158.

Harrison, M. I. (1994). *Diagnosing organizations: Methods, models, and processes* (2nd ed.). Thousand Oaks, CA: Sage.

Harrison, M. I., & Shirom, A. (1999). *Organizational diagnosis and assessment: Bridging theory and practice.* Thousand Oaks, CA: Sage.

Hasenfeld, Y. (1983). *Human service organizations.* Englewood Cliffs, NJ: Prentice-Hall.

Hasenfeld, Y. (Ed.). (1992). *Human services as complex organizations.* Newbury Park, CA: Sage.

Hasenfeld, Y. (2000). Social welfare administration and organizational theory. In R. Patti (Ed), *The handbook of social welfare management* (pp. 89–112). Thousand Oaks, CA: Sage.

Hasenfeld, Y., & English, R. A. (Eds.). (1994). *Human service organizations.* Ann Arbor: University of Michigan Press.

Hassard, J. (1993). *Postmodernism and organizational analysis: An overview.* In J. Hassard & M. Parker (Eds.), *Postmodernism and organizations* (pp. 1–23). London: Sage.

Hassard, J., & Parker, M. (Eds.) (1993). *Postmodernism and organizations.* London: Sage.

Hearn, J., & Parkin, P. W. (1987). *"Sex" at "work": The power and paradox of organization sexuality.* New York: St Martin's Press.

Hearn, J., & Parkin, P. W. (1993). Organizations, multiple oppressions and postmodernism. In J. Hassard & M. Parker (Eds.), *Postmodernism and organizations* (pp. 148–162). Newbury Park, CA: Sage.

Heidegger, M. (1977). *The question concerning technology and other essays.* New York: Harper and Row.

Hepworth, D., Rooney, R., & Larsen, J. (1997). *Direct social work practice: Theory and skills* (5th ed.). Pacific Grove, CA: Brooks/Cole.

Hersey, P., & Blanchard, K. H. (1977). *Management of organizational behavior: Utilizing human resources* (3rd ed.). Englewood Cliffs, NJ: Prentice-Hall.

Herzberg, F. (1966). *Work and the nature of man.* Cleveland, OH: World Publishing.

Hess, P. M., & Mullen, E. J. (Eds.). (1996). *Practitioner-researcher partnerships: Building knowledge from, in, and for practice.* Washington, DC: National Association of Social Workers Press.

Heydebrand, W. V. (Ed.). (1973). *Comparative organizations: The results of empirical research.* Englewood Cliffs, NJ: Prentice-Hall.

Heyman, R. (1994). *Why didn't you say that in the first place? How to be understood at work.* San Francisco: Jossey-Bass.

Hirsh, S. (1992). *MBTI team building program: Team members' guide.* Palo Alto, CA: Consulting Psychologists Press.

Hodgkinson, V. A., & Toppe, C. (1991). A new research and planning tool for managers: The national taxonomy of exempt entities. *Nonprofit Management & Leadership, 1,* 404–414.

Hutchinson, J. G. (1967). *Organizations: Theory and classical concepts.* New York: Holt, Rinehart and Winston.

Hyde, C. (1992). The ideational system of social movement agencies: An examination of feminist health centers. In Y. Hasenfeld (Ed.), *Human services as complex organizations* (pp. 121–144). Newbury Park, CA: Sage.

Hyde, C. (2000). The hybrid nonprofit: An examination of feminist social movement organizations. *Journal of Community Practice, 8*(4), 45–67.

Iannello, K. P. (1992). *Decisions without hierarchy: Feminist intervention in organization theory and practice.* New York: Routledge.

Iglehart, A. P., & Becerra, R. M. (1995). *Social services and the ethnic community.* Boston: Allyn & Bacon.

Jacobsen, W. (1998). Defining the quality of practitioner researcher. *Adult Education Quarterly, 48*(3), 125–138.

James, W. (1950). *The principles of psychology (Vols. 1 & 2).* New York: Dover. (Original work published in 1890).

Jansson, B. S. (1999). *Becoming an effective policy advocate: From policy practice to social justice.* Pacific Grove, CA: Brooks/Cole.

Jansson, B. S., & Simmons, J. (1986). The survival of social work units in host organizations. *Social Work, 31,* 329–343.

Jaques, E. (1951). *The changing culture of the factory.* London: Tavistock Institute.

Jaques, E. (1990, January-February). In praise of hierarchy. *Harvard Business Review,* 127–133.

Jenkins, S. (1980). The ethnic agency defined. *Social Service Review, 54,* 249–261.

Kanter, R. M. (1977). *Men and women of the corporation.* New York: Basic Books.

Kanter, R. M. (1979). Power failure in management circuits. *Harvard Business Review, 57,* 65–75.

Kanter, R. M. (1987). Power failure in management circuits. In J. M. Shafritz & J. S. Ott (Eds.), *Classics of organizational theory* (pp. 349–363). Chicago: Dorsey.

Kanter, R. M. (1989). *When giants learn to dance.* New York: Simon and Schuster.

Kast, F. E., & Rosenzweig, J. E. (1972). General systems theory: Applications for organization and management. *Academy of Management Journal, 4,* 447–465.

Katz, D., & Kahn, R. (1966). *The social psychology of organizations.* New York: Wiley.

Kaufman, H. (1960). *The forest ranger.* Baltimore, MD: Johns Hopkins University Press.

Kellner, D. (1998). Postmodernist as social theory: Some challenges and problems. *Theory, Culture and Society, 5* (2–3), 239–269.

Kelly, R. M. (1991). *The gendered economy: Work, careers, and success.* Newbury Park, CA: Sage.

Kettner, P. M. (2002). *Achieving excellence in the management of human service organizations.* Boston: Allyn and Bacon.

Kettner, P. M., Daley, J. M., & Nichols, A. W. (1985). *Initiating change in organizations and communities: A macro practice model.* Monterey, CA: Brooks/Cole.

Kettner, P. M., Moroney, R. M., & Martin, L. L. (1999). *Designing and managing programs: An effectiveness-based approach* (2nd ed.). Thousand Oaks, CA: Sage.

Kikert, W. (1993). Complexity, governance, and dynamics: Conceptual explorations of public network management. In J. Kooiman (Ed.), *Modern governance: New government-society interactions* (pp. 191–204). London: Sage.

Kilmann, R. H., Saxton, M. J., Serpa, R., & Associates. (1985). *Gaining control of corporate culture.* San Francisco: Jossey-Bass.

Kirk, S. A., Siporin, M., & Kutchins, H. (1989). The prognosis for social work diagnosis. *Social Casework, 70,* 295–307.

Knights, D. & Willmott, H. (1989). Power and subjectivity work: From degradation to subjugation in social relations. *Sociology, 23,* 535–538.

Koen, S. (1984). *Feminist workplaces: Alternative models for the organization of work.* Ph.D. dissertation. Union for Experimenting Colleges, University of Michigan Dissertation Information Service.

Kondrat, M. E. (1999). Who is the "self" in self-aware: Professional self-awareness from a critical theory perspective. *Social Service Review, 73,* 451–477.

Koontz, H. (1961). The management theory jungle. *Academy of Management Journal, 4*, 174–188.

Kramer, R. M. (1981). *Voluntary agencies in the welfare state.* Berkeley: University of California Press.

Kroeger, O., & Thuesen, J. M. (1988). *Type talk.* New York: Dell.

Lakey, B., Lakey, G., Napier, R., & Robinson, J. (1995). *Grassroots and nonprofit leadership: A guide for organizations in changing times.* Philadelphia: New Society Publishers.

Lash, S., & Urry, J. (1987). *The end of organized capitalism.* London: Polity.

Lawler, E., Nadler, D., & Cammann, C. (Eds.). (1980). *Organizational assessment.* New York: Wiley.

Lawrence, G. (1993). *People types & tiger stripes* (3rd ed.). Gainesville, FL: Center for Applications of Psychological Type.

Lawrence, P. R., & Lorsh, J. W. (1967). *Organization and environment: Managing differentiation and integration.* Boston: Graduate School of Business Administration, Harvard University.

Lawrence-Lightfoot, S. (1999). *Respect: An exploration.* Cambridge, MA: Perseus Books.

Lawson, H. (1985). *Reflexivity: The postmodern predicament.* London: Hutchinson.

Lechich, A. J. (2000). Home care in jeopardy. *Care Management Journals, 2*, 128–131.

Leifer, R. (1989). Understanding organizational transformation using a dissipative structure model. *Human Relations, 42*(10), 899–916.

Levy, B. S. (1994). *The empowerment tradition in American social work.* New York: Columbia University Press.

Lewis, J. A., Lewis, M. D., Packard, T., & Souflee, F., Jr. (2001). *Management of human service programs* (3rd ed.). Belmont, CA: Brooks/Cole.

Lewis, J. A., Lewis, M. D., & Souflee, F. (1991). *Management of human service programs* (2nd ed). Pacific Grove, CA: Brooks/Cole.

Likert, R. (1961). *New patterns of management.* New York: McGraw-Hill.

Lincoln, Y., & Guba, E. (1985). *Naturalistic inquiry.* Beverly Hills: Sage.

Lindenberg, M. (1999). Declining state capacity, voluntarism, and the globalization of the not-for-profit sector. *Nonprofit and Voluntary Sector Quarterly, 28*, 147–167.

Linstead, S. (1993). Deconstruction in the study of organizations. In J. Hassard & M. Parker (Eds.), *Postmodernism and organizations* (pp. 49–70) London: Sage.

Lohmann, R. A. (1989). And lettuce is non-animal: Toward a positive economics of nonprofit action. *Nonprofit and Voluntary Sector Quarterly, 18*, 367–383.

Lohmann, R. A. (1992). *The Commons: New perspectives on nonprofit organizations and voluntary action.* San Francisco: Jossey-Bass.

Lohmann, R. A., & Lohmann, N. (2002). *Social administration.* New York: Columbia University Press.

Louis, M. R. (1980). Surprise and sense making: What newcomers experience in entering unfamiliar organizational settings. *Administrative Science Quarterly, 25*(2), 226–251.

Lugones, M. C., & Spelman, E. V. (1983). Have we got a theory for you! Feminist theory, cultural imperialism and the demand for "the woman's voice." *Women's Studies International Forum, 6*(6), 573–81.

Lum, D. (1996). *Social work practice and people of color: A process-stage approach* (2nd ed.). Pacific Grove, CA: Brooks/Cole.

Lum, D. (2000). *Social work practice and people of color: A process-stage approach* (4th ed.). Pacific Grove, CA: Brooks/Cole.

Lyotard, J. F., & Thibaud, J. L. (1985). *Just gaming.* Manchester, UK: Manchester University Press.

Macduff, N., & Netting, F. E. (2000). Lessons learned from a practitioner-academician collaboration. *Nonprofit Voluntary Sector Quarterly, 29*, 46–60.

Mann, M. (1986). *The sources of social power. Vol. I: A history of power from the beginning to A.D. 1760.* Cambridge: Cambridge University Press.

Mannheim, K. (1936). *Ideology and utopian* (L. Wirth & E. Shils, trans.). New York: International Library of Psychology, Philosophy of Scientific Method.

Marcuse, H. (1991). *One dimensional man: Studies in the ideology of advanced industrial society.* Boston: Beacon.

Martin, C. (1997). *Looking at type: The fundamentals.* Gainesville, FL: Center for the Applications of Psychological Types.

Martin, J., & Frost, P. (1996). Organization culture war games: Struggle for intellectual dominance. In S. R. Clegg, C. Hardy & W. R. Nord (Eds.), *Handbook of organization studies* (pp. 598– 621). London: Sage.

Martin, L. L. (2000). The environmental context of social welfare administration. In R. J. Patti (Ed.). *The handbook of social welfare administration* (pp. 55–67). Thousand Oaks, CA: Sage.

Martin, L. L., & Kettner, P. M. (1996). *Measuring performance of human service programs.* Thousand Oaks, CA: Sage.

Martin, P. Y. (1990). Rethinking feminist organizations. *Gender & Society, 4*(2), 182–206.

Martin, P. Y., & O'Connor, G. G. (1989). *The social environment: Open systems applications.* New York: Longman.

Maslow, A. H. (1943). A theory of human motivation. *Psychological Review, 50,* 370–396.

Mayo, G. E. (1933). *The human problems of an industrial civilization.* Boston: Harvard Business School, Division of Research.

McGregor, D. M. (1957). The human side of enterprise. *Management Review, 46,* 22–28, 88–92.

McGregor, D. M. (1960). *The human side of enterprise.* New York: McGraw-Hill.

McKelvey, B. (1982). *Organizational systematics: Taxonomy, evolution classification.* Berkeley: University of California Press.

Meenaghan, T. M., & Gibbons, W. E. (2000). *Generalist practice in larger settings: Knowledge and skill concepts.* Chicago: Lyceum.

Merton, R. K. (1952). Bureaucratic structure and personality. In R. K. Merton, A. P. Gray, B. Hockey, & H. C. Selvin (Eds.), *Reader in bureaucracy* (pp. 261–372). Glencoe, IL: Free Press.

Metzendorf, D., & Cnaan, R. A. (1992). Volunteers in feminist organizations. *Nonprofit Management & Leadership, 2*(3), 255–269.

Michels, R. (1951). *Political parties.* New York: Dover.

Miller, J. (2001). Social workers as diagnosticians. In K. J. Bentley (Ed.), *Social work practice in mental health.* Pacific Grove, CA: Brooks/Cole.

Millman, M. & Kanter, K. (Eds.). (1975). *Another voice: Feminist perspectives on social life and social sciences.* Garden City, NY: Doubleday.

Mintzberg, H. (1979). *The structuring of organizations.* Englewood Cliffs, NJ: Prentice-Hall.

Mizruchi, M. S., & Galaskiewicz, J. (1993). Networks of organizational relations. *Sociological Methods and Research, 22,* 46–70.

Mondros, J. B., & Wilson, S. M. (1994). *Organizing for power and empowerment.* New York: Columbia University Press.

Morgan, G. (1986). *Images of organizations.* Newbury Park, CA: Sage.

Morgan, G. (1997). *Images of organization* (2nd ed.). Thousand Oaks, CA: Sage.

Morris, R., & Lescohier, I. H. (1978). Service integration: Real versus illusory solutions to welfare dilemmas. In R. C. Sarri & Y. Hasenfeld (Eds.), *The management of human services.* New York: Columbia University Press.

Münsterberg, H. (1922). *Hugo Münsterberg, his life and work.* New York: Appleton.

Myers, K. (1998). *Introduction to type* (6th ed.). Palo Alto, CA: Consulting Psychologists Press.

Myers, K., & Kirby, L. (1994). *Introduction to type: Dynamics and development, exploring the next level of type.* Palo Alto, CA: Consulting Psychologists Press.

National Association of Social Workers. (1996). *NASW Code of Ethics.* Washington, D.C.

Netting, F. E, Kettner, P. M., & McMurtry, S. L. (1998). *Social work macro practice* (2nd ed.). New York: Longman.

Netting, F. E., & Rodwell, M. K. (1998). Integrating gender into human service organization, administration, and planning curricula. In J. Figueira, F. E. Netting, & A. Nichols-Casebolt (Eds.), *The role of gender in practice knowledge* (pp. 287–321). New York: Garland.

Nkomo, S. M. (1993). The emperor has no clothes: Rewriting "race in organizations." *Academy of Management Review, 17,* 487–513.

Nyden, P., Figert, A., Shibley, M., & Burrows, D. (1997). *Building community: Social science in action.* Thousand Oaks, CA: Pine Forge Press.

Oakeshott, M. J. (1962). *Rationalism in politics and other essays.* New York: Basic Books.

O'Connor, M. K., & Netting, F. E. (1999). Teaching students about collaborative approaches to organizational change. *Affilia, 14*(3), 315–328.

Odendahl, T., & O'Neil, M. (Eds.). (1994). *Women and power in the nonprofit sector.* San Francisco: Jossey-Bass.

O'Donnell, S. M., & Karanja, S. T. (2000). Transformative community practice: Building a model for developing extremely low income African-American communities. *Journal of Community Practice, 7*(3), 67–84.

Oster, S. M. (1992). Nonprofit organizations as franchise operations. *Nonprofit Management & Leadership, 2*(3), 223–238.

Ouchi, W. G. (1981). *Theory Z.* Reading, MA: Addison-Wesley.

Oxford University Press Staff. (2000). *Oxford dictionary of American usage and style.* New York: Berkley Publishing Group.

Parker, M. (1992). Post-modern and organizations or postmodern organization theory? *Organization Studies, 13* (1), 1–17.

Parker, M. (1993). Life after Jean-Francois. In J. Hassard & M. Parker (Eds.), *Postmoderism and organizations* (pp. 204–212). London: Sage.

Parsons, T. (1956). Suggestions for a sociological approach to the theory of organizations. *Administrative Science Quarterly, 1,* 63–85.

Patti, R. J. (Ed.). (2000). *The handbook of social welfare management.* Thousand Oaks, CA: Sage.

Perlmutter, F. D. (Ed.). (1988). *Alternative social agencies: Administrative strategies.* New York: Haworth.

Peters, T. J., & Waterman, R. H., Jr. (1982). *In search of excellence.* New York: Harper and Row.

Pfeffer, J. (1981). *Power in organizations.* Marshfield, MA: Pitman.

Pifer, A. (1983). The nongovernmental organization at bay. In B. O'Connell (Ed.), *America's voluntary spirit.* New York: Foundation Center.

Piven, F. F., & Cloward, R. A. (1971). *Regulating the poor: The functions of public welfare.* New York: Pantheon.

Platt, R. (1989). Reflexivity, recursion, and social life: Elements for a postmodern sociology. *Sociological Review, 37*(4), 636–667.

Power, M. (1992). Modernism, postmodernism, and organization. In J. Hassard & D. Pym (Eds.), *The theory and philosophy of organizations: Critical issues and new perspectives.* London: Routledge & Keagan Paul.

Rauch, J. B. (Ed.). (1993). *Assessment: A sourcebook for social work practice.* Milwaukee, WI: Families International, Inc.

Reamer, F. G. (1995). *Social work values & ethics.* New York: Columbia University Press.

Reamer, F. G. (1998). *Ethical standards in social work: A critical review of the NASW code of ethics.* Washington, DC: National Association of Social Workers Press.

Reddin, W. J. (1970). *Managerial effectiveness.* New York: McGraw-Hill.

Reed, M. (1993). Organizations and modernity: Continuity and discontinuity in organization theory. In H. Hassard & M. Parker (Eds.), *Postmodernism and organizations* (pp. 163–182). Newbury Park, CA: Sage.

Reed, M. (1996). Organizational theorizing: A historically contested terrain. In S. R. Clegg, C. Hardy, & W. R. Nord (Eds.), *Handbook of organization studies* (pp. 31–56). London, England: Sage.

Reitan, T. C. (1998). Theories of interorganizational relations in the human services. *Social Service Review, 73,* 285–309.

Resnick, H., & Patti, R. J. (Eds.). (1980). *Change from within: Humanizing social welfare organizations.* Philadelphia: Temple University Press.

Richmond, M. (1917). *Social diagnosis.* New York: Russell Sage Foundation.

Ritzer, G. (1980). *Sociology: A multiple paradigm science* (rev. ed.). Boston: Allyn and Bacon.

Rodwell, M. K. (1987). Naturalistic inquiry: An alternative model for social work assessment. *Social Service Review, 6,* 231–246.

Rodwell, M. K. (1998). *Social work constructivist research.* New York: Garland.

Roethlisberger, F. J., & Dickson, W. J. (1939). *Management and the worker.* Cambridge, MA: Harvard University Press.

Rogers, R. E. (1975). *Organizational theory.* Boston: Allyn and Bacon.

Rossi, P., & Freeman, H. (1993). *Evaluation: A systematic approach* (5th ed.). Beverly Hills: Sage.

Rothman, J. (1995). Approaches to community intervention. In J. Rothman, J. E. Erlich, & J. E. Tropman, (Eds.), *Strategies for community intervention* (5th ed.) (pp. 26–63). Itasca, IL: F. E. Peacock.

Rothman, J. (Ed.). (1999). *Reflections on community organization: Enduring themes and critical issues.* Itasca, IL: F. E. Peacock.

Rothman, J., Erlich, J. E., & Tropman, J. E., (Eds.). (1995). *Strategies for community intervention* (5th ed.). Itasca, IL: F. E. Peacock.

Rothman, J., Erlich, J. E., & Tropman, J. E. (Eds). (2001). *Strategies for community intervention* (6th ed.). Itasca, IL: F. E. Peacock.

Ryan, W. P. (1999, January–February). The new landscape for nonprofits. *Harvard Business Review,* 127–136.

Sackman, S. A. (1993). *Cultural knowledge in organizations: Exploring the collective mind.* Newbury Park, CA: Sage.

Salamon, L. M. (1987). Partners in public service: The scope and theory of government-nonprofit relations. In W. W. Powell (Ed.), *The nonprofit sector: A research handbook* (pp. 99–117). New Haven, CT: Yale University Press.

Salamon, L. M. (1993). The marketization of welfare: Changing nonprofit and for-profit roles in the American welfare state. *Social Service Review, 67,* 16–39.

Salamon, L. M., & Anheier, H. K. (1992). In search of the non-profit sector II: The international classification of nonprofit organizations. *Voluntas, 3,* 125–152.

Schein, E. H. (1989). Reassessing the "divine rights" of managers. *Sloan Management Review, 30*(2), 63–68.

Schein, E. H. (1992). *Organizational culture and leadership* (2nd ed.). San Francisco: Jossey-Bass.

Schneider, R. L., & Lester, L. (2001). *Social work advocacy.* Belmont, CA: Brooks/Cole.

Scott, W. G. (1961). Organization theory: An overview and an appraisal. *Academy of Management Journal, 4,* 7–26.

Scott, W. G., & Mitchell, T. R. (1972). *Organization theory: A structural and behavioral analysis* (rev. ed.). Chicago: Dorsey.

Scott, W. R. (1992). *Organizations: Rational natural and open systems* (3rd ed.). Englewood Cliffs, NJ: Prentice-Hall.

Seashore, S., Lawler, E., Mirvis, P., & Cammann, C. (Eds.). (1983). *Assessing organizational change.* New York: Wiley.

Selznick, P. (1948). Foundations of the theory of organization. *American Sociological Review, 13,* 25–35.

Senge, P. M. (1990). *The fifth discipline: The art and practice of learning organization.* New York: Doubleday.

Shafritz, J. M., & Ott, J. S. (1987). *Classics of organization theory* (2nd ed.). Chicago: Dorsey.

Shafritz, J. M., & Ott, J. S. (1996). *Classics of organization theory* (4th ed.). Fort Worth, TX: Harcourt, Brace College Publishers.

Shafritz, J. M., & Ott, J. S. (2001). *Classics of organization theory (5th ed.).* Fort Worth, TX: Harcourt College Publishers.

Sherwood, D. A. (Ed.). (2000). *Charitable choice: The challenge and opportunity for faith-based community services.* Botsford, CT: North American Association for Christians in Social Work.

Shoichet, R. (1998). An organization design model for nonprofits. *Nonprofit Management & Leadership, 9*(1), 71–88.

Simon, H. A. (1946). The proverbs of administration. *Public Administration Review, 6,* 53–67.

Simon, H. A. (1947). *Administrative behavior.* New York: Macmillan.

Simon, H. A. (1957). *Administrative behavior* (2nd ed.). New York: Macmillan.

Smircich, L., & Calás, M. (1987). Organizational culture: A critical assessment (pp. 228–263). In F. Jablin, L. Putnam, K. Roberts, & L. Porter (Eds.), *Handbook of organizational communications.* Newbury Park, CA: Sage.

Smith, A. (1776). Of the division of labour. In *An inquiry into the nature and causes of the wealth of nations* (pp. 5–15). Printed for W. Strahan and T. Cadell in the Stand, London.

Smith, D. H. (1999). The effective grassroots association, Part one: Organizational factors that produce internal impact. *Nonprofit Management and Leadership, 9*(4), 443–456.

Smith, D. H. (2000). *Grassroots associations.* Thousand Oaks, CA: Sage.

Starbuck, W. H., & Milliken, F. J. (1988). Executives' perceptual filters: What they notice and how they make sense. In D. C. Hambrick (Ed.)., *The executive effect: Concepts and methods for studying top managers* (pp. 35–65). Greenwich, CT: JAI.

Stogdill, R. M., & Coons, A. E. (1957). *Leader behavior, its description and measurement.* Columbus: Ohio State University Press.

Sumariwalla, R. D. (1976). *UWASIS II: A taxonomy of social goals and human service programs.* Alexandria, VA: United Way of America.

Tannenbaum, R., & Schmidt, W. H. (1958). How to choose a leadership pattern. *Harvard Business Review, 36,* 95–101.

Taylor, F. W. (1911, 1947). *Scientific management.* New York: Harper and Row.

Taylor, F. W. (1916). The principles of scientific management. *Bulletin of the Taylor Society.* An abstract of an address given by Dr. Taylor before the Cleveland Advertising Club, March 3, 1915.

Thayer, F. C. (1981). *An end to hierarchy and competition: Administration in the post- affluent world* (2nd ed.). New York: New Viewpoints.

Thompson, J. D. (1967). *Organizations in action.* New York: McGraw-Hill.

Thompson, P. (1993). Postmodernism: Fatal distraction. In J. Hassard & M. Parker (Eds.), *Postmodernism and organizations* (pp. 183–203). Newbury Park, CA: Sage.

Tieger, P., & Barron-Tieger, B. (1992). *Do what you are: Discover the perfect career for you through the secrets of personality type.* Boston: Little, Brown.

Toffler, A. (1970). *Future shock.* New York: Random House.

Trice, H. M., & Beyer, J. M. (1993). *The cultures of work organizations.* Upper Saddle River, NJ: Prentice-Hall.

Tuominen, M. (1991). Caring for profit: The social, economic, and political significance of for-profit child care. *Social Service Review, 65,* 450–467.

Turner, F. J. (1994). *Social work treatment: Interlocking theoretical approaches* (4th ed.). New York: Free Press.

Turner, J. H. (1987). Toward a sociological theory of motivation. *American Sociological Review, 52,* 15–27.

Van Maanen, J. (Ed.). (1979). *Qualitative methodology.* Newbury Park, CA: Sage.

Van Maanen, J. (Ed.). (1983). *Qualitative methodology.* Newbury Park, CA: Sage.

Van Maanen, J., Dabbs, J. M., Jr., & Faulkner, R. R. (Eds.). (1982). *Varieties of qualitative research.* Newbury Park, CA: Sage.

Van Til, J. (1988). *Mapping the third sector: Voluntarism in a changing social economy.* Washington, DC: The Foundation Center.

Walker, A. H., & Lorsch, J. W. (1968). Organizational choice: Product vs. function. *Harvard Business Review, 46,* 129–138

Warren, R. L. (1971). *Truth, love and social change.* Chicago: Rand-McNally.

Weber, M. (1922). Bureaucracy. In H. Gerth & C. W. Mills (Eds.), *Max Weber: Essays in sociology.* Oxford, UK: Oxford University Press.

Weber, M. (1946). *From Max Weber: Essays in sociology* (H. H. Gerth & C. W. Mills, trans.). New York: Oxford University Press.

Weber, M. (1947a). *The methodology of social sciences.* Glencoe, IL: Free Press.

Weber, M. (1947b). *The theory of social and economic organization* (A. M. Henderson & T. Parsons, trans.). New York: Macmillan. (First published in 1924).

Weick, K. E. (1995). *Sensemaking in organizations.* Thousand Oaks, CA: Sage.

Weiner, M. E. (1990). Trans-organizational management: The new frontier for social work administrators. *Administration in Social Work, 14*(4), 11–27.

Weiner, N. (1948). *Cybernetics.* Cambridge, MA: MIT Press.

Wheatley, M. J., & Kellner-Rogers, M. (1996). *A simpler way.* San Francisco: Berrett-Koehler Publishers.

Whyte, W. F., Jr. (1948). *Human relations in the restaurant business.* New York: McGraw-Hill.

Whyte, W. H., Jr. (1956). *The organization man.* New York: Simon & Schuster.

Wiesendanger, B. (2000). Star quality. *Working Woman* (May).

Wilkerson, A. E. (1988). Epilogue. In F. D. Perlmutter (Ed.), *Alternative social agencies: Administrative strategies* (pp. 119–128). New York: Haworth.

Williams, R. (1977). *Marxism and literature.* Oxford: Oxford University Press.

Willmott, H. (1993). Strength is ignorance; slavery is freedom: Managing culture in modern organizations. *Journal of Management Studies, 30*(4), 515–552.

Wilson, F. (1996). Research note. Organizational theory: Blind and deaf to gender. *Organizational Studies, 17,* 825–842.

Wineburg, B. (2001). *A limited partnership: The politics of religion, welfare, and social service.* New York: Columbia University Press.

Wolff, J. (1977). Women in organizations. In S. Clegg, & D. Dunkerley (Eds.), *Critical issues in organizations* (pp. 7–20). London: Routledge & Kegan Paul.

Woods, M. E., & Hollis, F. (2000). *Casework: A psychosocial therapy (5th ed.).* Boston: McGraw-Hill.

Young, D. R. (2001). Organizational identity and the structure of nonprofit umbrella associations. *Nonprofit Management & Leadership, 11,* 289–304.

Zald, M. (1970). Political economy: A framework for comparative analysis. In M. Zald (Ed.), *Power in organizations* (pp. 221–261). Nashville: Vanderbilt University Press.

NAME INDEX

SUBJECT INDEX